MODERN
MILITARY
GEOGRAPHY

Edited by

FRANCIS A. GALGANO
Villanova University

EUGENE J. PALKA
US Military Academy at West Point

W0007677

Routledge
Taylor & Francis Group

NEW YORK AND LONDON

First published 2011
by Routledge
711 Third Avenue, New York, NY 10017, USA

Simultaneously published in the UK
by Routledge
2 Park Square, Milton Park, Abingdon, Oxon OX14 4RN

Routledge is an imprint of the Taylor & Francis Group, an informa business

© 2011 Taylor & Francis

Typeset in Palatino by
Florence Production Ltd, Stoodleigh, Devon

Library of Congress Cataloging in Publication Data
Modern military geography / [compiled by] Francis A. Galgano, Eugene J. Palka.
       p. cm.
    Includes bibliographical references.
   1. Military geography.   2. Military geography—History.   I. Galgano, Francis A.
(Francis Anthony)   II. Palka, Eugene Joseph.
   UA990.M64 2010
   355.4'7--dc22   2010014727

ISBN 13: 978-0-415-87094-8 (hbk)
ISBN 13: 978-0-415-87095-5 (pbk)
ISBN 13: 978-0-203-84439-7 (ebk)

If we know that the enemy is open to attack and also know that our men are in a condition to attack, but are unaware that the nature of the ground makes attack impracticable, we have gone only halfway towards victory.

(Sun Tzu, *The Art of War*)

Contents

Foreword

MODERN MILITARY GEOGRAPHY IS a major new text that explores in depth the basic and varied relationships between geography and the conduct of military conflict. As the editors tell us, the underlying fundamental conceptual principle around which this volume is organized and crafted is the assumed synergy between geography and military operations wherever they may occur. In the chapters that follow, we see this theme played out in many different scenarios and operational theatres whether in local topographic and hydrographic settings, climate and coastal conditions, broader scenes related to biological and health issues, environmental issues that affect regional security, or even more provocatively evolving geopolitical realities in different geographic settings. All involve some dimension wherein the character of the area or place exerts a profound influence upon the real or potential military conflict.

Lieutenant Colonel ret. (Associate Professor) Francis Galgano and Colonel (Professor) Eugene Palka are both professional military officers and professional academics and geographers. They are extremely well qualified, based on their past research and publications, to co-author and compile a well organized and representative set of essays that explore in detail historic and contemporary studies that illustrate the force of geographic realities upon the planning, conduct, and outcome of military operations.

The book opens with an introductory section (Part I) on the nature of military geography. Three introductory chapters provide a contextual setting for the reader who may be new to either geography or military geography but is eager to come to grips with this vitally significant subfield of geography. This introductory section of the book is then rounded out with several chapters that focus on the relationship between environmental issues and regional security or insecurity, as well as a chapter on the legacy of military lands in the US. An analytical approach to examining and assessing the link between environment and regional security is included, and this is a very useful addition for both student and professional as they seek better understanding of the complexity of these issues and to enhance their own capabilities to explain and assess them.

Part II provides case studies of historic and operational military geography in settings ranging from Iraq and Bosnia to the Anglo-Boer War in southern Africa. This section also includes topics as disparate as medical geography and streams and military landscapes. Finally, Part III focuses on applied military geography that includes the actual effects of biophysical factors on military operations in history as well as contemporary settings, and the impact and role of location and physical geography on geopolitical hotspot potential theatres of military operations in Asia. Both of these sections of the text offer a lively and convincing sampling of historic and recent military operations that present both successes and continuing challenges stemming from the imperative of geographic realities.

Military geography has a long history in the US, and a major point of its lineage may be traced to the US Military Academy at West Point where both Colonel Palka and Lieutenant Colonel Galgano have taught. At West Point, one may still find sketches of the topographic outlines of battlefields drawn by none other that Cadet George McClellan, later a key leader of Union forces during the Civil War. A course in military geography has long been popular with cadets at West Point, and this text is indeed ideally suited for use in such a course, whether at USMA or any number of other colleges or universities where offered. All of the contributors are or have been professional military officers or have substantial military experience and interest, and thus bring the combination of expertise as geographers as well as military specialists to their writing and analysis of the battlefields and operations under consideration.

Altogether, the editors and contributors are to be congratulated for writing and compiling a cogent and very well illustrated set of essays that explain the relationship between geography and military performance, and why it is important to the understanding of historic as well as contemporary military planning and operations. I believe this volume will be of great benefit to students and professionals alike who seek a realistic and timely explanation of the field of military geography as seen in the case studies and analytic discussions found in *Modern Military Geography*.

Clifton W. Pannell
University of Georgia

Preface

THIS BOOK OF CONTRIBUTED chapters by subject-matter experts provides an overview and analysis of salient contemporary and historical military subjects from the military geographer's perspective. Factors of geography have had a compelling influence on battles and campaigns throughout history. However, geography and military affairs have gained heightened attention during the past two decades, and military geography is the discipline best situated to explain them. Hence, the premise of this book and its contents are founded on the principle that geographic knowledge of space, place, people, and scale provides essential insights into contemporary security issues, and promotes the idea that such insight is critical to understanding and managing significant military problems at local, regional, and global scales.

We have titled this book *Modern Military Geography* because we intend for it to connect contemporary topics in military geography to the roots of the discipline. The book is divided into three parts—*Introduction to Military Geography, Historical and Operational Military Geography,* and *Applied Military Geography*—and each offers chapters that address salient issues in military geography. Each section is prefaced by an introduction that explains the importance of its content and links together the chapters. The first section of the book begins with three chapters that lay the foundation. The first chapter examines the history, scope, and recent developments within military geography in the US. The second and third chapters are complementary in that they are intended to provide non-military professionals and non-geographers with the basic concepts needed to understand fully the material presented throughout the remainder of the book. The second section uses classic historical and contemporary case studies to demonstrate the important linkages between military operations and key elements of the human and natural landscape. The final section presents a series of topics that encompass modern problems in military geography. Thus, this book is one of the few that addresses military problems from peacetime to war.

Finally, our book does not have an agenda. Instead, it is focused on academic military geography to support what is needed in the classroom. The book is written by professional geographers and military officers who are also credentialed geographers. Thus, we bring clear expertise to both sides (i.e. academic geography and professional military) of the subject and have a unique understanding of what is needed to support a military geography course.

Francis A. Galgano
Eugene J. Palka

PART I

Introducing military geography

G EOGRAPHIC INFORMATION has been used to support military operations for as long as history has been recorded. This is because there is a clear and fundamental link between geography and military operations—military operations take place in distinct operational environments such as jungles, deserts, oceans, and cities. They also take place in different operational contexts such as peacekeeping, disaster relief, civic action, and of course combat operations; thus, they are in part shaped by the nature of the natural and human landscape. Military operations have evolved through time with changes in military technology and with their scope. Different operational environments and contexts require different types of geographic information; consequently, military geography offers a unique and important vantage point from which to study the nature of military operations and their relationship with discrete landscapes and operational environments at diverse scales.

A geographer seeks to answer the question "Why is it like this here?" By their very nature, military operations are geographic: they occur in places; and places contain unique physical environments, climates, and culture systems. In essence, military operations involve time, space, and the nature of what exists within the confines of that time and space—this is an inherently geographic perspective. Military operations are a complex three-dimensional array of actions that have to be arranged in time and space. Geographers understand the components and processes—terrain, weather, climate, and people—that affect military operations in time and space. Military geography then is the application of geographic information, tools, and technologies to military problems across the spectrum of military operations from peacetime to war. Military geographers are uniquely qualified to examine the linkages between military operations and the nature of the space in which they take place because like all geographers they apply an integrated, multidisciplinary approach.

1

Through the centuries, the geographic nature of warfare has been obvious to military leaders; however, it was only during the nineteenth century that the distinct subfield of military geography could be identified. As warfare has evolved in complexity through two World Wars, countless low-intensity conflicts, the explosive growth in military technology, a proliferation of stability and support missions, and now the Global War on Terror, it has become impossible for one leader to keep pace with the ever-increasing demands for accurate and timely geographic information. Military planners have also acknowledged the complex linkages between terrain and cultural systems, as well as the extreme difficulty in understanding and predicting their impact. Modern military operations, which include a wide spectrum of potential wartime and peacetime endeavors, demand more precise and complex analyses of physical and cultural landscapes. This reality is the genesis of this book.

Military Geography has grown considerably as an academic subject during the past two decades. For example, the number of university geography programs offering Military Geography courses has grown by nearly a factor of four since 2001. This growth has been fueled in part by the collapse of the Soviet Union and transition from a bi-polar strategic world in 1989, through a decade of ethnic violence and peace-keeping operations, and now asymmetrical warfare and the Global War on Terror. These events demanded an increasing volume of ever more sophisticated geographic analyses, and clearly sparked interest in an academic subdiscipline that was essentially dormant—at least in the US—since the end of the Vietnam War. Without question the global geopolitical situation since the end of the Cold War and events following 9/11 have demonstrated the need for increased geographic awareness and research as military efforts shifted to peacetime and stability and support operations, but also the complexity of wartime operations as part of counter-terror operations have generated renewed public and academic interest as well.

Before 1998, the last published volume on military geography was *Military Geography* by Louis C. Peltier and G. E. Pearcy. Since 1998, seven legitimate Military Geography books have been published. Clearly, 1998 was a watershed year, and in that year *Military Geography for Professionals and the Public* by John Collins and *Battling the Elements* by Harold Winters were published. In 2001, Eugene Palka and Francis Galgano published an edited volume titled *The Scope of Military Geography: Across the Spectrum from Peacetime to War*. This was the first of two books published by Palka and Galgano that attempted to address the full spectrum of military operations from the perspective of the military geographer. Their second book, *Military Geography: from Peace to War*, was published in 2005 and incorporated analyses from Iraq and Afghanistan, as well as discussing topics such as military land management and base closure and re-alignment. Three other books have appeared on the market. National Geographic published *Battlegrounds* in 2003, Blackwell a new title by Rachel Woodward (*Military Geographies*) in 2004, and Oxford University Press one edited by Colin Flint (*The Geography of War and Peace*) in 2005.

We have titled this book *Modern Military Geography* because we intend for it to connect contemporary subjects in military geography to the roots of the discipline. It is our intention to bring out this theme in the introductory section and reinforce it throughout the book. It is our belief that, in order for the reader to truly understand the scope of military geography, we would, out of necessity, have to present the full spectrum of subject matter and not focus on discrete aspects of military geography such as historical case studies or critical geographies. Thus, this book is organized into three discrete sections. In the first, *Introduction to Military Geography*, it is our aim to introduce the reader to military geography as a discipline, i.e. present its historical background, traditional subject matter, methodologies, and pedagogies. In the second part of the book, *Historical and Operational Military Geography*, we present the reader with a set of timeless case studies that illustrate linkages between warfare and geography. However, in that this is a more contemporary publication, we present not only historical case studies from the Civil War and the era of twentieth-century warfare, but also case studies that focus on the aftermath of the shattering of Yugoslavia, as well as Operation Enduring Freedom (Afghanistan), and Operation Iraqi Freedom. Finally, we complete our précis of modern military geography in the closing section, titled *Applied Military Geography*. In this section, we introduce the reader to a broad spectrum of contemporary military geography topics such as disaster relief operations, military land management and training analogs, ethnic warfare, issues relating to effective sovereignty and terrorism, and the rise of China as a military power, to name a few.

It would be impossible to overemphasize the importance of military geography during wartime. The dependence on geographic information has been fundamental to training, equipping, and deploying forces overseas throughout history; hence, relevant regional and systematic geographies routinely provide essential informational considerations to support decision-making. Ironically, most geographers are not military professionals and most military professionals are not geographers. Given this dilemma, we have created the introductory section of the book to provide all readers with a common understanding of military geography as a discipline, as well as a common introductory foundation in military science and geography. Finally, in this section of the book we intend to focus the reader on the seminal contemporary geographic issues affecting the discipline.

In *Chapter One*, Eugene Palka explains the history, scope, and recent developments of military geography in the US. This chapter will also provide the reader with a basic understanding of the nature and scale of geographic analyses, as well as common methods used by military geographers. The second and third chapters are complementary in that they are intended to provide non-military professionals and non-geographers with the basic concepts needed to understand fully the material presented throughout the remainder of the book. In *Chapter Two*, Frank Galgano presents an elementary introduction to military science for the layperson. Similarly, in *Chapter Three*, he introduces basic concepts in geography so that the non-geographer can approach the material in this book with a solid understanding of geographic terms, concepts, and methods. In chapters four through six, we present a set of related topics that are of seminal importance to modern military geographers—the undeniable linkage between environmental change, environmentally induced instability, and issues of military strategy and planning. Kent Butts offers an important synopsis of the evolving concept of environmental security in *Chapter Four*, and illuminates how it is influencing military decision-making at the strategic level. In *Chapter Five*, Amy Krakowka uses environmental security as a framework for analysis to examine the nexus between non-sustainable practices, environmental change, and latent ethnic conflict, and how they combined to trigger the genocide in Rwanda in 1994. At the strategic level, Eugene Palka examines the strategic imperatives engendered by the melting of Arctic sea ice. His examination of this complex geopolitical issue in *Chapter Six* is an excellent example of the dynamic geographic interactions of environmental change, international law, competition for resources, and military strategy. Finally, Bill Doe illustrates the fundamental link between military forces and the land in *Chapter Seven*. In this chapter, he provides a historical perspective of how the armed forces acquire and use land, as well as the environmental challenges associated with responsible land management.

Collectively, the chapters of Part I demonstrate the understandable utility, if not necessity, of military geography in the modern world. As long as military forces are used to solve problems, during peace and wartime, geographic variables must be considered as an integral part of all military plans and operations.

Chapter one
Military geography in the US
History, scope, and recent developments

EUGENE J. PALKA

Introduction

MILITARY GEOGRAPHY emerged from the overlap between geography and military science, and in one respect is a type of applied geography, employing the knowledge, methods, techniques, and concepts of the discipline to military affairs, places, and regions (Palka 2003). The subfield can also be approached from a historical perspective (Davies 1946; Meigs 1961; Winters 1998; Palka and Galgano 2000, 2005), with emphasis on the impact of physical or human geographic conditions on the outcomes of decisive battles, campaigns, or wars. In either case, military geography has continued to keep pace with technological developments and military doctrine to effectively apply geographic information, principles, and tools to military situations or problems across the spectrum from peacetime to wartime (Corson and Palka 2004).

In the landmark publication *American Geography: Inventory and Prospect* (1954), Joseph Russell reported that military geography had long been recognized as a legitimate subfield in US academic geography. Despite the occasional controversy surrounding the subfield since his assessment (Association of American Geographers 1972; Lacoste 1973), and the dormant period it experienced within US academic geography during the Vietnam era, military geography displayed unquestionable resilience by the end of the twentieth century. Moreover, the turbulent years of the first decade of the twenty-first century have served as a catalyst for new opportunities within the subfield.

Throughout the twentieth century, professional and academic geographers made enormous contributions to the US Military's understanding of distant places and peoples. Within most university libraries, one is apt to encounter a substantial collection of Area Handbooks authored initially by geographers during wartime. Some of the work by geographers within the *Department of Defense (DoD)* remains classified, but a significant amount of literature is in the public domain or considered "open source." A brief examination of the roles and contributions of geographers within the DoD enables one to appreciate the discipline's far-reaching impact on military affairs (Munn 1980). The trend continues today with hundreds of geographers employed by the Defense Intelligence Agency (DIA), the National Geospatial Intelligence Agency (NGA), and other organizations. Additionally, these agencies rely on the contributions of academic geographers and open-source literature more than ever before.

While most recognize the utility of military geography during a time of war, the subfield has also been important during peacetime, providing an important forum for the continuing discourse among geographers, military planners, political officials, and government agencies, as each relies upon geographic information, tools, and techniques to address a wide range of problems within the national security, humanitarian assistance, and installation management arenas. This chapter traces the history of military geography as a conscious field of study, chronicles its origin and development within the US, highlights recent developments, provides a current assessment, and proposes an agenda for the future.

Military geography's early roots

The use of geographic knowledge to support military decision-making likely predates written history. Thompson (1962) traced the first use of military geography to Megiddo, near present day Haifa, Israel, where the Egyptians battled the armies of several Levant States in 1479 BC. Later historical writings are replete with examples of famous military leaders whose actions were influenced by their interpretation of geographic factors. Thucydides' history of the Peloponnesian War from 431–404 BC (Meigs 1961), Xenophon's account of the march of 10,000 Greek mercenaries across Asia Minor to the shores of the Black Sea in 400 BC (Rouse 1964), and Caesar's geographic insights during the Gallic Wars from 60–55 BC (Edwards 1939), are a few examples of the dozens of ancient works that include a military geographic perspective.

As a formal field of study, military geography was a European innovation, with the French, Germans, and British pioneering most of the work during the nineteenth and early twentieth centuries. Theophile Lavallée's (1836) *Géographie physique, historique et militaire* is generally regarded as the first publication exclusively devoted to military geography. The field gained added notoriety one year later when Albrecht von Roon (1837), a captain on the Prussian General Staff (and later a famous War Minister), published a work containing detailed physiographic descriptions of military regions of Europe.

6

During the late nineteenth and early twentieth centuries, military geography appeared under the rubric of "grand strategy" as it was applied to national objectives (Peltier and Pearcy 1966). Lieutenant Brown's (1885) military geography of the US and Canada was one of the earliest US publications devoted exclusively to the subfield, but his effort went largely unnoticed because it was written for use as a textbook at the Infantry and Cavalry Schools. With *The Influence of Seapower upon History, 1660–1783*, Mahan (1890) provided the first widely recognized US contribution to the field and laid the foundation for what was later to become strategic geography.

Although there were relatively few US publications on military geography at the turn of the twentieth century, the British continued to develop a significant body of literature and provided landmark works during the era by Maguire (1899), Mackinder (1902), May (1909), and MacDonnell (1911). These comprehensive works were clearly indicative of the maturity of the subfield in Great Britain at that time, and proved to be influential on US perspectives in later years.

Military geography in the US

At the turn of the twentieth century, several unpublished papers and lectures devoted to military topography were used for instructional purposes at the US Military Academy at West Point, the Command and General Staff College at Fort Leavenworth, and the Army War College at Carlisle (Thompson 1962), but none of the papers reached a wider audience or entered into the geographic literature. Some authors provided examples of military geography, if only indirectly, within the context of other publications. In *American History and Its Geographic Conditions*, Semple (1903) included chapters on the geography of the Civil War, and sea and land operations during the war of 1812, viewed from her classic environmental deterministic perspective. Brigham (1903) used a similar approach in his chapter on the Civil War, in *Geographic Influences in American History*.

World War I

The first formal demand for military geography in the US emerged during World War I. US geographers initially assisted the war effort by providing written descriptions of the physical landscapes surrounding major training camps throughout the country. These descriptions were subsequently printed on the backs of training maps and were used to teach basic terrain analysis skills to leaders and soldiers. The military geographic emphasis at that time, and throughout the war, was on the physical geographic aspects of the battlefield, envisioned primarily as the domain of ground forces. A total of fifty-one members of the

Association of American Geographers (AAG) participated in World War I and/or the Peace Conference that followed (Martin and James 1993). Regardless of whether they served in the Military or Civilian Service, or conducted research within academia, the emphasis was on applying geographic principles and knowledge to solving the Military's wartime problems. D.W. Johnson (1917) published *Topography and Strategy in the War*, but his later work, *Battlefields of the World War, Western and Southern Fronts: A Study in Military Geography* (Johnson 1921), became a widely recognized military geographic publication stemming from the war years. The most lingering effect of World War I on military geography was the notion that the subfield focused exclusively on wartime military problems.

World War II

When the US entered World War II, US geographers again provided widespread support to the war effort. By 1943, over 300 geographers were working in Washington, in the Office of Strategic Services, War Department, Intelligence Division, and in the Army Map Service (Martin and James 1993). During the war, military geographers progressed beyond collecting and compiling data, to providing continual assessments of both the physical and human geography of specific regions. These efforts culminated in the *Joint Army and Navy Intelligence Studies (JANIS)*, which were essentially the regional geographies of selected countries and theaters. Regional studies were helpful not only to commanders and military planners, but also to the Army quartermaster and the research and development teams who were responsible for designing uniforms, vehicles, equipment, weapons, and materials.

Within academia, training programs specifically designed for military personnel spurred widespread interest in military geography. Poole (1944) proposed a formal agenda for training military geographers, and aspects of his syllabus were instituted at universities and military schools alike. Throughout the war, numerous articles and studies were published on various aspects of military geography (Ackerman 1945; Palka and Lake 1988). Arthur Davies' "Geographical Factors in the Invasion and Battle of Normandy" (1946) evolved as one of the best-known military geographic publications during the period and continues to be regarded as a classic analysis.

Military geography continued to thrive after the war as many geographers returned to academia and shared their wartime experiences and perspectives via publications and lectures (Committee on Training and Standards in the Geographic Profession 1946; Mason 1948*a*, *b*). The subdiscipline continued to be taught as a standard course offering in numerous geography departments throughout the country and the Committee on Military Geography was well-established within the AAG. The Committee's purpose was to advise professional military schools on the design and implementation of military geography courses within their respective programs (Renner 1951). The subfield remained unquestionably relevant during the initial stages of the Cold War era, and the Korean War served as another catalyst for continued growth. In *American Geography: Inventory and Prospect* (Russell 1954) confirmed the healthy status of the subfield, but reinforced the perception that military geography was restricted to wartime concerns.

The Vietnam War

Prior to the US involvement in the Vietnam War, a number of military geography publications appeared in the disciplinary literature. "The Potential of Military Geography" (Peltier 1961) proclaimed the legitimacy and utility of the subfield. Meigs (1961) analyzed geographic factors that influenced the outcome of the Peloponnesian War, and drew comparisons with World War II operations in North Africa and Sicily. Jackman's article, "The Nature of Military Geography" (1962), was a widely cited publication that provided a clear, concise, theoretical perspective on military geography. Although unpublished, Thompson (1962), under the mentorship of Preston James, chronicled the history of military geographic thought and the development of its theoretical underpinnings. *Military Geography* (Peltier and Pearcy 1966) was published a few years later, and was the most comprehensive and focused publication on the topic, serving as the guidepost for the subfield between the end of World War II and the mid-1990s. The legitimacy of the subfield was reinforced in the AAG's special bulletin, *Geography as a Professional Field* (1966), which featured a section entitled "Careers in Military Geography" (Palka 2003).

During the Vietnam War and its aftermath, military geography lost its appeal among university geography programs, and within the AAG. The scarcity of contemporary publications, the absence of a specialty group within the AAG, the reduced numbers of AAG members claiming military geography as a topical proficiency, the scant number of course offerings at universities, and the lack of any dissertations in the subfield from 1969 to 1982 (Browning 1983), was clear evidence of the declining popularity of the subfield.

Throughout the mid-1960s and early 1970s, anti-war sentiments and a general mistrust of the federal government prompted geographers to become increasingly concerned with being socially, morally, and ecologically responsible in their research efforts and professional affiliations with government agencies. Contributing to the war effort in Vietnam came to be regarded as irresponsible by many members of the AAG. The controversy surrounding the Vietnam War cast an enduring shadow on military geography throughout the 1970s. In hindsight, the adverse effect of the unpopular war was understandable, if not predictable. The applied wartime focus of military geography, perceived for many years as its *raison d'être*, came under intense scrutiny, and, without alternative applications, the subfield lost its appeal within academia, despite the widespread applications within the DoD and other government agencies.

The post-Vietnam era

In the aftermath of the Vietnam War, Cold War tensions remained and shifted to other locations. Despite the success of US military operations in Grenada and Panama during the early and mid-1980s, the justification for those incursions was controversial, and so there was little renewed interest in military geography among academic geographers. Nevertheless, a few publications managed to surface within the literature. Some employed military geographic studies as a means to analyze regional conflicts (Soffer 1982), or to assess the security implications of land-use patterns (O'Sullivan 1980; Soffer and Minghi 1986). Others such as Munn (1980) reinforced the Military's continued interest in the subfield and outlined the role of geographers within the DoD. Within military literature, Garver (1981, 1984) and Galloway (1984, 1990) compiled an excellent collection of contemporary readings for use in their military geography course at West Point, and Palka (1987, 1988) examined the routine requirement for geographic perspectives and tools in military planning. Reaching a wider audience were Winters (1991), who discussed the influence of geomorphologic and climatologic factors in his historical account of a Civil War battle, and O'Sullivan (1991), who provided extensive treatment of the relationships between terrain and small unit engagements.

During the latter stages of the Cold War the boundaries between political geography, military geography, and military intelligence became blurred, an almost inevitable condition foreseen decades earlier by Jackman (1962). In some instances, military geography merged with political geography, while in other cases (O'Sullivan and Miller 1983; Soffer and Minghi 1986), it overlapped with military intelligence (O'Sullivan 1991). At the same time, the use of applied geography towards peace (as opposed to war) initiatives gained popularity (Pepper and Jenkins 1985; O'Loughlin and van der Wusten 1986, 1993). Throughout the 1980s, military geographers within academia were plagued by the subfield's image, perceived ambiguity, and questionable legitimacy.

Desert Shield and Desert Storm

War in the Persian Gulf proved to be another catalyst for military geography. The reliance on geographic information was fundamental to training, equipping, and deploying forces to Southwest Asia during the Gulf War. Satellite imagery, aerial photographs, computer-assisted cartography, the global positioning system, geographic information systems, and a wide range of map types and scales were routinely used to develop plans and conduct operations at all echelons (Corson and

Palka 2004). Regional and systematic geographies re-emerged, and once again provided essential information to support decision-making processes from the outset of Desert Shield to the end of Desert Storm.

The end of the Cold War

The fall of the Berlin Wall and the demise of the former USSR prompted significant changes in the National Security Strategy of the US (Shalikashvili 1995). The dramatic shift in strategic orientation warranted substantial changes in the size, force structure, and disposition of the US Military. While the numbers of "forward deployed" units were decreased considerably, the country's involvement in *military operations other than war (MOOTW)* increased at an unprecedented rate. Between 1989 and 1997, the Military participated in forty-five operations other than war, more than triple the total number conducted during the entire Cold War era from 1947 to 1989 (Binnendijk 1998).

The end of the *Cold War* provided an opportune time to re-examine the scope of military geography (Anderson 1993; Palka 1995; Palka and Galgano 2000; O'Sullivan 2001). For Russell (1954) and Jackman (1962), military geography included the whole range of geographic research as it applied to military problems. Both, however, conceptualized military problems within a wartime context. Contemporary military problems have proven to be significantly different from those that were envisioned by either Russell or Jackman (Palka 1995; Palka and Galgano 2000; O'Sullivan 2001; Palka and Galgano 2005). To be sure, security remains the fundamental concern of the U.S. Military, but throughout the 1990s, there was a considerable expansion of activities in the humanitarian sphere (Anderson 1994; Palka 1995) and environmental security realm (Butts 1993, 1994).

Military operations in Bosnia and Kosovo also served to introduce a new range of military problems, as operations shifted between peacetime and wartime endeavors. The concept of MOOTW was replaced by a new doctrinal term, *Stability and Support Operations (SASO)*, which better characterized the intent and nature of the dynamic and fragile military missions that were undertaken along the spectrum from peace to war.

The Global War on Terror

The attacks of 11 September 2001 on the World Trade Center in New York City marked the beginning of the Global War on Terror (GWOT). A new kind of warfare emerged in Afghanistan in 2001 and in Iraq in 2003. Throughout both the Afghanistan and Iraq campaigns, US forces have had to conduct *full-spectrum operations*. No longer able to enjoy the luxury of focusing on specific peacetime, SASO, or combat operations in a consecutive manner, forces have been required to undertake operations concurrently across the spectrum. Complicating matters more are the complex human and physical geographies of both countries and the multitude of insurgent groups that are involved. The GWOT will present military geographers with a "target rich" environment for their research or applications for the foreseeable future.

Recent developments and a current appraisal

Wartime necessity coupled with heightened public interest has historically increased the demand for military geography (Palka and Henderson 2008). The subfield is currently more visible than at any time since World War II. Recent developments have not only provided a tremendous boost to the subdiscipline, but also have paved the way for even greater success in the future.

First, the end of the Cold War and the Military's subsequent involvement with MOOTW (and later SASO) has generated wider-ranging possibilities for military geographic studies (Goure 1995; Gutmanis 1995; Palka 1995; Palka and Galgano 2000, 2005). Geographic applications to support warfighting, although invaluable, have not always been popular. Indeed, such applications encountered significant resistance and may have actually contributed to the decline of the subfield during the Vietnam era. Humanitarian and peacekeeping missions, however, have been much less disputable and appear to be extremely attractive to a larger audience and new generation of geographers (Palka and Galgano 2005).

Second, books by Collins (1998), Winters (1998), and Palka and Galgano (2000, 2005) filled a void that had existed for more than a quarter of a century. For the first time since Peltier and Pearcy's 1966 publication, comprehensive works on military geography are available for use as college textbooks. In *Military Geography for Professionals and the Public*, Collins (1998) considers a wide range of environmental conditions, employs historical vignettes, and addresses warfare at the tactical, operational, and strategic levels. In *Battling the Elements*, Harold Winters (1998) highlights the impacts of weather, climate, terrain, soils, and vegetation on the outcomes of important military operations. He clearly illustrates from a historical perspective that the physical settings in which battles are fought are neither passive nor presumable. Rather, environmental components are active agents that have the potential to shape conflict and decisively influence the outcome. Winters demonstrates in a compelling fashion that the relationships between the environment and combat are highly variable, often unpredictable, and always formidable. In *The Scope of Military Geography*, Palka and Galgano (2000) retain the wartime focus of traditional military geography, yet broaden the scope of the subfield to incorporate a wide range of MOOTW as well as peacetime endeavors. Their book emphasizes the synergy between geography and military operations across a spectrum from peacetime to war and takes into account the current nature of military activities. Their more recent publication, *Military Geography from*

Peace to War (2005) takes into account the significant events that had transpired since their earlier work, e.g. the wars in Kosovo, Afghanistan, and Iraq, the transition from MOOTW to SASO, and the Army's campaign to exercise environmental stewardship on its installations.

Third, the establishment of a military geography specialty group within the AAG has generated renewed interest and enthusiasm among academics. Since the 1996 meeting of the AAG in Charlotte, multiple sessions have been scheduled during the annual conference to accommodate a wide range of papers within the subfield. A major strength of the organization is the balanced participation from academics, planners, military personnel, and government professionals. Moreover, the range of experience among members, from graduate students to professors emeritus, ensures continuity of key issues and themes, yet promotes a thorough mixing of ideas and perspectives.

Fourth, recent technological advancements continue to highlight the capabilities of geographic tools to facilitate problem-solving at multiple scales. Corson and Minghi (1996a) showcased the applications of *Powerscene* (a computer-based terrain visualization system) to revolutionize making boundaries. They further elaborated on the utility of *Powerscene* during the negotiations of the Dayton Peace Accords (Corson and Minghi 1996b), and, in so doing, rekindled a traditional military geographic concern with boundaries, a topic that dates back to World War I (Russell 1954; James and Martin 1979). More recently, the wars in Afghanistan and Iraq have contributed to an unprecedented use of technology on the battlefield to support accurate targeting, the prevention of fratricide and collateral damage, enhanced situational awareness, intelligence gathering, and battle damage assessments (Corson and Palka 2004).

Fifth, military geography is resurfacing in professional military schools. An article in *Parameters* by the former chairman of the Department of National Security and Strategy at the Army War College, entitled "The Immutable Importance of Geography," provides a case in point (Hansen 1997). More recently, members of the AGS visited Fort Leavenworth to consult with General Petraeus as the concept of the human terrain and analysis team (HTAT) was designed and implemented to enhance cultural understanding among deploying units. Veterans of the Afghanistan and Iraq campaigns display an increased awareness of military geography as they pass through their professional development schools and interact with faculty or members of HTATs who reach out to support Army units who are deployed.

Finally, the combined efforts of military geographers and geologists have resulted in four highly successful international conferences in 2003, 2005, 2007, and 2009. In each case, fifty to seventy-five professionals and academics have come together to deliver a wide range of outstanding research papers, participate in field trips, and engage in scholarly debates and discussions. Häusler (2009) provides a superb, detailed account of the participants, presentation topics, major themes, and resulting publications.

Beyond the horizon

As a continuously evolving subfield, military geography displays tremendous momentum in this first decade of the twenty-first century. Several paradigm shifts are already underway that ensure steady progress. First, many have moved beyond the traditional, narrowly construed focus on wartime military problems, and have taken into account peacetime concerns. Ironically, peacetime concerns have always consumed a far greater percentage of the Military's time and effort, yet until recently military geographers have generally ignored these areas.

A second emerging transition involves embracing two contemporary military realms, SASO and environmental security. These areas continue to represent fertile ground within an expanded military geography. Both spheres have evolved during the post-Cold War era and appear destined to command a significant amount of attention within the subfield in the future. Expansion into these new realms will maximize the subfield's potential by enabling academics and practitioners to address military problems across the entire spectrum of contemporary military employment scenarios from peace to war.

Stability and support operations include: nation assistance; security assistance; humanitarian assistance and disaster relief; support to counter-drug operations; peacekeeping; arms control; combating terrorism; shows of force; noncombatant evacuation; and support to domestic civil authority (Palka and Galgano 2005). Recent examples are too many to list, but have been well publicized. Trends suggest that the US Military will continue to be called upon to respond to refugee problems, floods, earthquakes, hurricanes, and forest fires, domestically and abroad. Additionally, the Military continues to be actively involved in operations to improve infrastructure and health conditions throughout Latin America, Africa, Asia, and the Pacific (Shannon and Sullivan 1993; Binnendijk 1998; Palka and Galgano 2005). These types of missions are innately geographic and afford ideal opportunities for military geographers to apply their expertise to noble causes and showcase military geography as a versatile, problem-solving subdiscipline.

Environmental security has been an integral part of the country's National Security Strategy since 1991. Annual updates have expanded the concept based on input from national and international forums, which recognize that environmental issues have major impacts on health and economies, and are increasingly viewed as threats to development and political stability (Butts 1993). The environment is not a new security concept, but in the past it has generally been regarded as the victim rather than the cause of conflict (Butts 1994). Today the environment plays an unquestionable role in regional stability, and it has become a fundamental military concern during peacetime training.

The US Military is linked to environmental security in several respects. First, the former can be employed to resolve conflicts resulting from regional instability prompted by environmental problems (Palka 2008). Second, in support of the country's National Security Strategy, the Military is involved in a wide range of security assistance scenarios to help host countries resolve their internal environmental problems. In such instances, the US Military has helped host governments to improve fisheries, construct water-supply systems, implement flood control, develop irrigation, construct sanitary landfills, administer forest management programs, and perform wildlife protection and management (Butts 1993). Third, the DoD is one of the most important environmental resource managers in the world, overseeing 25 million acres of domestic holdings and more than 2 million acres of land abroad. Thus, environmental stewardship is a fundamental military concern during peacetime (Shaw et al. 2000).

Expansion into the SASO or environmental security arenas does not necessitate abandoning traditional themes in military geography. Broadening the military geographic perspective enables practitioners to keep pace with contemporary military concerns and ensures the continued growth and relevance of the subfield.

Another paradigm shift that has been underway targets the generic classification schemes previously employed to distinguish or categorize work in military geography. Introduced initially in Palka (1999), Figure 1.1 enables one to organize research themes and clarify the boundaries of the subfield in order to reduce traditional ambiguities and enhance coherence. The model is based on the parameters of context, scale, approach, and perspective. This design is capable of addressing military problems across a full spectrum of employment scenarios, from peacetime to war. The scheme also identifies the magnitude of the operation (scale), and the nature of the geography involved (approach). By also indicating the perspective (applied or historical), this model provides a comprehensive, yet useful, method for organizing and classifying research in military geography. Perhaps most importantly, the model conceptualizes the scope of the subfield and provides an organizational construct.

Conclusion

Within US academia, military geography has evolved from infancy during the course of the twentieth century. The subfield acquired additional interest and stature during the course of the world wars and the Korean conflict, only to have its legitimacy questioned during the Vietnam era. After a period of stagnation during the 1970s and early

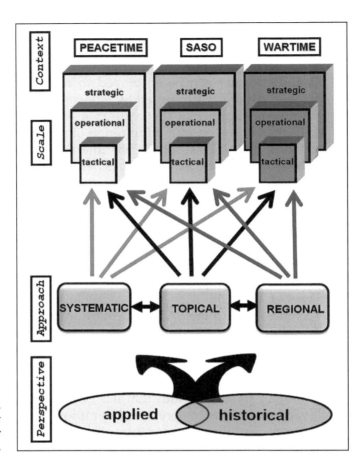

Figure 1.1
The scope of military geography. *Source*: after Palka (1999).

1980s, military geography rebounded during the 1990s and has accelerated throughout the first decade of the twenty-first century.

For most of the past decade, elements of the US Military have been present in nearly half the countries of the world, actively engaged in training, peacekeeping, humanitarian assistance missions, environmental security, and stability and support operations. Additionally, the Military has been deployed to Afghanistan since the fall of 2001 and to Iraq since the spring of 2003. Meanwhile, those units remaining at home stations in the US or abroad are charged with continually preparing to respond to crises across the full range of military operations from humanitarian assistance to fighting and winning major theater wars. The problems encountered within each of these scenarios are varied, complicated, and often unexpected. Many of the problems, however, are innately geographic. Thus, the tools, techniques, and knowledge of the geographer can be fundamentally relevant and unquestionably useful in solving military problems anywhere along a spectrum from peace to war.

Military geographers, be they systematic, regional, or technical specialists, can enhance the success of military operations through

16

professional writing, guest lectures in military units, seminars with the senior leadership of the military, and formal teaching at the military's institutions of higher learning. Indeed, historical precedents have long been established in each of these cases (Poole 1944; Forde 1949; Warman 1954; Jackman 1971).

The current emphasis on SASO is indicative of the US's global commitment, yet also reflective of the increased flexibility (since the end of the Cold War) to employ military forces in a wide range of humanitarian scenarios. Similarly, the commitment to environmental security has been expressed in our National Security Strategy since 1991. These relatively recent changes in the US Military's orientation demand a military geography that is broader in scope and capable of focusing on the full range of contemporary military problems in peacetime and in war. Current full-spectrum operations in both Afghanistan and Iraq remind us that the core of traditional military geography is still of timeless value to the Military, and will continue to be an integral aspect of all plans and operations during armed conflicts. Yet, now more than ever before, geographers specializing in various subfields or regions can make substantial contributions to the Military's humanitarian relief efforts and environmental programs by recognizing the previously untapped potential of the subfield. The synergistic effect of recent publications, an active specialty group within the AAG, the endless possibilities afforded by SASO and environmental security, and the continuing demand for military geography within theaters of war, will continue to propel the subfield into the twenty-first century.

Editor's Note: This chapter is a significantly revised and updated version of a chapter previously published in: Palka, Eugene J. 2003. "Military geography: its revival and prospectus." In *Geography in America at the dawn of the 21st century*, Gary L. Gaile and Cort J. Willmott (eds). 503–13. Oxford: Oxford University Press.

References Cited

Ackerman, Edward A. 1945. "Geographic training, wartime research, and immediate professional objectives." *Annals* 35: 121–43.

Anderson, E. 1993. "The scope of military geography." Editorial. *GeoJournal* 31(2): 115–17.

——. 1994. "The changing role of the military." Editorial. *GeoJournal* 34(2): 131–2.

Association of American Geographers. 1972. "Minutes of the annual business meeting, Boston, 18 April 1971." *Professional Geographer* 24(1): 36–9.

Binnendijk, Hans (ed. in chief). 1998. *Strategic assessment*. Washington, DC: Institute for National Strategic Studies, National Defense University.

Brigham, Albert Perry. 1903. *Geographic influences in American history*. Boston: Ginn & Co.

Brown, Lieutenant W. C. 1885. *Military geography*. Fort Benning, GA: United States Infantry and Cavalry School.

Browning, Clyde E. 1983. *A bibliography of dissertations in geography: 1969 to 1982*. Studies in Geography 18. Chapel Hill, NC: University of North Carolina, Department of Geography.

Butts, Kent Hughs (ed.). 1993. *Environmental security: what's DOD's role?* Special Report of the Strategic Studies Institute. Carlisle, PA: US Army War College.

——. 1994. *Environmental security: a DOD partnership for peace*. Special Report of the Strategic Studies Institute. Carlisle, PA: US Army War College.

Collins, John M. 1998. *Military geography for professionals and the public*. Washington, DC: National Defense University Press.

Committee on Training and Standards in the Geographic Profession. 1946. "Lessons from the war-time experience for improving graduate training for geographic research." *Annals* 36: 195–214.

Corson, Mark W. & Julian V. Minghi. 1996a. "*Powerscene*: application of new geographic technology to revolutionise boundary making." *IBRU Boundary and Security Bulletin* (Summer).

——. 1996b. "The political geography of the Dayton Accords." *Geopolitics and International Boundaries* 1(1): 77–97.

Corson, Mark W. & Eugene J. Palka. 2004. "Geotechnology, the U.S. military, and war." In *Geography and technology*, Stanley D. Brunn, Susan L. Cutter, & J.W. Harrington, Jr. (eds) Dordrecht, the Netherlands: Kluwer Academic Publishers.

Davies, A. 1946. "Geographical factors in the invasion and battle of Normandy." *Geographical Review* 36(4): 613–31.

Edwards, H. J. (trans.). 1939. Translated from Caesar, *Gallic Wars*, Loeb Classical Library. London: William Heinemann.

Forde, H. M. 1949. "An introduction to military geography." *Military Review* 28: 30–6, 55–62.

Galloway, Colonel Gerald E., Jr. (compiler). 1990. *Readings in military geography*. West Point, NY: Department of Geography, US Military Academy.

Garver, Colonel John B., Jr. (compiler). 1981. *Readings in military geography*. West Point, NY: Department of Geography & Computer Science, US Military Academy.

Garver, John B., Jr., & Gerald E. Galloway, Jr. (compilers). 1984. *Readings in military geography*. West Point, NY: Department of Geography & Computer Science, US Military Academy.

Goure, Daniel. 1995. "Non-lethal force and peace operations." *GeoJournal* 37(2): 267–75.

Gutmanis, Ivars. 1995. "United States international policies and military strategies in the era of defunct aggressor." *GeoJournal* 37(2): 257–66.

Hansen, David G. 1997. "The immutable importance of geography." *Parameters* (spring): 55–64.

Häusler, Hermann. 2009. *Report on national and international military geo-conferences held from 1994 to 2007*. MILGEO. Nr. 30 E. Vienna: Institute for Military Geography, Austrian Ministry of Defence and Sports, April.

Jackman, Albert. 1962. "The nature of military geography." *Professional Geographer* 14: 7–12.

——. 1971. "Military geography" In *Research institute lectures on geography, special report ETL-SR-71*, Roger A. Leestma (ed.). Fort Belvoir, VA: US Army Engineer Topographic Laboratories.

James, P. E. & G. J. Martin. 1979. *The Association of American Geographers: the first seventy-five years, 1904–1979*. Washington, DC: Association of American Geographers.

Johnson, D. W. 1917. *Topography and strategy in the war*. New York: Henry Holt.

——. 1921. *Battlefields of the world war, western and southern fronts: a study in military geography*. Research Series No. 3. New York: American Geographical Society.

Lacoste, Yves. 1973. "An illustration of geographical warfare: bombing of the dikes on the Red River, North Vietnam." *Antipode* 5(2): 1–13.

Lavallée, T. S. 1836. *Géographie physique, historique et militaire*. Paris.

MacDonnell, Colonel A. C. 1911. *The outlines of military geography*. London: Hugh Rees.

Mackinder, Halford J. 1902. *Britain and the British seas*. New York: D. Appleton.

Maguire, T. Miller. 1899. *Outlines of military geography*. Cambridge: Cambridge University Press.

Mahan, Alfred Thayer. 1890. *The influence of sea power upon history, 1660–1783*. Boston: Little, Brown.

Martin, Geoffrey J. & Preston E. James. 1993. *All possible worlds: a history of geographical Ideas*. New York: John Wiley.

Mason, Charles H. 1948*a*. "The role of the geographer in military training." *Bulletin of the American Society for Professional Geographers* (April): 7.

——. 1948*b*. "Role of the geographer in military planning." *Annals* 38(1): 104–5.

May, Colonel Edward Sinclair. 1909. *An introduction to military geography*. London: Hugh Rees.

Meigs, Peveril. 1961. "Some geographical factors in the Peloponnesian War." *Geographical Review* 51(3): 370–80.

Munn, Alvin A. 1980. "The role of geographers in the Department of Defense." *Professional Geographer* 32(3): 361–4.

O'Loughlin, J. & H. van der Wusten. 1986. "Geography of war and peace: notes for a contribution to a revived political geography." *Progress in Human Geography* 10(3): 434–510.

——. 1993. "Political geography of war and peace." In *Political geography of the twentieth century: a global analysis*, P. J. Taylor (ed.). London: Belhaven Press.

O'Sullivan, Patrick. 1980. "Warfare in suburbia." *Professional Geographer* 32(3): 355–60.

——. 1991. *Terrain and tactics*. New York: Greenwood Press.

——. 2001. *The geography of war in the post Cold War world*. Lewiston, NY: Edwin Mellen Press.

O'Sullivan, Patrick & Jesse W. Miller, Jr. 1983. *The geography of warfare*. New York: St Martin's Press.

Palka, Eugene J. 1987. "Aerial photography." *Infantry Journal* (May–June): 12–14.

——. 1988. "Geographic information in military planning." *Military Review* 68(3): 52–61.

——. 1995. "The US Army in operations other than war: a time to revive military geography." *GeoJournal* 37(2): 201–8.

——. 1999. "Military geography at the dawn of the twenty-first century." Paper presented at the Annual Convention of the Association of American Geographers, Honolulu, HI, 23–27 March.

——. 2003. "Military geography: its revival and prospectus." In *Geography in America at the dawn of the 21st century*, Gary L. Gaile and Cort J. Willmott (eds), 503–13. Oxford, UK: Oxford University Press.

——. 2008. "Potential effects of climate change on the U.S. Army, regional instability, and war." In *Climatic change & variation: a primer for teachers*, William A. Dando (ed.). 175–9. Washington, DC: National Council for Geographic Education.

Palka, Eugene J. & Francis A. Galgano (eds). 2000. *The scope of military geography*. New York: McGraw-Hill.

——. 2005. *Military geography from peace to war*. New York: McGraw-Hill.

Palka, Eugene J. & Joseph P. Henderson, 2008. *A bibliography of military geography*, 2 vols. West Point, NY: US Military Academy Press.

Palka, Eugene J. & Dawn Lake. 1988. *A bibliography of military geography*. 4 vols. West Point, NY: US Military Academy Press.

Peltier, Louis C. 1961. "The potential of military geography." *Professional Geographer* 13(6): 3–4.

Peltier, Louis C. and G. Etzel Pearcy. 1966. *Military geography*. Princeton, NJ: D. Van Nostrand.

Pepper, David & Alan Jenkins (eds). 1985. *The geography of peace and war*. Oxford: Basil Blackwell.

Poole, Sidman P. 1944. "The training of military geographers." *Annals* 34(4): 202–6.

19

Renner, George. 1951. *Instructor's manual for political and military geography*. New York: US Air Force Reserve Officer Training Program, Headquarters Continental Air Command Directorate, Mitchell Air Force Base.

Roon, Capt. Albrecht Theodor Emil Graf von. 1837. *Militarische Landerbeschreibung von Europa*, vol. 1. *Mittel-und Sud-Europa*. Berlin.

Rouse, W. H. D. 1964. *The march up country*. A translation of Xenophon's *Anabasis*. Ann Arbor, MI: University of Michigan Press.

Russell, J.A. 1954. "Military geography." *American Geography: Inventory and Prospect*, P. E. James and C. F. Jones (eds.), 484–495. Syracuse, NY: Syracuse University Press.

Semple, Ellen Churchill. 1903. *American history and its geographic conditions*. Boston: Houghton, Mifflin.

Shalikashvili, John M. 1995. *National military strategy of the United States of America*. Washington, DC: US Government Printing Office.

Shannon, Hon. John W. & General Gordon R. Sullivan. 1993. "Strategic force—decisive victory: a statement on the posture of the United States Army, fiscal year 1994." Presented to the Committees and Subcommittees of the United States Senate and the House of Representatives, First Session, 103rd Congress.

Shaw, Robert B., William W. Doe, Colonel Eugene J. Palka, & Thomas E. Macia. 2000. "Where does the U.S. Army train to fight? Sustaining army lands for readiness in the 21st century." *Military Review* 80(5) (September–October): 68–77.

Soffer, Arnon. 1982. "Topography conquered: the wars of Israel in Sinai." *Military Review* 62(4): 60–72.

Soffer, Arnon & Julian V. Minghi. 1986. "Israel's security landscapes: the impact of military considerations on land uses." *Professional Geographer* 38(1): 28–41.

Thompson, Edmund R. 1962. *The nature of military geography: a preliminary survey*. Ph.D. dissertation. Syracuse, NY: Syracuse University.

Warman, Henry J. 1954. *Geography—backgrounds, techniques and prospects (for teachers)*. Worcester, MA: Clark University Print Shop.

Winters, Harold A. 1991. "The battle that was never fought: weather and the Union mud march of January 1863." *Southeastern Geographer* 31(1): 31–8.

——. 1998. *Battling the elements: weather and terrain in the conduct of war*. Baltimore, MD: Johns Hopkins University Press.

Chapter two
Military science for the non-professional

FRANCIS A. GALGANO

Introduction

NOT ALL USERS OF THIS BOOK are military professionals and, thus, may not have a working knowledge of military organizations, doctrine and concepts, types of operations, and weapons. This chapter is included to provide the non-professional with baseline information needed to understand the material presented in this book. This chapter should by no means be considered a complete synopsis of military organizations, weapons, and doctrine as it is only designed to meet the needs of the chapters in this book.

This chapter essentially uses US military structure and doctrine as its baseline; however, the author makes no claim that it mirrors perfectly US doctrine and terminology. Instead, using US doctrine and structure as a framework, terminology and concepts are explained for the sole purpose of clarifying material on a very generic basis. The other reason that we have decided not to mirror exactly US terminology and doctrine is that it changes so frequently that this chapter may appear to be out-of-date before it is published. For example, we use the term *Military Operations Other Than War* (MOOTW) to classify non-combat operations. This term was effectively employed by the US armed forces during the late 1990s but was inexplicably discarded and replaced with a series of terms that are less descriptive, and certainly less useful.

This chapter is organized to provide first an overview of military command structure and levels of war, which are inherently geographic in nature. This is followed by a concise overview of military units and a brief discussion of different types of major weapon systems. Finally, the chapter addresses military operations, differentiating combat operations and forms of maneuver from MOOTW. More detailed and extensive background material can be found by visiting the Defense Link Website (US Department of Defense 2009), GlobalSecurity.org (2009), and the Federation of American Scientists (2009).

The military structure

Military operations, in their traditional sense, emanate from some form of national command authority such as a president, dictator, or other form of national leader. A national military staff and perhaps a minister of war or secretary of defense advise the national leader. This group collectively determines national objectives, force structure, and military strategy. The precise organization and interrelationships of this national structure vary from state to state. In the US, the Department of Defense (DoD) is the agency charged with co-ordinating all aspects of national security. The DoD includes its combat components, the Army, Navy, Air Force, and Marine Corps, as well as non-combat organizations such as the National Security Agency (NSA) and Defense Intelligence Agency (DIA). During war or other national emergencies, the DoD has authority over the Coast Guard, which normally belongs to the Department of Homeland Security (US Department of Defense 2009).

The DoD command structure was redefined by the Goldwater–Nichols Act of 1986 (Summers 1992). This law redesigned the command structure and introduced the most important changes to the DoD since its inception. The Goldwater–Nichols Act redefined the chain of command, which now runs from the President, through the Secretary of Defense, to *Combatant Commanders* (i.e. CINCs) who command all military forces within an area of responsibility. Therefore, in the US system, command and strategic direction of the armed forces flows from civilian leadership directly to military leaders in the field, and this civilian leadership is referred to as the *National Command Authority (NCA)* (Guidebook 2008; US Department of Defense 2009).

The Chairman of the Joint Chiefs of Staff and the service Chiefs of Staff, who are collectively responsible for the readiness of the various military branches—but are not in the chain of command—leads the military advisory staff (Summers 1992). By law, the Chairman of the Joint Chiefs of Staff is the highest ranking military officer in the US and each military service, under the direction of its chief of staff, is responsible for organizing, training, and equipping military units for use by CINCs so that they may execute strategic directives given by the NCA (Guidebook 2008).

Actual command of US forces in the field is accomplished under the direction of the *Unified Combatant Commands (UCC)*, of which there are ten: six regional and four functional. Each UCC is a joint military command composed of forces from two or more services. Additionally, each UCC has a well-defined mission, and each is organized either on a geographic basis, also called an *Area of Responsibility (AOR)*, or on a functional basis. Each UCC is commanded by a senior officer of four-star rank and the UCCs are *joint commands*. Thus, the commander of each UCC has the distinct task of translating strategic guidance from the NCA into action in the field. The map given in Figure 2.1 illustrates the geographic

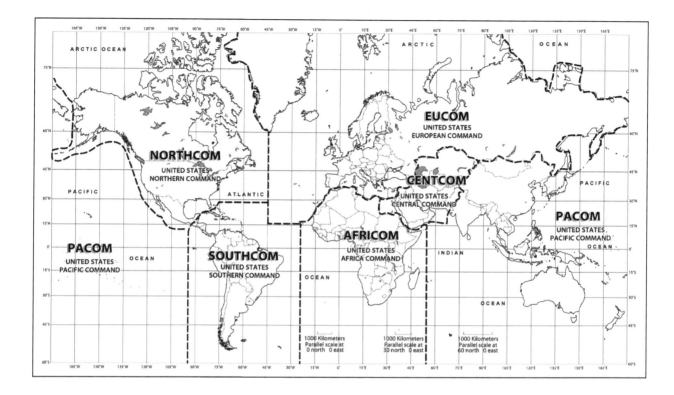

Figure 2.1
A map of geographic regions assigned to UCCs as of July 2009.

AORs of the regional UCCs, and the data given in Table 2.1 delineates key information about each UCC (Guidebook 2008).

Levels of military operations

Military operations occur within three levels of war, i.e. strategic, operational, and tactical. The levels of war are not independent; they are complementary and there should be a common thread at all levels. *Strategy* is defined as the art and science of developing and using political and military force as needed during peace and war to achieve national objectives (Department of the Army 1997*b*, 2001). Thus, at the strategic level, the NCA determines national objectives, and, in times of war, these objectives drive the scope and direction of military policy. When articulating a national strategy, the NCA usually delineates a goal, or an *end*, along with sequence of events (i.e. *ways*), and the forces and resources (i.e. *means*) to be used in achieving the goal. Using a football game as an example, a coach may use a defensive strategy to win a game by running the ball, thereby using up time, and keeping the other team's offense off the field. A classic example of national military strategy was the *Germany First* strategy employed by the US and its allies during World War II (Weigley 1973).

23

Table 2.1: Regional and functional commands

Regional commands

Command	Home base	AOR
United States Northern Command (NORTHCOM)	Peterson Air Force Base, Colorado	North American homeland defense and co-ordinating homeland security with civilian forces
United States Central Command (CENTCOM)	MacDill Air Force Base, Florida	Egypt through the Persian Gulf region, into Central Asia.
United States European Command (EUCOM)	SHAPE (Supreme Headquarters Allied Powers Europe), Belgium USEUCOM HQ in Stuttgart, Germany	Europe and Israel
United States Pacific Command (PACOM)	Camp H. M. Smith, Oahu, Hawaii	The Asia-Pacific region, including Hawaii
United States Southern Command (SOUTHCOM)	Miami, Florida	South, Central America, and the surrounding waters
United States Africa Command (AFRICOM)	Kelley Barracks, Stuttgart, Germany for now; to be relocated to African continent	Africa excluding Egypt and Saharan Africa

Functional commands

Command	Home base	AOR
US Special Operations Command (SOCOM)	MacDill Air Force Base, Florida	Provides special operations for the Army, Navy, Air Force, and Marine Corps
US Joint Forces Command (JFCOM)	Naval Support Activity Headquarters (Norfolk) and Suffolk, Virginia	Supports other commands as a joint force provider
United States Strategic Command (STRATCOM)	Offutt Air Force Base, Nebraska	Covers the strategic deterrent force and co-ordinates the use of space assets
United States Transportation Command (TRANSCOM)	Scott Air Force Base, Illinois	Covers global mobility of all military assets for all regional commands.

Strategy has to be translated into successful military operations by linking and co-ordinating efforts in time and space. This is the operational level of war, or *operational art*, which is defined as the use of military forces to achieve strategic goals through the design, organization, integration, and conduct of campaigns, major operations, and battles (Department of the Army 2001). The UCCs employ operational art, in concert with strategic direction received from the NCA, to develop *campaigns* and *operations*. Operational art is the process by which commanders effectively use resources to achieve strategic objectives;

otherwise, war would be a set of disjointed engagements, with attrition as the only measure of success (Defense Technical Information Center 2009). Continuing with the football analogy, the operational level of the coaches' strategic design would perhaps entail running up the middle early in the game to tire the opposing defense, then running sweeps with speedier players later in the game to capitalize on fatigued defenders.

Strategy and operational art will ultimately result in battles. *Tactics* or the tactical level of war is defined as the employment of units in combat (Department of the Army 1997). This is the level of war at which battles are planned and executed to achieve military goals. Activities at this level focus on the spatial arrangement and movement of combat units in relation to each other, the military operating environment, and the enemy to achieve objectives (Guidebook 2008). Once again employing our football analogy, tactics are the individual plays and formations used by the coach to take advantage of the opposing team's weaknesses.

There is a clear geographic hierarchy to the levels of war, and military geographers typically study them at the macro- and microgeographic levels (see Figure 2.2). *Macrogeography* is the large-scale analysis of military problems and environments, usually at the strategic and operational level of war. At the macro level, military geographers link strategy to geographic concepts such as strategic choke points, transportation nodes, global water or energy resources, movement corridors, strategic deployment, and the size and shapes of states. At the tactical level of

Figure 2.2
Definitions and scope of macro- and microgeographic analyses.

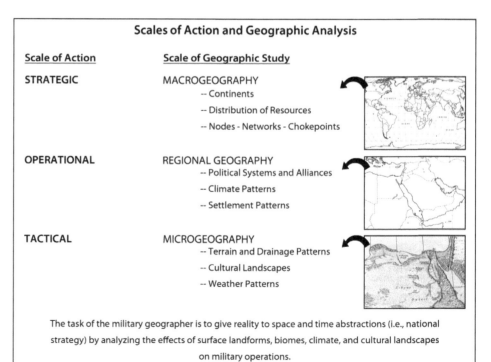

Scales of Action and Geographic Analysis

Scale of Action	Scale of Geographic Study
STRATEGIC	MACROGEOGRAPHY -- Continents -- Distribution of Resources -- Nodes - Networks - Chokepoints
OPERATIONAL	REGIONAL GEOGRAPHY -- Political Systems and Alliances -- Climate Patterns -- Settlement Patterns
TACTICAL	MICROGEOGRAPHY -- Terrain and Drainage Patterns -- Cultural Landscapes -- Weather Patterns

The task of the military geographer is to give reality to space and time abstractions (i.e., national strategy) by analyzing the effects of surface landforms, biomes, climate, and cultural landscapes on military operations.

war, military geographers characteristically study military problems at the *microgeographic* level, which includes small-scale, very detailed studies of terrain, vegetation, drainage patterns, soils, road networks, urban street patterns, and weather effects.

Military units and basic weapons systems

Military units

Military units are classified by type, function, and size (see Figure 2.3). There are many types of military units ranging from combat units (e.g. infantry, armor, and artillery) to combat support (e.g. military police) and logistical functions (e.g. quartermaster and transportation). For our purposes, we will focus on combat units: i.e. infantry, armor, cavalry, engineer, aviation, air defense artillery, and artillery. The discrete unit symbols associated with each type of unit are given in Figure 2.3. However, on the modern battlefield, we seldom see pure combat units. They are characteristically grouped together in *combined arms teams* of two or more types of units called a *task force*. These groupings are based on the mission to be accomplished, and in large measure influenced by the geography of the battlefield. For example, a task force maybe infantry-heavy in an urban or heavily forested environment, but may change to a tank-heavy configuration in a more open situation such as a steppe or desert (Department of the Army 1997).

Figure 2.3
Diagram illustrating unit symbols for various military units.

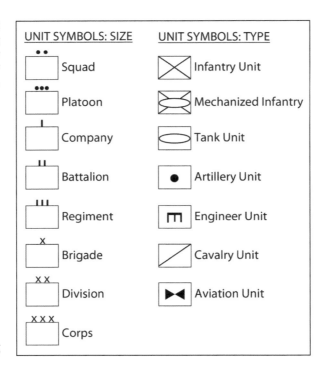

26

Military units are also classified by size, and the appropriate unit symbols are given in Figure 2.3. The *squad* is the basic military unit. It consists of about seven to ten soldiers, and is led by a sergeant. Three or more squads are grouped into a *platoon*, which includes forty soldiers or four to five major weapons (e.g. tanks). A *company* is a military unit, typically consisting of 75–200 soldiers. Most companies are formed of three to five platoons, although the exact number may vary by unit type, mission, and structure. In artillery units, the company is called a "battery" and is called a "troop" in cavalry units.

A *battalion* is a unit of about 500–1500 soldiers, usually consisting of between three and six companies, and typically commanded by a lieutenant colonel. A tank battalion would have about fifty tanks and an artillery battalion would have about twenty-four guns. Some battalion-sized units are called squadrons (e.g. cavalry and aviation units). A battalion is generally the smallest military unit capable of independent operations. The battalion is usually part of a regiment, group, or a brigade, depending on the organizational model used by that service. The bulk of a battalion will ordinarily be homogeneous with respect to type (e.g. an infantry battalion or a tank battalion), although there are many exceptions based on task organization (Department of the Army 1997).

A *regiment* is a military unit composed of a variable number of battalions and commanded by a colonel. Depending on the nation, military branch, mission, and organization, a modern regiment resembles a *brigade*, in that both range in size from a few hundred to 5000 soldiers (three to seven standard battalions). Generally, regiments and brigades are grouped into divisions. The modern regiment/brigade's size varies from country to country. Squads, companies, battalions, and regiments/brigades are normally considered tactical units because they plan and conduct day-to-day battles, usually at small spatial scales (Department of the Army 1997).

A *division* is a large military unit consisting of around 15,000–20,000 soldiers. In most armies, a division is composed of several brigades, and, in turn, several divisions make up a *corps*. In most modern armies, a division tends to be the smallest combined arms unit capable of sustained independent operations due to its self-sustaining role as a unit with a range of combat troops and suitable combat support forces. A modern US mechanized division will have about 300 tanks, 300 armored fighting vehicles, 6000 infantry, 72 guns, and 60 attack helicopters (Department of the Army 2001). The division normally operates at the tactical level, but during recent conflicts they have assumed an operational role.

Basic military weapons

Perhaps the largest of the ground weapons is the *tank*. A tank is a tracked, armored fighting vehicle designed with offensive and defensive capabilities. Firepower is normally provided by a large-caliber main gun in a rotating turret and secondary machine guns. Its heavy armor and all-terrain mobility provide protection for the crew, allowing it to operate on the battlefield. The infantry's cousin to the tank is the armored personnel carrier or *armored fighting vehicle (AFV)*. AFVs are light, armored fighting vehicles designed for the transport of infantry. They usually have only a machine gun, although variants carry recoilless rifles, anti-tank guided missiles, light cannon, or mortars. Fire support to soldiers is provided by artillery units, which use howitzers or guns. A *howitzer* is a type of artillery piece that is characterized by a relatively short barrel and the use of comparatively small explosive charges to propel projectiles with a steep angle of descent. By contrast, a longer barrel, larger propelling charges, higher velocities, and flatter trajectories characterize a gun. *Mortars* are cheap, simple, indirect-fire weapons, usually carried by infantry troops. *Mortars* fire explosive shells at very high arcs, but over relatively short ranges.

Although they have been used during previous wars, the *improvised explosive device (IED)* has gained major notoriety during recent fighting in Iraq. An IED is a bomb constructed and deployed in ways other than in conventional military action. They may be comprised of conventional military explosives, such as an artillery round, attached to a detonating mechanism, or may be homemade devices triggered by a variety of mechanisms. A highly specialized variant is the *explosively formed penetrator (EFP)*, also known as an explosively formed projectile. This is a device with a self-forging warhead, or a self-forging fragment, which is a special type of shaped charge designed to penetrate armor. They were first developed during World War II.

Aircraft are divided between fixed- and rotary-wing types. Fixed-wing aircraft include fighters and fighter-bombers, bombers, and transports. Rotary-wing aircraft consist of utility helicopters, gunships or attack helicopters, and scout helicopters. A *fighter* aircraft is designed primarily for attacking other aircraft, as opposed to a *bomber*, which is designed primarily to attack ground targets by dropping bombs. Fighters are comparatively small, fast, and maneuverable, and are the primary means by which armed forces gain air superiority. At least since World War II, air superiority has been a key component of victory in conventional warfare. An *attack helicopter*, also known as a helicopter gunship, is a military helicopter armed for attacking infantry, armored vehicles, and structures, using automatic cannon and machine-gun fire, rockets, and precision guided missiles. Many attack helicopters are also capable of carrying air-to-air missiles.

Two new types of air weapons that have gained importance during the past two decades are the cruise missile and un-manned aircraft. A *cruise missile* is a guided missile that carries an explosive payload and uses a jet engine. Cruise missiles are designed to carry a large conventional or nuclear warhead many hundreds of miles with great accuracy.

Modern cruise missiles can travel at supersonic or subsonic speeds, are self-navigating, and fly very low to avoid radar. In general, cruise missiles are distinct from *unmanned aerial vehicles (UAVs)* in that they are used as weapons and not for reconnaissance. UAVs, or drones, are flown remotely (they are not autonomous aircraft) and can serve in a reconnaissance role and fire missiles.

Primary modern seaborne weapons include the destroyer, cruiser, aircraft carrier, and submarine. In naval terminology, a *destroyer* is a fast and maneuverable warship intended to escort larger vessels and defend them against submarines and aircraft. Destroyers are armed with guns, torpedoes, missiles, and anti-submarine weapons. A *cruiser* is a large warship intended for individual raiding and protection missions. Today the cruiser provides primary air defense to a fleet and carries an array of missiles. The *aircraft carrier* is a warship designed for deploying and recovering aircraft, thus acting as a seagoing airbase. They permit a naval force to project air power without having to depend on local bases. Finally, the *submarine* is a ship that can operate independently underwater.

Types of operations

Military operations can be divided into two broad categories: wartime or combat operations; and operations other than war. The wartime spectrum encompasses offensive and defensive operations, and various forms of maneuver. Operations other than war have proliferated greatly since the end of the Cold War and comprise an array of missions predicated on assisting governance and establishing stability.

Wartime operations

Offensive operations are the decisive form of war, and are used to defeat an enemy, secure important terrain or resources, or expel enemy forces from a region. Offensive operations permit a force to retain the initiative and dictate tempo. Offensive operations culminate when the enemy is defeated or the friendly force achieves its objectives. A classic example occurred at the end of the 1991 Gulf War, when allied forces terminated operations once Iraqi forces were expelled from Kuwait (Spiller 1992). Additional goals of offensive operations include: disrupting enemy coherence; securing or seizing terrain; denying the enemy resources; fixing the enemy in place; or gaining information about an enemy (Department of the Army 2001).

There are five basic forms of maneuver associated with offensive operations: the envelopment, turning movement, infiltration, penetration, and frontal attack. These forms of maneuver are not normally used independently, and are usually combined into a sequence of events that attack the enemy differently, which explains why we see military units

29

move across the battlefield in the way they do. From a geographic perspective, terrain, weather, climate, and cultural landscapes greatly influence the selection of a form of maneuver and often dictate the flow and tempo of operations once they begin.

The *envelopment* is a form of maneuver in which the attacker attempts to avoid direct contact with enemy defenders by seizing objectives in the enemy rear (see Figure 2.4). The objective is to surround the enemy. At the tactical level of war, envelopments focus on capturing important terrain features and interdicting enemy supply or withdrawal routes (Department of the Army 2001). The *turning movement* (see Figure 2.5) is a form of very deep envelopment during which the attacking force is focused on bypassing the enemy altogether and seizing important terrain objectives deep in the enemy rear, forcing them to retire from their forward positions. By creating such a deep threat, the attacker compels the enemy to attack or withdraw rearward, thus "turning" them out of defensive positions. Successful turning movements normally require greater operational depth than other forms of maneuver (Department of the Army 2001).

An *infiltration* is a form of tactical-level maneuver during which the attacker uses small units to exploit gaps in enemy defenses to reach a position in the enemy rear (see Figure 2.6). The key planning parameters with this form of maneuver are stealth and surprise; thus, geographic considerations are very important. Although infiltration attacks can be very disruptive, they are rarely decisive because the small size of the attacking units lacks the mass required to bring about a decision (Department of the Army 2001).

A *penetration* attack is designed to rupture enemy defenses on a very narrow front to dislocate the defensive system (see Figure 2.7). A commander will resort to a penetration when enemy flanks are not vulnerable or time does not permit another form of maneuver. Penetrations are usually directed into the strength of the enemy defense; hence, they risk higher casualties (Department of the Army 1997). A *frontal attack* is the least favored form of maneuver because the attacking force engages the defenders along their entire front and seeks to destroy or fix an enemy in place (see Figure 2.8). A frontal attack engages the enemy over the most direct approaches; consequently commanders will normally only use it when they possess overwhelming combat power, or can take advantage of favorable terrain and weather (Department of the Army 2001).

Regardless of the form of maneuver, a force may use one of four types of offensive operations, sequentially or in combination, as part of the maneuver to achieve an objective. The four types of offensive operations are the movement to contact, attack, exploitation, and pursuit. For example, a penetration may employ a movement to contact to find the enemy front, and then transition to an attack once the enemy force is

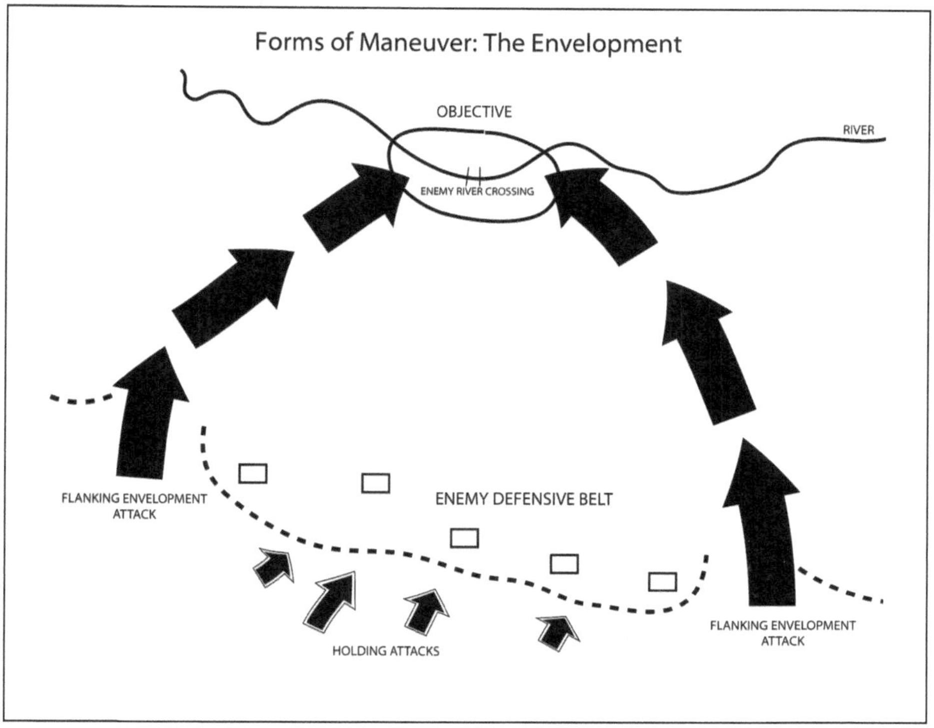

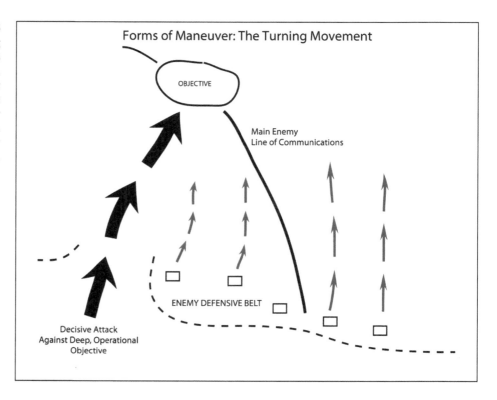

Figure 2.4
Diagram illustrating the principal elements of envelopment. Envelopment avoids enemy strength by focusing its decisive attack against an objective in the enemy rear, with the objective of capturing or destroying the enemy force.

Figure 2.5
Diagram illustrating the principal elements of a turning movement. A turning movement attacks a critical node deep in the enemy's rear area, thus causing them to be turned out of their defensive positions.

31

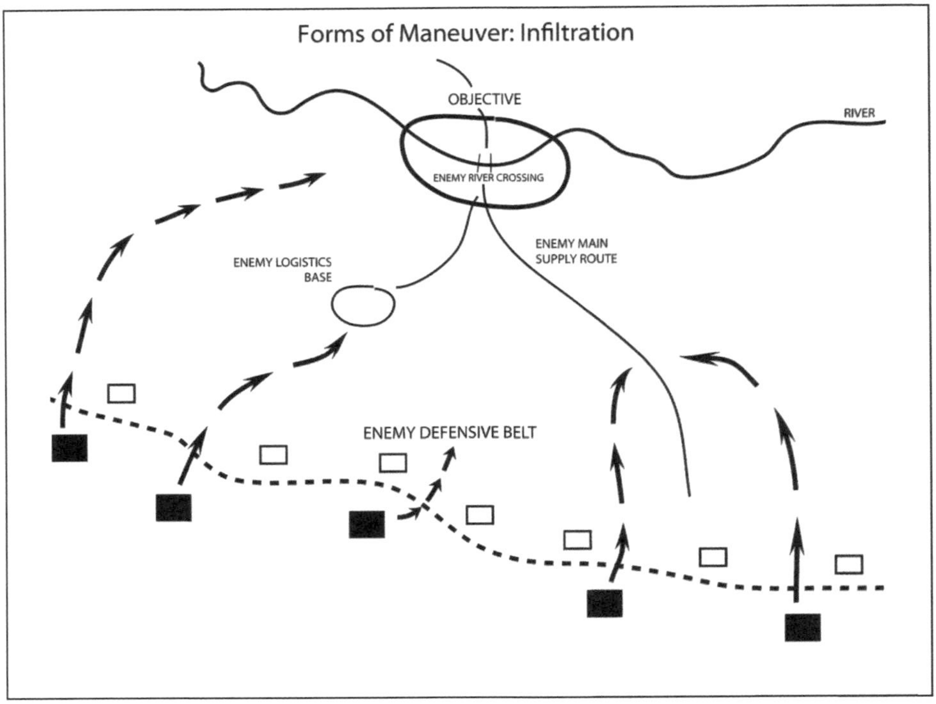

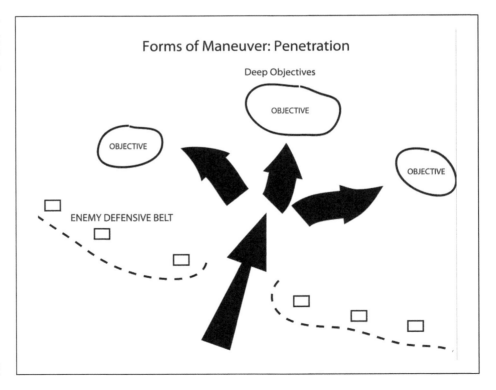

Figure 2.6
Diagram illustrating the principal elements of an infiltration. This form of maneuver uses covert movement by small units to penetrate gaps in an enemy defensive belt.

Figure 2.7
Diagram illustrating the key components of a penetration.

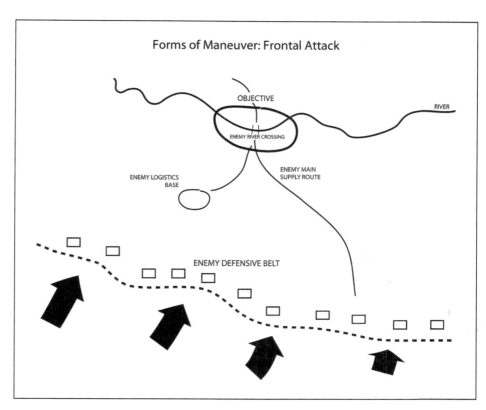

Figure 2.8
Diagram illustrating a
frontal attack.

found. Finally, when the enemy front is penetrated, the friendly force may transition to an exploitation and pursuit to destroy the enemy.

A *movement to contact* is designed to develop the situation and establish or regain contact. Units conducting a movement to contact seek to make contact with the smallest force possible. Once contact is achieved, the commander has five options: attack, defend, bypass, delay, or withdraw. An *attack* is an offensive operation that destroys or defeats enemy forces, seizes and secures terrain, or both. Attacks may be hasty or deliberate, depending on the time available. Hasty attacks take place when circumstances call for instantaneous action with available forces, in contrast to a deliberate attack that is used when there is time to develop plans and co-ordinate preparations. *Exploitations* and *pursuits* usually occur in sequence following a successful attack. Exploitations usually follow a successful attack and are intended to disorganize the enemy in depth, and disintegrate the integrity of their dispositions to the extent that they have no alternative but to surrender. A pursuit is a type of offensive operation designed to trap an enemy attempting to escape (Department of the Army 1997, 2001).

Defensive operations are not a decisive form of warfare, and a commander will resort to a defensive strategy to defeat an enemy attack, buy time, economize forces, or develop conditions favorable for offensive

operations (Department of the Army 2001). There are several types of
defensive operations, and they, too, are strongly influenced by geography. For example, the Russians have historically traded their vast
geographic space for time, taking advantage of inhospitable climate
conditions, mud, and poorly developed road systems to stymie enemy
attacks (Winters 1998).

Mobile defenses are focused on destroying attacking forces by permitting the enemy to advance into an area in which they can be counterattacked. The defending force seeks a geographic advantage to hinder
the attacker and enhance the defense. In contrast, the *area defense* is
designed to hold ground. The classic area defense draws the enemy
into a well-developed series of positions to break up enemy forces by
firepower. *Retrograde operations* are employed to move units away from
the enemy to gain time, preserve forces, or preclude combat under unfavorable circumstances (Department of the Army 2001).

Military Operations Other Than War

MOOTW comprise the use of military capabilities and forces across a
wide range of operations that fall short of war, and can be divided into
stability and support operations. These operations have been employed
throughout history, but their use has increased since the end of the Cold
War (Binnendijk 1998; Palka 2000). MOOTW focus on preventing violent
confrontations, resolving conflict, promoting peace, and supporting
civil authorities, but may also involve elements of combat operations
(Department of the Army 2000).

Stability operations

The US uses its forces in *stability operations* outside the country to
promote national interests and sustain regional and global stability. By
creating stability, the US hopes to promote peace and viable economic
conditions. Military units are ideal for stability operations because they
are equipped and organized to control land, populations, and situations
for extended periods in austere environments. Stability operations are
used to influence conditions in hostile environments and they include
developmental and co-operative activities during peacetime, but may
also use coercive measures during crises (Department of the Army 2001).
Stability operations are diverse, continuous, and often long term. For
example, the US maintained military forces on the Sinai Peninsula for
more than three decades to maintain peace and stability between Israel
and Egypt.

In an ideal scenario, stability operations focus on deterring or pre-
empting conflict. During a crisis, military units may be used to resolve
a conflict or prevent escalation by force, or they may keep violent conflict
from spreading. Stability operations are used to provide a secure

34

environment that permits civil authorities to reassume control following hostilities. There is a broad range of stability operations (Department of the Army 2001; Guidebook 2008):

- *Peace operations* encompass peacekeeping operations and peace enforcement operations conducted to support diplomatic efforts to establish and maintain peace.
- *Peacekeeping operations* are undertaken with the consent of all major parties to a dispute. They are used to aid the implementation of ceasefire agreements, or to support diplomatic efforts.
- *Peace enforcement operations* are enacted to apply or threaten military force to compel compliance with resolutions designed to maintain or restore peace. Peace enforcement operations normally do not require the consent of all parties.
- *Operations in support of diplomatic efforts* are used to establish peace and order before, during, and after conflicts, and may incorporate preventive diplomacy, peacemaking, and peace building.
- *Foreign internal defense* includes participation by civilian and military agencies of one government to free and protect the society of another government from subversion, lawlessness, and insurgency.
- *Security assistance* refers to a cluster of programs that supports national objectives by providing equipment, military training, and other services to foreign nations.
- *Support to insurgencies* is when the NCA employs forces to support insurgencies that oppose regimes that threaten national interests or regional stability. These are operations normally given to Special Forces (i.e. Green Berets, Navy Seals, etc.).
- *Support to counterdrug operations* uses military forces to interdict drug shipments along national borders and is a form of domestic support operation.
- *Counterterrorism* includes offensive measures taken to prevent, deter, and respond to terrorism. Military forces usually participate in the full array of counterterrorism actions, including strikes and raids against terrorist organizations and facilities.
- *Antiterrorism* operations are defensive measures used to minimize the vulnerability of individuals and property to terrorist attacks.
- *Noncombatant evacuation operations* are used to relocate civilian noncombatants from locations in a foreign state to secure areas. These operations involve citizens whose lives are in danger either from the threat of hostilities or a natural disaster.
- *Arms control* operations support treaties and enforcement agencies. Military forces can assist in locating, seizing, and destroying weapons after hostilities, or escort deliveries of weapons and material to preclude loss or unauthorized use, inspecting and monitoring production and storage facilities, or training foreign forces to secure weapons and facilities.

- *Show of force* operations are used to bolster and reassure allies, deter potential aggressors, and gain or increase influence.

Support operations

Support operations use military units to assist civil authorities as they prepare for, or respond to, crises and to relieve suffering. In these scenarios, military units provide essential support, assets, or specialized resources to help civil authorities manage situations beyond their capabilities. Support operations are important because they meet immediate needs for a restricted time, until civil authorities can do so using their assets (Department of the Army 2001).

Domestic support and foreign humanitarian assistance are the two broad forms of support operations. *Domestic support operations* use military units and capabilities to supplement the resources of local governments and organizations. Domestic support operations oblige careful co-ordination among governmental and non-governmental organizations. *Foreign humanitarian assistance* missions are usually conducted to relieve the results of natural or man-made disasters. Military units are used to supplement or complement efforts of the host nation, and are normally very limited in scope and duration, focusing on timely aid to resolve an immediate crisis. There are several forms of support operations:

- *Relief operations* are used to support the efforts of state, local, and host nation authorities after a disaster. These operations focus on recovery of critical infrastructure and on the wellbeing of supported populations.
- *Support to civil law enforcement* involves activities related to counterterrorism, counterdrug operations, civil disturbances, and general support to civil law enforcement organizations. Military support involves providing resources, training, or augmentation within the bounds of the law.
- *Community assistance* is a broad range of activities that provides support and maintains a strong connection between the military and civilian communities.

References cited

Binnendijk, H. (ed.). 1998. *Strategic assessment*. Washington, DC: Institute for National Strategic Studies, National Defense University.

Defense Technical Information Center (DTIC). 2009. *Overview of operational art*. www.dtic.mil/doctrine/jrm/opart.doc [accessed 30 April 2010].

Department of the Army. 1997. *FM 101-5, staff organizations and operations*. Washington, DC: US Government Printing Office.

———. 2001. *FM 3-0, operations*. Washington, DC: US Government Printing Office.

Department of Defense (DoD). 2009. Defense link. www.fas.org/pubs/index.html [accessed 30 April 2010].

Federation of American Scientists (FAS). 2009. *Publications and reports*. www.fas.org/pubs/index.html [accessed 30 April 2010].

Globalsecurity.org. 2009. *Military: defense policy and programs.* www.globalsecurity.org/
military/index.html [accessed 30 April 2010].

Guidebook. 2008. *Organization and functions guide.* Director of Administration and
Management. US Department of Defense. www.defenselink.mil/odam/omp/pubs/
GuideBook/ToC.htm [accessed 30 April 2010].

Palka, E. J. 2000. "Military geography: its revival and prospectus." In *Geography in
America at the dawn of the 21st century,* Gary L. Gaile and Cort J. Willmott (eds). London:
Oxford University Press.

Spiller, R. J. 1992. *Combined arms in battle since 1939.* Fort Leavenworth, KS: Command
and Staff College Press.

Summers, H. G. 1992. *On strategy II: a critical analysis of the Gulf War.* New York: Dell.

Weigley, R. F. 1973. *The American way of war, a history of the United States military strategy
and policy.* Bloomington, IN: Indiana University Press.

Winters, H. A. 1998. *Battling the elements: weather and terrain in the conduct of war.*
Baltimore, MD: Johns Hopkins Press.

Chapter three
An introduction to geography for non-geographers

FRANCIS A. GALGANO

Introduction

THIS CHAPTER IS provided to give the non-geographer a condensed overview of the discipline and a familiarization with geographic terms, themes, concepts, and methodologies. As with the previous chapter, this is not intended to be a complete introduction to geography in a traditional sense. Instead, it is designed to inform the reader (who may be a non-geographer) to ensure an understanding suitable for the content of this book.

Defining geography

Unfortunately, many people associate geography with knowledge of maps, lengths of rivers, names of countries and their capital cities, and the location of natural resources (Getis et al. 2008). Clearly, this type of factual knowledge has its place in geography because it permits us to position events, locations, and phenomena in a useful spatial setting. However, knowing and understanding *why* they exist in discrete places is significantly more important, and that is the true relevance of geography (Holt-Jensen 1999). Thus, geography is much more than simply knowing place names, cartography, and locations. Geographers attempt to understand places and the interconnectivity between them, and accordingly, military geographers focus their efforts on understanding the nexus between military operations and the landscape. To understand this nexus, the military geographer must understand the dynamics and processes of the natural and human landscape as well as their spatial and temporal patterns (Winters 1998).

The investigation of spatial variability—how and why things differ from place to place—gives purpose and methodology to geography (Lanegran and Palm 1978). Geography is further defined by the study of how spatial patterns develop through time, thus an awareness of locations is only an important initial step in understanding why things are where they are, and what events and processes determine change and distribution over time. For example, contemporary military questions may include: "Why have latent ethic divisions, non-sustainable practices, and environmental change conspired to trigger violent conflict in some places, and not in others?" or "Why have twenty of the world's most important battles been fought in a geographically confined space in Belgium and northeastern France?" By answering such questions, military geographers focus their enquiry on the interface between people, governments, and their relationship to the physical environment (Getis et al. 2008). Hence, geography—and military geography—is about space and the content of space (Palka 2003). Because military geographers usually employ an integrating approach in their enquiries, they are cognizant of the variety of processes affecting a place.

Geography and military geography have gained great importance during the past two decades given the pace of globalization, the collapse of the Soviet Union, and the aftermath of 9/11 (Janelle et al. 2004; Palka 2003). Each of these important global dynamics has a fundamental geographic origin, and geography is the only discipline dedicated to understanding how and why natural and human processes differ from place to place. The chapters in this book are designed to give the reader a basic knowledge of many of the salient security issues that shape our world. Additionally, knowledge of the ongoing geographic research agenda is central to grasping and understanding global security issues that dominate the modern world. The security implications of environmental change, the proliferation and security concerns associated with ungoverned space, the cumulative effects of population growth, global water resources, terrorist networks, and the problematic effects of non-sustainable practices in marginal environments have clear spatial dimensions, and geography is the discipline best situated to explain them (de Blij et al. 2007).

Subfields of geography

Geography is an integrating discipline and its core is defined by space, place, landscapes, and the interaction of processes (Livingstone 1992). Geography has two important divisions: physical and human geography, and the two broad branches include many subfields that overlap with other disciplines (see Figure 3.1). The focus of each subfield is not on shared subject matter, but instead on spatial manifestations of the subject material. The geomorphologist does not focus on rock structure, nor does the political geographer concentrate on politics, and, clearly, the military geographer does not focus on military science. More accurately, military geographers—like their colleagues in other subfields—approach their subject from a spatial perspective, emphasizing linkages between earth space and military activity, and the important

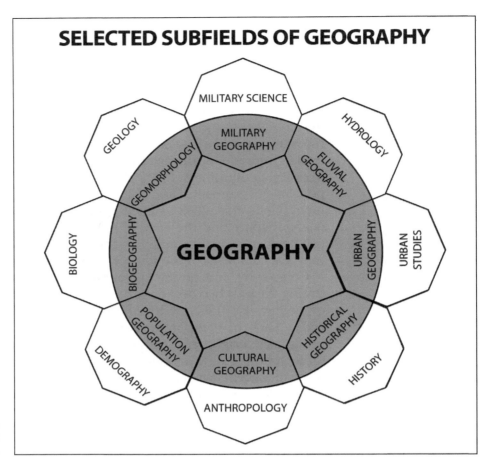

Figure 3.1
Selected geographic subfields.

themes of interaction, location, scale, distribution, and diffusion of security-related issues and processes (Palka 2003). Military geographers, however, also focus on the study of military operating environments (i.e. places and regions) by applying geographic information, tools, and technologies (Palka and Galgano 2005). Since the character of the area of operations, in its entirety, conditions any type of military operation, military geographers are drawn from across the spectrum of geographic subfields.

Geographic subfields are not isolated and the subdivisions are characterized by three overarching interests. First is the spatial variation of physical and human processes and their manifestations on the environment. Second is an examination of the systems that connect physical processes and human activities at one place with other places. Finally, regional analysis is a unifying and enduring theme regardless of the subdiscipline (Getis et al. 2008). Hence, it is at the regional level of synthesis that geographers can relate all aspects of the natural and human landscape to explain physical, cultural, political, economic, security-related, and social patterns to define the unique properties of places and their linkages to others (Peltier and Pearcy 1966).

By contrast, some geographers devote their research to the examination of unique types of phenomena for specialized study, rather than discrete portions of earth surface. Thus, *systematic geographers* concentrate their interest and research on a specific aspect of the physical or human landscape, rather than a defined space. For example, a fluvial geomorphologist employs the principles and physical laws of geomorphology to the discrete study of hydraulics, sedimentation, and landform evolution of fluvial channels, which are limited by a unique set of interactions.

Geography and its traditions

The breadth of geographic subject matter necessitates a simple, logical organizing principle for presentation to people unfamiliar with the discipline. Regardless of its complex outward appearance, geography demonstrates a consistency of purpose achieved through the recognition of four unifying traditions within which all geographers work: the earth science tradition; the culture–environment tradition; the spatial tradition; and the area analysis tradition (Pattison 1964; Robinson 1976).

Likewise, military geographers work within this framework, and the chapters of this book reflect the constancy and interrelationship between these timeless themes. In fact, the chapters demonstrate that the four geographic traditions are not only an organizational expediency, but also recognize that, although distinctive, they are at the same time interwoven. For example, the earth science tradition is the branch of geography that addresses the earth as the habitat of humans and employs physical geography to demonstrate the continuing and pervasive influence of the environment on military operations. Examples of this tradition are illustrated in chapters 8 through 15, which illustrate the influence of the physical environment on military operations using a historical, case study approach.

Humans interact with their habitat, and the environment may have a profound effect on people as well. This is the culture–environment tradition, within which population and distributions, patterns of social and political organization, and the development of the cultural landscape manifestly influence the nature of military operations (Peltier and Pearcy 1966). Hence, this theme is distinctive, but linked to the earth science tradition, because behaviors occur within the context of the physical realities of military operating environments. For example, in Chapter 5, Amy Richmond Krakowka demonstrates the linkages between people and their environment in Rwanda, and the influence of the environment on the ethnic violence that occurred there in 1994. Similarly, in Chapter 19, Joseph Hupy presents an example of the profound and long-lasting imprint of warfare on the environment by describing the alteration of the landscape near Khe Sanh in Vietnam.

The spatial tradition can be found at the heart of all military geographic inquiry, and it is clearly the unifying theme in all geographic research (Livingstone 1992; Holt-Jensen 1999). Maps, geographic information systems, GPS, remote sensing, and statistical methods are among the techniques employed by military geographers when exploring spatial patterns and the interconnectivity between natural and human systems. This tradition is principally concerned with the spatial patterns of weather, climate, landforms, and people; however, scale, movement, and areal relationships are also fundamental to the spatial theme (Robinson 1976). Hence, this tradition defines spatial patterns of interaction between humans and their environment, which are often the root cause of many violent conflicts. In Chapter 7, Bill Doe follows this tradition in his examination of military lands in the US.

Perhaps the strongest influence in military geographic research evolved from the area analysis tradition (Peltier and Pearcy 1966). Since it is the task of the military geographer to give reality to space and time abstractions such as strategy, operational art, and tactics by analyzing the effects of places and environments, area analyses are one of its principal unifying methodologies. As part of the area analysis tradition, the military geographer examines all aspects of the environment to develop an integrated story explaining the complexity, relevant dynamics, advantages, and disadvantages of a given place with respect to a military operation. To demonstrate the role of the area analysis tradition, Steven Oluić, in Chapter 13, examines the complex military operating environment in Bosnia, and how these factors of geography influenced the civil war and ethnic violence that occurred there during the early 1990s.

Basic geographic concepts

Like every discipline, geography incorporates a set of fundamental concepts that unite all subfields, frames its research, and determines answers to the study of the landscape. This is of course true of military geographers as they strive to answer their unique version of the common geographic questions: "What is the operating environment like?" "Why is it like this here?" and "How will it affect operations?" Certainly, these three questions are embedded in the geographer's interest in the variability of earth space and they are linked to core geographic traditions.

To answer these questions, the military geographer draws upon a common set of terms, concepts, and methodologies that lend structure to their study of operational environments. Geography is a spatial science and the common thread in all research is the recognition of spatial patterns. This is the necessary point of departure for understanding the nexus of military problems and the landscape (Peltier and

Pearcy 1966). Thus, like their colleagues, military geographers are concerned with spatial and temporal patterns, such as the behavior of cultural groups, the spatial extent of regions, the patterns of climatic and weather phenomena, and important attributes of the physical landscape along with the fundamental dynamics that trigger those patterns and relationships (Jackman 1962).

To the military geographer, then, the concept of space explains the way processes and dynamics cause things to be distributed, as well as the temporal patterns associated with phenomena that lend uniqueness to places. Thus, the military geographer understands that the content of places and dynamics of phenomena are structured and explainable:

- Places and phenomena have location, direction, and distance with respect to other places.
- Places and phenomena have size and scale.
- Places and phenomena have physical structure and cultural content.
- The nature of places and phenomena changes over time.
- Places and phenomena are related.
- Places and phenomena can be generalized into regions.

Location

The seminal geographic question is, of course, "Where is it?" Hence, knowing and understanding location is essential because it explains so much about discrete occurrences and places on the landscape. Location can be expressed in a variety of ways; the most useful method should be chosen depending upon the situation. Consequently, geographers view location from two important perspectives, absolute and relative.

To the geographer, *absolute location* is a way of describing the position of a place by using a precise co-ordinate system or other means of establishing an exact location. Thus, absolute location provides a means to describe exactly the position of places so that they can be placed in earth space. The geographer has several formal methods by which to articulate absolute location: latitude and longitude, state plane, or perhaps Universal Transverse Mercator co-ordinates. Geographers, however, may also employ informal means to describe absolute location. For example, seat 5, row G, section 21 of a stadium, or the corner of 5th and Main Street are useful indicators of absolute location as well (de Blij et al. 2007). Regardless, absolute location is unique to discrete places and has understandable value in spatially organizing places or placing them on a map, in measuring distance between places, in determining the direction between places, or in giving legal definition to a place (Getis et al. 2008).

Thus, absolute location is very useful for mapping and research purposes, such as describing the exact location of a study site, and it is useful to the military geographer because it permits the identification of discrete places, such as where battles or operations occur. However, it is of only limited value in that it offers little insight into spatial interconnectivity, which helps the military geographer explain why things are where they are. Hence, the use of *relative location* provides the military geographer with the position of a place or phenomenon relative to the location of other places or phenomena, and is a much more powerful concept. To the military geographer, relative location communicates spatial connectivity and interdependence. For example, Omaha Beach, one of the five D-Day invasion beaches, is located at 49° 22′ N, 2° 52′ W. However, this absolute location does not explain the physical characteristics of the place, or inform the military geographer as to why this location was selected as one of the D-Day invasion sites, given the hundreds of kilometers of suitable coastline in northern France. Davies (1946) illustrated the value and power of relative location in his detailed explanation of the geographic reasons why Normandy was selected as the invasion site, given that there were actually better invasion beaches available to the Allies, and he demonstrated how the choice was driven by Normandy's geographic connection to other places, or relative location (see Figure 3.2).

Given that geographers distinguish different methods of relating location, they also make a distinction between a place's *site* and *situation*. Site refers to the characteristics of the local setting or internal aspects of

Figure 3.2 Factors of relative location that led to the selection of Normandy as the D-Day invasion site in 1944. Normandy was selected over more favorable coastal areas because of its advantages linked to its location. *Source*: after Davies (1946).

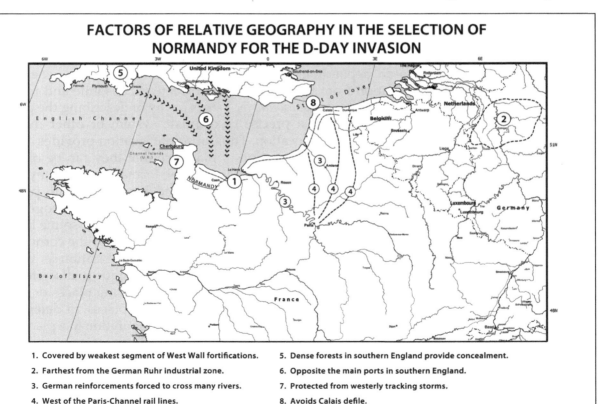

FACTORS OF RELATIVE GEOGRAPHY IN THE SELECTION OF NORMANDY FOR THE D-DAY INVASION

1. Covered by weakest segment of West Wall fortifications.
2. Farthest from the German Ruhr industrial zone.
3. German reinforcements forced to cross many rivers.
4. West of the Paris-Channel rail lines.
5. Dense forests in southern England provide concealment.
6. Opposite the main ports in southern England.
7. Protected from westerly tracking storms.
8. Avoids Calais defile.

a place, and in the military geographic context, may include such attributes as relief, climate, vegetation, soil composition, mobility potential, street patterns, and the availability of water. If certain aspects of a place—or site—appear to afford a distinct advantage to a military commander, then, potentially, it may be selected as a site for a battle. Situation, on the other hand, refers to the external relations of the place and is an expression of relative location with particular reference to the geographic significance of the place in question (de Blij et al. 2007).

Distance is another location-related concept employed by geographers. Distance links locations and may be viewed in both an absolute and a relative sense. The spatial separation between points, usually measured by some known standard (e.g. miles or kilometers), defines absolute distance. In contrast, relative distance translates linear measurements into other, more meaningful, spatial relationships. For example, two routes of march from a starting point to an objective point that may be potentially used by an army may be of nearly equal length. However, the absolute distance may be less important in selecting a route, because the longer of the two may have more favorable terrain and thus, though longer, may actually take less time.

Size and scale

Along with location, size and *scale* are perhaps the most important concepts employed by geographers in their examination of natural and human landscapes; issues of scale have always been central to geographic theory and research (Abler et al. 1992). Size and scale lend relative dimensions to places and phenomena. Geographic scale is defined as the representation of real-world phenomena at a certain level of generalization (de Blij et al. 2007). For example, when we say that a place is large or small, we are normally addressing the character and physical dimensions of the place. Generalization is significant because the earth can never be examined or represented in its full complexity. Thus, scale is necessary because of its effect on the degree to which geographic information is digested and generalization refers to the quantity of detail included in an analysis; it is fundamentally an issue of simplification, but also includes aspects of selection and enhancement of features of particular interest. For example, as military geographers examine smaller sections of the landscape, they tend to deal with more detailed data regarding terrain and human landscapes (Getis et al. 2008).

Places and their military attributes

Places are unique and manifest discrete natural and cultural attributes that differentiate them from other places. This is important to the military geographer because their attributes lend strategic, operational, and tactical importance to places, and furnish them with character, potential, and meaning (Peltier and Pearcy 1966). Military geographers are concerned with identifying and analyzing the details of the attributes of places, especially in recognizing the interconnectivity between natural and human landscapes.

The study of geography has established that places matter. Each place is unique and demonstrates a discrete set of geographic imperatives. Furthermore, places interact, thus creating compelling and sometimes difficult dynamics and conditions within which military units must function. Military geographers typically think of places as *military operating environments*, each exclusively influenced by the interrelationship of a distinct set of geographic variables. The scale of a place is, in a military sense, a function of the level of war (see Figure 3.3). At the strategic level, a place or operating environment may be an entire continent. At the operational level, it may be a region or country. At the tactical level; it could be something as small as a city block.

Karl von Clausewitz captured the nature of place when calling the military operating environment "terrain," and in his view "terrain" was composed of "the territory and inhabitants of the whole theater of war" (von Clausewitz 1976: 67). Furthermore, von Clausewitz demonstrated that the operational significance of the operating environment varies with the mission, organization, and type of military units involved, technology, and current circumstances: in other words, site remains constant, but situation changes over time. So too, then, must a military geographer's assessment of place.

Thus, the military operating environment is the sum total of all factors of the natural and cultural landscape that shape and control military

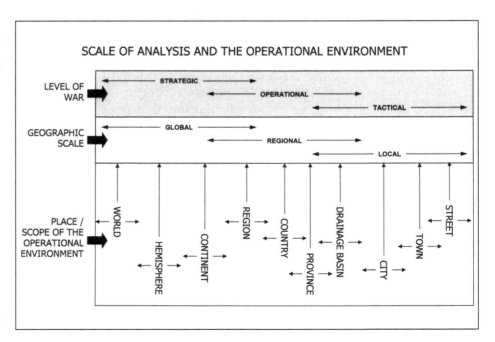

operations during peacetime or war (Galgano 2005). The military operating environment is composed of a place's weather and climate, its landforms and topography, human populations, networks, systems and cultural landscapes. In the final analysis, an examination of a place, from a military perspective, typically results in an assessment of:

- key terrain—strategic areas and selected critical targets/objectives
- surface structure—movement corridors and terrain compartments, natural obstacles
- critical topographic features—relief, hydrologic features, landforms, vegetation
- transportation networks and nodes—road systems, railroads, ports, airfields
- resources and host nation support—clean water, medical facilities, living facilities
- logistical requirements—medical, specialized equipment
- observation and concealment: ground and air
- human landscapes.

Regions

The *region* is a contemporary concept used by geographers to define and describe an area of earth space that is part of a larger whole. Regions can be characterized by physical characteristics, human characteristics, or their functional characteristics (de Blij et al. 2007). As a way of describing discrete spatial zones, the concept of the region is important and used among many geographic subfields, and each describes areas in terms of its branch of geography. For example, physiographic region is a term used by geomorphologists, a drainage basin is a highly specialized region employed by fluvial geographers, and a bioregion is a term used in biogeography (Getis et al. 2008).

The distinguishing characteristics of regions directly imply several important ideas. Each region has a unique absolute location and is distinguished by distinctive natural and human characteristics; hence, no two places can be the same. However, the physical and cultural characteristics of places, in fact, do demonstrate patterns similar to other areas (Getis et al. 2008). For example, a military geographer studying desert operating environments will find similar landforms, soils, weather patterns, and perhaps agricultural techniques in others. Thus, geographic consistency exists; therefore, a geographer can recognize and define regions that express internal consistency and external difference from adjacent areas. However, geographers concentrate on important unifying similarities to establish regional boundaries (de Blij et al. 2007).

Military geographers typically focus on the study of formal and functional regions. A *formal region* is an operating environment that manifests homogeneity with respect to a distinctive natural or cultural attribute (de Blij et al. 2007). The formal region is a substantial area within which a legitimate generalization may be made with respect to an attribute. For example, a subtropical steppe area would form a unique formal climate region with distinctive temperature and precipitation patterns, vegetation, soils, landforms, and perhaps cultural landscapes. Consequently, a formal region is based on tangible (e.g. landforms, vegetation, industry, soils, agriculture, religion, or language) and sometimes statistically derived features such as per-capita income, birth rates, or human indices.

In contrast to the formal region, a *functional region* is a spatial system with interdependent components, and its defined geographic extent is a function of the dynamics of the system under study. The functional region has unity in the manner of its operational connectivity, not a sense of static content; the defining characteristics of functional regions are interaction and connection. A military geographer may define a functional region based on military alliances, trade organizations, terrorist cells, or areas linked by a common ethnic dynamic.

Military regional analysis: the environmental matrix

History and contemporary events have demonstrated that there is a clear link between military operations and geography. Factors of geography have had a compelling influence on battles throughout history. In recent times, the influence of geography on peacetime military operations and operations other than war has been equally pervasive (Palka 2003). Likewise, the important geographic concepts of location, time, space, scale, and distance must be considered during the planning and execution of any military operation. Consequently, the military geographer is compelled to employ an integrating approach to study an operating environment and ascertain how geography may potentially influence an operation. Even at the smallest tactical scale, operating environments are complex. Thus, the best analyses benefit from an integrated methodology that offers a comprehensive framework against which an informed analysis can be conducted.

The development of a military strategy involves the selection of objectives, a method, and sequence of employment, and the movement of military power to an objective area. In a wartime scenario, the ultimate purpose of a strategy is to weaken or destroy the enemy's ability to resist, and different strategies have been pursued. The most fundamental strategy is the employment of military force to annihilate or force an enemy to capitulate. A different form of strategy is a more limited, and annihilation is thought to be impossible or unattainable because military power is inadequate. Insurgent forces use this type of strategy to prosecute political–military objectives (Galgano 2005). Insurgents seldom seek decisive battle. As an alternative, they employ military force at selected times and places with the objective of wearing down their opponent. Today, in the context of operations other than war, a field commander may be presented with a set of difficult and confounding variables in a very complex operating environment. In that situation, the commander is not preparing for battle, but is perhaps planning for a multifaceted disaster relief or peacekeeping operation (Palka 2003).

Clearly, political objectives, economic wherewithal, and the means available influence strategy. In one situation, the destruction of enemy forces may be the objective, but in another taking terrain to strangle the opponent by denying needed supplies may be more suitable. Nevertheless, regardless of the strategy, the success of any military operation—in peacetime and during war—depends on a sound plan that takes into account a cogent analysis of the military operating environment. A methodology by which we may examine the geographic significance of the military environment is the *environmental matrix*, which is defined as the sum of all factors that operate in a place, and which can have an effect on the successful execution of any operation (Garver 1975; Galgano 2005). The environmental matrix includes both physical and cultural components of the landscape, and assumes that the military operating environment is the manifestation of the combined effects of the natural and human landscapes and processes (Peltier and Pearcy 1966). The matrix, however, is only a methodology for analysis, and is *not* a predictive tool, hence care must be taken to re-evaluate significant elements of the matrix continuously because they can vary considerably for different periods, different areas, and different culture groups. The elements of the environmental matrix are given in Figure 3.4.

The physical, or natural, elements of the matrix define the basic features of the physical landscape, which essentially forms the template upon which a military force must operate. In addition to location and place, they include the features of weather and climate, water, topography and relief, soils, plant and animal life, and resources (see Figure 3.4). In their countless combinations, the natural elements of the matrix are the physical framework of the military operating environment. Their careful analysis as discrete factors and as an integrated whole provides insight into the possibilities and limitations associated with mounting any form of military operation in a given place (Galgano 2005). Thus, they need to be understood by themselves; more importantly, they need to be understood and appreciated as they occur in natural combinations, for that is how they are constituted at differing scales and in various operating environments (Garver 1975; Jackman 1962). Physical elements of the matrix include:

Location

Location in reference to space is probably the single most important aspect of an environment's physical make-up as it establishes weather patterns, climate, biomes, landforms, and culture systems.

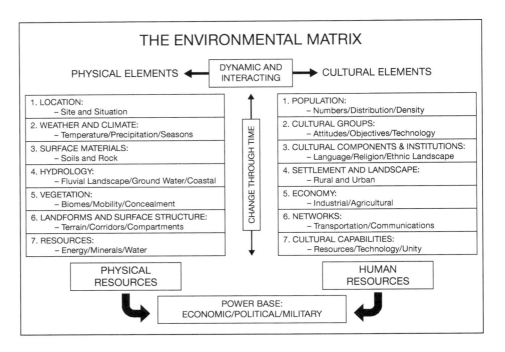

Figure 3.4
The environmental matrix is defined as the sum of all factors that operate in a place, and which can have an effect on the successful execution of any operation. The environmental matrix includes both natural and cultural components of the landscape, and assumes that the military operating environment is the manifestation of the combined effects of the natural and human landscapes.

Landforms and surface structure
From the military perspective, the analysis of landforms and surface structure offers important insight into characteristics such as movement corridors, terrain compartments, obstacles, and the location of critical resources.

Hydrology
The features most important in terms of military operations are land surface drainage systems, such as streams, lakes, ponds, wetlands, swamps, glaciers, snowfields, and coastal waters. In most cases these are viewed as obstacles to military operations; however, rivers and amphibious operations can provide a force with unprecedented mobility.

Weather and climate
Perhaps the most completely pervasive factors that influence military operations on a day-to-day basis are the weather and climate. Weather is the short-term state of the atmosphere. Most places have persistent

and relatively predictable weather patterns. Climate is the long-term construct of weather at a given place and is classified in terms of long-term averages of temperature and precipitation data.

Surface materials

There are many varieties of surface materials (e.g. soils, rock, ice, or sand), some highly productive and some essentially worthless; however, regardless of their relative value, collectively soils make an important contribution to the military environment in terms of mobility, visibility, and health.

Vegetation

Plants seldom grow alone, but rather in groups or combinations called biomes. The type of vegetation and the productivity of the biome give an indication of climatic conditions. Vegetation has a significant effect on all types of military activities, and it must be considered carefully in planning operations, to include the potential effect of vegetation on movement, concealment, cover, observation, airdrops, the availability of fuel, shelter, food, and construction material.

Mineral resources

The earth provides humans with many products, which can be used directly or processed into useful goods. Mineral resources are significant not only as fundamental requirements of modern industrial society, but also because they may figure prominently in territorial disputes.

The natural elements of the environmental matrix are complemented by significant cultural or human elements, which must be taken into account before considering a military operation. In summary, cultural aspects of the matrix include: population and distribution; culture systems, traits, and institutions (e.g. language, religion, and political units); settlement patterns; economic pursuits; networks of transportation and communication; and the cultural/technological capabilities of the society. Physical and cultural elements of the matrix are closely interrelated throughout the operating environment; however, their combinations and interrelationships are in no way constant, and the proportion of the whole contributed by each element varies from place to place. Furthermore, the elements themselves change through time. Various combinations of the physical elements present different possibilities to human development. Because humans are present in differing numbers, because ways of doing things vary from one group to another, cultural settings vary as much as physical settings.

Population

From the geographic perspective, the seminal human variable correlates to population and demographics: numbers, distribution and patterns, movement, and density.

51

Cultural groups

The manner in which humans live and make a living in an area is not the same for all peoples. Even given essentially the same physical setting, two different groups may create very dissimilar cultural landscapes. Differences exist largely because traditions, or learned ways of behaving, of one group differ from those of another. So do the material manifestations—the houses, the roads, the fields, the equipment, and the settlement patterns—of one group differ from those of another. The sum of the traditions for any distinctive group of people and of the material manifestations of those traditions is called culture.

Cultural institutions

In the contemporary world there are many cultural institutions, which leave their imprint upon the landscape. There are others less easy to recognize that, nevertheless, have profound effects in creating differences and similarities between cultural groups. Any full understanding of the cultural environment must make allowance for these cultural institutions.

Settlement patterns and land use

Perhaps the most common indicators of human presence and activity in a region are their dwellings and other buildings, which suggest how they use the land. Individually, the house furnishes clues to the way a group lives in a region and suggests other forms, which have been created. Types and arrangements of dwellings differ among cultures and can tell much about a people.

Economies

Settlement and land use are partly adapted to the physical setting, but they also reflect the main activities by which human groups make a living. The most concentrated and complex groupings evidence the economy of manufacturing and commerce, wherein most of the individuals are not directly concerned with securing a livelihood through agriculture, but rather through the transformation of raw materials into manufactured products.

Networks of transportation and communication

The transportation and communication network ties the whole human habitat together through roads, highways, railroads, power lines, pipelines, air terminals, port facilities, and electronic/digital means.

Cultural capabilities

As has been noted, development by different cultural groups, particularly in agriculture and industry, varies significantly among states and
regions.

In summary, the integration and analysis of interacting physical and human elements of the matrix define the limitations and opportunities within a given operating environment. Each place is unique and influenced differently by facets of the matrix; thus, distinctive and precise analyses are required for each operation, which are scale and time independent (Galgano 2005). The differentiation of the world into unique areas is the result of a multitude of processes through which nature and humans determine the contents of space; consequently, our analyses have to be precise, and broad-brush generalizations about one segment of a region may not apply to another (Garver 1975). Thus, the environmental matrix is the product of successive modifications by physical and cultural processes that have been ceaselessly active in the past and will continue in the future. Every area is constantly in flux and military plans must be made to account for this flux. Accordingly, the analysis of a given military operating environment is also a continuing process and forms an important component in the study of military geography.

References cited

Abler, R. F., M. G. Marcus, & J. M. Olson (eds). 1992. *Geography's inner worlds: pervasive themes in contemporary American geography*. New Brunswick, NJ: Rutgers University Press.

Davies, A. 1946. "Geographical factors in the invasion and battle of Normandy." *Geographical Review* 36(4): 123–42.

de Blij, H. J., A. B. Murphy, & E. H. Fouberg. 2007. *Human geography: people, places, and culture*. New York: John Wiley & Sons, Inc.

Galgano, F. A. 2005. "The environmental matrix." In *Readings in military geography*, F. A. Galgano (compiler), 8th edn. West Point, NY: US Government Printing Office.

Garver, J. B. 1975. "The environmental matrix." In *Readings in military geography*. West Point, NY: US Government Printing Office.

Getis, A., J. Getis, & J. D. Fellmann. 2008. *Introduction to geography*. 8th edn. New York: The McGraw-Hill Companies, Inc.

Holt-Jensen, A. 1999. *Geography: its history and concepts*. 3rd edn. Thousand Oaks, CA: Sage.

Jackman, A. 1962. "The nature of military geography." *Professional Geographer* 14: 7–12.

Janelle, D. G., B. Warf, & K. Hansen (eds). 2004. *World minds: geographical perspectives on 100 problems*. Dordrecht: Kluwer Academic.

Lanegran, D. A. & R. Palm. 1978. *An invitation to geography*. 2nd edn. New York: McGraw-Hill.

Livingstone, D. N. 1992. *The geographical tradition*. Cambridge, MA: Blackwell.

Palka, E. J. 2003. "Military geography: its revival and prospectus." In *Geography in America at the dawn of the twenty-first century*, Gary Gaile and Cort J. Willmott (eds). Oxford, UK: Oxford University Press.

Palka, E. J. & F. A. Galgano (eds). 2005. *Military geography from peace to war*. New York: The McGraw-Hill Companies, Inc.

Pattison, W. D. 1964. "The four traditions of geography." *Journal of Geography* 63: 211–16.

Peltier, L. C. & E. G. Pearcy, 1966. *Military geography*. Princeton, NJ: D. Van Nostrand Company, Inc.

Robinson, J. L. 1976. "A new look at the four traditions of geography." *Journal of Geography* 75: 520–30.

von Clausewitz, K. 1976. *On war*. Oxford World's Classics. New York: Oxford University Press.

Winters, H. A. 1998. *Battling the elements*. Baltimore, MD: Johns Hopkins University Press.

Chapter four
Environmental security
A growing force in regional stability

KENT HUGHES BUTTS

Introduction

MODERN MILITARY GEOGRAPHERS must contend with much more than the hedgerows of Normandy or the logistics-paralyzing mud of the South Pacific. The security milieu and the role of the military have changed dramatically, requiring a broader approach to security and a better understanding of the causes of conflict. Globalization has reduced the friction of distance and created expectations of economic growth and affluence to match Western lifestyles. So, too, globalization is exacerbating the gap between the haves and have-nots that is putting many developing states in danger of failing, and creating ungoverned spaces ripe for extremist ideology and exploitation by international crime organizations. As the global population rises toward an estimated 2050 level of 9.2 billion, it will exceed the natural resource base of many states, erode governmental legitimacy, destabilize regions, and promote intrastate conflict over increasingly scarce resources (Hardee and Jiang 2009).

Environmental issues are now a major factor in regional stability and state security, affecting the supply and demand sides of these problems. Notwithstanding the two brief force-on-force phases of the Gulf Wars, the major issue confronting the military establishment since the end of the Cold War is conflict rooted in environmental security issues. This chapter explores the relationship of environmental issues to national security, explains the definitional framework that underpins the use of *environmental security* by the US Government, and discusses the trends that will make environmental security central to US foreign policy objectives and an important military role for the near future.

The concept of environmental security

Because of its interdisciplinary nature and the variety of backgrounds and motivations that security analysts bring to the debate, there will always be disagreement on what constitutes environmental security. For example, the literature is replete with typologies of environmental conflict, with concepts based on variables such as climate change, development, migration, and resource scarcity. This is good, for it encourages multiple disciplines to examine the dimensions of environmental conflict, bringing their own methodologies and skill sets to better inform the debate and offer richer solutions to policymakers. Fortunately, this is possible because security studies have moved decisively to include a spectrum of explanatory concepts in this important field of study, one of which is environmental security.

In his article "The Renaissance of Security Studies," Dr Stephen Walt made clear what the security studies field of academia considered relevant subject matter. He stated that, "Security studies assume that conflict between states is always a possibility and that the use of military force has far reaching effects on states in society. Accordingly, security studies may be defined as the study of the threat, use, and control of military force" (Walt 1991: 214). However, he went on to say that legitimate security studies research may explore the "conditions that make the use of force more likely, the ways that the use of force affects individuals, states, and societies, and the specific policies that states adopt in order to prepare for, prevent, or engage in war" (Walt 1991: 214). Increasingly, environmental issues were recognized as the conditions that make the use of force more likely; thus, they affect security.

After the Cold War, NATO revised its strategic concept to reflect the new security milieu; in addition to traditional defense matters, future threats to Allied security would come from instability caused by unaddressed social, political, economic, and environmental issues (NATO 1991). In his congressional testimony on security threats facing the US, Director of National Intelligence Admiral Dennis Blair explained further:

> Climate change, energy, global health and environmental security are often intertwined, and while not traditionally viewed as "threats" to U.S. national security, they will affect Americans in major ways. Such a complex and unprecedented syndrome of problems could cause outright state failure, or weaken pivotal states counted on to act as anchors of regional stability.
>
> (Blair 2009: 41)

Today, the chief threat to US national security issues is regional instability, and environmental security issues are a major element of this problem.

While academics and some environmental groups may disagree on the definition of environmental security, it is important to understand that there is an accepted definition of environmental security in the US interagency community, which drives a common US Government approach to environmental security and policies related to that definition. It was informed by the research and findings of Tad Homer-Dixon's work, and reflects much of the theoretical contributions of Alexander Carius and Kerstin Imbusch in their four dimensions of the environmental security nexus (Carius and Leitzmann 1999). Environmental security is a process whereby solutions to environmental problems contribute to national security objectives (USEPA 1999). When environmental factors affect national security issues, as defined by the US National Security Strategy, they become environmental security issues and legitimate subjects for address by the diplomatic, developmental, and defense sectors of government.

In 1986, the Goldwater–Nichols Department of Defense Reorganization Act amended the National Security Act of 1947 and required the President to issue a National Security Strategy to guide US foreign policy. When President Ronald Reagan signed his 1988 National Security Strategy it included threats to US interests from the Soviet Union's nuclear arsenal, and "the dangerous depletion or contamination of natural endowments of some nation's soil, forest, water, and air" that "create potential threats to the peace and prosperity that are in our national interests as well as the interests of the affected nations" (The White House 1988: 6). Other National Security Strategies followed suit, stating that environmental issues cause, trigger, or exacerbate conflict (The White House 1991, 1997). Thus, conflict over access to, or control of, natural resources that threatens regional stability may threaten US national security interests. So, too, co-operation between regional countries to prevent transnational environmental crime, such as over-fishing by foreign-flag trawlers or illegal logging, which promotes confidence building and communication, may enhance US national security interests.

Typically, environmental issues affect US national security interests when they: serve to threaten those interests; serve as confidence-building measures; or threaten the human security of state populations. Thus, the Department of Defense (DoD) role has been to "deter or mitigate the impacts of adverse environmental actions leading to international instability" (Goodman 1993: 2). The Department of State emphasizes the environmental and natural resource competition dimensions of conflict: "Environmental security refers to a range of security issues caused or exacerbated by such demographic and environmental factors as population growth, competition for resources (namely food, fuel and water), urbanization, migration, health issues, and, in some instances, climate change" (Harnish 2009: 1). At the US Environmental Protection Agency (EPA) there has been an emphasis on environmental security as a confidence-building measure: "It encompasses the idea that cooperation among nations and regions to solve environmental problems can help advance the goals of political stability, economic development, and peace" (USEPA 1999: 1).

In 1991, the US and the Soviet Union co-sponsored the Madrid Conference hosted by Spain. The objective of the conference was to create a peace process between Israel, certain Arab countries, and the Palestinians. The process methodology called for creating multilateral fora in which the Israelis and the Palestinians would participate. The subjects chosen for the fora were water, environment, refugees, economic development, and arms control (Israeli Ministry of Foreign Affairs 1991). Thus, for three of the five issues the environment played a primary role, and agreements reached through this process still govern the sharing of water resources between Israel and its neighbors. When examining the significance of environmental phenomena in their spatial context it is important to consider not just the negative impacts of threats to stability from resource conflict, but also these potentially positive implications as confidence-building measures.

The *Westphalian system* of the nation state has long guided practitioners of foreign policy. While it has retained its importance and primacy among security strategists, the rise of the concept of human security has increased awareness of the impact of environmental issues on state legitimacy. The 1994 *Human Development Report* by the United Nations Development Programme was a watershed in elevating the importance of the human condition to security studies (United Nations Development Programme 1994). Human security, rather than state power alone, increasingly determines the stability of regions.

When US national security interests are threatened by regional instability, that instability increasingly comes not from major power meddling, but from the inability of countries to meet the demands placed on the political system by a population seeking freedom from want and freedom from fear. These systemic demands increasingly include drought, food insecurity, pandemics, and resource conflict. Governments that lack legitimacy are vulnerable to extremist ideology, and are more likely to fail or experience intrastate conflict over scarce resources. Environmental issues directly affect the ability of governments to provide for the needs of their people and are, thus, an element of human security and a critical variable in state legitimacy.

The US experience in Afghanistan and Iraq demonstrated the limitations of military power and the pyrrhic victory of regime change without creating a government capable of providing for its population's human security needs, demonstrating the link between state and human security concepts. Environmental issues are now seen as an essential element of post-conflict sustainable development and stability, so much so that the DoD has crafted *Directive 3000.05, Military Support for Stability,*

Transition, and Reconstruction Operations (Department of Defense 2006).

It states that the immediate goal of stability operations "is to provide the local populace with security, restore essential services, and meet humanitarian needs." It states significantly that "stability operations are a core U.S. military mission . . . they shall be given priority comparable to combat operations" (DoD 2006: 2). Similarly, the Department of State has created the Office of the Co-ordinator for Reconstruction and Stabilization (S/CRS) (Department of State 1997). This interagency organization seeks to build governmental capacity in order to bring stability in a post-conflict environment or to prevent conflict, and thus focuses upon the ability of the government to successfully address human security (Bankus 2009). The latest thinking on combining the traditional state-centric, hard-security paradigm with the human security-based focus on soft power and governmental legitimacy can be found in the CSIS *Commission on Smart Power Report* (CSIS 2007).

As the case of Rwanda demonstrates, many developing countries have multiple national groups within their political borders with the potential for, or long simmering, ethnic conflict. When the government is composed disproportionately of a particular group, then other ethnic groups often assume that the resources of the country are not being evenly distributed. If the country experiences economic difficulties, the government will likely be accused of unfairly reducing benefits to the regions of the country populated by the other ethnic groups, with the potential to undermine political stability. To the degree that the developed world can provide sustainable development aid and build the host nation's capacity for successful natural resource and environment management, it creates a more positive milieu in which these groups may seek national identity and a feeling of belonging, and builds governmental legitimacy.

Environmental threats to security

The US is faced with a group of environmental challenges that will directly affect regional stability and US national security interests for the foreseeable future. These challenges include combating terrorism, climate change, food security, and freshwater scarcity. They are not mutually exclusive, but often affect one another and are themselves affected by such trends as globalization, population growth, urbanization, and disease.

Combating terror

The Global War on Terror was the *raison d'être* for the Bush administration and has been regularly listed as the principal US national security issue, as well as the rationale for many foreign-policy decisions. The US Combating Terrorism Strategy, written by the National Security Council, had four objectives, one of which was to diminish the underlying conditions that terrorists seek to exploit (National Security Council 2003). This objective was subsequently broadened to include the concept of countering ideological support for terrorism. For many developing countries the primary underlying condition of terrorism is poverty, which stems often from environmental degradation and non-sustainable exploitation of natural resources. Republic of the Philippines President Gloria Macapagal-Arroyo makes the case for a balanced approach to terrorism that emphasizes the need to address the underlying conditions that foster terrorism: "We have to fight poverty in the places where they can recruit their support" (Green 2005: 27). This phenomenon is not limited to Southeast Asia. In the North Caucasus, where some republics have 80 percent unemployment and the per capita gross domestic product is half that of Russia, poverty and other socioeconomic issues are driving the populace into rebel organizations with ties to international Islamic terrorists groups. In the words of Moscow Carnegie Center's Alexi Malashenko, "Fundamentalist Islam is a form of social protest" (Buckley 2005: 4).

Environmental problems challenge governments and make it difficult for them to satisfy human security demands placed upon the political system. Terrorists seek to exploit this to their advantage. Hamas and Hezbollah gained power on Israel's borders by providing basic services to the people: "By providing what governments have not, these insurgents have gained legitimacy, psychologically conditioned these populations, and created an area from which they can safely operate" (Gregson 2005: 2). Thus, sustainable development is the key to governmental legitimacy in developing countries. When a shortage of fresh water, widespread disease, natural or man-made disasters, or food security issues beset a population, governmental legitimacy is challenged and extremist ideology is given opportunity. These issues are growing in importance in much of the Muslim world, from North Africa to Southeast Asia. Within this Islamic crescent lies the bulk of the world's conventional petroleum reserves and three declared nuclear states.

Climate change

Global environmental change is already changing the world's political landscape, making the resource base upon which stable governments depend more dynamic than ever before. With climate change, the security priorities of those governments will change, and necessitate forming new alliances, building resilience and adaptation mechanisms for their economies, and broadening the role of their militaries. Hence, climate change may be characterized as affecting US national security at three levels. At a global level, climate change affects moisture patterns and energy retention, and will have a direct impact on earth systems and reduce the resources upon which human kind depends.

At a geopolitical level, more powerful storms, droughts, and increased migration will affect the US homeland. Rising sea levels and loss of habitable space are creating new geopolitical areas of concern and complicating the work of defense planners to project power, influence regional events, and maintain forward bases like Diego Garcia (Reynolds 2007). The surprising melting of the Arctic sea ice has already ignited geopolitical competition for the 25 percent of global energy resources thought to underlie the polar region, with Russian explorer Artur Chilingarov throwing down the gauntlet by saying, "the Arctic has always been Russian" (Zellen 2007: 1).

At the regional level, changes in climate will threaten the survival of fragile states, create opportunities for extremist ideology and insurgencies, put at risk access to strategic fuel and mineral resources, and create instability that threatens US national security interests (United Nations Environment Programme 2009). Speaking of global climate change in the new Quadrennial Defense Review (QDR) (Department of Defense 2006), Under Secretary of Defense Michelle Flournoy explained,

> I believe that over time, as the results of this manifest, it's going to be an accelerant. It's going to accelerate state failure in some cases, accelerate mass migration, spread of disease, and even possibly insurgency in some areas as weak governments fail to cope with the effects of global climate change.
>
> (Flournoy 2009)

A warmer planet will experience rising sea levels. Glaciers will melt and remove the seasonal water flow management system that prevented floods and provided river water for irrigation during the dry season. Prolonged droughts in arid areas will result in declining crop yields, starvation, and forced migration. Increased rainfall from more powerful storms will spread waterborne disease and change agricultural patterns. The Intergovernmental Panel on Climate Change (IPCC) has predicted a devastating melting of the Tibetan Plateau glaciers, which feed the major rivers of Asia, and the weakening of the South Asia monsoons (Intergovernmental Panel on Climate Change 2007). This will directly impact the security of the world's two most populous countries, China, which is struggling with drought in agriculturally rich areas of the country, and India, which in 2009 experienced its weakest monsoon season and worst drought in the last 40 years, with 23 percent lower than average rainfall in the major rice- and grain-producing areas (Agarwal 2009).

Food security

The availability of food is a growing and contentious issue that affects developed as well as developing countries. Europe now expects large influxes of immigrants by 2020 as climate change affects arable land and agriculture in North African countries. A loss of as much as 75 percent of the arable land could be expected in North and sub-Saharan Africa from drought and over-farming (Castle 2008). The Ogallala aquifer that runs from the northern Great Plains south into Texas supports a large portion of US grain production. The aquifer has been over-pumped for years, and portions of Texas have been removed from cultivation because the aquifer is drying up. Global rice stock figures for 2007–8 by the US Department of Agriculture showed rice stocks of only 72 million tons, half its peak of 2000–1 and the weakest since 1983–4. Asian aid agencies fear an inability to feed the hungry and the corresponding price rise for rice is creating political tensions in many Asian countries. President Macapagal-Arroyo of the Philippines hosted a food summit in April 2008 to demonstrate her concern about falling rice production and a doubling of prices since 2004 (Associated Press 2008). China is predicting grain harvest drops of another 10 percent because of global warming. Complicating this is competition for grain by meat producers meeting the demands of an increasingly affluent Chinese middle class for animal protein (Toy 2007). The dynamics of the food market and rising fertilizer costs make it difficult for governments to maintain crop production to support growing populations in increasingly arid climates.

Water scarcity

Water is an opportunity for either peacemaking or a cause of future conflict, or both. Well-respected academics will argue persuasively that for thousands of years no nations have gone to war specifically over water resources (Wolf et al. 2005). However, policymakers such as Ariel Sharon and Boutros Boutros-Ghali speak with equal passion about the role of water in international conflict. Intrastate conflict over water has certainly occurred, and Sharon explains that the 1967 war in the Middle East actually began two years earlier when Israel intervened to prevent the diversion of the Jordan River headwaters by Syria (Sharon and Chanoff 1989). For these reasons, whether as a standalone issue or a multiplier effect for pre-existing tensions, water will play an increasingly important role in regional stability and security. Water has also proven to be an excellent vehicle for negotiating co-operative agreements between countries with existing hostilities and promoting communication and co-operation.

Water security is a critical variable in the sustainability of cultures and governments. Climate change is affecting the distribution and retention of water in many critical areas. Global temperature rise is melting glaciers that once stored water for increasingly large urban populations and agriculture. Geographic shifts in rainfall pattern are already creating forced migration and conflict in Muslim states critical to the US effort to combat terrorism. Water is essential to industrial and agriculture production, and frequently governs the location of profitable industries. The economic growth of both India and China is dependent upon increasingly scarce freshwater resources. Following the dynamic pattern of water scarcity in regions that are critical to US national security interests is essential to managing conflict and maintaining stability.

The global political implications of environmental security for US foreign policy are significant. The environmental threats discussed above provide a framework of analysis with which to determine the priority regions, functions, and countries of US foreign affairs. The effects of these trends will vary temporally and spatially in regions that are important to US national security.

Conclusions and recommendations

The DoD is already doing much to address environmental security; however, much remains to be done. Security analysts should think of the military establishment as a resource to apply to all security problems, to include environmental change. The military need not lead, but could provide essential resources or bring leverage to bear on security issues being addressed by other organizations. Doing so may make the difference between success and failure.

Environmental security has been demonstrated to be a process wherein environmental problems can be used to contribute to national security objectives, both in reducing tensions over environmental issues and by using commonly held environmental problems as confidence-building measures to bring together countries that may themselves have other sources of tension. The military has an interest in environmental security because it has a mission of promoting regional stability and has found preventing conflict much cheaper than introducing combat forces. In addition, because of their benign nature environmental security issues lend themselves to promoting multilateral co-operation in regions of significant tensions such as South Asia and Northeast Asia. Both US and host nation militaries are uniquely suited for addressing many environmental security issues. The military has good communications, a presence on the frontiers and in border areas, relatively good transportation assets, technical expertise, an existing security mission, and the role of preparing for disasters and other crisis. Moreover, involving the military creates military support for civil authority, builds legitimacy, and adds a resource with which the government may address the human security demands on the political system.

References cited

Agarwal, V. 2009. "India: Monsoon season ends with devastating drought." *Wall Street Journal* (1 October). http://article.wn.com/view/2009/10/01/Indias [accessed 9 November 2009].

Associated Press. 2008. "Rising rice prices spark concerns." 27 March. http://www.ap.org/ [accessed 9 November 2009].

Bankus, B. C. 2009. "Environmental security in peacekeeping operations." In *African environmental and human security and AFRICOM in the 21st Century*, Helen Purkitt (ed.). Youngstown, NY: Cambria Press.

Buckley, N. 2005. "Insurgency in North Caucasus spreads out from Chechnya: poverty and heavy handed security forces are boosting support for Islamist rebel groups." *Financial Times* (29 August). www.ft.com/cms/s/0/f10df062-1828-11da-a14b-00000e 2511c8.html [accessed 30 April 2010].

Blair, D. C. 2009. "Annual threat assessment of the intelligence community for the Senate Select Committee on Intelligence." *Statement for the Record* (February).

Carius, A. & K. M. Leitzmann. 1999. *Environmental change and security: a European perspective*. New York, NY: Springer-Verlag.

Castle, S. 2008. "Europe's leaders warned of big rise in migration." *New York Times*. www.nytimes.com/2008/03/07/world/europe/07iht-migrate.4.10815080.html?_r=1 [accessed 30 April 2010].

Center for Strategic and International Studies (CSIS). 2007. *Commission on smart power report*. Washington, DC: Center for Strategic and International Studies. http:// media.csis.org/smartpower/071105_CSIS_Smart_Power_Report.pdf [accessed 30 April 2010].

Department of Defense (DoD). 2006. *Quadrennial defense review report 2006* Washington, DC: US Government Printing Office. www.globalsecurity.org/military/library/ policy/dod/qdr-2006-report.htm [accessed 9 November 2009].

Department of Defense (DoD). 2006. *Directive 3000.05, military support for stability, transition, and reconstruction (SSTR) operations*. Washington, DC: US Government Printing Office.

Department of State, 1997. *Environmental diplomacy: the environment and U.S. foreign policy*. Washington, DC: US Government Printing Office.

Flournoy, M. 2009. *Remarks on the quadrennial defense review*. Washington, DC: Center for Strategic and International Security. 29 April. Transcript by Federal News Service.

Goodman, S. W. 1993. *Statement before the United States Senate Committee on armed services, subcommittee on military readiness and defense infrastructure*. Washington, DC: Senate Committee on Armed Services Subcommittee on Strategic Forces. http://armed-services.senate.gov/statemnt/980324wg.htm [accessed 30 April 2010].

Green, W. 2005. "Family comes last, interview with Philippine President Gloria Macapagal Arroyo." *TIME Asia* (6 June).

Gregson, W. C. 2005. "Ideological support: attacking the critical linkage." In *The struggle against extremist ideology*, Kent Hughes Butts & Jeffrey C. Reynolds (eds), 21–9. Carlisle, PA: Center for Strategic Leadership.

Hardee, K. & L. Jiang. 2009. *How do recent population trends matter to climate change?* Washington, DC: Population Action International.

Harnish, R. L. 2009. *Environmental security information memo for the secretary*. Washington, DC: United States Department of State.

Intergovernmental Panel on Climate Change (IPCC). 2007. *IPCC fourth assessment report: climate change 2007 (AR4)*. Cambridge, UK: Cambridge University Press. www. ipcc.ch/publications_and_data/publications_and_data_reports.htm [accessed 30 April 2009].

Israeli Ministry of Foreign Affairs. 1991. *The Madrid framework*. www.mfa.gov.il/ MFA/Peace%20Process/Guide%20to%20the%20Peace%20Process/The%20Madrid%2 0Framework [accessed 30 April 2010].

National Security Council (NSC). 2003. *National strategy for combating terrorism*. Washington, DC: US Government Renting Office.

NATO. 1991. *The alliance's new strategic concept*. North Atlantic Treaty Organization. www.nato.int/cps/en/natolive/official_texts_23847.htm [accessed 30 April 2010].

Reynolds, P. 2007. "Russia ahead in arctic 'gold rush'." BBC News, 1 August, http:// news.bbc.co.uk/2/hi/in_depth/6925853.stm [accessed 30 April 2010].

Sharon, A. & D. Chanoff. 1989. *Warrior: the autobiography of Ariel Sharon*. New York, NY: Simon & Schuster.

Toy, M. A. 2007. "Climate change threatens China's food supply." *Sydney Morning Herald* (24 August). www.smh.com.au/news/environment/climate-change-threatens-chinas-food-supply/2007/08/23/1187462441067.html [last accessed 9 November 2009].

United Nations Development Programme (UNDP). 1994. *Human development report.* New York, NY: Oxford University Press. http://hdr.undp.org/en/media/hdr_1994_en_contents.pdf [accessed 30 April 2010].

United Nations Environment Programme (UNEP). 2009. *From conflict to peacebuilding: the role of natural resources and the environment.* www.unep.org/publications/search/pub_details_s.asp?ID=3998 [accessed 30 April 2010].

USEPA. 1999. *Environmental security: strengthening national security through environmental protection.* Washington, DC: US Government Printing Office.

Walt, S. M. 1991. "The renaissance of security studies." *International Studies Quarterly* 35: 211–39.

The White House. 1988. *The national security strategy of the United States.* Washington, DC: US Government Printing Office.

———. 1991. *The national security strategy of the United States.* Washington, DC: US Government Printing Office.

———. 1997. *The national security strategy of the United States.* Washington, DC: US Government Printing Office.

Wolf, A., A. Kramer, A. Carius, & G. Dabelko. 2005. "Water can be a pathway to peace, not war, global policy forum." Worldwatch Institute. www.worldwatch.org/node/79 [accessed 30 April 2009].

Zellen, B. 2007. "The new Cold War: global warming reveals hidden riches beneath the polar sea, causing Arctic resource conflicts to heat up." *Security Innovator*, Boulder, CO: University of Colorado, http://securityinnovator.com/index.php?articleID=12387&sectionID=43 [accessed 30 April 2009].

Chapter five
The environment and regional security
A framework for analysis

AMY RICHMOND KRAKOWKA

Introduction

THE LINK BETWEEN VIOLENT conflict and environmental degradation is a matter of some polemic. Recent events, however, have exhibited a connection between environmental stress and conflict because these stresses intensify latent ethnic and political fissures, thus undermining security. Evidence suggests that this trend will persist because environmental change will continue to stress marginal and frontier environments in places with inherently weak governance. These events have inspired an acceptance of the relationship between regional stability and environmental factors, and represent fertile ground for military geographic analysis because of their clear temporal and spatial dimensions (Butts 1994; Homer-Dixon and Levy 1995).

The strategic division of the world during the Cold War usually ensured that adequate control was exerted over proxy regimes to preclude regional hot spots from escalating into violent confrontations. The proliferation of ungoverned space, however, combined with diluted superpower control over former surrogate regimes since the end of the Cold War, has enabled festering ethnic and political enmities to erupt into violent conflicts often triggered by environmental stress (Renner 2002). This dilemma is aggravated by non-sustainable environmental practices, migration, and resource shortages (Schwartz and Randall 2003; Gleditsch, Nordås, and Salehyan 2007). This chapter does not contend that the nature of modern conflict is new; in fact, insurgency, ethnic clashes, and civil war are ancient modes of warfare. It does maintain, however, that global environmental stress is enabling an increase in the frequency of conflicts with an environmental component. Furthermore, environmentally triggered conflict is fueled by dynamic, complex, and interacting environmental processes. Consequently, a framework for analysis is useful to understand causes and consequences.

65

With conflicts in Somalia, Bosnia, Rwanda, East Timor, and Kosovo as the precedent, the use of Western and United Nations (UN) military force to address humanitarian dimensions of regional conflict has been now well established, although UN and Western leadership has approached these commitments with acute reluctance (Dulian 2004). Nonetheless, conflicts with an environmental component coupled with divisive ethnic dimensions, such as those observed in Rwanda, have increased pressure on the West and the UN to commit military resources to stability efforts (Drapeau and Mignone 2007).

In fact, strategic policy documents produced by the US National Security Council (NSC 1991) and Department of Defense (DoD 2005) have delineated US strategic interests in environmentally enabled instability. The environment first became an element in the US National Security Strategy in 1991, when the NSC pointed out that, "stress from environmental challenges is already contributing to political conflict" (NSC 1991: 2; Butts 1994). By 2005, the DoD identified environmentally related instability as a fundamental strategic concern because of evidence that environmental stress was an important contributor to contemporary conflicts. Furthermore, environmental conflict typically manifests itself along ethnic lines, thus making its international management difficult (DoD 2005).

The environment, security, and conflict

The incidence of environmentally triggered conflict is not new. Researchers have offered compelling evidence that suggests the role of environmental stress in precipitating warfare in ancient China and the collapse of the Mayan, Anasazi, and Akkadian civilizations (Gibbons 1993; Abate 1994; Diamond 2005; Mays 2007; Zhang et al. 2007). Recent examples in Chiapas (Mexico), Rwanda, Somalia, and Darfur seem to indicate the nexus of environmental stress and violent conflict is a reality and that the specter of contemporary environmental change and resource scarcity may prompt an increase in violent conflict (Homer-Dixon 1999; Schwartz and Randall 2003).

Environmental stress alone does not necessarily trigger violent conflict. Evidence suggests that it enables violent conflict when combined with weak governance and social fragmentation, to affect an escalation of violence, typically along latent ethnic divisions. The spatial distribution of contemporary environmental stress is pervasive, but not uniform. Contemporary trends, however, indicate that environmentally driven violence is concentrated in the developing world or other regions with extreme social fragmentation and stratification (Homer-Dixon 1999; Gleditsch, Nordås, and Salehyan 2007). Developing states are more susceptible to environmentally triggered violent conflict because they are, characteristically, more dependent on the environment for their economic productivity, have higher concentrations of *subsistence farming*, and have manifested weak governance during the past decade (Homer-Dixon 1999; Galgano 2007).

Weak governance is a seminal problem in the developing world and, since 1990, the number of failing states has increased. The World Bank (Kaufmann, Kraay, and Mastruzzi 2003) examined *effective sovereignty* by monitoring six key metrics as a means of quantifying the level of governance. Their findings suggest that, of 187 states examined, 92 exhibited considerable levels of political instability and can be categorized as failing states. In the category of *government effectiveness*, 75 states exhibit significant levels of ineffectiveness, and 20 of those indicated an alarming drop in government control since 1998 (Kaufmann, Kraay, and Mastruzzi 2003). Table 5.1 shows the links between governance, the environment, and stability; it illustrates the 15 states with the least effective governments and 15 states with the most effective, demonstrating the global dichotomy in governance. The states that are bold have experienced environmentally related violence during the past decade. Table 5.1 also indicates those states that have recently experienced violence with a significant environmental component. It is useful to note the correlation between governance, violence, and key environmental indicators.

Ungoverned space is problematical because these places have large areas that are outside of effective government control and, thus, can be affected severely by humanitarian disasters, environmental stress, and ethnic conflict. This is because they typically lack effective institutions and the financial and material resources to safeguard the population from the effects of environmental stress (Galgano 2007). Consequently, this raises the complexity of the problem for government leaders as well as directors of non-governmental organizations and intergovernmental bodies as they attempt to develop relief strategies, especially without an effective framework for understanding the nature of the conflict and its environmental underpinnings (deMenocal 2001).

Environmental conflict: causes and results
Environmental stress will play a pervasive role in future conflicts because the economic well being of about one-half of the world's population is tied directly to the land, thus making agricultural space, water, fuel, and forested space critical environmental indicators, especially considering anticipated population growth and projected climate change. This is important because nearly 2 billion people do not have access to clean drinking water (Gleick 2008), and nearly 75 percent of the world's most impoverished inhabitants are subsistence farmers attempting to live on increasingly smaller plots of land. Drought, *desertification*, deforestation, soil erosion, and exhaustion are major problems in these regions. These are compounded by the fact that
67 although agricultural space, *biomass fuels*, and water are renewable

Table 5.1: Level of governance, 1996–2002, and key environmental indicators

State (rank)	Governance index[1]	Human development index[2]	Percent of land under agriculture	Annual freshwater withdrawals, percent of resources
Somalia (198)	−1.99	—	70.50	54.83
Congo Dem Rep (197)	−1.94	0.41	—	—
Iraq (196)[3]	−1.76	—	22.91	121.31
Afghanistan (195) [4]	−1.74	—	58.34	42.29
Liberia (194)	−1.74	0.80	26.99	711.33
Burundi (193)	−1.65	0.41	91.16	2.85
Haiti (192)	−1.55	0.53	57.69	0.90
Rwanda (191)	−1.48	0.45	45.00	1.58
Sudan (190)	−1.47	0.53	56.32	124.40
Angola (189)	−1.44	0.45	46.03	0.24
Congo (188)	−1.44	0.55	—	—
Myanmar (187)	−1.43	0.58	16.61	4.84
Sierra Leone (186)	−1.42	0.34	39.10	0.24
Central African Rep (185)	−1.39	0.38	8.26	0.02
Ivory Coast (184)	−1.38	0.43	—	—
United States (15)	1.54	0.95	45.41	17.12
United Kingdom (14)	1.55	0.95	—	6.58
Australia (13)	1.62	0.96	58.19	4.86
Austria (12)	1.66	0.95	40.92	3.84
Liechtenstein (11)	1.66	—	43.75	—
Sweden (10)	1.73	0.96	7.73	1.73
Denmark (9)	1.74	0.95	62.90	21.17
New Zealand (8)	1.74	0.94	64.38	0.65
Singapore (7)	1.76	0.92	1.78	—
Norway (6)	1.77	0.97	3.44	0.57
Netherlands (5)	1.78	0.95	13.57	72.18
Iceland (4)	1.84	0.96	22.75	0.12
Finland (3)	1.88	0.95	7.34	2.31
Luxembourg (2)	1.89	0.94	49.42	—
Switzerland (1)	1.97	0.96	38.13	6.36

[1] Aggregate governance index derived from Kaufmann, Kraay, and Mastruzzi (2003). This index was developed by an examination of six metrics (i.e. voice and accountability of the government; political stability and absence of violence; government effectiveness; regulatory quality; rule of law; and control of corruption) during four periods between 1996 and 2002. A more negative score indicates weaker governance.
[2] Human development index provides a composite measure of three dimensions of human development: life expectancy, adult literacy, and standard of living. See http://hdr.undp.org/en/.
[3] Iraq governance data was recorded before the 2003 US–led invasion.
[4] Afghanistan governance data was not recorded for 2002, after the *Taliban* was ousted from power.

resources, in many places non-sustainable practices are depleting them far beyond their renewal capacity (Homer-Dixon 1999).

This scenario is made more problematic because anticipated population growth, especially in the developing world, will result in higher per capita consumption rates, exacerbating extant non-sustainable practices. Thus, it is anticipated that environmental stress will make an increasingly significant contribution to three modes of conflict: 1) ethnic/racial warfare enabled by environmental stress and population pressure; 2) civil warfare instigated by environmental stress and economic collapse; and 3) limited-scale interstate wars along an adjacent border. Although these are essentially local-scale events, they do have the potential to become major regional wars that defy global management (Homer-Dixon 1999; Drapeau and Mignone 2007).

Defining environmental security

This chapter is focused on the link between *environmental security* and conflict, and offers an analytical framework to assess how environmental stress affects intrastate confrontations. This relatively narrow approach is adopted because one accepted definition of environmental security, i.e. "a general physical, social, and economic well-being" (King 2000: 4) is rather broad and frankly not useful for planning and systematic conflict analysis. This definition suggests that environmental security encompasses a broad spectrum of human–environmental interactions. Thus, it is my purpose to focus on the destabilizing effects of environmental stress on state and regional security, and consider how it enables violent conflict.

Researchers have offered a number of specialized environmental security definitions. One definition is presented by Butts (1994), which states that it entails environmental issues that undermine the stability of democratic regimes. Other researchers have offered definitions that are more inclusive. Glenn, Gordon, and Perelet (1998: 4) defined environmental security as, "a set of factors that threaten peace world wide and includes environmental instability that degrades public safety from environmental dangers caused by natural or human processes due to ignorance, accident, mismanagement, or design." Homer-Dixon and Levy's (2006: 190) definition is concise, but ignores natural environmental cycles: "ecocide, or a set of human-induced practices that degrade the environment to the extent that it cannot sustain normal social, political, or economic activity."

For this analysis, I propose a comprehensive definition of environmental security, which is consistent with links between people, governance, and natural environmental stressors. I view environmental security as a process involving environmental risk analysis based on multifaceted linkages between anthropogenic and natural processes that destabilize the environment and contribute to instability or conflict. The fundamental components of environmental security include: 1) environmental processes that undermine governments and promote instability; and 2) environmental processes that trigger civil conflict.

A framework for analysis

Since 1990, violent conflicts have occurred in Bosnia, Kosovo, Croatia, Rwanda, Ivory Coast, Burundi, Angola, Nigeria, Sudan, Turkey, Azerbaijan, Georgia, Kashmir, Myanmar, Sri Lanka, Iraq, and Palestinian Territories (Kaufman 1996; Renner 2002). It would be too simplistic, and probably incorrect, to assert that environmental stress instigated each of these conflicts, and too difficult to disaggregate their human and environmental components because they are interrelated and complex. Therefore, if we attempt a proactive approach to mitigate environmentally enabled conflict, it is useful to develop an analytical framework from which we can make informed assessments (Butts 1994). This framework must account for *anthropogenic* and natural environmental processes and recognize fundamental ethnic, economic, cultural, and political issues behind regional instability, understanding that each place is different (Homer-Dixon 1999).

Detractors of this perspective of conflict analysis argue that conflicts result solely from politico-military factors, which are minimally influenced by environmental stress at best, and perhaps allude to *environmental determinism*. Environmental stress and scarcity result from the combined influence of anthropogenic effects on the environment in conjunction with the vulnerability of the ecosystem. Scarcity and stress contribute to conflict only under certain circumstances, but there is no deterministic link between these variables (Percival and Homer-Dixon 1995). Clearly, not all violent episodes are alike and the influence of environmental stress on conflict will vary in magnitude from example to example. Nonetheless, there is compelling evidence that indicates that environmental stress does enable violent conflicts (Gibbons 1993; Abate 1994; Homer-Dixon 1999; Renner 2002; Schwartz and Randall 2003; Diamond 2005; Gleditsch, Nordås, and Salehyan 2007; Mays 2007; Zhang et al. 2007).

The relationships between food, population growth, climate, environmental resources, and environmental stress are evident in many developing states (Homer-Dixon 1999). This *Malthusian* paradigm generates much disagreement among scholars. Both factions, however, have to agree on an undeniable outcome that was manifest in Rwanda in 1994: population growth and environmental stress, superimposed over latent ethnic and political divisions will, in the end, be solved one way or another. History and events suggest that their resolution can be violent (Diamond 2005). Thus, I propose a framework for conflict analysis that identifies sources of environmental stress and linkages to political, cultural, economic, and ethnic dimensions. The framework is developed after the work of Butts (1994), Percival and Homer-Dixon (1995), Homer-Dixon (1999), and Diamond (2005). The framework is not intended to be predictive or proscriptive, only an analytical tool to account for dynamic and complex factors that contribute to environmentally enabled conflict.

The framework (Figure 5.1) is not a checklist because such inventories tend to disconnect intrinsically linked factors into artificially discrete variables. Instead, the framework forms the basis for a narrative explaining links between environmental stress and conflict. The framework suggests that environmentally enabled conflict evolves from four fundamental processes: 1) non-sustainable practices that degrade ecosystems; 2) natural environmental change or events; 3) governance and governmental practices; and 4) human activity and processes. These processes form the basis of the framework and are not mutually exclusive: they take place concurrently, and occur at the intersection of the natural landscape and human activity. So too are the outcomes: 1) resource shortages; 2) ecosystem degradation; 3) loss of agricultural productivity; 4) disease; 5) economic decline; 6) population change; 7) decline of effective governance; and 8) violent conflict.

The Rwandan genocide of 1994

The 1994 Rwandan conflict resulted in the *genocide* of the hundreds of thousands of ethnic Tutsi and Hutu sympathizers, and was the largest atrocity during 35 years of conflict (Department of State 2002). Although the 1994 outbreak was the most vivid, violence between ethnic Hutu and Tutsi was not unique to that episode; it was only the most disastrous and most widely covered. Between 1959 and 1994, thousands of Hutu

Figure 5.1
The environmental security framework for conflict analysis.

Environmental Security Framework for Conflict Analysis

DESTABILIZING PROCESSES

1. Non-sustainable processes

   e.g., over-extraction of resources, non-sustainable agricultural practices, poor land use planning, deforestation, ecosystem contamination

2. Natural environmental change/events

   e.g., climate change, climate variability, extreme weather events, natural disasters, invasive species

3. Government activities

   e.g., persecution, banking policy, corruption, economic policy, military activity

4. Human activity

   e.g., ethnic conflict, land tenure practices, cultural practices, population growth, migration, existing infrastructure

OUTCOMES

1. Resource shortage (e.g., water, energy, food, bio-fuel)

2. Ecosystem degradation (e.g., soil, forest, air)

3. Loss of agricultural productivity

4. Disease (e.g., AIDS, epidemic, genetic)

5. Economic decline (e.g., loss of market, currency devaluation)

6. Population change (e.g., migration, structure)

7. Government effectiveness (e.g., institutional collapse)

8. Violent conflict (e.g., ethnic, civil war, interstate war)

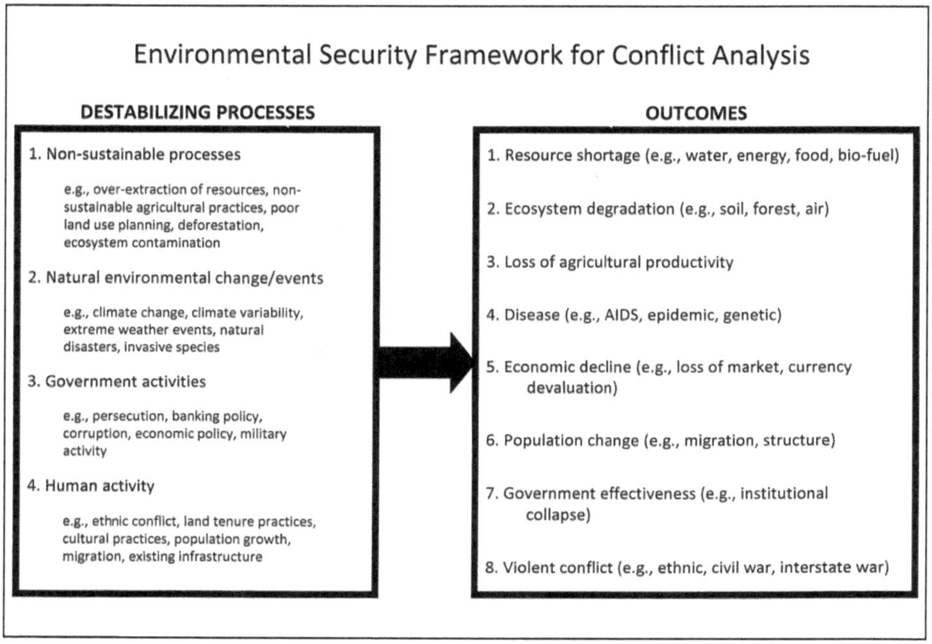

and Tutsi were slaughtered as part of the political struggle to gain control of Rwanda following Belgian colonial rule. However, the salient variables that differentiate this event are that non-sustainable environmental practices, drought, decreased agricultural output, rapid population growth, and economic collapse had destabilized Rwandan society, exacerbating ethnic divisions, and eroded the government's ability to sustain a secure living environment (Percival and Homer-Dixon 1995; Dulian 2004).

The 1994 genocide was carried out by two extremist Hutu militia groups, the *Interahamwe* and the *Impuzamugambi*, between April and July. Some estimates put the death toll between 800,000 and 1,000,000, which represents about 75 percent of the Tutsi population and about 11 percent of Rwanda's total population (Newbury 1995). This scale of killing is particularly gruesome because the weapon of choice was the machete, and the UN estimates that 1000 Rwandans were hacked to death every 20 minutes during the height of the genocide (Melvern 1999). So, then, how did the nexus between ethnic friction, ineffective governance, and environmental stress come together to enable mass murder?

Culture, society, and governance

The distinction between Hutu and Tutsi is not expressly ethnic or racial, but rather is best described as economic. The Hutu are farmers and the Tutsi pastoralists who were more economically prosperous. Tutsi dominated the region politically and simply labeled the indigenous people "Hutu." Hence, Hutu came to be a trans-ethnic identity associated with subjugation (Mitchell 1997). The Belgians, seeking an explanation for the complex society they found in the colony, framed the Hutu–Tutsi distinction as one of race. They issued racial identification cards, giving preferential treatment to Tutsis for administrative and economic positions, further deepening latent ethnic divisions (Newbury 1995). Independence came in 1961, and Rwanda entered a 35-year period of civil unrest, conflict, and forced migration, punctuated by periods of relative calm (Diamond 2005).

The downing of the Rwandan President's plane on 6 April 1994 was the catalyst for the start of the genocide, and the killing was well organized with government support (Department of State 2002). By the time it started, Hutu militia were 30,000 strong and organized nationwide. Furthermore, there were widespread examples of government soldiers participating in the violence as well (Department of State 2002). The orgy of violence was to continue—as the West stood by—until the *Rwandan Patriotic Front* (RPF) seized control of the country and effectively ended the violence in mid-July 1994 (Mitchell 1997).

Setting the stage: Rwandan population growth

Perhaps the seminal environmental stressor in Rwanda was its population density and the spiral of ecosystem degradation it caused.

Rwanda is situated in East Africa (see Figure 5.2), which has the highest regional population growth in the world, averaging about 4.1 percent, with a doubling time of 17 years. Rwanda is one of the world's most densely populated states, and most densely populated in Africa: its 1995 population was about 7.5 million with a growth rate of 4.7 percent. To make matters worse, large internal refugee displacements pushed increasing numbers of people into environmentally sensitive areas (Percival and Homer-Dixon 1995).

Explosive population growth was enabled by a number of interrelated human factors: adoption of non-native crops; improved sanitation and health care; and relative political stability, which opened up once contested areas for farming. Characteristics of Rwanda's natural landscape facilitated population growth as well. Rwanda has comparatively higher relief and moderate temperatures. This is important because lower temperatures curtail vector populations, thus limiting the spread of disease (Diamond 2005). Rwanda also experiences moderate amounts of rainfall in two seasonal peaks (Figure 5.2), which permits year-round farming, and limits nutrient leaching. Furthermore, volcanic soils are fertile, and the geologic structure establishes conditions for a sustainable groundwater supply. Therefore, sustainable farming practices should permit Rwandans to produce crops to support a growing population (Mitchell 1997; Diamond 2005).

By 1994, however, population growth, migration, and non-sustainable farming practices dangerously degraded the environment and diminished food output beyond acceptable levels. Rwanda's population growth meant that there was little useful arable land left for cultivation. Furthermore, about one-half of all farming in Rwanda is conducted on hill slopes greater than 10 degrees. Over-cultivation and cultivation on marginal land led to increased erosion and decreased soil fertility (Clay, Reardon, and Kangasniemi 1998). Consequently, Rwanda was transformed from one of the region's leading producers in per capita food production in 1980, to one of its worst by 1990. Although total food output increased by 10 percent between 1980 and 1990, per capita production declined by nearly 20 percent (Percival and Homer-Dixon 1995). The basic problem was that population growth was nearly exponential, but its food production increased at something approximating a linear rate that had begun to decline. Environmental stress damaged the agricultural system and food production decreased. Consequently, as food became scarce and internal migration became commonplace, a dangerous strain was placed on latent ethnic divisions and the government began to lose legitimacy (Diamond 2005).

Land use and ecocide

The environmental underpinnings of Rwanda's environmental degradation are associated with rapid population growth and a series of non-sustainable land use practices, which were underscored by a

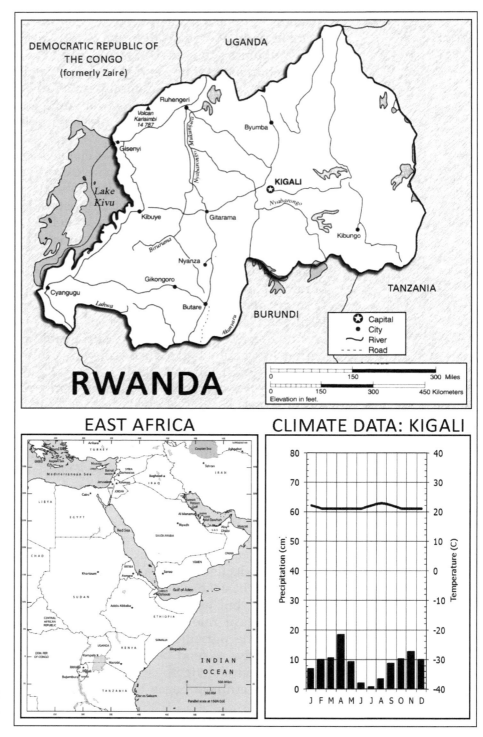

Figure 5.2
Map of Rwanda and East Africa.

decade-long drought. By 1990, Rwanda had experienced 15 years of relative calm and prosperity. It established a trade surplus built on coffee and tea exports, and attracted substantial development investment by the World Bank and other Western institutions. By every measure, it appeared that Rwanda was a model African state (Diamond 2005). Events conspired, however, to destroy this illusion and perhaps trigger the 1994 genocide. The first was a steep decline in world coffee and tea prices, which the Rwandan economy could not absorb, and, as a result, subsequently collapsed. This was followed by withdrawal of external monetary support. The second factor was environmental, which quickly exposed extant non-sustainable land use practices that over-stressed the environment. During the early 1990s, a major drought affected East Africa, and Rwanda in particular. Rainfall totals declined by as much as 30 percent, but, more importantly, the drought revealed a set of fundamental environmental land use problems, namely deforestation, soil erosion, and soil exhaustion (Newbury 1995; Diamond 2005).

Rwanda's large population depended on subsistence farming, which was pushed into marginal land. Remarkably, even though Rwanda was a relatively prosperous state, population growth was not offset by farming technology and more efficient farming practices. Instead, more land was placed under the plow. Thus, by 1985, all arable land in Rwanda, discounting that devoted to parks and other government land use, was under cultivation (Percival and Homer-Dixon 1995). To make this happen, forests were clear-cut and marshes were drained, exposing slopes to runoff and erosion; this limited the percolation of precipitation into the groundwater table. Fallow periods were shortened, resulting in soil exhaustion. Deforestation led to severe soil erosion and a lowering of the water table to the extent that streams began to run dry. Thus, when the climate began to change into a decadal drought cycle, the ability to irrigate was lost. Clear-cutting was also the result of Rwanda's high fuel-wood consumption, which was using 2.3 million cubic meters more than it was producing (Mitchell 1997).

The final variable in this *ecocide* was the *land tenure* practices used by Rwanda's farmers. The normal farm plot in 1980 was about 2.5 acres per family. As the population grew, additional arable land was tilled, yet food production could not accommodate the number of mouths to feed. Furthermore, the average farm plot was reduced to less than one acre per family as custom normally dictated that the oldest son would inherit the family farm. Once all of the arable land was taken, younger siblings had to remain at home; hence, family farms were split almost infinitesimally, and larger families had to be fed by increasingly small and unproductive farm plots (Clay, Reardon, and Kangasniemi 1998).

The basic components of Rwanda's environmental security framework are summarized in Figure 5.3. The seminal problem was that Rwanda had a large, densely concentrated population that depended on the land for resources that were rapidly diminishing, resulting from

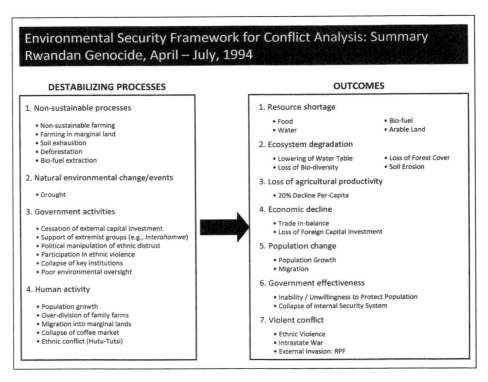

Figure 5.3
Framework summary
for Rwanda.

non-sustainable practices and environmental change. About 90 percent of Rwandans were engaged in subsistence agriculture on increasingly smaller plots of land with declining productivity and, by 1994, population had clearly outpaced food production. These environmental factors, combined with the collapse of the global coffee market, latent ethnic problems, and political competition perhaps pushed this society over the edge.

Summary and conclusions

Environmental security is, for the purpose of this analysis, defined as a process involving environmental risk analysis based on an understanding of the complex interactions between anthropogenic and natural processes that destabilize the environment and contribute to instability or conflict. To operationalize this definition I propose an analytical framework that is not proscriptive or predictive; rather it is a method for organizing the varied, dynamic, and complex environmental factors that produce regional instability and enable violent intrastate conflict. The framework for environmental security analysis is intended to form the foundation for a narrative explaining links between environmental stress and conflict to include: non-sustainable practices that degrade ecosystems; natural environmental change or events; governmental practices; and human activity.

No two conflicts are the same, thus accentuating the need for careful assessments of regional and local conditions to understand how ethnic, economic, and political tensions are affected by environmental stress. The Rwanda example demonstrates the fundamental problem with this type of analysis: factors of the human landscape and environmental stress are not mutually exclusive. They are complicated and inextricably linked, making it difficult to quantify how much the environment has enabled a violent conflict. Nonetheless, the Rwandan example also demonstrates that population growth and severe environmental stress caused by non-sustainable practices, superimposed over latent ethnic and political divisions, will, in the end, be solved sometimes very violently.

Complex, interacting factors enabled Rwanda's genocide, and military geography offers compelling insight and an especially valuable vantage point from which to conduct an analysis of conflict and environmental security. Rwanda's genocide, like other violent conflicts, had profound roots in long-standing ethnic distrust, politically charged manipulation, and weak governance; however, economic disparity and environmental stress were certainly contributing factors. In Rwanda's case, a principally rural society that depended heavily on subsistence agriculture and resource extraction from the environment proved particularly vulnerable to the effects of environmental stress, which threatened its stability even before the 1994 genocide. Evidence suggests, however, that by 1994 these stresses, combined with economic collapse and weak governance, precipitated a three-month-long episode of violence the likes of which the world has seldom witnessed.

References cited

Abate, T. 1994. "Climate and the collapse of civilization." *Bio Science* 44(8): 516–19.

Butts, K. H. 1994. *Environmental security: a DoD partnership for peace.* Strategic Studies Institute Special Report, Carlisle, PA: US Army War College Press.

Clay, D., T. Reardon, & J. Kangasniemi. 1998. "Sustainable intensification in the highland tropics: Rwandan farmers' investments in land conservation and soil fertility." *Economic Development and Cultural Change* 46(2): 351–77.

deMenocal, P. B. 2001. "Cultural responses to climate change." *Science* 292(5517): 667–73.

Department of Defense (DoD). 2005. *The national defense strategy of the United States of America.* Washington, DC: US Government Printing Office.

Department of State. 2002. "Department of State legal analysis of 1994 Rwandan genocide." *American Journal of International Law* 96(1): 258–62.

Diamond, J. 2005. *Collapse.* New York: Penguin Books.

Drapeau, M. D. & B. K. Mignone. 2007. "Culture, conflict, and . . . climate?" *Science* 316(5831): 1564.

Dulian, A. 2004. Rwandan genocide. *International Affairs* 50(4): 40–4.

Galgano, F. A. 2007. "A geographic analysis of ungoverned spaces." *Pennsylvania Geographer* 44(2): 67–90.

Gibbons, A. 1993. "How the Akkadian empire was hung out to dry." *Science* (News Services) 261(5124): 985.

Gleditsch, N. P., R. Nordås, and I. Salehyan. 2007. *Climate change and conflict: the migration link.* Coping with Crisis Working Paper Series. International Peace Academy. www.ipacademy.org [accessed 30 April 2010].

Gleick, P. 2008. *The world's water, 2006–2007.* Chicago, IL: Island Press.

Glenn, J. C., T. J. Gordon, & R. Perelet. 1998. *Defining environmental security: implications for the U.S. Army.* M. Land Holm, ed. Atlanta, GA: Army Environmental Policy Institute.

Homer-Dixon, T. F. 1999. *Environmental scarcity and violence.* Princeton, NJ: Princeton University Press.

Homer-Dixon, T. F. & M. A. Levy. 1995. "Environment and security." *International Security* 20(3): 189–98.

Kaufman, C. 1996. "Possible and impossible solutions to ethnic civil wars." *International Security* 20(4): 136–75.

Kaufmann, D., A. Kraay, & M. Mastruzzi. 2003. *Governance matters III: governance indicators for 1996–2002.* The World Bank, World Bank Institute, Global Governance Department and Development Research Group.

King, W. C. 2000. *Understanding environmental security: a military perspective.* The Center for Naval Warfare Studies. Newport, RI: Naval War College Press.

Mays, L. W. 2007. "Water sustainability of ancient civilizations in Mesoamerica and the American Southwest." *Water Supply* 7(1): 229–36.

Melvern, L. 1999. "The record of killing by machete was 1,000 every 20 minutes." *Times* (London) (4 March): 15.

Mitchell, T. 1997. *Rwanda and conflict.* International Conflict and the Environment: Rwanda Case, Case No. 23, Trade and Environment Database. www.american.edu/ted/ice/Rwanda.htm [accessed 30 April 2010].

National Security Council (NSC). 1991. *National security strategy of the United States.* Washington, DC: US Government Printing Office.

Newbury, C. 1995. "Background to genocide: Rwanda." *Issue: A Journal of Opinion* 23(2): 12–17.

Percival, V. & T. Homer-Dixon, 1995. *Environmental scarcity and violent conflict: the case of Rwanda.* Occasional Paper. Project on Environment, Population and Security, Washington, DC: American Association for the Advancement of Science and University of Toronto. www.library.utoronto.ca/pcs/eps/rwanda/rwanda1.htm [accessed 30 April 2010].

Renner, M. 2002. "The anatomy of resource wars, Worldwatch Paper 162." In *State of the world library*, Thomas Prough (ed.). Danvers, MA: Worldwatch Institute.

Schwartz, P. & D. Randall. 2003. *An abrupt climate change scenario and its implications for United States national security.* www.edf.org/documents/3566_AbruptClimateChange.pdf [accessed 30 April 2010].

Zhang, D. D., J. Zhang, H. F. Lee, & Y. He. 2007. "Climate change and war frequency in eastern China over the last millennium." *Human Ecology* 35: 403–14.

Chapter six

Climate change and potential regional instability in the Arctic

EUGENE J. PALKA

Introduction

GEOGRAPHERS ARE CONSTANTLY reminded that changes to the natural environment can have profound social, political, and economic impacts. Observed increases in global average air and ocean temperatures, widespread melting of ice and snow, and rising global average sea level provide unquestionable evidence of global climate change (IPCC 2007). Many expect that climate change will have a particularly negative impact on those regions of the world where people struggle to subsist on marginal lands. Just as concerning, however, are those sparsely populated and under-utilized regions of the far north that are now attracting considerable interest as climate change promises to unleash their previously untapped potential.

The *Arctic* has long been recognized as an important storehouse for fossil fuels, but, except for Alaska's North Slope and onshore and offshore development in Arctic Russia and Norway, the region remains largely under-developed because of cost factors associated with its austere location and harsh environment. Historically, the *Northwest Passage* has been of little utility because it was choked with ice for most of the year. Global warming trends, however, have the potential to open the Arctic to increased oil and natural gas exploration, and avail new shipping routes, as the areal extent of sea ice continues to decrease. Such a scenario might not unfold without considerable debate, if not dispute, between several countries. Canada, Russia, Denmark, Norway, and the US each has considerable interest in, if not sovereign claims to, parts of the region. If current trends continue, climate change and competing interests could conceivably transform the Arctic frontier into one of the most contentious regions in the world (Goodman 2007).

This chapter examines recent patterns of sea ice in the Arctic and considers the impact of the continued warming trend on the far north as it relates to navigability through the Northwest Passage, accessibility to minerals and oil deposits beneath the Arctic Ocean, and regional stability. I begin with a brief geography of the Arctic, discuss the historical background of the Northwest Passage, and mention some of the pertinent aspects of the *Law of the Sea Treaty*. I describe ongoing climate change in general and introduce the strategic and military issues that this may raise among Canada, Russia, the US, Denmark, and Norway.

A brief geography of the Arctic

One might generally choose to define the "Arctic" as the earth's surface area north of the Arctic Circle (or latitude 66½ degrees north), the parallel north of which the sun does not rise in mid-winter or set in mid-summer. An expanded and more useful definition often includes the land north of the latitudinal limit of normal tree growth and those oceans affected by Arctic water masses (Thomas and Goudie 2000). The Arctic Ocean, at the core of the region, covers 13,960,100 square miles and is historically covered with ice for most of the year (National Geographic 2007; Figure 6.1). Five countries (Russia, Canada, United States, Norway, and Denmark) have mainland territory, islands, and/or portions of their continental shelf that extend north of the Arctic Circle. Given its vast territory extending north of the Arctic Circle, the former USSR and present-day Russia have continued to develop mineral deposits (such as nickel in the Norilsk area) and fossil fuels in this contiguous land.

Over the past four centuries, aside from a few expeditions, the world's northernmost countries have historically not had much interest in the Arctic Ocean. Recently, however, global warming has reduced the areal extent and thickness of the Arctic's sea ice. This warming trend has prompted tremendous interest in three specific areas. First, the Arctic in general, and the Northwest Passage in particular, could become open to international shipping, a scenario that would save several thousand miles for routes between Europe and Asia, while creating environmental and security concerns for several countries, especially Canada. Second, oil and gas deposits previously considered inaccessible might be open to exploration. The USGS estimates that more than 22 percent of the world's untapped oil and gas reserves are located north of the Arctic Circle (USGS 2008). Some estimate that more than 10 billion metric tons of hydrocarbons are buried beneath the seafloor of the Arctic Ocean (Geotimes 2007). Third, adjacent countries now have the motivation to field scientific expeditions to acquire the evidence necessary to justify extending their coastal economic zones beyond 200 nautical miles.

It is not surprising that the seabed of the Arctic Ocean is not well surveyed, given its remote location, extreme environmental conditions, and limited utility in the past. Currently, however, all of the Arctic

Figure 6.1
The Arctic. *Source*:
adapted from
Geology.com (2008).

The Arctic Region

coastal countries are conducting hydrographic and geophysical surveys in order to better define the outer limits of their continental shelves (IBRU 2008). Of particular note is the Russian effort to claim the *Lomonosov Ridge* (see Figure 6.2). The country's claim was previously rejected by the "UN Commission on the Limits of the Continental Shelf" in 2002, but Russia's scientific exploration has only intensified, with hopes of acquiring convincing evidence to present before the commission again in 2009 (Geotimes 2007).

The Lomonosov Ridge is a distinct physical feature of the Arctic that stretches for more than 1800 km and rises approximately 3700 m above the floor of the Arctic Ocean (Rozell 2005). Discovered during the Soviet high-latitude expeditions in 1948 and named after Mikhail Lomonosov, the oceanic ridge divides the Arctic Ocean Basin into its two major components, the Eurasia and Amerasia Basins (Jakobsson et al. 2003). During the summer of 2007, Denmark launched a month-long expedition to prove that the underwater ridge was once attached to Greenland (a Danish territory), making it a geological extension of its territory

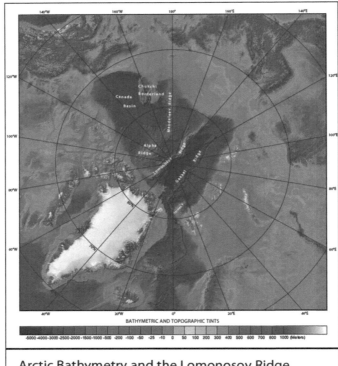

Figure 6.2
Arctic bathymetry
featuring the
Lomonosov Ridge.
Source: IBCAO (2008).

BATHYMETRIC AND TOPOGRAPHIC TINTS

Arctic Bathymetry and the Lomonosov Ridge

(Olsen 2007). More recently, in a perceived attempt to refute Russian findings, scientists from Canada and Denmark have co-operated in a joint study in an effort to prove that the ridge is an extension of the North American Continent (Boswell 2007). Claims to the submerged ridge will continue to be contentious if the Russian Natural Resources Minister is correct in his projection that the Lomonosov Ridge could yield as much as 5 billion metric tons of equivalent fuel (Energy Daily 2007).

The Northwest Passage: historical background

Another geographic feature of the Canadian Arctic that has gained considerable attention is the Northwest Passage. The Northwest Passage is a sea route that passes through Canada's Arctic Archipelago and connects the Atlantic and Pacific Oceans (see Figure 6.3). The quest for such a passage began in 1497 when King Henry VII dispatched explorer John Cabot to find a route from Europe to the Orient that would enable ships to avoid sailing around Africa (NASA 2007). Expeditions continued periodically through the 1800s without much success. Finally, in 1906, a Norwegian explorer, *Roald Amundsen*, and his crew became the first explorers to complete the passage entirely by sea, although the excursion

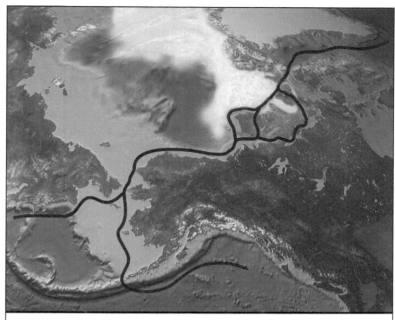

Figure 6.3
Northwest Passage.
Source: NASA (2006).

The Northwest Passage

lasted more than three years (Zorzetto 2006). The Northwest Passage is located approximately 800 km north of the Arctic Circle and approximately 1930 km from the geographic North Pole (NASA 2007). The benefits of an open passage would be significant for international trade, especially between Europe and Asia. Some of the current shipping routes between the two continents would be reduced by nearly 2500 miles, while oil and minerals from Alaska and the Canadian north could be more easily transported to European markets (Geology.com 2008). Unfortunately, for most of its discovered history, the passage has not been a feasible international shipping route due to low water in some areas and extensive ice blockades for most of the year.

The "fabled passage," however, might become a viable option in the near future thanks to global warming and the corresponding shrinking of the Arctic icecap and melting of sea ice. Based on the unprecedented changes in 2007 and 2008, some predict that the summer Arctic could be ice-free within a decade (Biello 2008).

Implications of the Law of the Sea Treaty

An accessible *Arctic Ocean* and an open Northwest Passage present numerous opportunities, especially for neighboring countries. However, potential access, use, and ownership are already highly debated.

83

The most promising document for regulating use is the Law of the Sea Treaty, which continues to evolve.

Formally known as the Third United Nations Convention on the Law of the Sea, or UNCLOS III, the treaty was adopted in 1982. Among its provisions, the treaty requires signatories to adopt regulations and laws to control pollution of the marine environment; it makes economic provisions; and it establishes jurisdictional limits on ocean areas that countries may claim, including a 12 mile *territorial sea* and a 200 nautical mile *exclusive economic zone* (Ridenour 2006). However, the treaty also stipulates that coastal states own the seabed beyond the 200 nautical mile zone and out to 350 nautical miles if it is an extension of their *continental shelf*, a point of contention that prompted ministers from Canada, Denmark, Norway, Russia, and the US to meet in Greenland for a two-day summit to discuss sovereignty issues in the Arctic (Reuters 2008). Meanwhile, the US recently completed a 1.2 million dollar seafloor mapping expedition confirming that Alaska's continental shelf extends more than 100 nautical miles further from the US coast than previously estimated (Lee 2007). Not to be outdone, Canadian Prime Minister Stephen Harper launched a 100 million dollar geomapping program in an attempt to identify oil, gas, and mineral deposits in the Canadian Arctic and to defend its sovereignty (CBS News 2008).

In addition to the problems with overlapping boundaries, an emerging (but fundamental) concern where the treaty falls short involves the question of who can transit the Northwest Passage. Canada considers the passage to be entirely within the historic internal waters of its Arctic Archipelago, which assumes there is no guaranteed right of innocent passage for foreign ships (IBRU 2008). The US, however, considers the multiple channels of the passage as straits used for international navigation, therefore assuming the right of transit passage for foreign ships (IBRU 2008). As the route becomes increasingly navigable for a greater part of the year, it is assumed that more countries will be interested in using the route to transport goods and materials between Europe and Asia. While tensions already exist between the US and Canada over the use of the Northwest Passage, arguments involving other countries may emerge over the use of sea routes through the central Arctic Ocean or the Northern Sea Route.

Climate change and projected impacts

While complicating matters even more, climate change and projected impacts also seem to be the catalysts necessary to advance the debate among bordering maritime countries. According to instrumental records of global surface temperature, which have been maintained since 1850, eleven of the twelve years from 1995 to 2006 rank among the twelve warmest years (IPCC 2007). While the median minimum extent of sea ice coverage was relatively constant between 1979 and 2000, there was a considerable reduction in the median minimum areal extent of sea ice between 2000 and 2005 (see Figure 6.4). Melting accelerated between 2005 and 2007, opening straits that had been previously choked with ice for most of the year. Based on the additional net melting that occurred between 2005 and 2007, the total minimum extent of ice coverage shrank from more than 5.3 million km in 2005 to a record low of 4.1 million km in 2007 (NSIDC 2008*a*; Figure 6.5).

The Northwest Passage was ice free for part of 2007, and, with the second lowest extent of ice cover recorded during the summer of 2008, it appears to have promise as a viable international, commercial shipping route in the near future (see Figure 6.6). One projection originating from the US National Snow and Ice Data Center (NSIDC) suggests that, if current warming trends continue, the Arctic Ocean could be ice free by 2060 (Zellen 2008). Existing climate projection models suggest that warming will continue through the twenty-first century with greatest warming over land and at most northern latitudes, and less warming over the Southern Ocean and parts of the North Atlantic (Homer-Dixon 2007; Figure 6.7).

Strategic–military considerations

As we postulate the impact on people and places around the world, we anticipate that climate change may adversely impact those regions of the world where people struggle to subsist on marginal lands (Goodman 2007; Gore 2006; Palka 2007). Yet, simultaneously, the continual warming of Arctic waters and the melting of sea ice in the Arctic may open up a

Figure 6.4
Change in sea ice cover.
Source: NASA (2007).

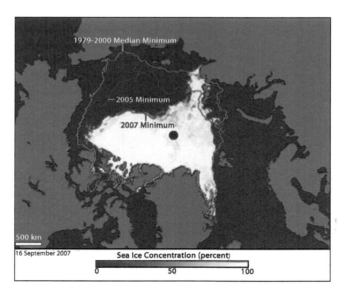

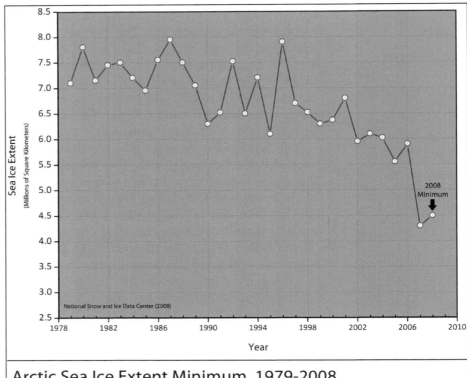

National Snow and Ice Data Center (2008)

Arctic Sea Ice Extent Minimum, 1979-2008

Figure 6.5
Arctic sea ice extent
minimum, 1979–2008.
Source: NSIDC 2008*a*.

Figure 6.6
Northwest passage open.
Source: NASA (2007).

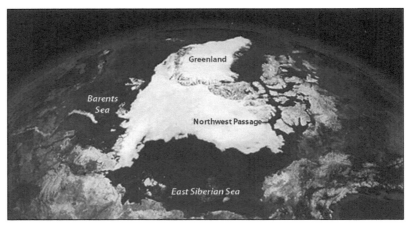

new frontier, along with access to previously untapped natural
resources. This presents a potentially volatile scenario as countries
compete for lucrative natural resources or vie for permission to use newly
available shipping routes.

The projected opening of the Northwest Passage is a recent development of tremendous economic interest to European, North American, and
Asian countries involved in international trade. The continued melting

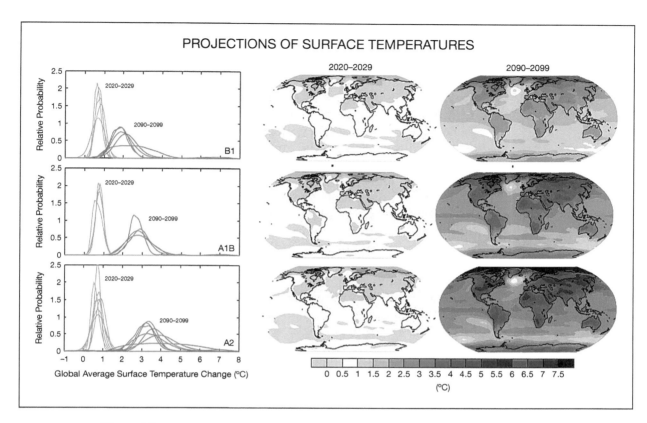

PROJECTIONS OF SURFACE TEMPERATURES

Figure 6.7
Models of global
climate change.
Source: IPPC (2007).

of ice in the Arctic has inspired the Russians to plant their flag under the North Pole, Canada to reassert their sovereign claims to the passage, and the US to become more sensitive about Alaska and the right of free passage (BBC News 2007; Zellen 2008). All three countries share interests in the improved access to potential oil and gas reserves. Canada has already taken measures to build bases and increase its military presence in the region, while Russia has undertaken extensive exploration underwater and conducted military overflights with its air force (Zellen 2008). Not to be overlooked is Denmark's statement of resolve on 13 August 2002, when a Danish icebreaker traversed Davis Strait to plant a flag on a barren plateau on Hans Island and claim a substantial amount of territory north of the 69th parallel (Polczer 2008). Canada responded three years later when a Navy vessel landed troops ashore to replace the Danish flag with a Canadian standard. Norway, with the longest tradition of Arctic exploration (Gjertz and Morkved 1998), is currently calling for a long-term system of governance for the polar region (Hundley 2007). Meanwhile, the country is intimately involved with expanding its oil, natural gas, and fishing industries into Arctic waters. And Norway and Russia continue to experience recurring incidents related to fishing grounds adjacent to Norway's Svalbard Islands.

87

As climate change continues to alter access to and through Arctic waters, adjacent countries will share concerns over access, use, sovereignty, security, and environmental protection. The implication for the Russian, American, Danish, Norwegian, and Canadian military forces would not necessarily mean a major shift from historical areas of interest, but it would likely prompt increased surveillance and/or presence of Air Force and Navy assets within the Arctic, and perhaps even ground forces from the US, Canada, and Russia.

The US has maintained a strong military presence in Alaska since World War II and continues to operate Army, Naval, and Air Force bases within the state. Surveillance of the Arctic is handled by existing systems on established installations and via air and underwater platforms. Russian submarines and surveillance aircraft have also frequented the Arctic region in the past, and, during the summer of 2008, the country launched a large-scale military exercise aimed at protecting its northern resources (Cook 2008).

Canada's efforts to exert its sovereignty have increased dramatically under Prime Minister Stephen Harper. Among Harper's initiatives are the production of up to eight Arctic offshore patrol ships, the deployment of military ice-breakers, and the installation of a remote sensing network (Environment News Service 2007). Harper also announced plans for an increased military presence that includes a new Army cold-weather training center at Resolute Bay and the construction of a deep-sea port for Naval and civilian purposes at Nanisivik, located on the north end of Baffin Island and strategically positioned at the eastern entrance to the Northwest Passage (redOrbit 2007). During the summer of 2008, Canada also launched a major military training exercise, named "Operation Nanook 08," with the specific aims of exerting sovereignty, demonstrating sovereignty and security, and learning how to better live off the land while operating in the northern environment (CTV News 2008).

Conclusion

The past three decades have included a series of disastrous climate and weather events around the globe. Future alterations could include: sea level rise; pronounced changes to temperature and precipitation patterns; and deviations to storm tracks (Dando 2007). Any or all of these anticipated climate changes could have significant impacts on people and their ways of life around the world. Moreover, many of these climate-related events can serve as catalysts for regional instability, even in the world's most remote and sparsely populated regions (Goodman 2007; Palka 2007).

The 2008 minimum extent of sea ice indicated a continuation of the downward trend of sea ice in the Arctic (NSIDC 2008*a*; see Figure 6.5).

While the 2008 minimum was slightly greater than during the summer of 2007, it is noteworthy that, for the first time since observations were recorded, ice had retreated away from the coast along the entire Arctic perimeter, opening both the Northeast and Northwest Passages (NSIDC 2008*b*).

Many anticipate that human-induced warming, the melting of Arctic ice-caps and sea ice, and associated rise in sea level will continue through the twenty-first century (Douglas et al. 2001; Harvey 2000; Victor 2004). Should these projected climate trends become a reality, then the Northwest Passage could conceivably be available (at least seasonably) as a viable maritime route, other routes could be available across the central Arctic Ocean, and access to the Arctic's store of fossil fuels and minerals would improve considerably. If such a scenario unfolds, then the Arctic could become the world's next contested frontier.

For now, Arctic claimants have agreed to let the UN rule on the conflicting territorial claims (McLaughlin 2008). In its current state, however, the Law of the Sea Treaty, the UN's primary tool that will serve as the basis for rendering decisions, seems inadequate for addressing several of the emerging issues. Meanwhile, the five Arctic coastal countries are positioning their military assets and continuing their surveys and mapping expeditions of their Arctic coastlines, continental shelves, and the Arctic Ocean floor.

References cited

BBC News. 2007. "Russia plants flag under N Pole." 2 August. http://news.bbc.co.uk/1/hi/world/europe/6927395.stm [accessed 30 April 2010].

Biello, D. 2008. "Fabled Northwest Passage open for business in the Arctic." *Scientific American* (27 August). www.scientificamerican.com/author.cfm?id=1013 [accessed 30 April 2010].

Boswell, Randy. 2007. "Canada draws line in the ice over Arctic seabed." *CanWest News Service* (Saturday 30 June).

CBS News. 2008. "Maps of Canada's Arctic will boost sovereignty: Harper," Tuesday 26 August, 6:18 p.m., CT.

Cook, B. 2008. "Russian army trains for Arctic resource war." *National Post Mobile* (Tuesday 24 June).

CTV News. 2008. "Canadian forces carry out Arctic training exercises." *CTV News Staff* (Monday 25 August).

Dando, W. A. 2007. *Climate change and variation: a primer for teachers.* Washington, DC: National Council for Geographic Education.

Douglas, B. C., M. S. Kearney, & S. P. Leatherman. 2001. *Sea level rise: history and consequences.* San Diego, CA: Academic Press.

Environment News Service. 2007. "Canada to fortify arctic sovereignty with new icebreakers." *Esquimalt* (British Columbia) (10 July).

Energy Daily. 2007. "Lomonosov ridge could bring Russians 5 billion tons of extra fuel." Moscow, Russia, 4 October.

Geology.com. 2008. "Northwest passage-map of Arctic sea ice: global warming is opening Canadian Arctic." http://geology.com/articles/northwest-passage.shtml [accessed 30 April 2010].

Geotimes. 2007. "Cold wars: Russia claims Arctic land." 1 August.

Gjertz, I. & B. Morkved. 1998. "Norwegian Arctic expansionism, Victoria Island (Russia) and the *Bratvaag* expedition." *Arctic* 51(4): 330–5.

Goodman, S. 2007. *National security and the threat of climate change*. Executive Director, Military Advisory Board, General Counsel, Washington, DC: The CNA Corporation.

Gore, A. 2006. *An inconvenient truth: the planetary emergency of global warming and what we can do about it*. New York, NY: Rodale.

Harvey, L. D. 2000. *Climate and global environmental change*. Harlow, UK: Pearson Education Ltd.

Homer-Dixon, T. 2007. "Positive feedbacks, dynamic ice sheets, and the recarbonization of the global fuel supply." Presentation at the Partners in Environmental Technology Technical Symposium and Workshop. Washington, DC, 4 December.

Hundley, T. 2007. "Arctic claims are poles apart." *Chicago Tribune* (24 August). Climate Ark, Climate Change and Global Warming Portal.

Intergovernmental Panel on Climate Change (IPCC). 2007. *Climate change 2007: the physical science. Summary for policymakers*. Paris: Fourth Assessment Report of IPCC Working Group I, Geneva, Switzerland: Intergovernmental Panel on Climate Change.

International Bathymetrical Chart of the Arctic Ocean (IBCAO). 2008.

International Boundaries Research Unit (IBRU). 2008. *Maritime jurisdiction and boundaries in the Arctic region*. Durham, UK: Durham University Press.

Jakobsson, M., A. Grantz, Y. Kristoffersen, & R. Macnab. 2009. "Physiographic provinces of the Arctic Ocean seafloor." *Geological Society of America Bulletin* 115(12): 1443–55.

Lee, J. 2007. *From cold to hot war: climate change and conflict in the 21st century*. Washington, DC: American University Press.

——. 2008. "New seafloor maps may bolster U.S. Arctic claims." *National Geographic News* (12 February).

Mclaughlin, K. 2008. "Arctic claimants say they will obey U.N. rules." *Reuters, UK*. Thursday 29 May, 3:24 p.m., BST. http://uk.reuters.com/article/idUKL288155 0420080529 [accessed 30 April 2010].

NASA. 2006. *World wind*. http://worldwind.arc.nasa.gov/download.html [accessed 30 April 2010].

——. 2007. "Northwest passage nearly open." *Earth Observatory*, 28 August. http://earthobservatory.nasa.gov/NaturalHazards/view.php?id=18964 [accessed 30 April 2010].

National Geographic. 2007. *College atlas of the world*. Washington, DC: National Geographic Society.

National Snow and Ice Data Center (NSIDC). 2008*a*. *Sea ice outlook: monthly reports*. Boulder, CO. http://nsidc.org/arcticseaicenews/ [accessed 30 April 2010].

——. 2008*b*. *Arctic sea ice news and analysis*. Boulder, CO. http://nsidc.org/arcticseaicenews/ [accessed 30 April 2010].

Olsen, J. M. 2007. "Denmark maps Arctic ridge in race for polar sovereignty." *International Herald Tribune*, Associated Press (Friday 10 August).

Palka, E. J. 2007. "Potential effects of climate change on the U.S. Army, regional instability, and War." In *Climatic change and variation: a primer for teachers*, W. A. Dando (ed.), 175–9. Washington, DC: National Council for Geographic Education.

Polczer, S. 2008. "Battle of the Arctic: expert says military conflict possible over vast resources." Canwest News Service. *Canada.com*, 24 March. www.canada.com/ [accessed 30 April 2010].

Reuters, 2008. "Arctic claimants say they will obey U.N. rules." Thursday 29 May. www.reuters.com/article/scienceNews/idUSL2881550420080529 [accessed 30 April 2010].

redOrbit News. 2007. "Harper announces army base, navy port to bolster Canada's claim to Arctic waters." 10 August. www.redorbit.com/news/business/1030020/harper_announces_army_base_navy_port_to_bolster_canadas_claim/index.html [accessed 30 April 2010].

Ridenour, D. A. 2006. "Ratification of the Law of the Sea Treaty: a not-so-innocent passage." National Policy Analysis, National Center for Public Policy Research, #542, August.

Rozell, N. 2005. "A fern grows in the Arctic Ocean." *Alaska Science Forum* (20 October). Article #1773.

Thomas, D. & A. Goudie (eds). 2000. *The dictionary of physical geography*. Oxford, UK: Blackwell Publishers.

US Geological Survey (USGS). 2008. "Circum-Arctic resource appraisal: estimates of undiscovered oil and gas north of the Arctic Circle." US Geological Survey Fact Sheet 2008-3049.

Victor, D. G. 2004. *Climate change: debating America's policy options*. New York, NY: Council on Foreign Relations.

Zellen, B. S. 2008. "Cold front rising: as climate change thins polar ice, a new race for Arctic resources begins." Volume 7(1), February 2008. Center for Contemporary Conflict. Monterey, CA: Naval Postgraduate School.

Zorzetto, A. 2006. "Canadian sovereignty at the Northwest Passage." ICE Case Studies, number 185.

Chapter seven

The legacy of federal military lands in the US

A geographic retrospective

WILLIAM W. DOE III

Introduction

THE HISTORICAL GEOGRAPHY and use of *military lands* associated with *military installations* within the US is an important and often misunderstood component of the federal landscape. Depending upon their use and military affiliation, military installations include forts, posts, camps, stations, bases, depots, annexes, and centers—in this chapter the term "base" is used comprehensively to describe all of these. The lands composing these bases are a complex and geographically diverse array of federally leased and owned spaces that are an important national asset, both for their primary use as military training and testing areas, and for their ecological and social/community contexts. These lands have evolved over the past 150 years to support the nation's defense requirements, providing an important legacy and footprint of our country's beginning, development, and westward expansion. These installations also reflect the changing paradigms of how the federal government has stationed and employed its military forces over two centuries (Doe and Palka 2009).

Today, military lands constitute over 30 million acres of federal land throughout the US, providing a critical resource for military training and testing activities. These lands also provide space for stationing of troops and housing their family members, and provide important social and economic benefits to surrounding communities. As will be discussed in this chapter, these installations also provide unintended environmental benefits to society, both in natural and cultural resources, given their unique locations and protection from outside development. In many instances, military lands have become primary refuge for many threatened and endangered species. Understandably, military activities on these lands can also be inherently destructive, resulting in a variety of environmental impacts that must be addressed and mitigated through regulatory enforcement and sustainable land management practices. Increasingly, these lands face public scrutiny and encroachment from private, public, and commercial sector activities near their boundaries. Thus, these lands and their legacy face new challenges from internal and external phenomena that have geographic, environmental, and social contexts and implications for the decades ahead. New and emerging land management approaches both inside and outside the installations are taking shape and will define the future for many of these lands.

Military lands in the US are defined as those federal lands controlled by the four armed services (i.e. Army, Air Force, Navy, and Marine Corps) in the fifty states and territories. These lands consist of both deeded ownership from the federal government and lands that are "withdrawn" by congressional approval from the overall federal land inventory. Typically, withdrawn lands are provided to the military for a period of 25–50 years, and most commonly involve lands from the Bureau of Land Management (BLM) in the Western US. They can be renewed with approval from Congress and upon completion of a complete environmental review. Although military forces may train on other public lands, and less frequently private lands for short periods, these lands are not typically referred to as military lands. In addition to the current footprint of military lands, there are many formerly used bases, which have been returned to the public or private sector. Some of these lands have retained many of their military characteristics, although they are no longer used for this purpose. One of the more illuminating examples of this is the former Army post, the Presidio of San Francisco, overlooking San Francisco Bay and the Golden Gate Bridge in northern California. In 1898, at the outbreak of the Spanish–American War, the Presidio became one of the Nation's premier military posts. In 1989, Congress determined the Presidio should be closed as a military post and, in 1994, its lands were transferred to the National Park Service to become part of the Golden Gate National Recreation Area (GGNRA). These lands constitute 1480 acres of high-value and relatively undisturbed coastal landscape and bluffs with wooded hilltops overlooking the San Francisco Bay. Today, the buildings, houses, and spaces, which were formerly used by the Army, are now residences and parks for a community of 2500 people and businesses for nearly 4000 people (National Park Service 2009). The complete story of this transformation of the Presidio from Army post to National Park is a fascinating and well-documented story of one legacy of military lands in the US (Benton 1998). Equally as fascinating is another story of military lands in the San Francisco Bay—the Island of Alcatraz. Although most notable for its period as a federal prison, the island was formerly developed and used by the Army as a Pacific Coast fortress in the mid-1950s to protect the growing city of San Francisco (Benton 1998).

Defining military lands and installations

The term military lands includes all land within the perimeter of a military installation, to include two primary areas: 1) *the cantonment*—the built up component or "city" that houses and supports military personnel and their families (larger cantonments can support up to 50,000 government employees, military personnel, and their families), and 2) the range and training complex consisting of live-fire ranges and maneuver areas for training and testing of personnel, units, and equipment (Doe and Palka 2009). There are over 3700 locations where the DoD manages land in the fifty states. To illustrate the geographical diversity of these locations, Figure 7.1 depicts 200 of the largest installation locations, which account for approximately 18 million, or about 60 percent, of the current total military land inventory. In Figure 7.1, the ownership of the lands is depicted for all four Armed Services. From the pie charts it is evident that the Army manages the largest percentage of lands (approximately 51 percent), while the Air Force manages about 38 percent of the inventory and the Navy/Marine Corps approximately

Figure 7.1
Map of 200 military installations in the US.

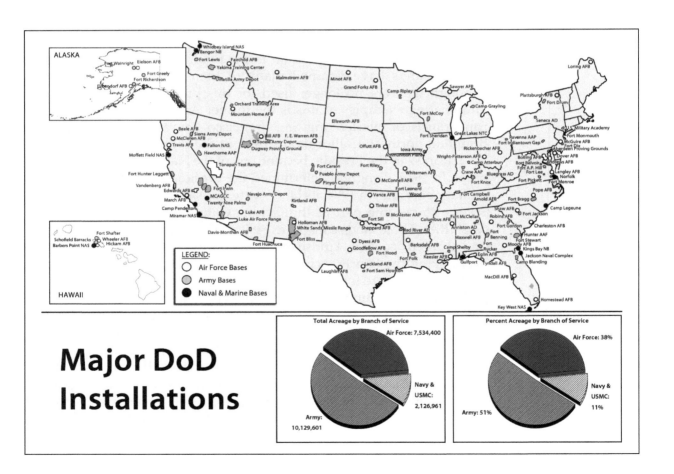

11 percent. The size of these installations can vary considerably, ranging from several thousand contiguous acres to over one million acres in size. The largest of these installations are located in the desert southwest where space and settlement have historically facilitated federal land acquisition (Doe et al. 1999; Doe et al. 2007).

The largest proportion of an installation is typically devoted to the training and testing missions, since extensive area is required to support firing of weapons systems, maneuvering of tracked and wheeled vehicles, landing of aircraft, docking of ships, tactical training, and other operational activities. The cantonment area houses the installation's military population and family members, and the majority of the infrastructure to support maintenance, logistics, and command and control of military units. The cantonment area is often referred to as the garrison area. Large military installations are essentially small cities, and just as a small town or city has basic infrastructure, so too does every military installation. Power-generating facilities, recycling centers, water treatment plants, transportation assets, for example, are all integral parts of the cantonment area.

Thus, the cantonment area is the built-up component of the installation and is designed to house and support military personnel and their families, as well as the logistics, maintenance, and operational facilities to support the various subordinate units that are assigned to the base. Within this densely populated life support area, one observes schools, one or more base exchanges (similar to large department stores), a commissary, service stations, numerous shops and fast-food establishments, movie theaters, craft shops, hospitals, a post office, an assortment of administrative buildings, and recreational facilities to support service members and their families. Additionally, there are various types of structures designed to house organizational units, their vehicles, aircraft, ships, weapons systems, and equipment. Motor pools, maintenance shops, warehouses, aircraft hangars, communications, and other facilities surround the headquarters and barracks of subordinate units assigned to the installation (Doe and Palka 2009).

The size and extent of the cantonment area corresponds to the size of the major unit and/or the variety of organizations and functions assigned to the installation. Base resident populations may range in size from a few hundred to over 84,000 in the case of Naval Station Norfolk (Military Times 2009), or 91,000 in the case of the Army's Fort Benning, Georgia (Military Times 2009). During the workday, base populations swell in numbers because of the influx of civilian employees from neighboring communities. Although each of the military services has slightly different facilities to support their specific mission, the cantonment areas are all very similar with respect to the layouts and functions that they perform (Doe and Palka 2009).

The planning, design, and construction of military installations is a multi-billion dollar business supported by commercial engineering firms

95

who have a close relationship with the Department of Defense (DoD). Standardized designs are often implemented to optimize use of space and to keep the military and civilian functions of a base separate. The design of family housing and schools engenders a close-knit neighborhood and community that supports service members and the constant deployments and stresses that accompany military life (Doe and Palka 2009). More recently, military residential areas have been built and maintained under long-term contracts with the commercial housing industry and have taken on remarkable resemblance to typical subdivisions within the civilian communities that surround them.

Historical evolution of military lands

The evolution of the US's military lands began in the late eighteenth century and early nineteenth centuries when the Army built a series of strategically sited forts along the coasts and inner waterways of the eastern states, as far west as the Mississippi River, to protect against foreign and internal attacks. One example, still an active military installation today, was the fortress built on the Hudson River at West Point, New York, which later became the site of the US Military Academy in 1802. West Point is currently the home for 4400 cadets, and several thousand staff, faculty, and family members (Doe 2009*b*; Doe and Palka 2009). Other examples from this era include inlet fortresses built along New York City's harbor (e.g. Forts Jay, Hancock, and Hamilton), and coastal fortresses along the East Coast and Gulf of Mexico, including Forts Morgan and Gaines in Alabama and the Pensacola Navy Yard in Florida (Balbach et al. 2008).

Army troops were first deployed westward in 1845 at the outbreak of the Mexican–American War, prior to major westward expansion by settlers. The beginning of the Indian Wars in 1860 brought numerous troops to Kansas and the Rocky Mountain states (see Figure 7.2). By the conclusion of the Civil War, the Federal Army had grown significantly and troops were stationed throughout the southern states, as well as throughout the midwest and west (see Figure 7.3). From 1850–95, a pattern of Army frontier forts was established across the plains, interior west, and coastal west to support the migration of settlers along established trail systems and the building of the continental railway system. Examples included Fort Scott and Fort Riley in Kansas, the latter being the post from which General George C. Custer's 7th Cavalry set out to meet their destiny at the Battle of Little Bighorn—one of the most famous confrontations of the Indian Wars (Balbach et al. 2008). Today, many of these original forts, such as Fort Larned, Nebraska, Fort Laramie, Wyoming, and Fort Union, New Mexico, are national historic sites managed by the National Park System, for public access and

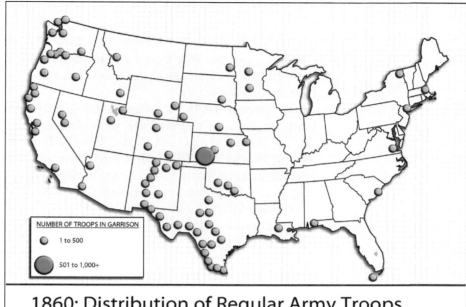

Figure 7.2
Map of US Army troop stationing—1860.

1860: Distribution of Regular Army Troops

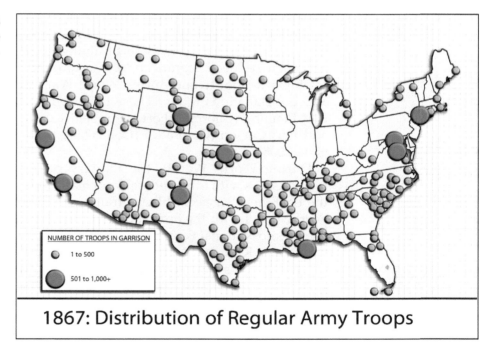

Figure 7.3
Map of US Army troop stationing—1867.

1867: Distribution of Regular Army Troops

historical remembrance. Many of these other original fort locations from the mid-1860s, such as Camp Collins on the banks of the Cache la Poudre River in the former Territory of Colorado, are no longer in existence, but became major population centers a century later, such as the city of Fort Collins along the Front Range of Colorado (Doe 2009*b*; Doe and Palka 2009).

The period 1900–50 witnessed a significant expansion of military lands in the US, particularly to mobilize and train forces for combat during World War I and World War II. Examples of bases constructed during World War I included Forts Monmouth and Dix in New Jersey, Fort Drum (originally Pine Camp) in New York, Fort Benning in Georgia, and Fort McClellan in Alabama (Balbach et al. 2008). Two examples of World War II expansions were lands acquired to support the Louisiana Maneuvers in the southeastern US in preparation for the land battle in Europe, and General Patton's armored training exercises in the Mojave Desert, as part of the Army's Desert Training Center in the Mojave Desert (along the intersection of the state boundaries of California, Arizona, and Nevada). The Louisiana Maneuvers area occupied 2.2 million acres (89,000 ha) of land, and more than 56 million acres (twice the current DoD landholdings) were used by General George Patton and his Armored Corps for tank training in anticipation of deployment to North Africa and Europe. Numerous base camps were established throughout the Mojave Desert and small towns began to grow around them (Bischoff 2000). The Mojave Desert today remains an important place for Army desert training, although the amount of land has been reduced significantly. Many of the original Army camps established prior to and during World War I and World War II remain active installations today. These include Fort Bragg (North Carolina), Fort Benning (Georgia), Fort Campbell (Kentucky), Fort Hood (Texas), and Fort Carson (Colorado) (Doe 2009*b*; Doe and Palka 2009; Balbach et al. 2008)

During World War II, the military built significant co-operative relationships with other federal land management agencies, particularly the US Forest Service. Military training in federal forests dates back to World War I with the activation of Camp Shelby in Mississippi within the DeSoto National Forest. In 1941, Fort Polk, Louisiana, was established within the Kisatchie National Forest for jungle warfare training, and Camp Hale was established in the White River National Forest of Colorado for military training in mountaineering and cold weather survival skills. Camp Hale became the home of the famous 10th Mountain Division during World War II. Similarly, the Marine Corps established the Mountain Warfare Training Center in the Humboldt-Toiyabe National Forest in 1951 to train personnel headed to the Korean War Theater (Doe 2009*b*; Doe and Palka 2009).

The Cold War era saw the continued establishment of perma- nent military installations to support the increasing size of the armed forces, although many units were stationed outside the US in Korea and Europe. This growth responded to the need to train and test long-range weapons systems, and to accommodate increased mobility for armored vehicles and massed formations of troops. During this era, significant developments occurred with respect to Air Force and Naval bases to support the arsenal of modernized weapons systems associated with the Cold War. Many of the lands acquired during this period, particularly for the US Air Force, remain active military installations, including major bases such as Little Rock AFB (Arkansas) and Edwards Air Force Base (California), as well as the US Air Force Academy in Colorado Springs, Colorado (Doe and Palka 2009).

During the last century, there was little public involvement in the military land acquisition process. Land transactions were generally handled through administrative actions linked to national security concerns. It was not until the late 1950s that land conflicts emerged, and policy-driven guidelines were established. These conflicts were driven by DoD expansion plans to acquire an additional 13 million acres in western states (Crotty 1995). Between 1945 and 1970 Congress allocated more than $100 billion for western military installations, making the DoD the biggest business in the west (Nash 1999). In response to the increased land demands by the DoD during the mid-1950s, Congressman Clair Engel of California convened the first hearings, known as the Engel Hearings, to address withdrawals of land from the public domain. The eventual outcome of these hearings was the establishment of the *Engel Act of 1958*, which established a key principle that DoD land withdrawals in excess of 5000 acres require an Act of Congress, with the attendant public hearings (Wilcox 2007). In short, this Act brought to a close the practice by which military land transactions were conducted without public scrutiny.

During the late 1970s and 1980s, two landmark decisions influenced the military footprint in the US, particularly in the west. The first, in 1979, occurred when the Carter Administration announced a plan to build the Intercontinental Ballistic Missile (ICBM) MX system on a racetrack encompassing some 25 million acres in the Great Basin region of Nevada and Utah (Crotty 1995). This plan was opposed by private landowners, federal land management agencies, and environmental groups. The Carter plan was defeated after the 1980 Presidential election, when Ronald Reagan became President and opted for the deployment of MX missiles in retrofitted silos, because of the enormous costs of the racetrack option and the significant opposition in the west. The second, the *Military Lands Act (PL 99-606)*, implemented in 1986, authorized several large land withdrawals in the west, but limited them to fifteen years, and required the preparation of extensive Environmental Impact Statements (EIS) (Wilcox 2007). It was also during these decades when the US public became more aware of environmental issues and the toxic legacy left behind from munitions and chemical production during the earlier war periods, as well as the Vietnam Conflict (Doe and Palka 2009).

The end of the Cold War during the early 1990s and the downsizing of the US Military led to a series of installation closures and consolidations under congressional mandate, known formally as *Base Realignment and Closure (BRAC)* (Balbach et al. 2008). While these changes affected many adjacent civilian communities, there was considerable effort made to turn these facilities and lands into local investments to spur economic growth.

Environmental and ecosystem contexts

In addition to the critical role that military lands play in providing training and testing space, they have become valued for their ecosystems and ecological value. This fact is somewhat counter-intuitive to the public, who envision bases as wastelands, covered by unexploded ordnance, craters, munitions waste, and other fragments of military activities. Indeed, some portions of these military lands, particularly the live-fire impact areas for ranges, are heavily impacted and contain dangerous and toxic constituents from munitions. However, these designated "sacrifice areas" represent only a small fragment of the overall military land inventory. In fact, most bases remain relatively or completely undisturbed from their pre-military occupation state, and often represent the only relatively undisturbed ecosystems in a region, particularly those areas where commercial development is rampant. One example of this phenomenon is Fort Carson, Colorado, in the city of Colorado Springs. When it was first established in the 1940s, Fort Carson (formerly Camp Carson) was geographically separated from the city, then a budding community of 50,000–75,000. Today, the perimeter of Fort Carson is surrounded by commercial and residential development as Colorado Springs has grown to become the second largest city in the state, with a population of over 350,000 (Doe and Palka 2009).

The maintenance of natural environments on military installations is critical to quality training for the armed forces. Installations in the US provide geographic analogs to many deployment areas where the military is engaged. Thus, they provide similar environmental conditions in which to train soldiers and test equipment (Doe and Bailey 2007; Doe et al. 2005; Shaw et al. 2000; Shaw and Doe 2005). The ability to use natural camouflage for cover and concealment, and to move across the landscape unimpeded, is also important to realistic training (Doe et al. 1999; Doe and Palka 2009).

As a result, many military lands have become, through somewhat unintended consequences, sanctuaries for hundreds of threatened and endangered species of flora and fauna. In comparison to other large federal land management agencies with much larger acreages, DoD lands contain a much larger population and proportion of threatened and endangered species, which are regulated under federal environmental laws (Stein 2008). Thus, the management of military land must not only support military use, but also account for species conservation and other multiple uses, such as forestry, grazing, and recreation. Over the past twenty years, the military has developed several key conservation and land management programs, such as the Integrated Training Area Management (ITAM) program and the Sustainable Range Program (SRP), to balance the requirements of training and conservation (Balbach et al. 2008).

Emerging land conflicts

Notwithstanding their inherent environmental advantages, the DoD's installation footprint is not without controversy. The management of species and other resources mandated by law has often come into conflict with military training needs. Examples of these conflicts abound, sometimes resulting in the closure of critical training ranges and assets or producing legal actions against the military. One of the more noteworthy cases was the closing of a critical multi-purpose firing range at Fort Bragg, North Carolina, during the late 1980s when the US Fish and Wildlife Service successfully stopped Army use because of violations of the Endangered Species Act (ESA) resulting from detrimental impacts to the red-cockaded woodpecker and its habitat. The policy and legal aspects of this case are well documented (Rubenson et al. 1993). In Hawaii, a newly constructed firing range was never opened when an endangered plant was discovered during a biological survey.

Many military lands, which were initially rural and very distant from large communities, are now surrounded by expanding residential and commercial development. This has created additional land use conflicts with surrounding communities. In the late 1990s the term *encroachment* was defined by the DoD as "the cumulative result of any and all outside influences that inhibit normal military training and testing" (US Government Accounting Office 2003: 1). These influences included noise complaints, zoning regulations, safety concerns for landing aircraft and munitions firing, and other issues. Encroachment issues initially resulted in a "we versus they" mentality that put the military and its surrounding neighbors at odds. However, in the past five years, an era of some co-operation has emerged on both sides. The DoD, other federal agencies, non-profit organizations, and local landowners have begun to creatively address and resolve encroachment issues through land use partnerships and collaboration. These strategies employ many different approaches such as alignments, easements, buffer zones, and zoning regulations. For example, the Army Compatible Use Buffer (ACUB) program allows the military to expend funds through non-profit organizations to support non-development of lands from private landowners surrounding an installation, thus reducing the potential for noise, dust, and other impacts on the installation's neighbors. Many of these strategies have emerged as communities grow and military land use becomes more constrained, and as some communities are threatened by BRAC actions. Buffer areas have recently been established adjacent to Fort Carson, Colorado, and Fort Riley, Kansas, through collaborative conservation. The successful implementation of these strategies is paramount if military lands and communities are to coexist for the future.

Twenty-first-century military lands

Several geopolitical factors have influenced the nature and extent of military lands in the US during the first decade of the twenty-first century. The majority of active duty forces have been deployed to Iraq and Afghanistan, leaving their families behind on military installations, and changing the frequency and intensities of training activities on military lands. Military forces stationed abroad in Europe have been drastically reduced and re-stationed back in the US, thus placing increased needs for housing and training space on some installations, such as Fort Bliss, Texas, and Fort Carson, Colorado. New weapons systems and technology, such as the unmanned aerial vehicle (UAV), have increased the need for land and airspace. These trends have collided with changing community notions of encroachment, development, and coexistence with their military neighbors. Thus, at the advent of the twenty-first century there are many challenges to how US military lands will be sustained. However, what remains unchanged are the inextricable links, memories, and importance that these military lands have to those who live, work, and train on them, and to the adjacent civilian communities that support and serve them.

References cited

Balbach, H., W. Goran, W. Doe, & A. Latino. 2008. "U.S. military installation land management history." Militarized Landscapes Conference, University of Bristol, UK, 3–7 September.

Benton, L. M. 1998. *The Presidio: from Army post to national park.* New York, NY: Northeastern University Press.

Bischoff, M. C. 2008. *The desert training center; California–Arizona maneuver area, 1942–44: Tucson, AZ: historical and archaeological contexts.* Technical Series 75, Statistical Research, Inc.

Crotty, W. 1995. *Post-cold war policy: the social and domestic context.* Chicago: Nelson-Hall Publishers.

Doe, W. W. 2009a. "Cold regions and mountain testing and training areas in the U.S." Proceedings, 8th International Conference on Military Geosciences, June 15–19, Vienna, Austria, *Submitted to Conference Proceedings.*

———. 2009*b*. "Introduction to sustainable military lands management." NR 550, online course content, Division of Continuing Education, Colorado State University, Fort Collins, CO. www.learn.colostate.edu/certificates/military-lands-management/ [accessed 30 April 2010].

Doe, W. W. & R. G. Bailey. 2007. *Military operating environments: an ecoregions framework to characterize U.S. Army testing and training lands as operational analogs.* Contract Report, CEMML, Colorado State University, September 2007.

Doe, W. W., T. J. Hayden, & R. M. Lacey. 2007. "Military land use: overview of DoD land uses in the desert southwest, including major natural resource management challenges." Invited paper, Proceedings from the DoD Strategic Environmental Research & Development Program (SERDP) Workshop—Southwest Region Threatened, Endangered, and At-Risk Species Workshop: Managing within Highly Variable Environments, Tucson, AZ, 22–26 October, www.serdp.org/Research/upload/SW%20TER-S%20Proceedings%20Final.pdf [accessed 30 April 2010].

Doe, W. W., Robert B. Shaw, Robert G. Bailey, David S. Jones, & Thomas E. Macia. 2005. "U.S. Army training and testing lands: an ecological framework for assessment." In *Military geography from peace to war*, E. J. Palka & F. A. Galgano (eds). New York, NY: McGraw-Hill.

Doe, W. W. and E. J. Palka. 2009. "America's military footprint: landscapes and built environments within the continental U.S." In *Engineering earth: the impacts of mega-engineering projects.* New York, NY: Kluwer.

Doe, W. W., R. B. Shaw, R. G. Bailey, D. J. Jones, & T. Macia. 1999. "Locations and environments of U.S. Army training & testing lands: an ecoregional framework for assessment." *Federal Facilities Environmental Journal* (autumn): 9–26.

Military Times Media Group. 2009. *Installations worldwide: 2009 guide.* www.militarytimes.com/military-installations-guide/ [accessed 30 April 2010].

Nash, G. D. 1999. *The federal landscape: an economic history of the twentieth century west.* Tucson, AZ: University of Arizona Press.

National Park Service. 2009. "A park for the 21st century: welcome to the Presidio of San Francisco." Brochure, the Presidio Trust, www.presidio.gov [accessed 30 April 2010].

Rubenson, D., J. Aroesty, & C. Thompsen. 1993. *Two shades of green: environmental protection and combat training.* Santa Monica, CA: Rand Corporation.

Shaw, R. B., W. W. Doe, E. J. Palka, & T. E. Macia. 2000. "Sustaining army lands for readiness in the 21st century." *Military Review* 80(5): 68–77.

Shaw, R. B. & W. W. Doe. 2005. "Training a global force: sustaining army land for 21st century readiness." In *Military geography from peace to war*, E. J. Palka & F. A. Galgano (eds). New York, NY: McGraw-Hill.

Stein, B. A., C. Scott, & N. Benton. 2008. "Federal lands and endangered species: the role of military and other federal lands in sustaining biodiversity." *BioScience* 58(4): 339–47.

US Government Accounting Office. 2003. *DOD approach to managing encroachment on training ranges still evolving.* GAO-03-621T. 2 April.

Wilcox, W. A., Jr. 2007. *The modern military and the environment: the laws of peace and war.* Lanham, MD: Government Institutes Press.

PART II

Historical and operational military geography

HISTORY HAS DEMONSTRATED that there is a clear and immutable link between military operations and geography. Factors of geography have had a compelling and sometimes decisive influence on battles throughout history. In recent times, the influence of geography on peacetime military operations and operations other than war has been equally pervasive. Likewise, the important geographic concepts of location, time, space, scale, and distance must be considered during the planning and execution of any military operation. Consequently, the military geographer is compelled to employ an integrating approach to study an operating environment and ascertain how geography may potentially influence an operation. Even at the smallest tactical scale, operating environments are complex. Therefore, the best analyses benefit from an integrated methodology that offers a comprehensive framework against which informed decisions can be made. To accomplish this task, military geographers have relied on a case study methodology using a historical and operational approach to dissect the linkages between military operations and the landscape.

Operational environments—the places where military operations take place—are unique and manifest discrete natural and cultural attributes. This is important to the military geographer because these attributes lend strategic, operational, and tactical importance to places, and furnish them with character, potential, and meaning. For this reason, military geographers are concerned with identifying and analyzing the details of places, especially in recognizing the interconnectivity between the natural and human landscapes. The study of geography has established that places matter. Each place is unique and demonstrates a discrete set of geographic imperatives. Furthermore, places interact, thus creating compelling and sometimes difficult conditions within which military units must function.

Karl von Clausewitz captured the nature of place when he called the military operating environment "terrain," and in his view "terrain" was composed of "the territory and inhabitants of the whole theater of war." Furthermore, von Clausewitz demonstrated that the operational significance of the operating environment varies with the mission, organization, and type of military units involved, technology, and current circumstances: in other words, site remains constant, but situation changes over time—thus geographic analyses must be dynamic and comprehensive. So too, then, must a military geographer's assessment of place.

Geography has long been studied by military leaders because of the indisputable link between the landscape and war. In that context, military geography has historically been related to the general military term *terrain analysis* by military officers. In fact, during the very early years of the discipline—especially in the US—military geographers focused essentially on such chorographic analyses and historical case studies. These types of studies are useful because, in a military context, the analysis of terrain gives purpose and application to the study of the operational environment. US *Field Manual 30-10 (Military Geographic Intelligence)* for many years provided a working definition of terrain analysis: "the process of analysis of a geographical area to determine the effect of natural and man-made features on military operations." Hence, in its simplest form, terrain analysis merely involves the description of the existing physical and cultural landscape, and an assessment of the impact of that landscape on military operations.

Clearly, this type of factual knowledge has its place in military geography because it permits us to position events, locations, and phenomena in a useful spatial setting. However, knowing and understanding why they exist in discrete places is significantly more important, and that is the true relevance of military geography. Thus, military geography is much more than simply knowing place names and describing aspects of a region. Modern military operations are very complex, and contemporary military geographers have to understand places and the interconnectivity between them; accordingly, they focus their efforts on understanding the nexus between military operations and the landscape. To understand this nexus, the military geographer must understand the dynamics and processes of the natural and human landscape as well as their spatial and temporal patterns.

Thankfully, military geography has evolved into a far richer integrative discipline that incorporates much more than descriptions of a geographic area and historical analyses of the effects of geography on battles. Today, military geographers seek to explain the *processes* that created a unique landscape through an understanding of geography and by using its distinctive spatial perspective. Nonetheless, historical analyses and case studies do serve a very useful purpose, and this methodology does assist military geographers as they strive to answer their unique version of the universal geographic questions: "What is the operating environment like?" "Why is it like this here?" and "How will it affect operations?" Certainly, these three questions are embedded in the military geographer's interest in the variability of earth space and they are linked to core geographic traditions.

To answer these questions, the military geographer draws upon the common theme that geography is a spatial science and the common thread in all research is the recognition of spatial patterns and the dynamics of the natural and human landscape that create that variability. This is the necessary point of departure for understanding the nexus of military problems and the environment. To the military geographer, then, the concept of space explains the way processes and dynamics cause things to be distributed, as well as the temporal patterns associated with phenomena that lend uniqueness to places. Thus, the military geographer understands that the content of places and dynamics of phenomena are structured and explainable.

The development of a military strategy involves the selection of objectives, a method, and sequence of employment, and the movement of military power to an objective area. Today, in the context of operations other than war, a field commander may be presented with a set of difficult and confounding variables in a very complex operating environment. In that situation, the commander is not preparing for battle, but is perhaps planning for a multifaceted disaster relief or peacekeeping operation. Clearly, political objectives, economic wherewithal, and the means available influence strategy. In one situation, the destruction of enemy forces may be the objective, but, in another, moving relief supplies into an austere region in response to a natural disaster may be the goal. Nevertheless, regardless of the strategy, the success of any military operation—in peacetime and during war—depends on a sound plan that takes into account a cogent analysis of the military operating environment.

A study of recent military history reveals the geographic nature of warfare. Contemporary operations in Afghanistan and Iraq have demonstrated the undeniable link between geography and military operations. Certainly, the skillful incorporation of terrain into battle planning by Lee, Rommel, MacArthur, and Patton are masterpieces in military geography. Consequently, the study of historical and operational military geography—in a case study format—has not lost its power to integrate the dynamics of the operational environment, the technology of warfare, and the human element of leadership.

In *Chapter 8*, Frank Galgano examines the characteristics of the fluvial landscape and its impact on military operations. In this chapter, he provides a geographic analysis of the role of rivers during the American Civil War, and presents a case study that demonstrates how the Union Army overcame barriers presented by the Mississippi River at Island No. 10 in 1863. Hendrik Smit, a South African, offers a unique and rare perspective of a campaign during the Boer War in *Chapter 9*. Smit's geographic analysis of the Northern Cape Campaign in 1899 illustrates the complex problems presented by distance, austere environments, and semi-arid conditions, as well as how various commanders adapted to the geographic conditions. Gene Palka examines an equally austere and imposing environment in *Chapter 10*. In his study of the US campaign to retake Attu in 1943, Palka illuminates the very difficult set of geographic problems that the Americans faced during their campaign in the Aleutians, which was the only battle fought on US soil during World War II. In *Chapter 11*, Gene Palka and Frank Galgano use the World War II Buna Campaign in New Guinea to illustrate the profound effect that disease can have on a military force. The amphibious landing at Inchon, Korea, in 1950 is perhaps one of the most decisive turning movements in military history. In *Chapter 12*, Frank Galgano evaluates the geographic challenges associated with this landing and describes how the very difficult geographic conditions perhaps contributed to the strategic brilliance of the plan.

The final three chapters are devoted to case studies that are more contemporary and focus on the compelling interactions of natural and human landscapes during post-Cold War military operations. In *Chapter 13*, Steve Oluić explains the historical geography of the former Yugoslavia and establishes the fundamental processes that led to the collapse and destabilizing ethnic violence in Bosnia during the early 1990s. In *Chapter 14*, Eugene Palka examines the operating environment in Afghanistan and its effect on Operation Enduring Freedom, and the continuing efforts to bring stability to this fractured human landscape. Finally, in *Chapter 15*, Eugene Palka, Frank Galgano, and Mark Corson provide a comprehensive overview of the events leading up to and following Operation Iraqi Freedom. In this chapter, they also impart a detailed analysis of the daunting physical landscape and very complex and perplexing human landscape, and its effects on the long, bloody conflict that ensued following the US invasion.

Collectively, the chapters of this section demonstrate the clear and unquestioned utility of military geography within a wartime context. As long as military leaders have to employ forces and fight battles in operational environments other than that of their homeland, then they must account for unknown and variable factors of terrain, vegetation, climate and weather, and the human landscape. History has demonstrated that these factors can be decisive.

Chapter eight
Streams and military landscape

FRANCIS A. GALGANO

Introduction

RIVERS HAVE ALWAYS played an important role in warfare. A river, with its meanders and floodplain, incorporates confounding geographic problems for an army. For example, Allied planners began preparing for the Rhine River crossings many months before the actual operation in March 1945 (MacDonald 1984), and the stunning success of the German Blitzkrieg into the Soviet Union in June 1941 was enhanced by carefully planned and executed river crossing operations that employed specially adapted tanks (Ziemke and Bauer 1987). The scope of military operations on the fluvial landscape is very broad and operations on rivers and inland waterways are typically brought together under the designation *riverine operations*. This chapter will examine how the fluvial landscape can influence military operations on the *strategic* and *tactical* scale, and present a case study demonstrating how a combined federal naval and land force overcame physical challenges presented by the Mississippi River during the American Civil War.

Rivers presented a nearly impassable obstacle to ancient armies. With improvements in technology, the ability to conduct river crossings improved as well, although these innovations did not guarantee success. The disastrous river crossing operations along the Rapido River in Italy during January 1944 (D'Este 1992) and failed Allied airborne operation to cross the Rhine in September 1944 (Ryan 1974) are testaments to this truth. The US Army's difficulty crossing the Sava River into Bosnia in January 1996 (see Figure 8.1) illustrates the complications associated with river crossing operations even when uncontested. Although rivers are ordinarily thought of as obstacles, they have been used as important highways by invading armies. Nowhere was this more evident than in the Western Theater of the American Civil War.

Figure 8.1
An M3 cavalry scout vehicle from the 1st Squadron, 1st Cavalry, crosses the Sava River into Bosnia-Herzegovina in January 1996. *Source*: US Army Photograph.

The role of rivers in military operations

The typical view of a riverine operation is that of a deliberate river crossing such as the crossing of the Rhine River during World War II, or more recently the Egyptian assault crossing of the Suez Canal during the 1973 Yom Kippur War (Herzog 1984). A deliberate crossing of a defended river is an operation that most soldiers would prefer not to risk. Nonetheless, these are common military operations. River crossings are associated with trepidation because they offer a capacity for defense that is nearly unequaled (Patton 1947).

A heavily defended river represents a nightmare for those who have to fight their way to the other side. Notwithstanding the disposition of an enemy force, operations on fluvial landscapes can be foiled by nature. A skillful enemy defending a crossing point can magnify the slightest terrain feature. Marshy approaches, steep banks, turbulent currents, unstable riverbeds, dense vegetation, and sheer bluffs can easily confound an operation. Furthermore, the relative impact of any one of these factors can be exaggerated in a matter of hours by a passing rainstorm or early-season thaw. All of these factors, taken together with difficult traffic control problems and confusing command relationships, must figure into the detailed planning for this type of operation (Spiller 1992).

Although operations on the fluvial landscape are typically thought of in the context of a crossing operation, they have other equally important roles in warfare. A river may be a part of a strategically vital region, and as such may represent *key terrain* such as the Hudson River during the American Revolution. In fact, the *strategic geometry* of that war dictated that, in order to be victorious, the winning side had to retain control of the river (Palmer 1969). Similarly, Harpers Ferry, a vital river gap through the mountains along the Potomac River, played a pivotal role in the early campaigns of the American Civil War (Foote 1958).

The typical role of a river is that of an obstacle that must be crossed. In this circumstance, the river is a barrier that can be exploited by a defending army. The river constricts and *compartmentalizes* movement, and usually presents a clear set of defensive advantages. History is replete with examples of rivers fulfilling this role. By way of example, the Rhine River has played a pivotal role throughout European history from the time of the Romans to World War II (Howard 1976). The grueling Italian Campaign during World War II included a series of river obstacles, which the Germans adroitly exploited to bog down the Allies (Doughty et al. 1996). In Korea, the final line of defense along the Pusan Perimeter depended heavily on defending the line of the Naktong River (Center for Military History 1989). The fortuitous seizure of the Remagen Bridge in March 1945 (MacDonald 1984) and the Israeli crossing of the Suez Canal during their counterattack in the Sinai in 1973 (Herzog 1984) are excellent examples of hasty river crossings.

A river may also serve as a *line of operation*. In this scenario, the river serves as the axis of the military operation and enhances mobility, logistics, and communications. A classic military operation of this nature occurred during the 1898 British campaign against the Khalifa in Egypt and Sudan. The British used the Nile River to link their principal base at Alexandria to their strategic objective at Khartoum (Macdonald 1985). In this same vein, operations on the Cumberland, Tennessee, and Mississippi Rivers during the American Civil War demonstrate the numerous advantages associated with rivers as lines of operations. Union forces exploited the inherent mobility and operational advantage offered by the rivers to penetrate deeply into the Confederate hinterland (Coombe 1996).

The American experience

American land and naval forces have conducted operations on fluvial landscapes since the Revolutionary War. The nature and frequency of these operations have depended largely on geography as well as the operational setting. For example, during the American Civil War, Union and Confederate forces in the west were inexorably tied to rivers because of the nature of the Mississippi basin, but less so in the Eastern Theater. Although operations on fluvial landscapes have not always been operationally decisive, they typically have made a significant contribution to the successful prosecution of a campaign (Fulton 1985).

Perhaps the most noteworthy military operations of the Revolutionary War were the fortification and battles for control of the Hudson River, which eventually led to the creation of Fortress West Point. These fortifications became necessary because the Hudson River was the strategic *center of gravity* of the American Revolutionary War, and the control of this important feature was decisive (Palmer 1969). Thus, not long after the start of the war, British and American forces sought to gain control of the strategic Hudson River–Lake Champlain–St Lawrence River waterway system, which was vital to the strategic geometry of the war for two reasons. First, it was the natural dividing line between New England and the mid-Atlantic colonies, and, by controlling it, the British could drive a wedge between the manufacturing and agricultural centers of the Colonies, thus fracturing the war effort. Second, this waterway physically connected the British bases in New York City and Montreal (see Figure 8.2). Consequently, possession of the waterway by the colonists was necessary to prevent concentration of British military effort and fragment their ability to act in unison (Palmer 1969).

During the War of 1812, American and British forces were once again engaged on waterways. Warfare on the fluvial landscape witnessed decisive engagements that substantially aided American efforts in two strategically important regions: Lake Erie and the St Lawrence River,

Figure 8.2
This map illustrates the strategic position of the Hudson River. The river was the geographic link between the principal British bases in New York City and Canada, and separated the New England Colonies from those in the mid-Atlantic and south.

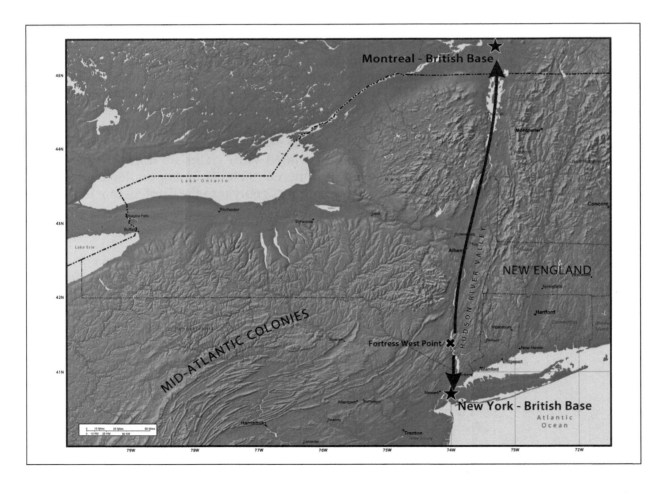

then later near New Orleans. In 1813, Commodore Perry assembled a fleet on Lake Erie to counter a British threat from Canada. He led this fleet to a series of important victories over British naval forces and gained control of the Great Lakes and St Lawrence River, permitting a subsequent American advance into Canada (Fulton 1985). The loci of the war shifted when the British moved against New Orleans in December 1814. As British naval forces assembled in the Gulf of Mexico, Americans under Commodore Patterson pulled together a small riverine force to oppose their advance. The small American river flotilla retreated and joined forces with General Andrew Jackson to defend New Orleans. During the land battles around the city, Commodore Patterson used his two largest gunboats, the *Carolina* and *Louisiana*, to harass British naval forces. This action materially aided in the British defeat at the gates of this strategically important city (Doughty et al. 1996).

The American Army and Navy fought a protracted form of low-intensity combat during the Seminole Wars (1835–42) in Florida. Land and naval forces operated jointly using the inlets, creeks, and swamps of the Florida Everglades to prosecute a frustrating war. Once again, the fluvial landscape served as a means of transportation and as a line of operation. The Seminole War also witnessed the building of highly specialized river craft, constructed to fight exclusively in the unique riverine environment, a unique characteristic of warfare that would reoccur during the American Civil War and later in Vietnam. Rivers require shallow-draft, stable watercraft capable of supporting heavy armament (Coombe 1996). Accordingly, American forces under Colonel W. J. Worth and Navy Lieutenant J. T. McLaughlin assembled a specialized fleet of flat-bottomed boats, floating batteries, canoes, and specialized troop transports to operate in the shallow swamps and rivers of the region (Fulton 1985).

The American Civil War witnessed riverine operations of all types and perhaps accounted for the most extensive riverine operations of any war (Coombe 1996). In the Eastern Theater, rivers tended to serve as obstacles to maneuver, requiring careful planning and extensive crossing operations. In the Western Theater, the Mississippi River and its major tributaries typically flowed parallel to Federal lines of advance and thus served as lines of operation. Hence, the American Civil War would also witness the evolution of highly specialized river craft, sometimes designed to deal with the unique physical characteristics of a specific river (Coombe 1996). Many of the most important Union victories were riverine campaigns and, perhaps more than any other battles, hastened the collapse of the Confederacy (Miles 1994).

The Civil War represented the zenith of American operations on fluvial landscapes until World War II and the Vietnam War. The immobile Western Front of World War I occasioned only minor, small-scale operations that had no considerable impact on the outcome of the war. However, operations during World War II necessitated a number of major river crossing operations, sometimes involving entire corps and armies. In Vietnam, operations in the Mekong River delta necessitated the creation of a joint Army–Navy Riverine Force. This force was composed of unique watercraft designed to contend with the operational requirements of the fluvial landscape (Fulton 1985). Not surprisingly, many of the Vietnam-era river craft looked remarkably similar to their Civil War-era cousins.

Streams and the Civil War landscape

At the start of the American Civil War, Federal strategy dictated a concerted drive down the Mississippi River to split the Confederacy and open it to Union commerce (i.e. the so-called Anaconda Plan, conceived by General Winfield Scott). In fact, each of the Western Theater's great rivers represented highways for invasion, and Federal armies would use them to pierce the left wing of the Confederate line (see Figure 8.3). No one was quicker to realize the importance of these rivers than General U. S. Grant and President Lincoln (Catton 1989). Lincoln saw the enormous geographic advantage this river system afforded the Northern cause all too clearly. Ownership of one or more of these rivers would bring about a major penetration of the western flank of the Rebel line and split the Confederacy. Furthermore, Lincoln saw possession of the

Figure 8.3
The rivers of the Western Theater. This map illustrates the dendritic drainage pattern of the rivers in the Mississippi River basin and their suitability as lines of operation for Union forces. *Source*: map adapted from Catton (1989).

Mississippi River as perhaps the singular objective of the war and he instructed General of the Armies Henry W. Halleck to impart this vision to his western commanders in a general memorandum in early February 1862, which stated, "The President regards the opening of the Mississippi River as the first and most important of all our military and naval operations" (The War of Rebellion 1883).

Ulysses Grant understood clearly that the Cumberland and Tennessee Rivers pointed directly into the heart of strategically important Tennessee (Grant 1885). A rapid penetration of this state and control of its rivers would unhinge Confederate General Albert Sidney Johnston's western flank and open Nashville and Chattanooga to easy Federal attack. Grant acted on this plan and, with the help of a powerful Union river flotilla, seized Forts Henry and Donelson in February 1862. This was a remarkable victory because Grant forced Johnston to withdraw the Confederate line south to Corinth, Mississippi, a retreat of 200 miles that gave the Union Army control of Kentucky, Nashville, and all of western Tennessee, almost without a fight (Catton 1989). Grant followed this success with a rapid advance down the Tennessee River to Pittsburg Landing, where the bloody Battle of Shiloh would be fought on 6 and 7 April 1862. While Grant's army fought for its life along the river bluff at Shiloh, another equally important battle was reaching its climax at Island No. 10 near the town of New Madrid, Missouri, along the Mississippi River (see Figure 8.3).

Physical setting: Eastern versus Western Theater

Riverine operations in the Eastern and Western Theaters of the Civil War were very distinct because of differences in their *physiography*. The Eastern Theater was confined to the region east of the Blue Ridge, between Washington, DC, and Richmond, and the landscape is composed of an Upland–Piedmont–Coastal Plain configuration (Fenneman 1938). The landscape includes a *trellis drainage pattern* with rivers that flow perpendicular to the coast, directly across the line of operations (see Figure 8.4). Consequently, eastern rivers were obstacles and the majority of operations were confined to deliberate river-crossing operations or securing fords.

The geographic implications of the fluvial landscape were very different in the Western Theater. The Mississippi River and its great tributaries flowed across a large inland-basin physiographic province (Fenneman 1938). This region includes a large area of horizontally bedded strata dipped slightly to the Gulf of Mexico with a characteristic *dendritic drainage pattern*. In this geographic setting, large rivers tend to flow south, perpendicular to Confederate lines. Therefore, rivers could be employed to breach and unhinge the Confederate defensive strategy in the west (Catton 1989).

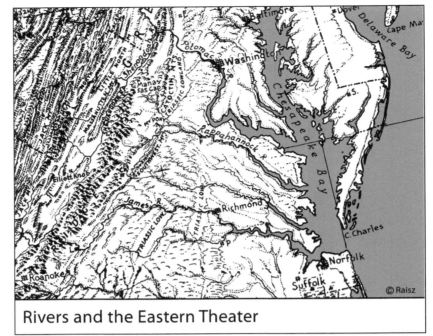

Figure 8.4
Trellis drainage pattern
of the Eastern Theater.
The region's major
streams flow
perpendicular to the
coast and across the
principal lines of
movement. *Source*: map
adapted from
Raisz (1957).

The magnitude of this geographic dilemma is clearly illustrated in Figure 8.3. The Cumberland River offers a direct line of advance to Nashville, which served as a major transportation hub and manufacturing center. Once the Confederate line was breached along this river at Fort Donelson, Nashville was doomed and there was little Rebel generals could do to prevent Union ironclads from wrecking railroad bridges and river ports as they freely rampaged down the Cumberland.

The loss of Fort Henry was even more problematic (see Figure 8.3). South of that fort, the Tennessee River penetrates central Tennessee and northern Alabama like a gigantic fishhook (Foote 1958). Once Grant seized Fort Henry in February 1862, the entire center of the Confederate line in the west was open to a river-borne Union advance, and, in fact, Union gunboats traveled as far south as Alabama, wreaking havoc as they went, destroying railroad bridges, river craft, and factories (Coombe 1996). Grant exploited this geographic advantage and rapidly advanced along the river to Shiloh in March and April 1862 (Catton 1989).

Simultaneously, as part of the Union's southward advance, another Federal army mounted an assault to seize the Confederate strongpoint blocking the Mississippi at Island No. 10 opposite New Madrid, Missouri (see Figure 8.3). Here, the Mississippi makes one of its gigantic meanders. The Union objective was Island No. 10, so-called because it was the 10th island south of the Ohio River's junction with the Mississippi (Nevin 1994). The geography of Island No. 10 made it of vital strategic importance; the island was selected by the Confederates as a major strongpoint because they were forced to abandon their major more northerly forts in Kentucky (see Figure 8.3), which were outflanked after the loss of Forts Henry and Donelson.

Island No. 10 was the only defensible terrain on the Mississippi, north of Memphis, and General P. T. G. Beauregard considered the retention of this fort essential to Confederate fortunes in the west (The War of Rebellion 1883). He saw Island No. 10 as the crucial strategic point along the Mississippi because it stood squarely in the way of the anticipated Federal advance south along the axis of the river. The location of Island No. 10 at the base of the meander, combined with the flooded banks along the Tennessee shore, sealed off river operations from New Madrid to Memphis. This compelled Beauregard to order the construction of a chain of forts on the island so that heavy guns could cover every possible approach along the river and the adjacent banks. The largest guns available to the Rebels were emplaced in the fortifications (The War of Rebellion 1883).

Island No. 10 was located (it no longer exists) at the base of a southerly meander, and the town of New Madrid was located at the top of the northerly loop of the Mississippi in 1862 (see Figure 8.5). The straight-line

Figure 8.5
Map of the New Madrid–Island No. 10 campaign. *Source*: Cowles (1895).

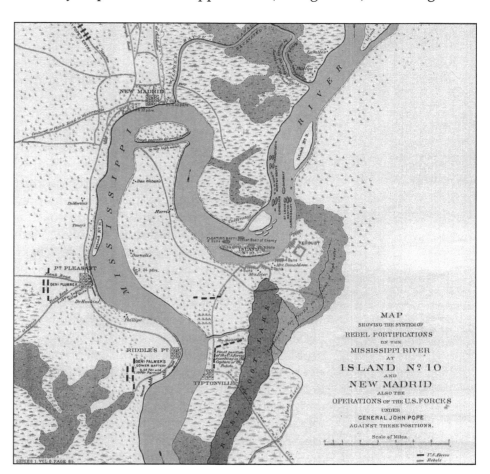

distance from Island No. 8 to New Madrid is about 10 miles, but is 24 miles by river. Likewise, the overland distance between Island No. 10 and Tiptonville is 10 miles, but 26 by water. Most of the land surrounding the fort was inundated and swampy, severely limiting movement to the levees adjacent to the river (The War of Rebellion 1883).

Reelfoot Lake (see Figure 8.5) is an artifact from the 1811 New Madrid earthquake and was an uncrossable barrier that prevented boat traffic (Coombe 1996). Therefore, an attack to capture the fort was possible only by crossing the river, or from the south by the road that passed through Tiptonville (Dodge 1897). The fort itself, deemed impregnable by many, consisted of a series of large earthen works with forty-nine heavy guns and 9000 veteran troops, supported by an additional five batteries on the Tennessee bank of the river (The War of Rebellion 1883). A floating battery and a small flotilla of gunboats augmented the land defenses. Therefore, Federal forces would have to fight a difficult twin battle: one against this formidable array of Confederate power; and the other, driven by geography, against inundated land, treacherous currents, and sandbars within the meander loop adjacent to the fort (Nevin 1994).

The battle for Island No. 10

General John Pope commanded a Federal army of 20,000 men, supported by the Union River Squadron under Flag Officer Foote (Nevin 1994). This combined force was given the mission of opening the northern stretch of the Mississippi to Memphis. Foote was no stranger to this type of operation. He was the naval commander who successfully captured Forts Henry and Donelson along with Grant in February 1862 (Catton 1989). Although the Federals greatly outnumbered the Rebels, the combination of fortifications and geography presented daunting physical obstacles. The only practicable land approach to the fort was along the western bank of the Mississippi via New Madrid, but, in order to get at the fort, Pope's army needed transports to cross the Mississippi and gunboats to silence shore batteries. However, powerful fortifications on Island No. 10 stood between the Federal army and the River Flotilla.

The battle began well for Pope. He seized New Madrid on 14 March, and wanted to send his soldiers across the river south of Island No. 10 to encircle and capture its garrison (Dodge 1897). However, this was problematic because Island No. 10 remained safe unless he crossed the river because two avenues of supply and escape remained open to the Rebels. Flag Officer Foote, on the other hand, decided it was too dangerous to push his ironclads and transports within range of the fort's heavy guns (Official Records 1884). Foote's plan was to begin a long-range bombardment (see Figure 8.6), but it quickly proved to be ineffective (Official Records 1884).

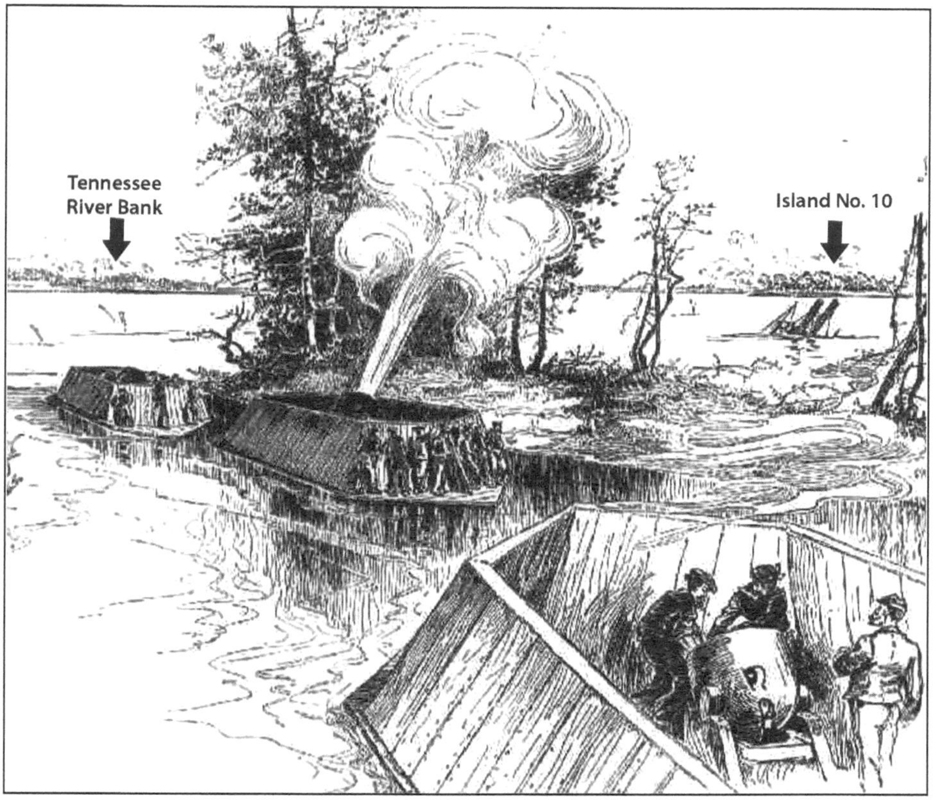

Tennessee
River Bank

Island No. 10

Figure 8.6
Union mortar boats
bombard Island No. 10
during Flag Officer
Foote's abortive attempt
to pound the island's
defenders into
submission. This view is
from the north with
Island No. 10 located in
the upper left of the
lithograph. *Source:*
Harper's Weekly.

In the interim, Pope's infantry attempted several courses of action to cross the river, but met with little success. After several weeks, Pope grew tired of Foote's ineffective bombardment and decided to attempt a novel plan to bypass the island. His formula was to cut a canal across the base of the flooded meander north of the "S" bend (see Figure 8.5). The proposed canal would directly connect the river from the area between Islands 8 and 9 and New Madrid. This shortcut would use the geography of the meander to bypass the island with the transports he needed to cross the river (The War of Rebellion 1883).

Engineers and a regiment of infantry dug the canal through flooded fields and tangled bottomlands, and devised ingenious tools to saw trees below the level of the floodwaters (The War of Rebellion 1883). Some 600 soldiers eventually dug a 50 foot-wide, 8 mile-long canal in three weeks. Finally, on 4 April, the levee above Island 9 was pierced and the transports rode the surge of floodwater safely to New Madrid. Simultaneously, two Union ironclads completed successful nighttime runs past the guns of Island No. 10. Now Pope had transports to ferry his army across the river and the big guns of the ironclads *Carondelet* and *Pittsburgh* to defeat shore batteries and cover his crossing (Dodge 1897).

The drive to take Island No. 10 from the rear began in earnest. On 6 April, the ironclads cleared Rebel batteries on the Tennessee shore and those opposite Point Pleasant (see Figure 8.5). The *Carondelet* and *Pittsburgh* attacked Watson's Landing on the morning of 8 April, then covered the crossing of Pope's army to the eastern bank of the river. Pope's troops quickly sealed off the escape routes by seizing Tiptonville and the narrow isthmus between the Mississippi and Reelfoot Lake. By noon, Island No. 10's garrison was cut off, and by 21:00 hours many of them surrendered. Early on 8 April (just as the Battle of Shiloh ended) the last Confederates surrendered to Pope's soldiers (Nevin 1994). This was a stunning victory, during which the Union Army reversed the geographic advantages of terrain and compelled the Confederates to surrender. More than 5000 Confederates were taken prisoner along with in excess of 100 captured guns and a mountain of ammunition (Foote 1958). The anchor of the Confederate left flank in the west was smashed with the loss of only a handful of Federal troops.

Summary of geographic factors

Unquestionably, geography had a profound effect on the battle for Island No. 10. The inundated terrain and meanders of the Mississippi River seemingly afforded the Confederates with an ideal, almost impregnable, fortress secure from land attack. The river channel was wide and at the highest levels in years. In order to cross the Mississippi, Pope's infantry required transports, which were blocked on the opposite side of the meander. To assist Pope, Union naval commanders were forced to contend with strong currents and sandbars in the meander as well as fighting the formidable fortifications. Hence, the meander played a diabolical geographic trick on the Union plan to seize the fort because the thin-skinned transports remained bottled up north of the island, separated from New Madrid by only 10 airline miles where the infantry remained idle. Union infantry commanders could only nibble at the periphery of the fort, blocked by swampy bottomland. Island No. 10 was approachable only by way of a single road through Tiptonville, and herein lay one irony of this battle. Once Pope's soldiers gained a foothold along the Missouri bank, this geographic advantage was reversed and the single-access road through Tiptonville became an Achilles' heel of the defenders.

Clearly, the most important geographic influence on the battle was the Mississippi River. The position and orientation of the meander presented a unique tactical puzzle to the Union Army. Moreover, the position of Island No. 10 at the base of the meander was fortuitous for the Rebels because the river current would force Foote's ponderous gunboats directly against the river batteries (see Figure 8.5). This problem was compounded because the river was at its highest flood stage in recent memory (The War of Rebellion 1883). The high water generated a current so strong that Union ironclads had to anchor themselves to the shore because their engines were not powerful enough to maintain position in the river. Foote's biggest problem however was the direction of flow. At Forts Henry and Donelson the rivers flowed north, hence a ship that took a disabling shot would drift back to Union lines. At Island No. 10, the situation was reversed. Here Foote had to contend with a southerly current, which would sweep a disabled ship south, into Confederate hands. This factor more so than any other caused him to rely on the seemingly timid long-range bombardment of the island (The War of Rebellion 1883).

Flooded banks and swamps were a key security factor for the Confederate forces assembled at Island No. 10. A land assault from the Tennessee side of the river was out of the question because of impassable swamps and bogs. This inundated land was reinforced by Reelfoot Lake, which connected with the Mississippi River some 14 miles to the south, and Reelfoot Lake was not easily crossed because it was thoroughly obstructed. Additionally, Pope's efforts to occupy the meander opposite Island No. 10 were similarly foiled by flooded land and bottomless swamps (The War of Rebellion 1883).

However, the security offered by the flooded land adjacent to the river and single road approach quickly turned into a major disadvantage for the Confederates. After capturing New Madrid on 14 March, Pope placed artillery at Riddles Point and south along the natural levee (see Figure 8.5). This ultimately reversed the relative advantage presented by the terrain and was significant for two reasons. First, Union batteries at Riddles Point commanded the river below Island No. 10, all but preventing re-supply by river craft. It also forced the Rebels to withdraw their small fleet of gunboats from the bend in the river, which would later facilitate the passage of Union ironclads on the evenings of 5 and 6 April (Coombe 1996). Second, the Riddles Point batteries controlled the land approaches to Tiptonville from the south. Since the land south of Tiptonville was flooded, movement had to take place on the single elevated road or along the natural levee, which was in easy range of Union artillery.

Conclusions

The battle for Island No. 10 was a key Union victory that opened the Mississippi River to Memphis, Tennessee, 150 miles to the south, and crushed Confederate plans to defend forward along the river. The battle is an excellent illustration of the influence of terrain on military operations and demonstrates the geographic obstacles associated with riverine operations. Union forces were able to overcome a heavily defended fort protected by bluffs and flooded land along a wide, swift river. This victory resulted in the capture of the entire Confederate garrison and a huge bag of heavy guns and ammunition with the loss of a handful of Union soldiers. The battle witnessed remarkable ingenuity in the construction of the canal to bypass Island No. 10. In terms of joint operations, it is a near textbook operation illustrating co-operation between land and naval forces during a time when there were no formal regulations mandating joint action.

Ironically, this important battle remains virtually unknown. Perhaps the battle was overshadowed by the bloody fighting at Shiloh, which was very controversial and captured the headlines in the Northern press. Furthermore, General Pope slipped quickly into oblivion after his catastrophic defeat at Second Manassas later that summer. Notwithstanding its relative obscurity, the battle for Island No. 10 was the first major engagement on the Mississippi River and was a model for a number of battles to come. In fact, when faced with a similar geographic problem at the meander opposite Vicksburg, Mississippi, in 1863, Union forces quickly dusted off the solution used at Island No. 10 and attempted to bypass its river batteries in much the same way. Unfortunately they met with failure and were forced into a protracted battle because the conditions of the Mississippi River could not support the scouring and maintenance of the canal long enough to float the transports across the meander, past the guns of Vicksburg.

Editor's note: This chapter is a revised and updated version of a public domain chapter previously published as Galgano, F. A. 2005. "Streams and the civil war landscape: the battle for Island No. 10." In *Military geography: from peace to war*. E. J. Palka and F. A. Galgano (eds), 11–34. New York, NY: McGraw-Hill Custom Publishing.

References cited

Catton, B. C. 1989. *Grant moves south*. New York, NY: Ballantine Books.

Center for Military History. 1989. *Korea, 1950*. Department of the Army, Center for Military History Publication 21-1, Washington, DC: US Government Printing Office.

Coombe, J. D. 1996. *Thunder along the Mississippi*. New York, NY: Bantam Books.

Cowles, C. D. 1895. *Atlas to accompany the official records of the Union and Confederate Armies*. Series 1, vol. 8. Washington, DC: US Government Printing Office.

D'Este, C. 1992. *Fatal decision: Anzio and the battle for Rome*. New York, NY: Harper Collins Publishers, Inc.

Dodge, T. A. 1897. *A bird's-eye view of our Civil War*. New York, NY: Da Capo Press.

Doughty, R. A., R. A. Flint, J. A. Lynn, M. Grimily, D. D. Howard, and W. Murray. 1996. *Warfare in the western world*. Lexington, MA: D. C. Heath and Company.

Fenneman, N. M. 1938. *Physiography of the eastern United States*. New York, NY: McGraw-Hill Book Company, Inc.

Foote, S. 1958. *The Civil War, a narrative: Fort Sumter to Perryville*. New York, NY: Random House.

Fulton, W. B., 1985. *Riverine operations. 1965–1969*. Department of the Army, Vietnam Studies, Washington, DC: US Government Printing Office.

Grant, U. S. 1885. *Personal memoirs of U. S. Grant*. New York, NY: Webster.

Herzog, C. 1984. *The Arab–Israeli Wars*. New York, NY: Random House.

Howard, M. 1976. *War in European history*. New York, NY: Oxford University Press.

MacDonald, C. B. 1984. *The last offensive*. The United States Army in World War II, The European Theater of Operations. US Army Center for Military History, Washington, DC: US Government Printing Office.

Macdonald, J. 1985. *Great battlefields of the world*. New York, NY: Macmillan Publishing Company.

Miles, J. 1994. *A river unvexed*. Nashville, TN: Rutledge Hill Press.

Nevin, D., 1994. *The road to Shiloh, early battles in the west*. Alexandria, VA: Time Life Books.

Official Records of the Union and Confederate Navies in the War of Rebellion. 1884. *Volume 22: Operations on western waters*. Washington, DC: US Government Printing Office.

Palmer, D. 1969. *The river and the rock*. New York, NY: Hippocrene Books.

Patton, G. S. P. 1947. *War as I knew it*. Boston, MA: Houghton Mifflin Co.

Raisz, Erwin. 1957. *Landforms of the United States*.

Ryan, C. 1974. *A bridge too far*. New York, NY: Simon & Schuster, Inc.

Spiller, R. J. 1992. "Crossing the Rapido." In *Combined Arms in Battle Since 1939*. Fort Leavenworth, KS: Command and Staff College Press.

The War of Rebellion: A Compilation of the Official Records of the Union and Confederate Armies. 1883. *Volume VIII: operations in Missouri, Arkansas, Kansas and the Indian Territories*. Washington, DC: US Government Printing Office.

Ziemke, E. F. and M. E. Bauer. 1987. *Moscow to Stalingrad: decision in the east*. Washington, DC: Center for Military History, US Army.

123

Chapter nine

Methuen's Northern Cape Campaign, Anglo-Boer War, 1899–1902

HENDRIK A.P. SMIT

Introduction

AT THE CLOSE OF THE nineteenth century and the dawn of the twentieth century, a devastating war raged in what is today known as the Republic of South Africa. Two small *Boer* republics took on the might of the British Empire, and between October 1899 and May 1902 Britain had to contend with an enemy that fought a skillful war of survival and independence.

At the end of the struggle in May 1902, Britain's military and economic superiority ultimately allowed them to defeat stubborn Boer resistance, ending the war with the signing of the peace accord in Vereeniging, south of Johannesburg. The war cost the two Boer republics their independence, and it devastated the landscape. Approximately 30,000 farms and more than forty towns, along with vast numbers of livestock, were destroyed during the course of the war. Casualties amounted to 28,647 soldiers, and more than 42,000 South African civilians of all races lost their lives in so-called *concentration camps*. This system was enacted by the British to deny Boer soldiers food and other support from the civilian population, and to weaken Boer resolve.

The *Northern Cape Campaign*, led by Lieutenant General Paul Sanford, the third baron Methuen, was the opening move of the initial British offensive. Although this campaign illustrates the influence of geography on a military campaign, it also conveys important lessons that transcend that particular period, and are perhaps applicable to operations today.

The importance of geography in war

O'Sullivan and Miller (1983) suggest that the fundamental strategic and tactical problems of warfare are geographic in nature. Historical analyses of battles certainly lend credence to this notion and serve to illuminate the nexus between geography and warfare. More recent studies, such as Winters (1998) and Palka and Galgano (2005), confirm this idea. The fact that geographic factors such as terrain, weather, and climate exert a pervasive influence on human and military activities is well known and thoroughly researched. Nevertheless, history also demonstrates that geographic factors were not always taken into consideration during military operations, often with dire results.

Two classic examples during which climate and terrain were fatally underestimated can be found in the Russian campaigns of Napoleon and Hitler (Blond 1995; Winters 1998). Numerous other examples demonstrating the crucial role played by geographic factors in military operations can be found in the international literature as has been recorded by, *inter alia*, Winters (1991), Metzger (1992), Bayles (1993), Galgano (1994), Puckett (1994), Palka and Galgano (2000, 2005), and Collins (2003). With particular reference to warfare in the South African region, the important influence of the human and natural landscape on warfare has been recorded by Opperman (1981), Perry (1996), and Pretorius (2002).

Geographic factors influencing the Northern Cape Campaign

> Therefore measure in terms of five things, use these assessments to make comparisons, and thus find out what the conditions are. The five things are *the way, the weather, the terrain* [author's emphasis], the leadership, and discipline.
>
> (Cleary 1988: 42).

Terrain

Control of the high ground has been traditionally regarded as a strategic and tactical imperative (Deighton 1985; Stephenson 2003). Control of high ground makes it possible to observe enemy movements and to employ effective fire against the enemy from long distances. These conditions also allow ample time to respond to enemy movements, or to hinder the enemy's ability to conduct effective reconnaissance. Both imperatives were amplified during defensive warfare and were conventional wisdom during the *Anglo-Boer War*. Given the acceptance of these principles, Boer forces fought the first two battles (i.e. Belmont and Graspan) from the hills overlooking the railroad to Kimberley. However, experience in the field during these battles forced Boer defenders to rethink traditional wisdom and to come up with new plans, which were better suited to their specific tactical circumstances. Among other things, they learned to make more innovative use of the diverse features of high ground and rivers for strategic and tactical purposes.

Similar to high ground, rivers are normally regarded as good
125 defensive positions. A river presents a set of difficult tactical planning

considerations to an army (Galgano 2005). From a tactical perspective, river characteristics such as length, depth, banks, size, discharge rate, velocity, and the number and size of *meanders* are important aspects that must be taken into consideration by an attacking force (Van den Berg 1997; Collins 1998; Winters 1998). Furthermore, the river affords abundant drinking water to defenders, while denying it to the attackers. In arid or semi-arid conditions, such as those experienced in South Africa, this can be a crucial advantage.

Each of the four battles during Methuen's Northern Cape Campaign took place on a relatively flat plain, between 1100–1200 m (3600–4000 ft) above sea level, dotted with *dolerite (diabase)* hills rising between 74–133 m (240–450 ft) above the surrounding plain (CDSM 1988; 1997). The plains are normally covered in long grass with patches of thorn trees and isolated anthills (see Figure 9.1). *Aardvark holes* and thorn bushes complicate movement at night much more than it seems at first glance (Pakenham 1979). Methuen had to cross two rivers as part of his campaign to take Kimberley. Of these, the Orange River is the larger of

Figure 9.1
Typical terrain of the Northern Cape seen from Magersfontein hills looking out towards Modder River.
Source: H. A. P. Smit.

the two, yet it played no role during the campaign, as the bridges were in British hands. However, the railroad crossed another river, the Modder, a couple of meters downstream of its confluence with the Riet River, thus forcing Methuen to deal with both. Given the technology of the time, these rivers formed a formidable obstacle to Methuen's force although they were both rather small.

Infrastructure

At the outbreak of the war, South Africa possessed good anchorages and harbors, all of which were in British hands. However, British problems began when they left the harbors—from that point on, movement of troops and supplies were largely restricted to the area traversed by railroad. This problem was compounded by a dire lack of transport animals in the region. Although the area was crisscrossed by numerous gravel and smaller farm roads, they were not suited to the movement of large military units (Breytenbach 1969). Methuen's principal advantage was that he had at his disposal a good railway line connecting Cape Town to Kimberley and the hinterland beyond. However, the railway was problematic for Methuen: it provided him with an excellent supply line, but it also tied him to a very narrow and predictable line of operation during his advance to Kimberley. Certainly, the Boers knew this, and destroyed bridges as well as vulnerable parts of the railroad, and concentrated their defense at critical points along the railway line.

A number of small settlements dotted the landscape. From a military perspective, these were insignificant, as they were not much more than a few houses and shops, servicing the surrounding communities. Kimberley was the only town of any importance in the region, and it became South Africa's first boomtown when diamonds were discovered in 1870. By 1882 it was the only South African city, and indeed in the Southern Hemisphere, with electric street lighting. Seventeen years later, on the eve of the outbreak of the Anglo-Boer War, Kimberley was the second largest city in the Cape Colony, outranked only by Cape Town, with a population of 20,000 Europeans and 30,000 Africans. It is estimated that it produced 90 percent of the world's supply of diamonds (Pakenham 1979).

Weather and climate

Weather and climate are perhaps the most pervasive factors that influence military operations at all levels of war. Exposure to *ambient air temperatures* beyond the 20–25°C (68–77°F) optimum range may result in excessive heat loss or gain to the human body, with significant physiological consequences. If this process continues, *thermoregulatory processes* will fail to maintain the body's core temperature, leading to *hypothermia* or *hyperthermia* (Morgan and Moran 1997). Both conditions can be fatal, and military leaders need to be aware of the dangers associated with exposing soldiers to extreme temperatures, and the effects they may have on their combat readiness (Blond 1995; Winters 1998). The Battle of Monmouth (28 June 1778), an example from the American Revolutionary War, illustrates the impact of weather on the outcome of battle. Following the battle, English forces under General Clinton reported 65 fatalities from battle injuries and another 59 from heatstroke (Wade 1998).

Like temperature, precipitation had an important influence on Methuen's campaign. This region of South Africa experiences a summer concentration of rainfall. Kimberley is approximately 30 km (19 miles) north of the Modder River and received between 300 and 750 mm (12–30 inches) of rain per year during the 10 years preceding 1899 (War Office 1899). According to the South African Weather Bureau, the average annual rainfall for this area is between 250 and 500 mm (10–20 inches). Rain usually results from thunderstorms and showers, sometimes accompanied with hail (Schulze 1986).

The average daily duration of sunshine is between 70 and 80 percent, even during the height of the rainy season, and the seasonal temperature pattern is typical of continental climates. Maximum temperatures for January (i.e. summer) are between 30 and 33°C (86–91°F), with extremes of up to 41°C (106°F). During July (i.e. winter), the maximum temperature is about 17°C (63°F), while extreme high temperatures can reach 28°C (82°F). Normal minimum temperatures during the summer (i.e. January) are 15°C (59°F) and 0°C (32°F) in winter (i.e. July), with extremes of 3°C (37°F) and –11°C (–9°F) respectively. Winds are usually northwesterly, attaining maximum speeds in the afternoon. During thunderstorms, strong and gusty southwesterly winds of short duration, accompanied by a sharp drop in temperature, are common features of this region (Schulze 1986). Thus, climate and weather conditions in South Africa were daunting and to the British soldiers, arriving in South Africa directly from the Northern Hemisphere winter, these conditions proved to be both unfamiliar and extremely trying. Dust, heat, relentless sun, sharp diurnal temperature variations, and the lack of freely available water were to negatively influence the fighting ability of British soldiers during the coming battles.

The Anglo-Boer War (1899–1902)

The Anglo-Boer War was a seminal event in South Africa, and more has been written about the conflict than any other in which South Africans have fought (Saunders 2001). This was also the bloodiest and most encompassing conflict between white people in Southern Africa, although it by no means limited its effects to the white population (Wessels 1991).

On 9 October 1899, Paul Kruger, the President of the *Zuid–Afrikaansche
Republiek (ZAR)*, sent an ultimatum to Britain that would lead to this

war, which was to have far-reaching consequences for southern Africa (Muller 1977; Pakenham 1979). This ultimatum expired on 11 October 1899, and the two Boer Republics, the ZAR and *Orange Free State (OFS)*, bound by a treaty, went on the offensive against the British Empire (Sleigh 1979; Scholtz, 1999).

Given that the Boer Republics were taking on the might of the British Empire, they would face a significant manpower disadvantage. At the start of hostilities, Britain had approximately 22,104 soldiers in, or on their way to, South Africa. Of these, 14,704 were posted in *Natal* (12,000 according to Pakenham 1979), and only 7400 were in the *Cape Colony*. Approximately 4900 Colonial soldiers augmented the British force already in South Africa. In contrast, the Boer Republics could muster between 61,500 and 78,000 men, which included soldiers from Germany, the Netherlands, France, Switzerland, Italy, Ireland, Austria-Hungary, Russia, and the US (Wessels 2001). Despite this apparently strong force, it must be borne in mind that Boers were mostly civilians, with little formal training, and that not more than approximately 47,000 of this force was ever at the front at any one time (Wessels 1991). Nonetheless, once the war began, the Boers struck quickly and shocked the British during the first few weeks. Boer armies invaded Natal and trapped Sir George White and 14,500 men at Ladysmith (Pakenham 1979). On the Kimberley front, Mafeking and Kimberley (see Figure 9.2) were besieged and other towns invaded (Wessels 1991).

Figure 9.2
Methuen's Northern Cape campaign. *Source*: J.A. Jacobs.

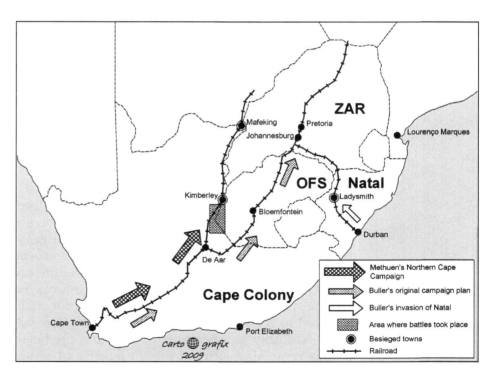

Figure 9.3
The opposing generals.
From left to right, Cronjé,
de la Rey, and Methuen.
Source: War Museum of
the Boer Republics,
Bloemfontein.

On 31 October, the supreme commander of the British forces in South Africa, General Sir Redvers Buller, arrived in Cape Town on board the *Dunottar Castle*. Up to that stage, Buller devised a simple strategy: mass his 46,000 men, 114 cannon, and forty-seven machine guns on the Northeast Cape front and launch a direct assault against the OFS and then the ZAR. However, the new realities of the war forced him to rethink this plan. Cecil John Rhodes, one of the favorite sons of the British Empire, was trapped in Kimberley, while White and his 14,500 men languished in Ladysmith (Miller 1999; Judd and Surridge 2002). Consequently, Buller decided to send Lieutenant General Paul Sanford, third baron Methuen, with 15,000 men to relieve Kimberley, while he would take 21,600 men to rescue White in Ladysmith (Waters 1904) (see Figure 9.2). Thus, it was on the harsh *veld* of the Northern Cape near Kimberley, opposed by Boers led by Generals Koos de la Rey and Piet Cronjé, that Lord Methuen was about to learn hard lessons of military geography and its pervasive influence on operations, weapons, and soldiers (see Figure 9.3).

Geography and battles of the North Cape Campaign

The Battle of Belmont (23 November 1899)

The opening battle of Methuen's Northern Cape Campaign took place at Belmont. Here, approximately 2000 Boers under General Jakobus Prinsloo took their position among the ridges east of Belmont Station, and, from the start, geography played a crucial role. The Boers knew that Methuen was forced to attack along the railway as it was the only effective means of supplying his large force. Furthermore, it was only the start of the rainy season and water for such a large force would be hard to come by on the arid Northern Cape veld.

Not only was Methuen linked to a predictable line of advance, but his army also suffered from a paucity of serviceable maps, thus daily reconnaissance was used to compile sketch maps (Waters 1904). The British topographer who compiled the sketch map used to depict the terrain of the battlefield underestimated the distance between the railway line and the Boer positions by a full 1000 paces. This error, coupled with the slower pace of the soldiers as they tried to advance during the night, brought the British to their assault positions much later than planned, thus negating the element of surprise and the cover afforded by darkness (Amery 1902; Breytenbach 1973). Despite the problems that the British encountered, the Boers eventually succumbed to Methuen's numerically superior force, and his army's highly effective artillery bombardment. By mid-morning, Boer resistance crumbled and Methuen could continue his march on Kimberley (Wessels 1991).

The Battle of Graspan (25 November 1899)

Two days later, General de la Rey positioned his troops in the hills east and west of the railway line between Graspan and Enslin. He had about 2000 soldiers under his command. The day was described as a "hot, blistering day, with the sun glaring pitilessly till the heavens looked like burnished brass" (Creswicke 1900: 93). Attacking British soldiers, unaccustomed to these conditions, suffered greatly in the heat, but once again Methuen skillfully used his artillery and overwhelming numbers to force the Boers to retreat (Amery 1902).

The Battle of Modder River (28 November 1899)

British manpower and technology proved capable of overcoming significant geographic disadvantages during the first two engagements of Methuen's campaign. However, the next geographic obstacle, the Modder River just north of its confluence with the Riet River (see Figure 9.4), would prove to be more difficult. Methuen's problems would also be compounded by the Boers who digested and correctly interpreted their geography lessons after their failures to defeat the British during the first two battles.

Because of their unsuccessful defensive battles at Belmont and Graspan, the Boers realized that the structure of the ridges in the region negated the traditional advantage of the high ground. According to Amery (1902), General de la Rey drew important geographic and tactical insights from his analysis of the Boer defeats at Belmont and Graspan. He realized that the steep hills, which were the choice position of the Boers, actually invited defeat. The concentration of Boer soldiers on the hills presented an ideal target for British artillery, while their convex shape enabled attackers to take cover in dead space, out of sight from defenders, once they had reached the base of the hill. The dead ground was then used by the British as a sheltered staging ground for their final assault against the defenders on the crests of the hills. Furthermore, the round dolerite (diabase) rocks that made up the hills improved the shrapnel effect of the British artillery. This increased the effectiveness

Figure 9.4
Destroyed railway
bridge and drift at
Modder River.
Source: adapted from
Anon (1901).

of the British bombardment and made the hills extremely dangerous hiding places (see Figure 9.5).

Consequently, the Boers decided to take up positions on the low ground along the southern banks of the Riet and Modder Rivers, rather than fall back onto the next line of hills as the British might have expected (Wessels 1991). From an analysis of modern aerial photographs and 1:50,000 scale topographic maps it is clear that the deeply dissected riverbanks of the Modder and Riet Rivers, and their soft *alluvial soil*, made this an excellent defensive position. The Modder is normally only 8 to 12 meters wide; however, heavy rains flooded both rivers so that they were about 25 meters ($\approx$ 90 ft) wide on the day of the battle. Between the stream channel and the edge of the floodplain, the banks rose with a gentle slope. This area was between 18 and 189 meters ($\approx$ 60–650 ft) wide and ended at the edge of the *floodplain* in an almost vertical wall, about 2 meters high, forming a natural *trench*. This enabled Boer soldiers to conceal themselves in the area between the river and this natural berm, and to fire from an upright position (Breytenbach 1971). The flat, featureless terrain over which the British attack had to come was used occasionally as a racecourse by the people of Kimberley, and, thus, formed the perfect field of fire (Amery 1902). This was further enhanced by the removal of vegetation before the British attack.

Approximately 2200 Boer soldiers occupied this natural defensive position, supported by five or six cannon and four *Pom-poms*. Because of his poor maps and reliance on incomplete terrain sketches, Methuen

Figure 9.5
The rocky terrain at
Gunhill, Battle of
Belmont. Note the
rounded dolerite
(diabase) rocks and the
convex shape of the hill.
Source: H. A. P. Smit.

failed to thoroughly analyze the area south of Modder River Station, as the open terrain made it extremely difficult to conduct effective reconnaissance. Furthermore, the smokeless ammunition used by the Boers, coupled to their excellent marksmanship, made it possible for them to pick off British scouts over long distances without giving away their positions. Thus, Methuen was forced to rely on simple—and incomplete—sketch maps of the Modder River, which only covered the immediate vicinity of the bridge. This level of terrain information was hopelessly inadequate, and he compounded the problem by not doing enough to gather better terrain information before ordering his troops into battle on 28 November. Thus, Methuen was effectively attacking blind, and two of the vital pieces of geographic information that he missed were the extent of the Boer positions to the east of the railroad, and the fact that the Riet River swung sharply to the south on the extreme eastern limit of the Boer positions (see Figure 9.6).

Lack of proper terrain information was exacerbated by Methuen's previous battle experiences at Belmont and Graspan, during which the Boers preferred to defend entrenched positions on the hills. Thus, it made perfect sense to him that the Boers would be waiting for him in the hills and ridges of Spytfontein rather than the banks of the Modder; he incorrectly concluded that the Boer positions along the river were only an outpost position, masking what he expected to be the main force at Spytfontein. As a result, Methuen's plan was to attack the Boers in the front and from the flanks. His misconception was aided because the

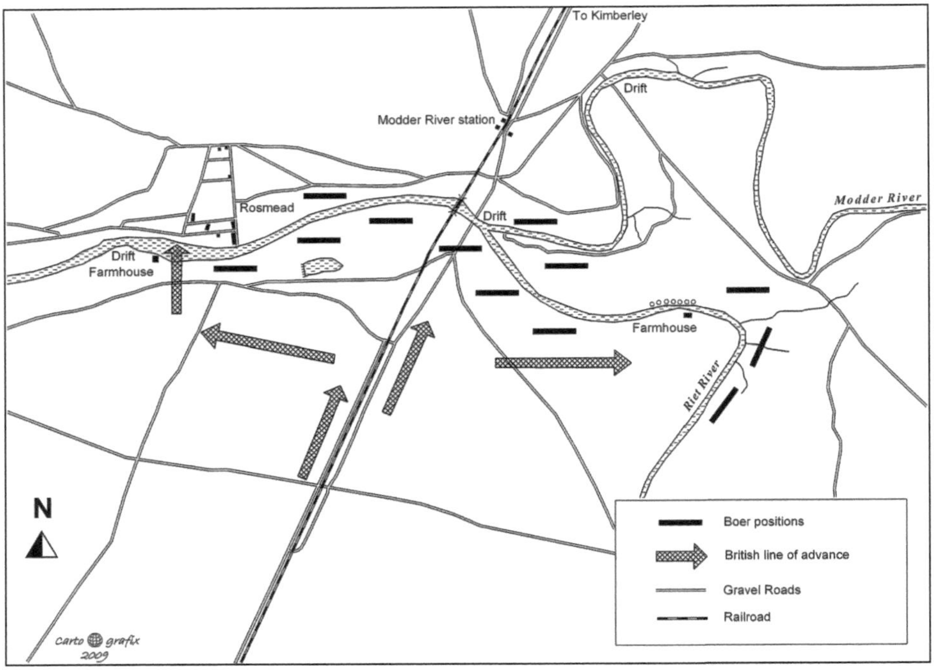

Figure 9.6
The battle of Modder
River. The absence of
contour lines on the map
indicates the extremely
flat terrain surrounding
the two rivers.
Source: J. A. Jacobs.

railroad effectively split the battlefield in two. To the east of the railroad, the British attack initially went as planned, strengthening Methuen's belief that the Boer positions were only manned by a small force.

However, at 08:00 the British columns were surprised by concentrated gunfire from the riverbank that pinned down the largest part of their force, making it impossible for them to counterattack. The Boers had orders to wait until the British were only 300 paces away before opening fire; however, their poor discipline caused them to start firing when the British were still 700 to 1200 paces away, saving Methuen from total disaster. Nevertheless, Methuen still lost many soldiers, and the attack on the east side of the railroad ground to a halt. To their horror, British soldiers that tried to maneuver around the Boer's eastern flank encountered the steep banks of the swollen Riet River and were enfiladed by Boer fire along their own right flank (Ackermann 1957). This action immobilized the largest part of the British force east of the railway.

As perilous as their tactical position was, the British soldiers were about to experience a terrible ordeal. Breytenbach (1971) suggests that, during the battle, temperature reached 43°C (110°F) on the bare soil where the British soldiers were trapped, and, according to Pakenham (1979), the temperatures reached 35°C (90°F) in the shade. Scottish soldiers, dressed in their traditional kilts, suffered most. The sun blistered their bare legs and this, aggravated by a terrible thirst, forced some soldiers to crawl back to the river to reach water (Creswicke 1900; Pakenham 1979). However, any movement across the flat, barren flood plain brought immediate response from the Boer sharpshooters, and the Coldstream Guards in particular lost many men in this way.

While the British soldiers were in a desperate situation, the Boers were right next to an abundant supply of fresh water from the Modder and Riet Rivers, and some even had the added advantage of the cool shade of the willow trees along the riverbanks. As the day wore on, the unbearable situation in which the British soldiers on the right flank found themselves lasted for more than ten hours (Colville 1901). During the rest of the battle, the flat terrain made effective communication by the British virtually impossible, as messengers were shot down even at extraordinarily long distances (Amery 1902).

On the left flank, west of the railway line, the British fared better. After the initial surprise of the Boer attack, British reserve forces marched west behind a low ridge and progressed unseen to about 2000 paces from the river on the Boers' right flank. It was at this point that General Pole-Carew and his men were met with fierce resistance from *Commandant* Greyling of the Boer forces who held a low hill and farmhouse 300 paces south of the Modder River, opposite the small village of Rosmead.

Greyling's men were guarding one of the *drifts* where it was possible to cross the Modder River. When Pole-Carew realized this, he redoubled his efforts to take the position, as it would give him the key to a foot-hold on the north bank. In this endeavor, geography came to his aid. A shallow *donga*, which the Boers failed to occupy, ran from his position to the channel of the Modder River. He sent his men along this ditch to attack Greyling's force. When a British cannon opened fire on Greyling and his men, and he found his unit under attack from two sides, he and his men fled over the river. By 11:30, Pole-Carew's force secured the drift and they crossed the river, took Rosmead, and began to roll up the Boer western flank. However, after this initial success, they were counterattacked by General de la Rey, and were forced back into Rosmead where they spent the night (Breytenbach 1971). That night General Cronjé decided to pull his troops back from the river, since he concluded that his Boer forces would not be able to hold the position against renewed British attacks the following day given the disparity in numbers (Wessels 1991). However, this time geography favored the British. Incredible as it might seem, the Boer generals failed to adequately guard a drift along the British left flank, which was the only place where the river could be easily forded. This enabled British soldiers to establish a foothold on the north bank, and compelled Cronjé's decision to retreat.

The Battle of Magersfontein (11 December 1899)

Following their evacuation of the Modder River position, General de la Rey decided that the Boer army would occupy their next position along a line of ridges called Magersfontein. This would put them directly across Methuen's axis of advance along the main rail line to his objective at Kimberley. Although only a relatively low ridge, Magersfontein commanded the area for miles around (see Figure 9.7). This time, however, the Boers would stay off the crests and dig trenches along the base of the ridge. By concealing their trenches, they intended to lure the British into an ambush and, at the same time, escape the effects of their superior artillery. The Boer position was strengthened because their trenches were much narrower than conventional trenches of the time. The Boers dug trenches that were about 1.2 meters deep and about 1 meter wide, which afforded maximum shelter as only the upper part of a soldier's body was exposed to the attackers—the lower body was sheltered from rifle fire and flying shrapnel (Breytenbach 1969).

Because of their ordeal at Modder River, Methuen rested his troops while reinforcements arrived, bolstering his force to 15,000 men, thirty-three cannons and sixteen machine guns. Meanwhile, positioned in their 7 kilometer-long defensive position, strengthened by five Krupp cannon and five Pom-poms, 8200 Boer soldiers waited for the British attack. Finally, the British force closed on the Boer position and, on 9 and 10 December, the British raked the hills with their cannon. This was the heaviest British bombardment since the attack on Sebastopol in 1854 during the Crimean War. However, the massive artillery barrage had an insignificant effect on the Boers because they were safely located in the trenches along the base of the ridge (see Figure 9.8).

Following the bombardment, the British attacked during the early morning hours of 11 December. An eyewitness of the battle, J. N. Brink (1940: 12), described conditions during the British night attack as "bitterly cold, very dark, and with thick clouds." In addition, it began

Figure 9.7
Magersfontein hills from a British perspective. The image illustrates the lack of shelter from incoming fire. *Source*: H. A. P. Smit.

to rain during the night, which eventually developed into a full-blown thunderstorm. Darkness forced Methuen to march his troops in closed formation to ensure that they did not get lost (Brink 1940; Kemp 1946; Ackermann 1957; Pakenham 1979). Major General H. E. Colvile (1901: 13) remembered the night as being "about as inky a night as I ever remember—one of those nights in which one literally cannot see one's hand." The night march ended in disaster as shortly before dawn British soldiers walked right into the trap. The Boers decimated the tightly massed columns of British infantry before they could open up their ranks for the final attack against the hills where they assumed the Boers were hiding (see Figure 9.9).

Once again, the British troops were trapped on the open veld, and, once again, the Scottish soldiers bore the brunt of the terrible African sun (Pakenham 1979). They took what scant cover they could as the bitterly cold night dawned into a blazingly hot day (Brink 1940). Breytenbach (1971) suggests that some of the Scottish soldiers were so sun burnt, that they had to receive medical attention after the battle, although they were not wounded. These allegations were confirmed by official British reports of casualties resulting from sunstroke found in the National Archives, Kew Gardens, London, UK (National Archives, War Office 108/89, Army Book 120, Casualties report for the period 26/12/99–26/2/00).

To make matters worse for the British, this time there were no dongas or drifts to aid their attack, and their subsequent frontal attacks against

Figure 9.8
The trenches at Magersfontein. The photograph illustrates the difference between the soft ground in front of the hills and the rocky terrain on the hills themselves. Note that this photo was probably taken after the Boers finally deserted the positions at Magersfontein two months later. At the time of the battle the trenches were not as extensive, or as wide, as portrayed here. *Source*: Adapted from Anon (1901).

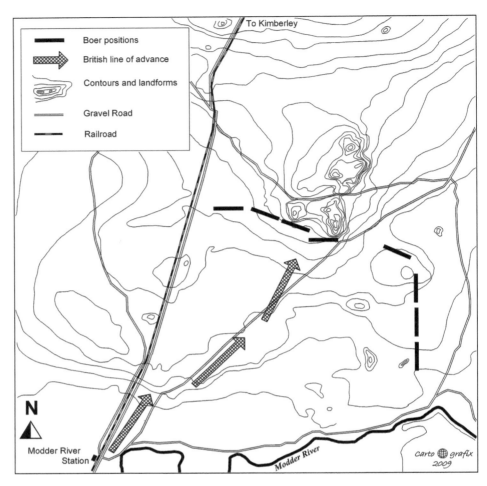

Figure 9.9
The Battle of Magersfontein.
Source: J. A. Jacobs.

the entrenched Boers failed dismally. When British commanders finally succeeded in extracting their men from the battlefield, they left behind 288 dead, 700 wounded, and 100 missing in action. In contrast, the Boers suffered only 71 fatalities and 184 wounded (Wessels 1991). Hence, the lessons learned from earlier efforts, and their accurate analysis of the geography of the battlefield, enabled the Boer commanders to exact a terrible toll on the British, making this one of the bloodiest battles of the war. It also halted Methuen's advance to Kimberley for more than two months.

Summary and conclusion

It is evident from the description of Methuen's campaign that geography played a pivotal role in the battles of Belmont, Graspan, Modder River, and Magersfontein. Boer generals and Methuen used the terrain to good effect, but both sides made fatal blunders. Limited transportation infrastructure forced Methuen to follow the rail line to Kimberley. Although it provided him with a fast, efficient means of transport, it also tied him to a narrow, predictable line of advance. The lack of horses and other livestock made him even more dependent on the railroad. These problems were well known to Boer generals and, thus, they could choose their best defensive positions with the knowledge that Methuen had virtually no other options. Consequently, this important quirk of geography permitted the Boers to concentrate their limited forces and fight the British at places of their choosing.

At Belmont and Graspan the numerical superiority enjoyed by the British forced the Boers from their positions in the hills. These battles highlighted other factors of geography as well. British artillery enjoyed increased effectiveness because of the dolerite rocks, which, by coincidence rather than insight, increased the efficiency of their bombardment. By occupying the hills, Boer forces were also concentrated in an easily recognizable area, affording the British artillery convenient targets. Furthermore, the convex shape of the hills aided the British by providing dead ground, which they exploited as footholds from which to launch their final attacks against defenders on the hilltops. For most of the Boer soldiers, being bombarded by British artillery was a terrifying psychological experience. However, the fact that the terrain aided the British effort did not escape General de la Rey and he would employ these hard-learned lessons in later battles, much to the regret of the British generals who failed to diagnose properly how the terrain aided their attack.

At the Modder River, the deep river channel afforded good shelter to Boer troops, while the exceedingly flat terrain over which the British had to attack formed an ideal kill zone. The nearest high ground was 16 kilometers (9.6 miles) away from the Modder and Riet Rivers, much too far to aid Methuen in his reconnaissance of the Boer positions. As a result, he pushed his forces across the river into an almost perfect ambush position. His soldiers paid dearly for his lack of proper terrain information and failure to insist on more aggressive reconnaissance.

The Boer ambush along the Modder was aided by the nature of the terrain. The flat plain, devoid of vegetation, offered little cover to British soldiers. The only natural cover was offered by anthills that dotted the landscape. The British were fighting a near-invisible foe from a perilous tactical position. Trying to outflank the Boers by moving eastwards, the British soldiers were foiled by the swollen Riet River. However, geography did offer the British a stroke of luck, which became the key to the battle. An undefended donga was exploited by General Pole-Carew to get his soldiers to the banks of the Modder River, and the drift opposite Rosmead allowed the British to establish a foothold on the north bank of the river. Cronjé's critical tactical error, driven by his faulty terrain appreciation, would cost him dearly. He neglected to guard the drift at

Rosmead with a sufficient force, thus enabling the British to get a foothold on the north bank. Once the British gained this foothold, Cronjé concluded correctly that the Boers would not be able to survive another assault by the enemy, and he withdrew his troops to Magersfontein.

The battles of Belmont and Graspan taught General de la Rey that to fight from exposed hilltops was not an effective tactical solution, while the nature of the battle at Modder River convinced him of the value of trenches and concealment. It also confirmed his belief that the soft ground would limit the effectiveness of the British artillery. With this in mind, he laid his trap for the British in front of the hills at Magersfontein and defeated Methuen by his skillful interpretation of geography.

Confounded by a lack of quality maps, Methuen depended on ground reconnaissance to make proper plans, and here, too, geography damaged his efforts. The lack of high ground denied Methuen the vital information he required for a thorough appreciation of battlefield conditions. As at Modder River, the extremely flat ground south of Magersfontein enabled the Boer sharpshooters to eliminate any attempt at reconnaissance close to the Boer trenches. With no nearby high ground from which to observe Boer movements and positions, Methuen was blind to the exact position and size of the Boer force, and, more importantly, to the effect of the artillery bombardment that preceded the infantry attack.

South Africa's climate and weather conditions led to almost unbearable hardships during the daylight hours of the battles. Scorching day temperatures, as well as the lack of available water, drained the strength of the British soldiers. Often British soldiers were demoralized by the heat, and also suffered physically to the extent that they had to seek medical attention. This was compounded by the lack of fresh water on the veld, which forced British soldiers into the open to seek water, exposing them to sniper fire. Prolonged exposure to these conditions caused hyperthermia in many soldiers. Even during the first stage of hyperthermia (i.e. heat exhaustion), symptoms such as profuse sweating, nausea, vomiting, and general weakness will degrade a soldier's ability and will to fight. During the second stage (i.e. heat or sunstroke) the victim has a rapid and strong pulse, exhibits psychotic behavior, and may slip into unconsciousness (Morgan and Moran 1997). The long hours of exposure to the brutal African sun caused symptoms like those described above, which directly or indirectly led to many casualties. At night, the total darkness made it difficult to advance, while the storm during the battle of Magersfontein and the accompanying bitterly cold night made effective attacks extremely difficult. The added effect of unusually dark nights was that the British invariably reached their objectives later than anticipated, negating the element of surprise and the concealment offered by darkness.

Although it will be an oversimplification to say that geography can account for the failure of Methuen's Northern Cape Campaign, it is certain that the *interpretation* of the geography of the battlefields influenced the results, and thus also the losses suffered during the campaign, proving that military geographic intelligence can indeed either be a powerful ally, or, in the absence thereof, a deadly adversary.

References cited

Ackermann, P. C. M. 1957. *Aardrykskundige invloede in die stryd tussen Brittanje en die Boere republieke met besondere verwysing na die Tweede Vryheidsoorlog.* Doktorale proefskrif, Universiteit van Suid Afrika.

Amery, L. S. 1902. *The Times history of the war in South Africa, 1899–1902 (Vol. II).* London, UK: Sampson Low, Marston & Company, Ltd.

Anon, 1901. *The Anglo Boer War, 1899–1900. An album of upwards of three hundred photographic engravings.* Cape Town, South Africa: Dennis Edwards & Co.

Bayles, W. J. 1993. "Terrain intelligence and battlefield success: A historical perspective." *Engineer* 23(3): 50–3.

Blond, G. 1995. *La Grande Armée.* London, UK: Arms & Armour Press.

Breytenbach J. H. 1969. *Die geskiedenis van die Tweede Vryheidsoorlog in Suid-Afrika, 1899–1902. Deel I: Die Boere-offensief, Oktober–November 1899.* Pretoria: Die Staatsdrukker.

———. 1971. *Die geskiedenis van die Tweede Vryheidsoorlog in Suid-Afrika, 1899–1902. Deel II: Die eerste Britse Offensief, November–Desember 1899.* Pretoria: Die Staatsdrukker.

———. 1973. *Die geskiedenis van die Tweede Vryheidsoorlog in Suid-Afrika, 1899–1902. Deel III: Die Stryd in Natal, Januarie–Februarie 1900.* Pretoria: Die Staatsdrukker.

Brink, J. N. 1940. *Oorlog en Ballingskap.* Kaapstad, South Africa: Nasionale Pers.

Chief Directorate Survey and Mapping (CDSM). 1988. South Africa 1:50 000 Topographic Map 2924 BA Modder River.

———. 1997. South Africa 1:50 000 Topographic Map 2824 DC Spytfontein.

Cleary, T. 1988. *The art of war.* Translation of the work by Sun Tzu. Boston, MA: Shambhala.

Collins, J. M. 1998. *Military geography for professionals and the public.* Washington, DC: National Defense University Press.

———. 2003. "Military geography." Presentation for Naval ROTC cadets at George Washington University, Washington DC.

Colville, H. E. 1901. *The work of the Ninth Division.* London, UK: Edward Arnold.

Creswicke, L. 1900. *South Africa and the Transvaal War.* Edinburgh, UK: T. C. & E. C. Jack.

Deighton, L. 1985. Introduction. In *Great battlefields of the world*, J. Macdonald. London, UK: Michael Joseph.

Galgano, F. A. 1994. "The landings at Anzio." *Military Review* 74(1): 69–73.

———. 2005. "Streams and the Civil War landscape: the battle for Island No. 10." In *Military geography: from peace to war*, E. J. Palka & F. A. Galgano (eds). New York, NY: McGraw-Hill Custom Publishing.

Judd, D. & K. Surridge. 2002. *The Boer War.* London, UK: John Murray.

Kemp, J. C. G. 1946. *Vir Vryheid en Reg.* Kaapstad, South Africa: Nasionale Pers.

Metzger, T. L. 1992. "Terrain analysis for Desert Storm." *Engineer* 22(1): 25–7.

Miller, S.M. 1999. *Lord Methuen and the British Army: failure and redemption in South Africa.* London, UK: Frank Cass.

Morgan, M. D. & J. M. Moran. 1997. *Weather and people.* Upper Saddle River, NJ: Prentice-Hall, Inc.

Muller, C. F. J. 1977. *Vyfhonderd jaar Suid-Afrikaanse geskiedenis.* Pretoria, South Africa: Academia.

National Archives, War Office 108/89, Army Book 120, casualties report for the period 26/12/–26/2/00.

Opperman, A. J. P. 1981. *Die slag van Majuba*. Johannesburg, South Africa: Perskor Uitgewery.

O'Sullivan, P. & J. W. Miller, 1983. *The geography of warfare*. London, United Kingdom: Croom Helm.

Pakenham, T. 1979. *The Boer War*. London, UK: Abacus.

Palka, E. J. & F. A. Galgano (eds). 2000. *The scope of military geography: across the spectrum from peacetime to war*. New York: McGraw-Hill Primis Custom Publishing.

Palka, E. J. & F. A. Galgano (eds). 2005. *Military geography: from peace to war*. New York, NY: McGraw-Hill Custom Publishing.

Perry, J. M. 1996. *Arrogant armies: great military disasters and the generals behind them*. New York, NY: John Wiley & Sons, Inc.

Pretorius, F. 2002. *Die invloed van landskap op die Anglo Boere Oorlog*. Unpublished manuscript.

Puckett, R. M. 1994. "The Rapido River crossings." *Military Review* 74(1): 73–6.

Saunders, C. 2001. "Historical reflections on the significance of the South African war." *Kleio* 33: 4–16.

Scholtz, L. 1999. *Waarom die Boere die oorlog verloor het*. Menlopark: Protea Boekhuis.

Schulze, B. R. 1986. *Climate of South Africa, part eight (general survey)*. Pretoria, South Africa: Weather Bureau.

Sleigh, D. 1979. *Ruiters teen die Ryk: die verhaal van die Tweede Vryheidsoorlog*. Goodwood: Nasou Beperk.

Stephenson, M. (ed.). 2003. *Battlegrounds: geography and the history of warfare*. Washington, DC: National Geographic.

Van den Berg, G. 1997. *24 Veldslae en Slagvelde van die Noordwes Provinsie*. Potchefstroom, South Africa: Potchefstroomse Universiteit.

Wade, D. R. 1998. "Washington saves the day at Monmouth." *Military History* 15(2): 46–56.

War Office. 1899. "Military notes on the Dutch Republics of South Africa." Compiled in Section B, Intelligence Division, War Office.

Waters, W. H. H. 1904. *The war in South Africa*. London, UK: John Murray.

Wessels, A. 1991. *Die Anglo–Boereoorlog, 1899–1902: 'n Oorsig van die verloop van die militêre stryd*. Bloemfontein, South Africa: Oorlogsmuseum van die Boererepublieke.

——. 2001. *They fought on foreign soil*. Bloemfontein, South Africa: Anglo Boer War Museum.

Winters, H. A. 1991. "The battle that was never fought: weather and the Union mud march of January 1863." *Southeastern Geographer* 31(1): 31–8.

——. 1998. *Battling the elements: weather and terrain in the conduct of war*. Baltimore, MD: Johns Hopkins University Press.

Chapter ten
The battle for Attu
Physical geographic challenges of the Aleutian Campaign of World War II

EUGENE J. PALKA

Introduction

THE WAR IN THE Aleutian Islands has been described as "the forgotten war" (Chandonnet 1993), "our hidden front," (Gilman 1944), and "the thousand-mile war" (Garfield 1969). Each of these characterizations alludes to the uncelebrated nature of the Aleutian Campaign and its relatively insignificant impact during World War II. Indeed, these references stem from the paltry number of publications that shed light on the bloody, yet little known, World War II struggle between the US and Japan in the North Pacific.

It is a little-known fact that one of the most extraordinary island battles of World War II occurred on US soil. As a percentage of the total forces involved, the battle to retake Attu was second only to Iwo Jima as the most costly battle of the Pacific Campaign (Garfield 1969). This information is further obscured by the difficulty in locating the tiny island of Attu on most maps. In some respects, the entire campaign in the Aleutians was nothing more than a footnote within the context of global war, or even war in the Pacific. Nevertheless, the battle to retake Attu came at a cost of 549 American lives, 1148 wounded, and 2100 other casualties who suffered from sickness, exposure, or non-battle injuries (Hutchison 1994). Not to be ignored were the millions of dollars of infrastructure and the multitudes of personnel, weapons, and equipment necessary to retake the Island. Although Japan initially captured the island unopposed, 2350 Japanese soldiers were later killed and the remaining 29 were taken prisoner (Hutchison 1994). Throughout the Aleutian Campaign, physical geographic conditions exacted a heavy toll on Japanese and US ground, sea, and air forces. Indeed, the remote location and extreme conditions prompted routine actions to require excessive time and resources. In the end, the harsh nature of the physical environment and the relative location limited the utility of Attu as key terrain, and questioned the logic of the Japanese incursion in the first place. The battle for Attu clearly demonstrated, however, the difficulty involved with conducting military operations in such forbidding environments and in remote locations. The harsh realities prompted immediate changes in US Army doctrine, weapons, uniforms, and equipment.

This chapter is an example of historical military geography explained within an operational and strategic context (Palka 2003). My intent is to describe the impact of the unique physical environment and remote location on military operations and to elaborate on some of the lessons that were learned by the US Military and subsequently applied elsewhere.

The physical setting

Location

The Aleutian Islands extend westward from the Alaskan Peninsula for more than 1200 miles, separating the North Pacific and the Bering Sea (see Figure 10.1). The arcuate chain of volcanic islands extends from east to west from about 165° west longitude to about 170° east longitude, and on the average sits astride the 53° north latitude parallel. Even a cursory glance at a map enables one to draw a number of general conclusions about the climate, vegetation, and geomorphologic characteristics of the Aleutian Islands.

While the absolute location of the Aleutians may enable one to form impressions regarding the physical nature of the place, the relative location of the chain, and specifically of Attu, is far more important to

Figure 10.1
The Aleutian Islands.
Source: Naval Historical Center (1993).

explaining why this site became a contested place during World War
II. Within the chain, Attu is located at the western extreme, and is
technically the easternmost point of the US, crossing the 180° line of
longitude (although the international dateline has been adjusted to curve
around Attu). To the casual observer, the Aleutians, and especially Attu,
are remotely located from both the continental US and Japan. The
straight-line distance, however, is significantly distorted by many of the
widely used map projections. A *polar projection* provides an illuminating
perspective, and reveals the importance of the relative location of Attu
to both the US and Japan (see Figure 10.2). Following a great circle route
depicted on the previous map, one might be surprised to note that the
island of Attu is only approximately 650 miles from the Japanese Kuriles
(see Figure 10.3). Most maps suggest that the logical and most direct
route from the West Coast of the US to Japan would pass through the
Hawaiian Islands. In reality, if traveling from San Francisco to Tokyo,
it is significantly shorter to travel via a route that passes along the
Aleutian Islands rather than passing through Hawaii. The former route
is actually about 1000 miles shorter than the latter (see Figure 10.4). Thus,
the significance of Attu's relative location was far more important than
its absolute location during the War in the Pacific.

Attu was uniquely located about mid-way between the more
populated areas of the Japanese and US homelands, and was perceived
to have utility as a forward base for limited incursions into the remote
territories of either country. Additionally, some believed that the island
could potentially provide a base to support operations to control the
North Pacific.

Figure 10.2
Relative location of the
Aleutian Islands.

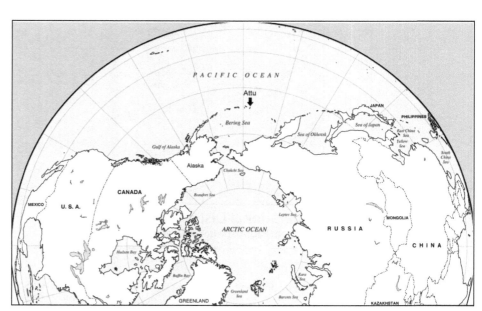

145

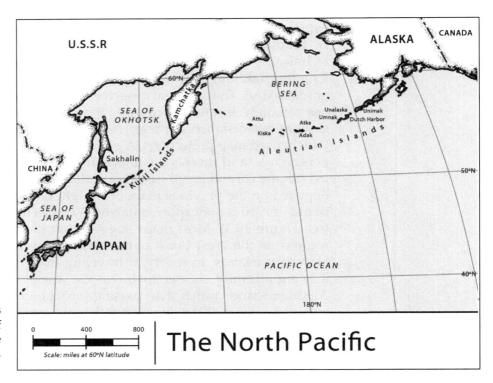

Figure 10.3
Relative proximity of
Attu to Japan's Kurile
Islands.

The North Pacific

Scale: miles at 60°N latitude
0 — 400 — 800

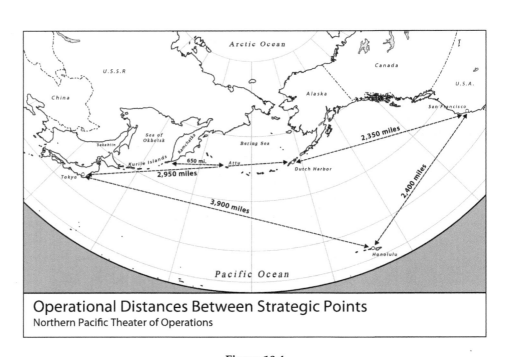

Operational Distances Between Strategic Points
Northern Pacific Theater of Operations

Figure 10.4
Actual distances between key points in the North Pacific. *Source*: adapted from Alaska
Geographic Society (1995*a*).

Physical geography

The physical environment found on Attu and throughout the Aleutians is one that presents a plethora of problems to military operations. The nature of the terrain, climate, weather, vegetation, soil, and seas combine to produce one of the most forbidding operating environments ever experienced by US military forces.

Terrain

The Aleutian Islands are the world's longest small-island *archipelago*, extending nearly 1200 miles. The Aleutians are comprised of approximately 120 islands, all of which are uniformly rocky and barren, and have volcanic origins (Department of the Navy 1993). The main islands are the exposed peaks of a submerged mountain range that separate the Bering Sea from the Pacific Ocean, and include fifty-seven volcanoes, twenty-seven of which are still active and exceed heights of 5000 feet (Faust and Bailey 1995). The inland mountains are conical in shape and are covered with volcanic ash, while the shorelines are comprised of jagged and submerged rock formations (Department of the Navy 1993).

Climate

The principal controls that combine to shape the Aleutian climate include latitude, ocean currents, air masses, and mountainous terrain. Average summer temperatures are 45°F, while winter temperatures average around 30°F (Faust and Bailey 1995). Although precipitation averages only about 50 inches annually, the chain averages 90 percent cloud cover and more than 200 days of measurable precipitation (Faust and Bailey 1995). A common characteristic is the ever-present high wind, which has a significant wind chill effect on temperatures and contributes to turbulent seas.

While the general climate of the Aleutians does not exhibit extremes of temperature or precipitation, the weather (regarded as the atmospheric conditions at a specific place and time) is highly localized and often unpredictable. The high latitude and rugged, mountainous terrain are subjected to the convergence of the tropical Japan Current and the Siberian air masses. This unique combination results in violent storms and extreme weather conditions, including blizzards, dense fog, turbulent seas, bone-chilling temperatures, and winds that can reach gusts of more than 140 miles per hour (Garfield 1969). "*Williwaws*" or sudden squalls that can reach gale force within half an hour are unique local phenomena that pose considerable problems for air and sea navigation.

Vegetation

Because of its proximity to Asia, Attu hosts some flora that is common to both Asia and the rest of the Aleutians (Faust and Bailey 1995). Like the majority of the Aleutian Islands, however, Attu is a treeless expanse of *tundra* void of any significant range of vegetation. Temperatures, high winds, and thin soils impose significant constraints and limit vegetational growth.

Most of the tundra is of the high-alpine type (as opposed to low-tundra found throughout much of the lowland areas of interior Alaska), void of any significant brush or shrubbery. Lowland areas on Attu and the other islands are covered with muskeg, a spongy carpet-like layer of vegetation that is underlain with discontinuous *permafrost*. During the warmer months, the muskeg presents a boggy, shifting surface that is difficult for even foot soldiers to traverse. The tundra, however, displays an assortment of wildflowers, fireweed, lichens, mosses, and wild grasses that combine to produce a colorful tapestry during the late summer and early fall.

Utility of Attu and the Aleutians?

Within the context of strategic geography, William Jacobs (1993) referred to the North Pacific as a "strategic backwater." He noted that the Aleutians were situated along a great circle route from the West Coast of the US to Japan, and that their occupation "appeared" to offer strategic advantages (Jacobs 1993). Many strategists, however, recognized the enormous challenges to military operations imposed by the natural environment of the North Pacific and questioned *any* rationale for securing the Aleutians. Even after the Japanese occupied Attu and Kiska, many argued that the wisest policy would have been to bypass the islands, just as US forces did later with many other Japanese-held islands in the South Pacific (Allard 1993).

Of all the islands in the Aleutians, Attu appeared to hold the most potential for both the US and Japan, simply because it was the western-most island in the chain and only 650 miles from the major Japanese military base at Paramushiro on the northern tip of the Kurile Islands. Yet the value of Attu was still controversial among military and political leaders of both countries. The island is located at great distance from any sizable concentration of people in either the US or Japan; it has no significant natural resources; nor has the island ever been populated by more than a few dozen Aleuts, who continue to practice a traditional, subsistence lifestyle. Finally, access to Attu is possible only via prolonged and hazardous travel across treacherous seas or through turbulent air.

Japanese strategy
There are a number of plausible, if not debatable, explanations for Japan's invasion and occupation of Attu and Kiska. Some sources conclude that the Japanese had long coveted Alaska and the Aleutians, and that many of the military leaders considered the poorly defended outposts in the chain as easy targets and a logical route for invading

North America (Department of the Navy 1993). Various intelligence sources anticipated Japan's seizure of the Aleutians to prevent the US from invading the Japanese homeland from the North (Hutchison 1944). Other intelligence estimates pointed to Japan's goal of thwarting US–Soviet communications in the North Pacific (Hutchison 1944). Still others dismissed both offensive and defensive strategic explanations and looked to psychological reasons. Garfield (1969), for example, claimed that the Japanese tried to psychologically offset their loss at Midway by seizing the undefended US territory in the Aleutians and draw attention to the latter. There is significant support for the explanation that, by seizing Attu and Kiska after the disastrous loss at Midway, Japan's political and military leaders were able to "save face," maintain high morale within the military, and retain popular support on the home front (Russell 1993; Nishijima 1993; Garfield 1969).

US strategy

In US political and military circles, the strategic importance of Alaska and the Aleutians dates back to the early 1920s (Braisted 1971). By the 1930s, military planners considered Alaska to be part of a strategic triangle linking Hawaii and Panama, and forming the basic framework for the US military strategy in the Pacific (Allard 1993). Despite the historical interest, however, there were no significant plans to fortify the Western Aleutians at the outbreak of hostilities with Japan.

The strategic situation began to change when the Japanese bombed Dutch Harbor on 3 and 4 June 1942, and then subsequently invaded Kiska and Attu on 6 and 7 June. Even after the uncontested occupations of Attu and Kiska, however, the Joint Chiefs of Staff considered the western extremes of the Aleutians to be insignificant within the context of global war in Europe and the Pacific (Morton 1989). The Joint Chiefs and US military strategists did not foresee the need to undertake substantial military operations in the North Pacific to retake either Attu or Kiska. Resources were deemed more critical elsewhere, the conditions for military operations were considered hazardous, and mainland Alaska did not appear threatened since the islands were more than 1000 miles from the state's heartland, and even more distant from the continental US (Morton 1989).

After persistent prodding from political officials and military leadership in Alaska, however, the Joint Chiefs began to entertain notions of retaking Attu and Kiska. Public pressure mounted with the perceived threat to Alaskan security. Another concern was the potential need to maintain sea and air lines of communication with the Soviet allies across the North Pacific, especially to ensure the continuous flow of lend–lease supplies (Jones 1969). Perhaps most important, however, was the American pride that was manifested in the pressing call to reclaim America's territory (Allard 1993). Hence, just as the Japanese incursion was motivated by psychological factors, so was the impetus for the US effort to retake Attu and Kiska.

149

Historical summary of the battle

Prior to the US mission to retake Attu and Kiska, Japanese troops occupied the two islands for approximately eleven months, becoming well entrenched in the process. Kiska was regarded as the primary objective because it provided potentially better air facilities, possessed a more satisfactory harbor, and included terrain that was more suitable for a base (Department of the Navy 1993). Additionally, US intelligence estimates considered Kiska to be more heavily fortified, so it posed the more imminent threat to Alaska. Nevertheless, the US plan called for Attu to be taken first because of a lack of logistics, sealift, and manpower necessary to assault the more heavily fortified Kiska (Coox 1993; Department of the Navy 1993).

The Joint Chiefs approved the US plan on 3 March 1943. A concerted aerial bombing campaign was initiated almost immediately to "soften up" the objectives. Emphasis was directed towards Kiska rather than Attu in an effort to conceal the US intentions, achieve the element of surprise, and further degrade the defenses at Kiska prior to invading. Aerial bombing shifted to Attu on 1 May in support of a scheduled *D-day* of 7 May 1943.

The US plan called for extensive air and naval gunfire support prior to and during the amphibious landings at five different beaches along the western half of Attu (Department of the Navy 1993; see Figure 10.5). Continuous reconnaissance flights were also planned. The US invasion force was scheduled to depart from Cold Bay in the Aleutians on 3 May, but poor weather and turbulent seas delayed sailing until 4 May (Department of the Navy 1993). Accordingly, D-day was also postponed until 8 May. With the assault force already at sea, D-day was again postponed because of dense fog, high winds, and hazardous surf conditions until 11 May.

Although they encountered difficulties with the dense fog and surf conditions, the US Seventh Division landed on the north shore around Holtz Bay and on the south shore at Massacre Bay with minimal resistance. The Japanese commander, Colonel Yasuyo Yamasaki, had concentrated his defense inland and had placed only coastal guns and a dozen anti-aircraft guns to oppose the anticipated landings (Coox 1993). Moreover, despite initial problems, the dense fog proved to be a mixed blessing to US forces. Although it virtually eliminated any air, naval gunfire, or artillery support, it concealed the landings from Japanese observation. By the end of the first day, about 3500 US soldiers had landed at Attu (Campbell 1995). Approximately 400 troops landed at Beach Scarlet, 1100 hundred at Beach Red, and 2000 at Beaches Blue and Yellow (Chandonnet 1993).

With the Japanese defense located on the high ground and well inland between Holtz and Massacre Bays, it quickly became apparent that the

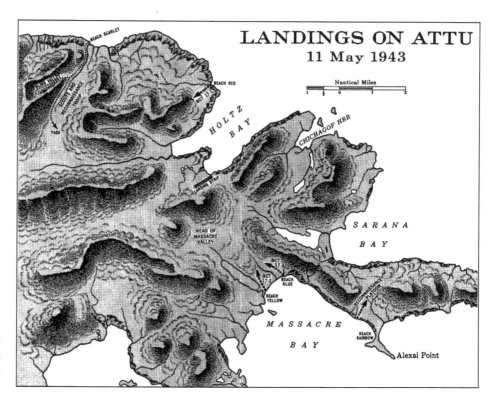

Figure 10.5
Landing beaches on
Attu. *Source*: Department
of the Navy (1993).

US operation would take much longer than the three days that were
initially anticipated. Moreover, the rugged nature of the terrain, boggy
tundra and mud, and extreme weather ensured an unexpectedly slow
rate of advance for US troops. By 17 May, more than 12,500 US troops
had landed on Attu, suffering more than 1100 casualties in the process
(Hutchison 1994). By 18 May, however, the US northern and southern
forces had linked up in the vicinity of Jarmin Pass and surrounded the
Japanese defenders in northeastern Attu (Hutchison 1994; see Figure
10.6).

Given the reinforced nature of the Japanese defensive positions, severe
weather that limited visibility and air and artillery support, and the
rugged nature of the terrain, the US attack was literally "reduced to a
crawl" from 18 to 28 May. Nevertheless, persistence prevailed, and by
29 May, Japanese forces on Attu were completely encircled. In a last ditch
effort, the remaining Japanese troops (estimated to be from 800–1,000)
conducted a suicidal counterattack against US positions. The initial
counterattack was repelled, yet the Japanese conducted successive
assaults, believing it was better to die with honor than to surrender
(Campbell 1995). In the hand-to-hand combat that ensued, virtually
every Japanese soldier was killed. The remaining survivors allegedly
committed suicide by blowing themselves up with hand grenades

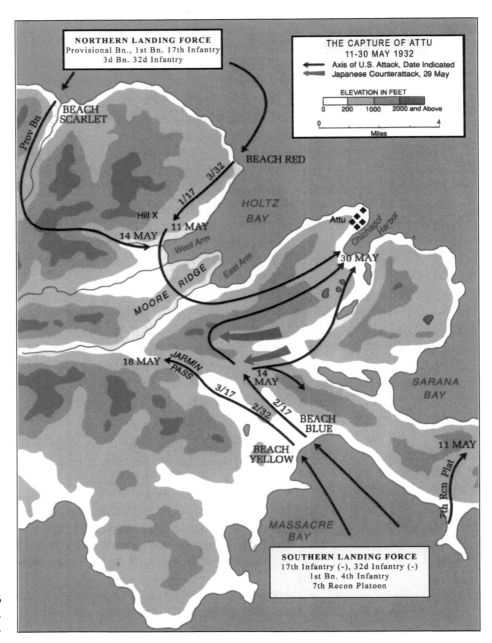

Figure 10.6
The tactical plan on Attu.
Source: US Army, 1992.

(Handleman 1943) or died from injections of morphine that were ordered by the Japanese commander (Campbell 1995).

On 29 May, Attu Island was secured. The cost of recapturing the tiny, rugged, and remote island came at a cost of 549 Americans killed, 1148 wounded, and 2100 suffering from exposure or disease (Hutchison 1994). Japanese losses totaled 2350 dead and twenty-nine prisoners of war (Hutchison 1994).

Geographic factors influencing the battle

The physical geography of the Aleutian Islands, and of Attu in particular, had a profound impact on the conduct of military operations. A plethora of factors, especially those relating to location, coastlines, weather, surf conditions, vegetation, and relief, posed continual challenges for the attackers and defenders alike. Throughout the battle to retake Attu, US and Japanese troops battled the elements and terrain, suffering immeasurably in some respects, and, in other instances, modifying their plans and tactics accordingly to overcome the adversity imposed by the physical environment.

Remote location

Attu's remote location was equally troublesome for both the Japanese and Americans. From the outset, operations were hindered by the lack of reliable maps of the island and charts of its adjacent waters, shortcomings attributed to the remoteness of the place. The island was distant from any military base or population center in either country. Once the Japanese attacked and seized the island, they encountered extreme difficulty as they tried to sustain operations and support the occupation force. Similarly, the US Military encountered a logistics nightmare as it attempted to muster, transport, and sustain the necessary forces, equipment, and supplies to retake the island.

Coastline and sea conditions

Attu's coastline is extremely rugged due to the volcanic origin of the island. Sea cliffs, rugged escarpments, and rocky outcrops along the coast presented major obstacles to amphibious landings of any type, especially during rough seas (see Figure 10.7). To make matters worse, the remote coastline was poorly mapped and much of the adjacent waters were uncharted. Moreover, the occasional sand beaches were often saturated with extensive piles of driftwood—8 to 10 feet high and situated 200 to 300 yards inshore of the normal beach because of recurring superstorms (Campbell 1995). Even its ideal harbors were unsuitable for large naval vessels (Department of the Navy 1993; Figure 10.8).

Sea conditions throughout the Aleutians had been considered unfavorable for naval operations long before the operation to re-secure Attu. Turbulent seas were made even more treacherous by the occasional incidence of *rogue waves* (Campbell 1995). The latter are great solitary waves or "super-crests" that tower over all others and occasionally include extra-deep troughs into which ships can drop and become subsequently submerged by the next crest (Bascom 1980). These conditions, coupled with extreme temperatures, limited visibility, high winds, and unreliable navigational aids, presented the ultimate environmental challenge to even routine naval operations.

Figure 10.7
Attu's rugged coastline
and austere location
presented challenges to
landing troops,
equipment, and logistics
supplies. *Source*: Official
US Navy photo,
1943; University of
Alaska, Fairbanks.

Figure 10.8
Soldiers improve the
landing site and unload
equipment in Holtz Bay.
Source: Official US Navy
photo, 1943.

Weather

Aspects of the island's weather that proved to be problematic included cold temperatures, extensive cloud cover, high winds, and dense fog. Inclement weather was decisive from the outset of the Aleutian Campaign, adversely affecting sea, air, and ground operations. D-Day was postponed on several occasions because of severe weather conditions. Cloe (1990) noted that of the 225 allied aircraft destroyed, 184 were attributed to adverse weather.

Dense fog proved to be a mixed blessing. While the fog effectively concealed the US amphibious landings from Japanese observation on D-Day, it also contributed to the initial US casualties. Four soldiers drowned when a transport prematurely dropped its ramp before hitting the beach, filled with water, and sank (Campbell 1995). Other injuries were incurred when the *Sicard* and *Macdonough* collided during the initial landing (Department of the Navy 1993). After the landing, the persistent fog served to conceal ground maneuvers for US troops, but it inhibited the use of air or artillery support. On occasion, the fog dissipated at inopportune times, exposing US troops who were out in the open to Japanese fire. At one point during a period of dense fog, a tragic battle was fought among US soldiers between their own sentries and litter bearers (Gilman 1944). Perhaps most important, dense fog limited the use of air or naval gunfire in support of the landing and subsequent offensive operations.

Persistent cloud cover had its greatest effect on air operations. Clouded skies reduced visibility and prevented the use of aerial reconnaissance during the operation's planning and execution stages. Throughout the attack, it also dictated when aerial fire support could be employed. Needless to say, breaks in the skies rarely coincided with those instances when support was needed most.

High winds proved to be hazardous to air and naval operations, contributing to turbulent seas and poor flying conditions. Ground troops felt the impact in the form of personal discomfort from the increased wind chill factor, and a disruption in the flow of logistics via sea or air. During stormy conditions, Aleutian gales reached speeds of up to 140 miles an hour (Garfield 1969). Under such adverse conditions, it was virtually impossible for ground troops to effectively operate weapons and equipment, or even erect and maintain suitable shelters. Williwaws (incredibly violent and impromptu gusts of cold wind) wreaked havoc and inflicted considerable damage to equipment caches, maintenance tents, first aid shelters, communication and weather stations, aircraft, and ships.

Cold temperatures proved to be a menace to both Japanese and US troops. Poorly equipped US soldiers suffered from more incidents of trench foot, immersion foot, and frostbite than they did from enemy fire (Handleman 1943; Figure 10.9). Vehicles, aircraft, weapons, and equipment functioned poorly or became inoperative in the extreme cold.

To exacerbate matters, the treeless tundra and partially frozen ground afforded little opportunity for ground troops to find shelter from the cold (see Figure 10.10).

Terrain and relief

The rugged terrain posed a considerable challenge to US troops during the attack. Steep slopes, rugged cliffs, extensive gullies, and elevations in excess of 4000 feet were made more difficult by the nature of the ground surface. Mud and boggy, shifting tundra ensured poor traction for vehicles and soldiers alike. Ground movement was slow and exhausting for foot soldiers, and the displacement of vehicles, weapons systems, and supplies was especially difficult. The evacuation of casualties was particularly troublesome (see Figure 10.11).

Because extensive use of mechanized or wheeled vehicles was simply impractical, or severely limited to isolated areas, the burden of transporting wounded and supplies literally fell on the shoulders of the foot soldier. Rugged relief, however, did not prove to be equally burdensome to the defenders who were situated in static positions. The Japanese had cached the supplies, weapons, and equipment necessary to defend the island. Moreover, they selected key inaccessible locations that afforded protection, as well as long-range observation and fields of fire.

Figure 10.10
Soldiers take cover from sniper fire in the boggy, shifting tundra near Massacre Beach. *Source*: Official US Navy photo, 1943; University of Alaska, Fairbanks.

Figure 10.11
With poor mobility and trafficability because of Attu's rugged landscape, troops struggle to evacuate a casualty. *Source*: Official US Navy photo, 1943; University of Alaska, Fairbanks.

Conclusion

Attu represented both "uncharted waters" and *terra incognita* to US military forces. Prior to the Aleutian Campaign, the US Military simply did not have the necessary training, weapons systems, vehicles, supplies, and equipment specifically designed for regions characterized by cold-wet climates, high winds, limited visibility, and rugged terrain. Consequently, the lessons learned were costly in terms of resources and casualties. In proportion to the number of troops employed, Attu ranked as the second most costly battle in the Pacific Theater, second only to Iwo Jima (Garfield 1969). Of the 3829 US casualties, a substantial number were classified as cold-weather injuries, and were the first combat cold injuries suffered by US troops in World War II (Garfield 1969).

The recapture of Attu and the subsequent seizure of Kiska did give the Western Aleutians back to the US. Control of the Aleutian Chain offered a potential "jumping off" point for an invasion of Japan. Moreover, occupation of the archipelago facilitated control of the North Pacific. It is debatable, however, whether the battles for Attu, and later Kiska, were strategically important, or whether their significance was merely psychological. Regardless, the lessons learned were later applied to operations in the Pacific and in Europe, and contributed immensely to success in both theaters.

The battle for Attu clearly revealed the profound, if not decisive, impact that physical geographic conditions can have on military operations at high latitudes. Fortunately, the experience prompted additional research and developments in a wide range of areas. Feedback from Army doctors studying Attu veterans resulted in various changes to Army footgear, clothes, tents, bedrolls, and food (Garfield 1969). Recovery of an intact Japanese Zero fighter plane facilitated training US fliers in combat strategy (Campbell 1995). In an effort to deal with the chronic problem of poor visibility, the Aleutians became an experimental proving ground for airborne search radar (Russell 1993). Perhaps most important, amphibious landing tactics were revised and subsequently applied elsewhere within the Pacific and European theaters with great success. Throughout the Aleutian Campaign and afterwards a wide range of technical modifications were made to aircraft and vehicles to enhance operability, durability, and survivability during weather and climate extremes. Finally, a number of different innovations were born out of US ingenuity at the lowest echelons during attempts to overcome challenges imposed by the physical environment. Examples included wicker mats to prevent howitzers from sinking into the mud when firing; "Marston mats" for use in building temporary runways in areas of boggy tundra or mud; and an A-frame cargo hoist (developed in Massacre Bay) used to unload cargo from shallow draft boats in austere bays. These innovations and others were subsequently refined, adopted, and employed elsewhere under similar circumstances. Thus, Attu proved to be a catalyst within the military's research and development community.

The battle for Attu has never been a celebrated part of US military history. Nor was the seizure or retaking of Attu of great military importance during World War II. It was, however, the only World War II battle fought on US soil, and the cost of seizing and retaking the tiny, volcanic island was unquestionably high to both the Japanese and Americans. In hindsight, the military utility of such a place remains questionable given the extensive resources and preparation necessary for any military force to seize, defend, and operate in such an austere and physically challenging environment.

Editor's note: This chapter is a revised and updated version of a public domain chapter previously published as Palka, E. J. 2005. "World War II in the Aleutian Islands: physical geographic challenges in the battle for Attu." In *Military geography: from peace to war*, E. J. Palka & F. A. Galgano (eds), 67–90. New York, NY: McGraw-Hill Custom Publishing.

References cited

Allard, Dean C. 1993. "The North Pacific Campaign in perspective." In *Alaska at War, 1941–1945: the forgotten war remembered*. Fern Chandonnet (ed.), 3–11. Anchorage: Papers from the Alaska at War Symposium, 11–13 November.

Alaska Geographic Society. 1995*a*. *World War II in Alaska*. Special edition of *Alaska Geographic* 22(4).

——. 1995*b*. *The Aleutian Islands*. Special edition of *Alaska Geographic* 22(2).

Bascom, Willard. 1980. *Waves and beaches*. New York: Anchor Press.

Braisted, William R. 1971. *The United States Navy in the Pacific, 1909–1922*. Austin, TX: University of Texas Press.

Campbell, L. J. 1995. "Arsenal of democracy." *Alaska Geographic* 22(4): 4–45.

Chandonnet, Fern (ed.). 1993. *Alaska at War, 1941–1945: the forgotten war remembered*. Anchorage: Papers from the Alaska at War Symposium, 11–13 November.

Cloe, Jolin Haile. 1990. *The Aleutian warriors*. Anchorage: Anchorage Chapter of the Air Force Association.

Coox, Alvin D. 1993. "Reflecting on the Alaska Theater in Pacific war operations, 1942–1945." In *Alaska at War, 1941–1945: the forgotten war remembered*, Fern Chandonnet (ed.), 39–42. Anchorage: Papers from the Alaska at War Symposium, 11–13 November.

Department of the Navy. 1993. *The Aleutians Campaign, June 1942–August 1943*. Washington, DC: Naval Historical Center.

Faust, Nina & Edgar Bailey. 1995. "The Aleutians: tiny islands in turbulent seas." *Alaska Geographic* 22(2): 4–33.

Garfield, Brian. 1969. *The thousand-mile war: World War II in Alaska and the Aleutians*. Garden City, NY: Doubleday.

Gilman, William. 1944. *Our hidden front*. New York: Reynal & Hitchcock, Inc.

Handleman, Howard. 1943. *Bridge to victory: the story of the reconquest of the Aleutians*. New York: Random House.

Hutchison, Devin Don. 1994. *World War II in the North Pacific: chronology and fact book*. Westport, CT: Greenwood Press.

Jacobs, William A. 1993. "American national strategy in East Asian and Pacific War: the North Pacific." In *Alaska at War, 1941–1945: the forgotten war remembered*, Fern Chandonnet (ed.), 13–17. Anchorage: Papers from the Alaska at War Symposium, 11–13 November.

Jones, Robert H. 1969. *The Road to Russia: United States lend–lease to the Soviet Union.* Norman, OK: University of Oklahoma Press.

Morton, Louis. 1989. *United States Army in World War II: the War in the Pacific. Strategy and command: the first two years.* Washington, DC: United States Army Center of Military History.

Nishijima, Teruo. 1993. "Recalling the Battle of Attu." In *Alaska at War, 1941–1945: the forgotten war remembered*, Fern Chandonnet (ed.), 109–12. Anchorage: Papers from the Alaska at War Symposium, 11–13 November.

Palka, Eugene J. 2003. "Military geography: its revival and prospectus." In *Geography in America at the dawn of the twenty-first century*, Gary Gaile & Cort J. Willmott (eds). Oxford: Oxford University Press.

Russell, James S. 1993. "The Aleutian Campaign." In *Alaska at War, 1941–1945: the forgotten war remembered*, Fern Chandonnet (ed.), 67–74. Anchorage, AK: Papers from the Alaska at War Symposium, 11–13 November.

United States Army Center of Military History. 1988. *United States Army in World War II: pictorial record. The war against Japan.* Washington, DC: United States Army Center of Military History.

——. 1992. *The U.S. Army campaigns of World War II, Aleutian Islands.* Washington, DC: United States Army Center of Military History.

Chapter eleven
Protecting the force
Medical geography and the Buna–Gona Campaign

EUGENE J. PALKA AND
FRANCIS A. GALGANO

Introduction

ARMY LEADERS AT ALL echelons are responsible for conducting risk assessments as an integral part of designing, planning, and executing training, regardless of whether it occurs at home station, elsewhere within the continental US, or overseas. Leaders have the same inherent responsibility when planning and orchestrating operational missions at home and abroad in both peacetime and war. An integral part of the planning process involves addressing the specific environmental health hazards that may be encountered in a specific place.

As a subdiscipline of geography, *medical geography* dates back to the late eighteenth century in England. The field gained significant credibility within US academic geography by the late 1940s. Two early founders of medical geography were Jacques May and Ralph Audy. Both developed much of their expertise during the course of their military experience.

Jacques May was educated in Paris and subsequently practiced medicine in Southeast Asia in the 1920s and 1930s. He also practiced in Vietnam prior to the war in Indochina, and was the head French doctor in Hanoi. May was the first to describe the cultural ecology of disease. He recognized that every disease revealed a specific distribution pattern, or geography, and that human behavior was an integral part of any disease complex. May was a prolific writer and many of his early works laid the foundation for medical geography, earning him the distinction as the "father" of the subfield in the US.

Ralph Audy traveled with the British Army throughout Southeast Asia, India, and Malaysia. He was a medical doctor who discovered the etiology of scrub typhus in Malaysia, and later served as the head of the Institute of Medical Research in that country. Audy later came to the US and served as the head of several research foundations. His concept of "health" has been adopted throughout medical geography and by the World Health Organization.

As Jacques May (1958) concluded, certain environments present distinct environmental hazards. All diseases have specific etiologies that can be described using basic physical geographic criteria. Primary consideration must therefore be given to identifying potential disease hazards, and subsequently protecting soldiers from acquiring diseases via implementing a wide range of preventive measures (such as immunizations, information briefings and pamphlets, protective clothing, specific types of personal hygiene, etc.). In the event that a disease is contracted, then proper treatment must be administered by trained medical personnel in a timely fashion, and all efforts must be made to prevent the spread of the disease.

Assessing health hazards of a particular region from a military perspective is yet another aspect of effective area analysis during operational planning. Medical geography specifically focuses on the interaction between people and their environment, and accentuates the activities that expose soldiers and civilians to health risks (Palka 1994, 2005). This particular subfield of geography is unquestionably relevant to military personnel from both a professional development and practical perspective.

Medical geography uses the concepts and techniques of the discipline to investigate a wide range of health-related topics. It explains the distribution of health and disease, and identifies efficient ways to intervene and distribute trained personnel and technology to provide effective health care. The subfield of medical geography is closely related to epidemiology, the study of epidemics and epidemic diseases. Epidemiology, however, tends to be focused on one or two scales. By comparison, medical geography is much broader—covering multiple scales that may range from a single house to a culture realm. Moreover, medical geography employs all of the systematic geographies at various scales over time, and, as such, is extremely integrative in its approaches. Finally, the scope of medical geography is not restricted to the presence or absence of disease, but considers the entire range of health concerns in a spatial context.

History is replete with examples of battles, campaigns, and wars, where far more casualties were attributed to disease than to enemy fire. This chapter provides an overview of medical geography and recalls the Buna–Gona Campaign of World War II as a means to emphasize the relevance of this particular subfield to military operations and warfighting.

Health versus disease

As a point of departure, we will consider the basic notion of health, a fundamental concern of all military units in virtually any context. *Health* is a state of complete physical, mental, and social wellbeing, and not merely the absence of disease or infirmity (Meade and Earickson 2000). Health is perhaps best understood as a continuing property that can be measured by an individual's ability to rally from a wide range and considerable amplitude of insults (Audy 1971). The latter include the impacts stemming from chemical, physical, infectious, psychological, and social stimuli. Insults may be best understood as an array of negative environmental aspects that affect a person and trigger a bodily response. Physical insults could refer to air quality, temperature, humidity, light, sound, atmospheric pressure, and trauma—just to name a few. Chemical insults might include pollen, asbestos, various pollutants, smoke, or even food. Infectious insults would include virus, *Rickettsia*, bacteria, fungi, protozoa, and helminthes. Moreover, psycho/social insults could involve crowding, isolation, fear, anxiety, excitement, humor, and/or alienation. Regardless of location, occupation, or lifestyle, every person is subjected to a continual range of insults from birth until death. Consequently, health is regarded as an ever-present measure of a person's total vitality. It is easy to see that, given the range of insults mentioned above, soldiers are routinely exposed to many, if not most of the possibilities during both peacetime training and war.

Disease refers to the alteration of living cells or tissues in such a way as to jeopardize their survival in their environment (May 1961). Medical geographers are concerned with several broad categories of disease. Congenital diseases are those that are present at birth. Chronic diseases are present or recurring over a long period. Degenerative diseases involve the impairment of an organ or the deterioration of its cells and the tissues. Finally, infectious diseases result from an invasion of parasites and their multiplication in the body. Given the various categories above, the military is most concerned with infectious diseases, because they can be contracted relatively easily and then subsequently spread throughout a unit. Moreover, given the routine medical screening that all soldiers undergo early in their career, the first three categories are rarely applicable to career soldiers, or even draftees.

Diseases may also be classified based on the conditions or contexts within which they occur. A deficiency disease comes about when one's diet is not varied enough to satisfy all of the body's demands. Substances important for health may be missing from the person's food intake for cultural or physical reasons. *Kwashiorkor* is a widespread example, and is due to a shortage of protein in the food eaten by some of the poverty-stricken residents of rice-growing areas of Africa and Southeast Asia. An occupational disease is caused by conditions at the workplace. For example, the chest disease, *silicosis*, has long been related to coal mining and the inhalation of harmful coal dust. In some cases, the disease may become quickly apparent, while, at other times, symptoms do not appear for many years after the occupation has ended. Stress diseases occur when environmental pressures are too great for an individual to bear.

Overcrowding in an urban area or one of many different types of social pressures could serve as the root of the problem. Senescent diseases are due to old age, rather than to environmental factors. Several types of heart failure would fall into this category. Obviously, the military is not concerned with senescent diseases; however, occupational and stress diseases are prevalent during both peace and war.

A third classification scheme that is routinely employed in undeveloped or underdeveloped countries of the world is based on the relationship between the disease and water. Waterborne diseases are ingested. Examples include typhoid, cholera, diphtheria, polio, and bacillary dysentery. Water-washed diseases are those that can be avoided with proper hygiene and other preventive measures. Typhus, plague, and various intestinal worms are examples of potential water-washed diseases that commonly occur under unsanitary conditions. With water-based diseases, people do not acquire the disease directly from the water; the vector requires water. Specific examples of diseases and their associated vectors include malaria (mosquito), river blindness (black fly), and schistosomiasis (snail). Given the global nature of the US Military's mission, each of the above water-related disease categories are of a special concern.

Key terms related to disease ecology

As is the case with any discipline, the lexicon of medical geography includes many basic concepts that must be understood and applied in the appropriate context. The following terms are interrelated and fundamentally important to the medical geographer, as he or she seeks to understand how diseases are acquired and spread to different locations. An *agent* is a disease-causing organism, including animals and viruses, ranging in size from one-celled organisms to parasitic worms and insects. A *host* is the organism infected by the disease agent. After being afflicted by an infectious disease, a host (person, animal, bird, or arthropod) supports the disease organism by providing lodgment or subsistence. A *reservoir* refers to a large number and concentration of hosts in a population, from which a disease may expand or diffuse. The infectious agent normally lives and multiplies within the reservoir. Thus, a reservoir may serve as a continuing source of possible infection for humans. A *vector* is a carrier of a disease and is capable of transferring the latter between hosts. The agent often goes through life cycle changes in form within the vector. The habitat of the vector may determine the location of the disease. Biological vectors (such as insects or rodents) are alive and provide the habitat for an agent to develop or multiply within prior to becoming infective. By comparison, non-biological or mechanical vectors such as water, soil, food, or fecal matter, are not essential for the agent's life cycle but may serve as a vehicle for transmitting the infectious agent.

Distribution and diffusion of diseases

In keeping with traditional practices, medical geographers are concerned with the questions of what is where and why—as it relates to their subfield. Locating specific places through geographic analysis, defining areal extents or regions, and identifying spread mechanisms are all research foci. Several terms are especially important to understanding the areal extent and diffusion of diseases. Unfortunately, for military personnel, however, missions in wartime routinely require personnel to venture into infested areas.

The term *epidemic* refers to a sudden and severe outbreak of a disease, leading to a high percentage of afflictions and a substantial number of deaths. A disease of *pandemic* proportions begins regionally and then spreads worldwide (as in the case of many forms of influenza or AIDS). *Endemic* refers to the situation where a disease is carried by many hosts in a condition of "near equilibrium," without leading to a rapid and widespread death toll among a population. A disease that is endemic within a population may gradually sap the strength from members or at least render them more vulnerable to other maladies. In either case, the endemic disease significantly decreases life expectancy. Endemic regions are areal extents that are best understood as reservoir areas where a large percentage of a population is host to a particular disease.

Medical geographers place tremendous reliance on the use of maps for conducting locational analysis, defining regions based on specific criteria, plotting incidence of disease, and graphically portraying diffusion. Indeed, the advent of medical geography can probably be traced to medical topography that evolved in Europe during the late eighteenth century (Meade et al. 1988). The earliest practitioners were medical personnel who recognized the tremendous utility of analyzing the spatial aspects of disease in order to find the root problem. Maps of the yellow fever and cholera epidemics of the late eighteenth and early nineteenth centuries were the first examples of disease maps. John Snow's 1854 dot map of cholera around the Broad Street water pump in London was perhaps the most famous of the early maps that convinced investigators of the utility of geography's most enduring tool.

In general, maps are two-dimensional representations of all or part of the earth's surface to scale. Many are designed to show a specific distribution of a particular phenomenon within a given area. Within medical geography, maps can address a wide range of topics ranging from specific diseases (see Figure 11.1), to deficiencies such as malnutrition or under-nutrition, to specific physical environments that provide the optimum habitats for a particular malady. Moreover, maps can be generated at various scales, enabling geographers to examine the areal extent of the disease in a global context, or focus on the particular region of concern. A current edition of *Goode's World Atlas* (Veregin 2004) provides several examples of maps (specifically cartograms) at the global

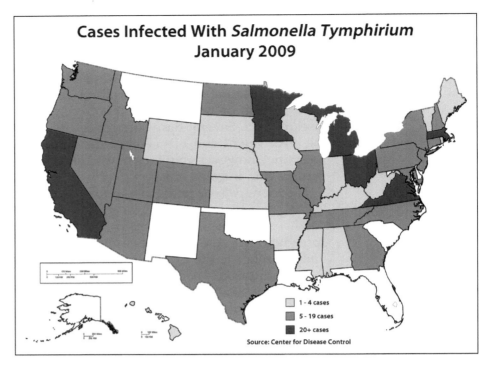

Figure 11.1
Map illustrating the
spatial distribution of
Salmonella typhimurium in
the US during January
2009. *Source*: Center for
Disease Control.

scale that graphically portray calorie supply, protein consumption, life expectancy, and the number of physicians per populations size. Each of these graphic representations enables one to assess the general health of a population in a particular place. Maps can also provide a revealing historical record of a particular disease. By plotting each occurrence for a given time period within a designated area, specific changes and trends can be observed (see Figure 11.2).

Disease ecology

Medical geographers have a long-established pattern of focusing research efforts into two major foci—disease ecology and medical health care. The latter is more recent and includes themes such as health services location, facility utilization, accessibility of health care, the relationship between health and poverty, and a number of different health care issues in undeveloped countries. Disease ecology has a much stronger tradition, and has sought to understand the relationships between health, disease, culture, and human/environmental interactions. The spatial ecology of disease and the geographic aspects of the health of populations provide fertile ground for medical geographers, ecologists, epidemiologists, and various specialists within medical science. More often than not, the map becomes the fundamental link between the disciplines. The following series of maps enables one to compare various diseases that occur within Africa (see Figure 11.3).

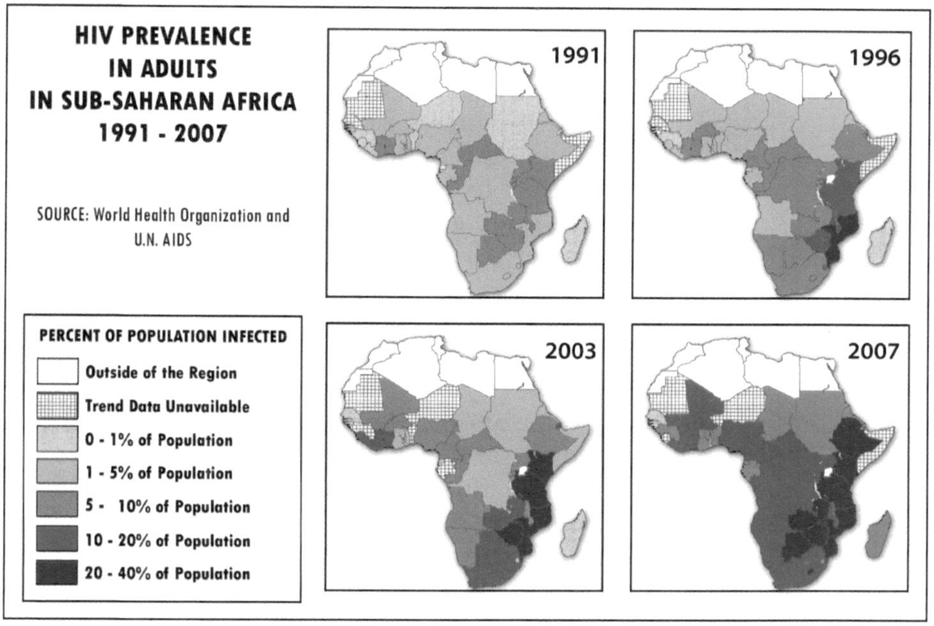

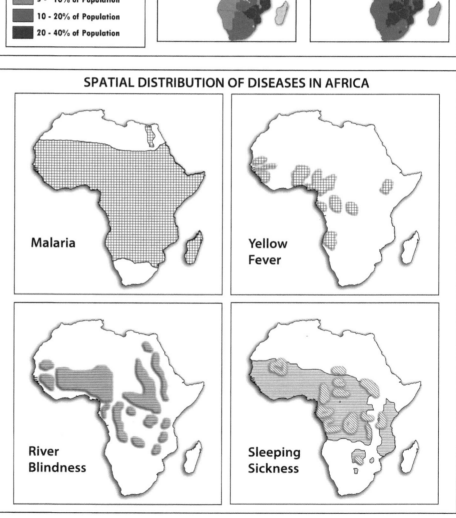

Figure 11.2
Spread of AIDS in Africa,
1991–2007. *Source*: World
Health Organization.

Figure 11.3
Various disease patterns
in Africa.

Each disease, however, requires a different environmental niche. Compare the climate, physiography, land-use patterns, population distribution, and vegetative biomes with the disease patterns. What questions do these patterns raise? What conclusions can you draw?

Given the patterns that emerge in the maps in Figure 11.3, it is tempting to arrive at premature conclusions, and to recall various discussions about environmental determinism. Cultural adaptations, however, have a significant impact on whether or not the population encounters a particular disease. Moreover, cultural beliefs have an influence on how various groups prevent or treat diseases. Cultural buffers refer to behavior or innovations that shield against disease. The examples are too many to list, but consider the following cultural generalizations. Many Chinese drink tea, not water. They must boil the water first to make tea; consequently, they experience few waterborne diseases. Europeans derive many similar benefits from drinking moderate amounts of wine instead of poor-quality water. Considering culture traits, sandals have proven to be a barrier to hookworms all over the world. Another simple innovation, the handkerchief, prompted the cessation of TB in many regions.

The triangle of human ecology

One model that facilitates the understanding of the relationship between health and a particular place is the triangle of human ecology, conceptualized by Meade et al. (1988). The triangle is formed by three vertices—population, behavior, and habitat, and encloses the state of health (see Figure 11.4).

Within the context of the model, habitat is that part of the environment within which people live. It includes houses, workplaces, settlement patterns, recreation areas, and transportation systems. The population considers humans as the potential hosts of various diseases. Factors affecting, and yet characterizing, the population include nutritional status, genetic resistance, immunological status, age structure, and psychological and social concerns. Behavior includes the observable aspects of the population and springs from cultural norms. It also affects who comes into contact with disease hazards and whether or not the population elects other alternatives.

The key to understanding the health of a population in a particular place is based on an appreciation of how the population, through its behavior, develops and interacts with its habitat. Virtually all diseases have an ideal habitat or natural nidus. Many exist in nature, independent of human activity, and are referred to as silent zones, unbeknownst to people until the latter come into contact with and contract the disease. The human factor, however, explains who, when, where, and why
168 people come into contact with various diseases. Through various beliefs

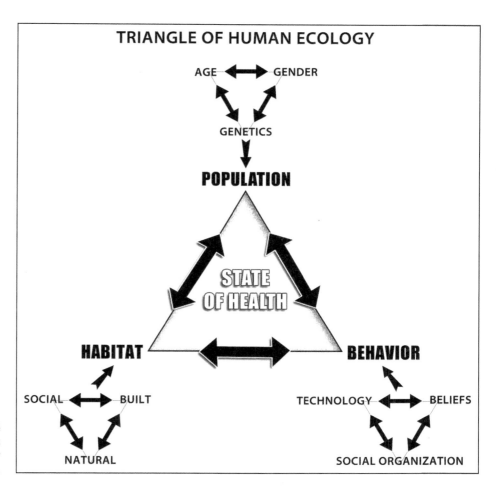

TRIANGLE OF HUMAN ECOLOGY

AGE ←→ GENDER

GENETICS

POPULATION

STATE OF HEALTH

HABITAT

BEHAVIOR

SOCIAL ←→ BUILT

NATURAL

TECHNOLOGY ←→ BELIEFS

SOCIAL ORGANIZATION

Figure 11.4
The triangle of human
ecology. *Source*: after
Meade et al. (1988).

and activities, humans may become exposed to a disease, enhance or reduce the spread of it, or establish a variety of cultural buffers as means of controlling the disease cycle (Palka 1994, 2005).

Nutrition and health

The triangle of human ecology emphasizes that the state of human health is linked to the interrelationships between people, their behavior, and the environment. "Good health" depends on much more than the successful avoidance of disease. A two-way interaction occurs between nutrition and health. A nutritional diet can enhance one's health, while deficiency diseases like *malnutrition* and *undernutrition* can have the opposite effect. Malnutrition results from deficiencies in protein, vitamins, or minerals within a person's diet. Caloric intake may be adequate, but the lack of a well-balanced nutritional diet has a negative impact on the body's ability to function. Perhaps more importantly, malnutrition renders a person more susceptible to other diseases or illness, and renders the person incapable of rallying from new insults. Whereas malnutrition is related more to a lack of protein rather than inadequate food, undernutrition is directly related to a lack of calories or the quantity of food intake. Like malnutrition, undernutrition renders a person more susceptible to other maladies, and thus lowers the state of health.

Both malnutrition and undernutrition have a distinct geography. The underlying patterns are related to both environmental and cultural factors. Environmental factors, including rainfall, temperatures, soil quality, sunlight, and relief, may limit crop varieties or harvests. Agricultural productivity can be further limited by periods of drought or other natural hazards. The latter can have a devastating effect on millions of people in underdeveloped countries, which are entirely dependent on subsistence agriculture.

Cultural preferences also play a part in both malnutrition and undernutrition. Given the population pressure in India, cattle could provide a much-needed source of protein, if not forbidden by Hinduism. Similarly, in various parts of the Middle East and northern Africa, hogs would provide the protein necessary to enhance the diet of many who are poverty stricken, yet Muslims will not consume pork. Even in the US, where there are far fewer deficiency diseases, people go hungry rather than consume any of the dog meat from the thousands of dogs that are killed daily in animal pounds across the country. Dogs could provide a much-needed source of protein to those in desperate need; however, a cultural bias prevents Americans from even considering such an option.

On a global scale, maps of calorie supply and protein consumption reveal a distinct pattern in *Goode's World Atlas* (Veregin 2004). While we could explain part of the pattern in terms of environmental factors and cultural preferences, we might also consider the impact of poverty on nutrition and health. Moreover, we might consider the availability of health care in the same locations, and then try to correlate all of the above factors with the map of life expectancy or to infant mortality rates in various countries.

With a better understanding of some of the basic concepts of medical geography, an appreciation of disease ecology, and an awareness of the impacts of nutritional-status environmental conditions on health, let us now turn to a historical vignette to emphasize the relevance of medical geography to military operations. Bear in mind that the Buna–Gona campaign is only a representative example. We can surely look to virtually any war and discover specific examples of where disease and/or adverse environmental conditions rendered soldiers and units combat ineffective.

The Buna–Gona Campaign

Introduction

Papua New Guinea (Figure 11.5) is the world's second largest island, located at 8° south latitude, and by late 1942 it became a lynchpin in the Allied strategy for stopping the Japanese in the Southwest Pacific (Weigley 1973). Papua (as it was known in 1942) is a land of soaring mountain ranges, impenetrable tropical jungle, low-lying coastal swamps, swollen rivers, and clouds of mosquitoes. The island's northern coast is a fever country, a landscape of torrential rains, insufferable heat, and tropical diseases, and it was here that US and Australian soldiers won a pivotal battle that halted the Japanese drive to seize Australia (Martin 1967; Milner 1989). However, the fighting cost the Americans some 10,879 casualties, and, of these, 7920 were caused by tropical illness, poor food and water, and appalling sanitary conditions because the jungle, a smothering tropical climate, and illness were also the enemy (Center of Military History 1990). As one veteran recalled:

> The men at the front in New Guinea were perhaps among the most wretched-looking soldiers ever to wear the American uniform. They were gaunt and thin, with deep black circles under their sunken eyes. They were covered with tropical sores. They were clothed in tattered, stained jackets and pants. Often the soles had been sucked off their shoes by the tenacious, stinking mud. Many of them fought for days with fevers and didn't know it . . . malaria, dengue fever, dysentery,

Figure 11.5
Map of the Pacific
Theater of Operations.

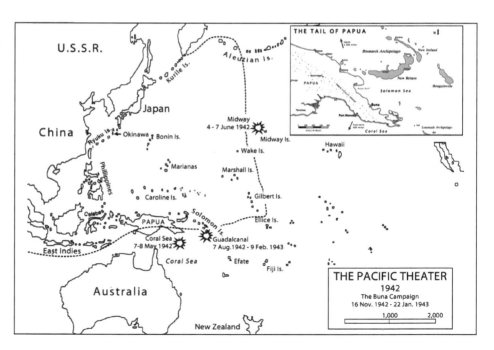

and, in a few cases, typhus hit man after man. There was hardly a soldier, among the thousands who went into the jungle, who didn't come down with some sort of fever at least once.

(Kahn 1943: 15)

Tropical disease and the stifling climate took a fearful toll of Allied soldiers (see Figure 11.6). Poor nutrition and unhealthy water compounded the effect of these problems. Not only did soldiers endure *malaria*, dengue fever, and other tropical illnesses; but they also suffered from food poisoning, *dysentery*, depression, and lethargy (Center of Military History 1990). The US 32nd Infantry Division was composed of soldiers from the American Midwest and they were not acclimated or physically prepared for the conditions. Furthermore, their equipment and diet were ill suited for the climate, and the medical staff was unprepared to deal with environmental conditions. Within two weeks after entering the jungle, the rate of sickness began to climb and it was not unusual for more than half the soldiers in an infantry battalion to

Figure 11.6
US soldiers in the dense tropical jungle. *Source*: US Army photograph.

be hospitalized. The casualty figures indicate that, for every two battle casualties, five soldiers were out of action because of a health-related problem (Milner 1989). It is remarkable that these soldiers were able to drive the Japanese out of Papua considering the harsh conditions and rates of non-battle casualties, which approached 80 percent in some units (Center of Military History 1990).

Geography and climate

A brief description of Papua's geography and climate is useful to explain the conduct of the battle and why disease played such a major role during the operation. The campaign took place on the elongated tail of the island Papua (see Figure 11.7) between Port Moresby and Buna, with the heaviest fighting taking place along the narrow strip of land along the northeastern coast of Papua centered on Buna (see Figure 11.8). The *coastal plain* was a mix of jungle, impassable swamps, coconut plantations, and open fields of shoulder-high *kunai grass* (Center of Military History 1990). The vegetation was very dense and it made for an ideal breeding ground for vectors such as mosquitoes, chiggers, fleas, ticks, rats, and biting flies (Milner 1989).

The coastal plain around Buna is low-lying and seldom exceeds 5 feet above mean sea level. Hence, the water table was very high and the prodigious rainfall inundated the landscape, with pervasive ponding and swamps. The highest ground is actually found along the coast and it was occupied by the Japanese, thus Allied soldiers were forced to live and fight in fetid swamps or on a few patches of dry ground where the water table was only inches below the surface. Consequently, Allied

Figure 11.7
Map of the "tail" of Papua delineating the locations of Port Moresby and Buna.

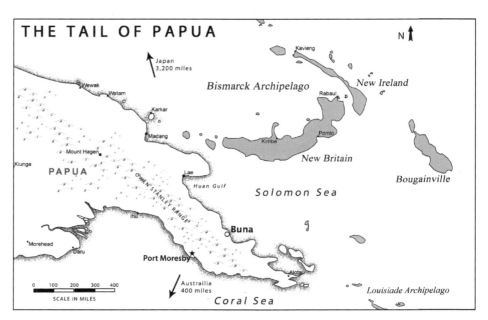

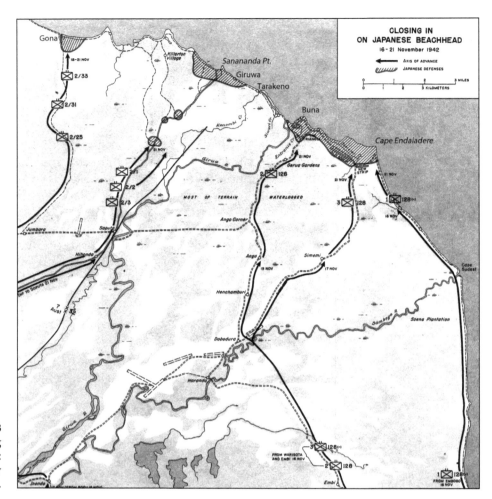

Figure 11.8
Map of the fighting around Buna. *Source*: Center of Military History (1995).

soldiers lived in a state of perpetual wetness. Their uniforms and boots rotted, skin ulcerated, food spoiled, and weapons rusted, and, although there was plenty of water, it was undrinkable (Kahn 1943). These conditions are highly conducive to the spread of tropical diseases and other health-related problems.

The region had no roads or other infrastructure except along the coastal margin. Dense jungle and swamps made mobility on foot difficult and virtually impossible by vehicle (Martin 1967). Heavy rains would inundate the jungle trails slowing the forward movement of supplies, and the distribution of food, water, and medical supplies was difficult. It was normal for units to go days without food, further wearing down immune systems. Extensive engineering was needed to carve roads out of this dense jungle (Milner 1989). Therefore, the distribution of fresh water, food, and medical supplies was accomplished by native porters, which was ineffective at best (Kahn 1943). Moreover, the dense vegetation made airdrops an uncertain proposition and only 50 percent of the drops reached Allied soldiers (Milner 1989).

Allied soldiers were also compelled to cope with the physical problems associated with Papua's tropical rainforest climate. Daily temperatures average near 29.4°C (85°F) throughout the year with daily maximums that hover near 37°C (100°F). Temperature and humidity conditions at Buna were such that soldiers experienced increasing physical discomfort. The climate problem was compounded because most of the fighting took place between November and January (i.e. summer); a period when precipitation, temperature, and humidity are highest. For example, during the month of December, the daily temperature range extends between 22 and 36°C (72–99°F), humidity averages 82 percent, and the area receives nearly 40 cm (16 inches) of rain on average (Center of Military History 1990). The effect of these conditions is evident in an entry of the field journal of Company F, 2nd Battalion, 128th Infantry Regiment for 9 December 1942: "What is left of the company is a pretty sick bunch of boys. It rained again last night, men all wet, and sleeping in the mud and water" (Milner 1989: 45).

Campaign summary: the fight for Papua

On 22 January 1943, elements of the US 32nd Infantry Division captured Buna. This was the culmination of a grueling, five-month counter-offensive to drive the Japanese back across the Owen Stanley Range (see Figure 11.7), and, in so doing, blunting their planned invasion of Australia (Milner 1989). The combined Australian–US force fought its way through rugged mountain rainforest and then across the coastal swamps and jungles. Victory here was important because it turned the tide of Allied fortunes in the Pacific.

By late spring, 1942 Allied prospects in the Pacific were bleak and they were confronted with a litany of military disasters: 250,000 soldiers surrendered at Singapore on 15 February; the British evacuated Rangoon on 7 March; the Dutch surrendered Java on 8 March; on 9 April Bataan surrendered; and, by 29 April, the Japanese controlled Burma. The Japanese Empire extended over a vast expanse of the Pacific and Southeast Asia (see Figure 11.5). In May 1942, a virtually unstoppable Japanese military machine launched a sea and land operation against Australia to administer the *coup de grâce* to Allied presence in the western Pacific. The first step was the seizure of Port Moresby, along the southern coast of Papua. Seizing Port Moresby would provide the Japanese with a staging area within striking distance of Australia, as well as bomber and fighter bases to cover their crossing of the Coral Sea.

On 1 May, a large invasion fleet steamed from the Japanese naval base at Truk with the mission of landing at Port Moresby. The fleet made passage through the New Britain Straits and into the Coral Sea where it was stopped by a small US carrier group. The so-called *Battle of the*

Coral Sea, fought on 7 and 8 May 1942, was important for a number of reasons. First, it marked the first defeat of the relentless Japanese drive across the Pacific since Pearl Harbor. Second, it was the first sea battle fought entirely between aircraft carriers. Third, it turned back the planned Japanese seaborne invasion of Port Moresby and perhaps saved Australia (Keegan 1989).

Initial fighting on Papua New Guinea

Although stunned by their defeat in the Coral Sea, the Japanese did not take long to continue their offensive against Port Moresby. They landed an invasion force near Buna on 21 July with the mission of taking Port Moresby from the landward side by crossing the formidable Owen Stanley Range. General Hori led this Japanese force across the island on a backbreaking march through the mountainous jungles, losing half of his force to the elements and disease along the way (Milner 1989). When the Japanese reached Iwibiwa Ridge near Port Moresby in early September, they were a shadow of the force that departed Buna the previous July. Consequently, on 18 September, General Hori ordered a retreat to the north coast. The Allies subjected the Japanese to intense bombing and pursuit by the Australian 7th and US 32nd Infantry Divisions (Center of Military History 1995). By 10 November, the Japanese were back at their start point near Buna Mission. However, the tables were now turned; it was the Allies that were exhausted and at the end of a tenuous supply line (see Figure 11.8).

The Allies were forced to cross the Owen Stanley Range in pursuit of the Japanese using narrow jungle trails over the mountains (see Figure 11.9). Thus, they were compelled to fight not only the Japanese, but also the tough environmental conditions for which they were ill prepared (Keegan 1989). Although ultimately victorious, the 32nd Infantry Division would pay a heavy price to drive the Japanese out of southeastern Papua. By the end of the battle, it suffered 10,879 casualties; however, disease would account for 7920 (Center of Military History 1990). Similarly, the Australians incurred disease-related casualties at a rate of six soldiers for every three killed by direct enemy action (Winters 1998). A complete listing of US casualties is given in Table 11.1, which illustrating the ratios between battle and non-battle casualties in the 32nd Infantry Division and other US units during the Buna campaign.

Disease, health and the Buna-Gona Campaign

The casualty figures in Table 11.1 are quite revealing. It is clear that the US Army was facing a medical disaster in terms of non-battle casualty rates and unit effectiveness. There were periods when commanders were uncertain if they could continue the fight because most of the soldiers were in the hospital, or too weak to fight effectively (Martin 1967). The reasons for these exceptionally high non-battle casualty rates

Figure 11.9
Soldiers and mules
negotiating the steep
Kakoda Trail over the
Owen Stanley Range.
Source: US Army
photograph.

Table 11.1: I Corps casualties: Buna–Gona Campaign (Sep. 1942–Jan. 1943)

Regimental combat teams	Beginning strength	Killed in action	Other deaths	Wounded in action	Sick in action	Total casualties
32nd Infantry Division						
126th Infantry	3791	266	39	816	2285	3406
127th Infantry	2734	182	32	561	2813	3588
128th Infantry	3300	138	29	557	2238	2962
41st Infantry Division						
163rd Infantry	3820	85	16	238	584	923
TOTAL	*13,645*	*671*	*116*	*2172*	*7920*	*10,879*

Source: *Center of Military History (1990).*

are explainable and are, in fact, understandable considering the state of our knowledge of medical geography and medical technology in 1942. This void was aggravated when combined with environmental conditions. The hot and exceedingly wet climate is a near-perfect breeding ground for infectious agents and vectors, some of which Westerners had never encountered up to this point (Milner 1989). Papua experiences in excess of 342 cm (135 inches) of rain per year, and Allied soldiers fought and wallowed in swamps and jungles along the north coast during the height of the rainy season. This much rainfall combined with poorly drained soils and a very high water table turned fighting positions and bivouac areas into cesspools. As time went on, Allied soldiers became increasingly susceptible to disease and infection as the oppressive heat and pervasive moisture weakened their immune systems. Furthermore, in these conditions, minor injuries quickly festered and required extensive medical treatment for even the healthiest individuals (Kahn 1943).

These debilitating conditions were exacerbated by logistical and leadership failures. Once they began fighting the Japanese near Buna, the Allies were at the end of a very long logistical tether in a region with virtually no infrastructure (see Figure 11.10). Although General MacArthur ordered an airlift, the pervasive clouds along the Owen Stanley Range, persistent rain, and dense tropical forest limited its effectiveness (Milner 1989). Food and medical supplies were in increasingly short supply. Water purification equipment became almost as important as tanks and artillery ammunition in Allied supply priorities.

Local tribes used rivers as open sewers and fouled nearly every stream (Kahn 1943). Other surface water supplies were equally unsafe because the water contained protozoa that caused dysentery that was so insidious it could reduce a 500-man battalion to platoon strength in a matter of days. Waterborne disease accounted for almost half of the disease-related casualties during this campaign. The combined effects of these conditions were profound. The average daily sick call rate in a World War II US division was 3.8 percent of its strength (i.e. roughly 15,000). The average daily sick call rate for the 32nd Division during the Buna–Gona Campaign was 24 percent. In some cases, units were reduced to 50 percent strength and had not even fired a shot in anger (Center of Military History 1990).

Leadership, water, and disease
In this setting discipline and leadership were critical; nevertheless, there were a number of significant lapses. Strict water and hygiene discipline was absolutely necessary, but the realities of warfare were stacked against the soldiers of the 32nd Division. Combat tends to take a heavy toll of junior leaders, and, as conditions deteriorated and increasing numbers of junior leaders were killed in action, discipline eventually

Figure 11.10
The lack of roads, combined with heavy rainfall, made ground resupply difficult during the Buna Campaign. In this image a supply convoy pushes through axle-deep mud. *Source*: US Army photograph.

broke down. Even ordinary things like water consumption resulted in large numbers of combat-ineffective soldiers. Field hygiene standards eroded as enemy action decimated the ranks of junior leaders and environmental conditions wore down soldier resolve and morale. An entry in the field journal of the 2nd Battalion, 128th Infantry Regiment for 12 December 1942 illustrates this point: "The men haven't washed for a month, or had any dry clothing" (Milner 1989: 67).

Large numbers of soldiers stopped shaving and washing; dirty uniforms quickly became filthy, but were not exchanged because clean ones were not available. Latrines were not prepared properly, or in many cases not at all, further contaminating the water supply. As the supply situation broke down, soldiers began drinking untreated water out of local streams. Even when chlorine tables made their way to the front, waterproof storage bags were a rarity and the tablets disintegrated before they could be used (Kahn 1943). Furthermore, water-heating equipment could not make it forward into the combat zone and there was no way for soldiers to properly clean cooking and eating utensils. In this type of hot and humid environment, these sorts of lapses were a recipe for the spread of debilitating water-washed and waterborne sickness. The acute diarrhea associated with dysentery became so bad that soldiers simply slit the backs of their trousers because they could no longer control their bowels (Milner 1989). Eventually, most of them dehydrated and collapsed requiring weeks of hospitalization.

The failure of the medical system and technology

The campaign in Papua was the first of its kind for Americans in World War II. In reality, Allied soldiers came into contact with endemic diseases for which they had no prior knowledge. The region included a host of diseases such as malaria, dengue fever, *scrub typhus, bacillary*, and *amebic dysentery*. These maladies were complemented by conditions such as *jungle rot, ringworm*, and *athletes foot* (Milner 1989). Soldiers quickly became more susceptible to these illnesses as their immune systems wore down. In most cases, the medical system was simply unprepared or at best overwhelmed. For example, the soldiers of the 32nd Division were inoculated for European typhus prior to their deployment or Papua. This was problematic because scrub typhus existed in this region and the initial inoculation had no effect on this disease.

The hot, humid climate was a haven for vectors, and mosquitoes, ticks, chiggers, and flies inhabited the area in prodigious numbers. US units, however, did not have adequate insect repellent, and mosquito netting was in short supply; hence, it was difficult to break the cycle of disease at the lowest and simplest level (Kahn 1943). Furthermore, there was a general shortage of *quinine* and *Atabrine* in the Pacific; when supplies could be brought forward, they quickly broke down because water-proofing methods were ineffective. In Papua, soldiers were issued these tablets in small paper pouches, which offered no protection in the near saturated conditions. Existing malaria remedies merely treated symptoms and the malaria would recur with increasing intensity requiring many soldiers to be evacuated. Finally, the hospitals that could move forward had inadequate sterilization equipment and infection was rampant (Center of Military History 1995).

Nutrition

Fighting in a tropical climate is exhausting business. Soldier health and unit efficiency can only be maintained if they are provided with the proper food in sufficient quantities, but this was problematical in Papua. The supply system was inadequate at best, and it was common for soldiers to go without food for days at a time (Martin 1967). Furthermore, the diet was not suited for the conditions, and the method of storage was inadequate. The primary component of the diet was an Australian canned beef product called Bully Beef by the soldiers. This notorious fare was packed in fish oil that broke down in the high temperatures of Buna's jungles and caused soldiers to wretch (Kahn 1943). Moreover, the storage tins quickly rusted along the seams because of the extreme humidity, thus allowing the beef to spoil. Hence, the starving soldiers had no choice but to eat spoiled, wretched food that brought on dysentery and food poisoning. Soldiers who survived those problems were still vulnerable to other illnesses as their general resistance eroded from poor nutrition (Milner 1989).

Equipment

In 1942, US soldiers did not have specialized uniforms and equipment designed for tropical environments. The standard infantry uniform was made of wool, which is entirely unsuitable for Papua's climate. Wool retains moisture and is an excellent insulator: both undesirable properties in a jungle. A decision was made to have each soldier's uniforms dyed in a mottled green pattern for camouflage (Milner 1989). This seemingly logical idea caused a great deal of difficulty for the soldiers. First, the dye ran once it was exposed to the humid conditions and heavy rain in the Papuan jungle, causing serious skin rashes, which became infected. Second, the dye stopped up the pores in the uniform material and they became unbearable in the extreme tropical heat (Milner 1989). Heat exhaustion and severe dehydration were quick to follow.

As already mentioned, waterproofing methods were inadequate. Soldiers could not be issued more than one or two days' worth of vitamins and other medications because the pills would disintegrate in the humid conditions (Martin 1967). The most basic items such as soap, socks, underwear, oral hygiene material, shaving equipment, and mosquito nets were in short supply. As the supply system deteriorated, clean uniforms were considered luxuries that received very low priory in light of heavy demands for ammunition (Milner 1989). Water purification equipment was in short supply and was too heavy to be brought forward. The net result was low morale and poor hygiene that permeated all ranks in the front lines.

Response to the medical disaster

By early December 1942, the influence of tropical conditions on soldier health and diseases such as dysentery, dengue fever, and malaria, combined with poor water supplies and bad nutrition, severely eroded the combat effectiveness of the 32nd Infantry Division. In most cases 250-man companies were reduced to platoon strength. The commander of the 2nd Battalion, 128th Infantry Regiment, noted in his unit history that, "all men display unmistakable signs of exhaustion and sickness" (Milner 1989: 68). By the third week of December 1942 the division was nearly combat ineffective.

It was at that point that LTG Eichelberger (I Corps commander) stepped in and established uncompromising hygiene and uniform policies to improve the health, discipline, and morale of the beleaguered infantrymen. He enforced shaving and washing requirements, and improved supply to ensure that there was ample clean water, quality hot food, and clean clothing for his soldiers. He redoubled efforts to airlift supplies into the combat area and demanded the improvement of trails to permit vehicles to bring forward hot food. These measures had an almost immediate effect on the overall strength of the 32nd Infantry Division.

By early January, the division had regained sufficient strength to at last defeat the Japanese forces around Buna Mission. Although LTG Eichelberger was able to alleviate the incapacitating effects of poor water supplies, dreadful hygiene standards, and nutrition problems, he had no remedy for the pervasive number of infectious agents in the region. US soldiers would continue to incur diseases such as malaria, typhus, and dengue fever until technology and our knowledge of medical geography improved.

Conclusion

It is often noted that the war in Papua was a war of mud, mountains, malaria, and mosquitoes. The cost of taking Buna was staggering, although the tally of killed and wounded to enemy action was relatively small. The war on Papua would drag on for another year until the island was cleared in September 1943. However, by that time equipment, medicine, and our knowledge of disease ecology improved to the extent that the near medical disaster experienced in the early fighting near Buna was not repeated.

Combat operations are challenging and the military operating environment (i.e. terrain, climate and weather, cultural landscape) further stresses demands on human endurance and unit effectiveness. Disease and sickness can destroy a unit's effectiveness even before shots are fired in anger, and force protection is an important aspect of all operations. Although the Buna–Gona Campaign appears extreme, it is actually a typical case. For example, in the World War II China–Burma–India Theater, 90 percent of all casualties were the result of disease and sickness. Likewise in the Southwest Pacific Theater 83 percent of all casualties were disease related, and, in spite of our vast improvements in medical technology and geographic awareness, some 67 percent of all casualties in Vietnam were related to the depredations of disease and sickness. As this study of the campaign to take Buna–Gona all too clearly shows, medical geography is fundamentally relevant to military operations in any context.

Editor's note: This chapter is a revised and updated version of a public domain chapter previously published as Palka, E. J. & F. A. Galgano. 2005. "Protecting the force: medical geography and the Buna Campaign." In *Military geography: from peace to war*, E. J. Palka & F. A. Galgano (eds), 35–66. New York, NY: McGraw-Hill Custom Publishing.

References cited

Audy, J. R. 1971. "Movement and diagnosis of health." In *Essays on the planet as a home*, P. Shepard & D. McKinley (eds), 140–62. Boston: Houghton Mifflin.

Center of Military History. 1990. *Papuan campaign*. Washington, DC: US Government Printing Office.

——. 1995. *Papua*. Washington, DC: US Government Printing Office.

Kahn, E. J. 1943. *G.I. jungle*. New York, NY: Simon & Schuster.

Keegan, J. 1989. *The Second World War*. New York, NY: Penguin Books.

Martin, R. G. 1967. *The GI war*. Boston, MA: Little, Brown & Company.

May, J. M. 1958. *The ecology of human disease*. New York: MD Publications.

——. 1961. *Studies in disease ecology*. New York: Hafner.

Meade, M S. & R. Earickson. 2000. *Medical geography*. New York: The Guilford Press.

Meade, M. S., J. W. Florin, & W. M. Gesler. 1988. *Medical geography*. New York: The Guilford Press.

Milner, S. 1989. *Victory in Papua*. Center of Military History, United States Army in World War II, The War in the Pacific, Washington, DC: US Government Printing Office.

Palka, E. J. 1994. "North Carolina: natural nidus for rocky mountain spotted fever." *North Carolina Geographer* 3: 1–16.

——. 2005. "Environmental hazards of leading tick-borne diseases in the eastern United States." *Pennsylvania Geographer* 43(2): 3–21.

Veregin, H. 2004. *Goode's world atlas*. 22nd edn. New York, NY: Rand McNally, Inc.

Weigley, R. F. 1973. *The American way of war*. Bloomington, IN: Indiana University Press.

Winters, H. K. 1998. *Battling the elements*. Baltimore, MD: Johns Hopkins Press.

Chapter twelve
The geography of amphibious warfare

FRANCIS A. GALGANO

Introduction

ON 15 SEPTEMBER 1950, the US X Corps reversed the tide of the Korean War with its decisive turning movement at Inchon, Korea. Operation Chromite was perhaps the most decisive amphibious *turning movement* in military history; however, despite its astonishing success, the landing was fraught with peril. *Amphibious operations* are perhaps the most difficult to plan and execute, and Operation Chromite was certainly no exception because the Americans had to overcome complex tidal conditions, difficult bathymetry, and poor beaches. However, for precisely those reasons the North Koreans essentially discounted a landing there. Thus, a successful landing at Inchon would yield an incalculable operational payoff. It was predictable that General Douglas MacArthur would think in these terms, and he was perhaps the only military leader of his day with the experience and credentials to pull off this operation in the face of its geographic difficulties.

The landing was challenged by significant geographic difficulties that would have turned away all but the most intrepid military leaders. MacArthur understood the inherent advantages associated with amphibious operations and the devastating effect of a deep turning movement against an unsuspecting enemy. Under his direction, the operation was highly planned and was predicated on the first-rate Army, Navy, and Marine Corps co-operation that he came to trust during his island-hopping campaigns against the Japanese (Utz 1994). His planners learned their business during World War II and they were highly skilled. Between their expertise and his unshakable nerve, the operation seemed destined to succeed if Chromite's timing could exploit the tides (Weintraub 2000).

This review is an example of historical military geography explained in a strategic and operational framework. In this chapter, we will examine geographic considerations that affect amphibious operations.

The geographic analysis of Operation Chromite will demonstrate how the geography of amphibious landings drives strategic decision-making. It is the goal of this chapter to demonstrate the influence of the unique set of problems associated with operations in the coastal zone, and their impact on military operations.

Amphibious operations

Three geographic spheres come together at the shoreline, thus making the zone of land–sea contact one of the more dynamic environments on earth. Consequently, an amphibious assault against a defended beach is perhaps the most difficult of military operations (Brown 1992). During an amphibious assault, the attacker crosses the *line of contact* at the shoreline after contending with rough sea conditions, waves, currents, and a host of other hydrographic problems; the attacker must then immediately face the enemy across an open beach.

The geographic reality of amphibious warfare is that there are a finite number of suitable landing beaches; hence, the defender characteristically has the advantages of time and space. The defender knows the terrain and surf conditions, while the attacker's information is usually imperfect. The defender typically has the luxury of time, and therefore can develop prepared defenses with elaborate fortifications and extensive obstacles (Brown 1992). Meanwhile the attacker is limited to operations during small windows of time when tides and surf conditions can support a landing. All of this is further complicated by the fact that the attacker is at the mercy of weather conditions.

Although physical obstacles make amphibious landings inherently risky, these operations do present an attacker with three fundamental advantages. First, an amphibious force has unprecedented mobility, compelling the defender to fortify long stretches of coastline. Second, the attacker holds the initiative and can employ the element of surprise. The advantage of being able to appear unexpectedly from over the horizon and quickly land on a stretch of beach cannot be overstated. Finally, the naval covering force can neutralize the heaviest fortifications.

US amphibious units would maximize these advantages repeatedly as they perfected amphibious doctrine during World War II and this was punctuated at Inchon. MacArthur appeared to grasp this when he insisted that Inchon remain as Operation Chromite's operational objective when virtually everyone tried to persuade against such a risky landing (Utz 1994).

Forms of amphibious warfare

Amphibious operations are intrinsically joint endeavors and they require the integration of naval, land, and air units. Defined as attacks launched from the sea by naval and landing forces against a hostile shore

(Department of the Army 1993), they are conducted for three purposes: 1) to prosecute further land-based operations; 2) to obtain bases and anchorages for future operations; and 3) to deny a base or region to an enemy.

Amphibious operations can be broken down into five discrete types of operations: *assaults*, landings, *withdrawals*, *demonstrations*, and *raids*. Of these, the most difficult and costly is the amphibious assault. An amphibious assault is a tactical landing on a defended beach. In this type of operation, the enemy defends the beach, and line of contact is the shoreline. In contrast, an amphibious landing is typically uncontested and accomplished against an undefended shoreline and the line of contact is some distance inland (Miller 1989).

Dunkirk is perhaps the most celebrated example of an amphibious withdrawal (Polmar and Mersky 1988). In this type of operation, the amphibious action is designed to extract a force. Amphibious demonstrations are conducted to deceive an enemy so that they cannot be used against operations elsewhere. The demonstration by a Marine division off the Kuwaiti coastline during the 1991 Gulf War pinned down sizable Iraqi reserves and is a classic example of this type of operation (Department of Defense 1992).

Finally, amphibious raids are conducted against land targets to gather intelligence, destroy vital targets, and deceive the enemy. The fundamental constraint of an amphibious raid is that the landing force is not intended to remain ashore once its task is completed. The raid against Dieppe in 1942 by a Canadian division is perhaps one of the more infamous examples of this type of operation (Polmar and Mersky 1988).

Characteristics of amphibious operations

Because of their complexity, amphibious operations have unique characteristics not shared with other types of military operations and, not surprisingly, geography plays a crucial role. The invasion force is by necessity self-contained, and must be capable of independent action. For this reason, distance is a key factor. Frequently, an amphibious force is projected hundreds, and sometimes thousands, of miles from its base. For example, during Operation Torch in November 1942, US amphibious units were transported from Norfolk, Virginia, across the Atlantic for landings in French North Africa (Morrison 1960).

Consequently, air and naval superiority are fundamental conditions because the landing force is usually transported in relatively slow, lightly armored ships. For instance, the entire focus of the Battle of Britain during the summer of 1940 was the destruction of the British RAF, so that the German Army could successfully cross the English Channel (Addington 1984). Thus, most amphibious operations are conducted only under the umbrella of friendly air cover. Anzio was selected as the landing beach for Operation Shingle in January 1944, even though Civitavecchia was a better landing site, in part because Anzio could be covered by Allied aircraft (Galgano 1993).

Finally, a significant feature of amphibious operations is detailed *terrain analysis*. In this case, terrain includes the ocean surface, sea floor, beach, and inland areas. A successful amphibious operation must account for waves, tides, bathymetry, sea floor material, beach slope and sediment type, nearshore currents, weather, and terrain beyond the beach. History is replete with examples in which the amphibious force struggled against the natural elements. For example, naval planners badly misjudged the tides at Tarawa and nearly precipitated a disaster (Russ 1975).

Amphibious doctrine: a geographic perspective

The amphibious doctrine employed at Inchon had its roots in the period just after the end of World War I (Morrison 1963). Amphibious warfare as we know it was developed, refined, and perfected by the US Marine Corps during the inter-war period. Although we take the contemporary mission of the US Marines as our principal amphibious force for granted, this was not always the case. This role was codified by a Joint Army–Navy Board decision in 1927, which stated that the Marines would be the proponent for developing doctrine for "land operations in support of the fleet for initial security and defense of advance bases and for such auxiliary landing operations as are essential for the prosecution of the naval campaign" (Parker 1970: 47).

Amphibious doctrine refined by the Marines during the inter-war period was the most highly evolved of its kind, and was based on the careful study of the geography of beaches and islands in the Pacific region. During the decade prior to World War II, they conducted practice landings in a variety of geographic settings to include atolls, mainland beaches, and barrier islands (Parker 1970). This resulted in a comprehensive doctrine, coupled with detailed plans for specialized equipment, weapons, and tactics to support the capture of heavily defended beaches (Costello 1981). This doctrine (i.e. Fleet Marine Force 1934, 1944) was adopted by the Army and was highly refined in practice during World War II, and Inchon was perhaps the denouement of this doctrine (Knox 1985).

Background and evolution

Today, the concept of an amphibious attack against a defended shoreline is a firmly established doctrine, but this was not always the case. Following World War I there was significant skepticism over amphibious attacks. Consequently, the Marines were going to have to prevail over significant professional inertia (Parker 1970).

The prevailing belief among military professionals in 1918 was that the prospects of a successful landing against a fortified beach were to be regarded with much skepticism (Brown 1992). There were many historical examples to support this belief. Popular logic was that the accuracy, power, and rapid-fire capability of modern weapons simply made killing too efficient for an amphibious assault to succeed. These views were cemented after World War I as the Allies digested the catastrophe at Gallipoli, which validated the prevailing attitude that amphibious assaults against modern firepower were hopeless (Addington 1984). The Gallipoli campaign ended in failure and ultimately cost the Allies 252,000 casualties (Brown 1992). Even though initial assaults were moderately successful, the Allies were pinned down on the beaches and a protracted war of attrition continued between March 1915 and January 1916. After the war, professional publications in Britain declared that amphibious operations were obsolete. Professional literature in the US indicated that most military professionals were doubtful of the future possibility of beach assaults in view of the Gallipoli failure (Weigley 1973).

However, in the early 1920s the Marines were seeking a definitive mission and they took a critical look at the Gallipoli operation. They were on the brink of fiscal extinction as Congress looked to make deep cuts in the military budget following World War I (Brown 1992). Although not a formal mission, the Marines always assumed the task of securing forward bases for the fleet. Marine leadership (specifically Commandant, MG John Archer Legeune) saw this mission as their new reason for existence in consideration of the perceived threat in the Pacific, and began to review critically the failure at Gallipoli.

The Gallipoli study was very successful and numerous Marine publications accurately demonstrated that Gallipoli was too badly handled to be used as an object lesson, except how not to conduct an amphibious operation (Weigley 1973). A progressive group of Marines led by Major Carl E. Ellis, considered by most to be the father of US modern amphibious doctrine, began writing and lecturing on the subject of amphibious assaults during the early 1920s. These labors benefited from the spreading awareness that Japan was a dangerous potential enemy, and a strategy was needed to cope with a future conflict in the Pacific. Ellis proposed that, "it will be necessary for us to project our fleet and landing force across the Pacific and wage war in Japanese waters" (Parker 1970: 46). This view received wider acceptance in the Navy as its leadership reached similar conclusions.

Between the wars: Orange Plan

The Marine Corps was retrieved from oblivion in large measure through the efforts of prescient thinkers such as Major Ellis and MG Legeune as well as the strategic evaluation of a future war against Japan. After World War I, the Joint Army–Navy Board developed the so-called Orange Plan to outline the strategy for a war against Japan. As the plan evolved, it became increasingly evident that the geography of the Pacific was a critical factor. The innumerable islands and *archipelagoes* that dotted that vast ocean were *key terrain* and would have to be seized if the US was going to prevail (Brown 1992). The original Orange Plan envisioned the war against Japan being fought in two phases: 1) a holding action by US garrison forces in distant island territories; and 2) the counterattack during which the fleet fights its way across the Pacific to relieve beleaguered forces, retake lost islands, and culminate the war in a fleet action against the Japanese (Weigley 1973).

However, geographic realities of a war in the Pacific began to alter the thinking of strategic planners because there were few bases between Hawaii and Manila to support the westward advance of the fleet, and operational distances were vast. The distance between San Francisco and Pearl Harbor is 2000 miles, and Pearl Harbor to Tokyo is 3400 miles. Without bases and anchorages along the way, the Navy could not contemplate fighting across such distances (Weigley 1973). Furthermore, the Japanese held a number of islands along the intended axis of advance. Hence, the concept of using Marines to capture enemy islands began to come sharply into focus as General Legeune summed up the geographic dilemma in 1921, "on both flanks of a fleet crossing the Pacific are numerous islands suitable for utilization by the enemy for radio stations, aviation, submarine or destroyer bases" (Parker 1970: 47).

War games designed to evaluate the Orange Plan changed the US strategic outlook in the early 1920s. They demonstrated that there was little hope that remote island garrisons in the Pacific could hold out for an extended time should the Japanese decide to attack. Hence, planning quickly shifted to the idea that the Japanese would seize and hold these islands, and, thus, would have to be retaken if the US meant to advance its fleet into Japanese waters (Weigley 1973). The war games indicated that fleet losses would be unacceptable if the US tried to retake the western Pacific without first securing enemy-held islands along the way (Weigley 1973).

Hence, Orange evolved and the massive naval battle that was expected to decide the war was discarded. Instead planners adopted a new approach: "the military and naval approach to the Far East should be made in a step-by-step mopping-up process by which all the islands enroute would be taken and occupied in passing" (Weigley 1973: 254). The new Orange Plan called for an island-hopping strategy to secure or take islands by assault and establish airfields, logistics bases, and anchorages to bring the Navy to within striking distance of Japan. The mission to execute this island-hopping campaign was given to the Marines because they appeared to be particularly suited to the mission and were already thinking in that direction (Parker 1970).

Major Ellis began a series of studies addressing the efficacy of taking a beach by assault. His focus was certainly in the Pacific where the geographic realities of the different types of islands presented the Marines with unique subsets of problems. Many islands were so small that there could be little or no deception as to where the main attack would fall, thus necessitating the development of specialized tactics, weapons, and landing craft (Weigley 1970). Furthermore, assaults had to be contemplated against *atolls*, volcanic islands in *island arc* systems, and *mainland beaches* on larger islands such as Okinawa and Japan itself. Each island type presented distinct geographic challenges.

Ellis proved to be a tireless and particularly foresighted thinker. Throughout the early 1920s he toured Pacific islands, assembled terrain and hydrographic intelligence, and developed new theories on amphibious assaults. He established a solid foundation upon which amphibious doctrine would be developed (Brown 1992). In 1921, he published a paper on how to take back Pacific islands. He was directed by General Legeune to undertake a detailed study to evaluate doctrine, tactics, and equipment needed to prosecute an amphibious war (Parker 1970). Unfortunately, Ellis met with a somewhat suspicious death in 1923 while touring the Japanese-controlled island of Palau. Nonetheless, his writings proved to be an important point of departure for a thirteen-year study that would result in the development of the doctrine that would ultimately win the Pacific war (Costello 1981; King 1946)

Operation Chromite, September 1950

The amphibious landing at Inchon was conducted on 15 September 1950 by the US X Corps, and it turned the tide of battle when things looked bleakest for the UN's forces. Prior to the landing, North Korean forces controlled nearly the entire Korean peninsula except for a small 140-mile perimeter surrounding the city of Pusan known as the Pusan Perimeter (see Figure 12.1). With the successful landing at Inchon, General MacArthur severed North Korean supply lines, drove the invaders north, and perhaps saved the UN forces from annihilation (Appleman 1992).

General MacArthur described the Inchon landing as having a 5000 to 1 chance of succeeding. Arlie Capps, a planning officer for the Inchon amphibious assault stated, "We drew up a list of every conceivable natural handicap and Inchon had 'em all" (Utz 1994: 16). Most problematic was Inchon's 32-foot *tidal range*, which was compounded by a sinuous channel with tricky currents, wide mud flats, poor beaches, and large seawalls. On MacArthur's side were a very capable amphibious planning team and absolute surprise. The amphibious assault led to the recapture of Seoul and severed completely North Korean lines of communication, smashing their offensive in the south. The turning movement at Inchon utterly crippled the North Korean Army (Center of Military History 1989).

Operation Bluehearts: early planning
MacArthur directed planning for an amphibious attack against the North
190 Koreans during the first weeks of their offensive because it was the most

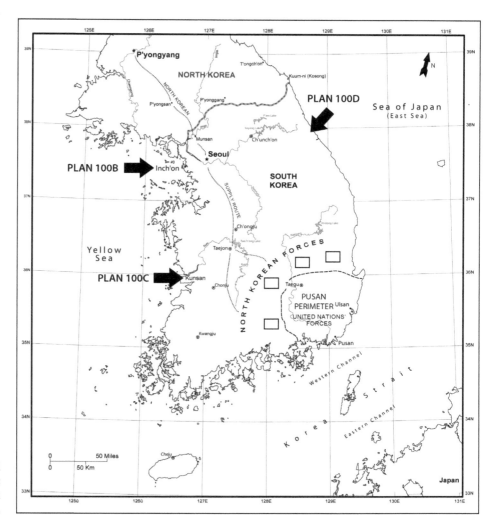

Figure 12.1
Situation map. *Source*:
Adapted from
Knox (1985).

powerful tactical tool at his disposal (Appleman 1992). His original plan,
Operation Bluehearts, called for an amphibious landing behind the
North Korean advance on 22 July 1950, but it was scrapped as the pace
of the North Korean offensive quickened and more US units were
committed to the peninsula. Undeterred, MacArthur remained focused
on the possibilities of a deep amphibious turning movement to rupture
North Korean lines of communication. Under his orders, Colonel D. H.
Galloway assembled an unusually talented group of planners to prepare
contingency plans. During the first weeks of July 1950, they developed
a series of detailed plans and the operation was re-designated Operation
Chromite (Utz 1994).

Chromite called for an amphibious landing during September, chiefly
191 to take advantage of tidal conditions and calmer seas (Center of Military

History 1989). Galloway's team furnished three different plans. Plan 100B called for a landing at Inchon combined with a simultaneous counter-attack by the 8th Army north from the Pusan Perimeter. Plan 100C proposed a landing at Kunsan on the western coast of the peninsula, much closer to the Pusan Perimeter. Plan 100D called for a landing on the eastern side of the Korean peninsula at Chumunjin (see Figure 12.1). Planners knew that MacArthur favored a landing at Inchon, hence it was the best developed of the three (Weintraub 2000). On 20 July 1950, MacArthur selected Plan 100B because, in his estimation, Inchon was the most decisive location.

The unexpected success of the North Korean attack, combined with a paucity of combat-ready US units, dimmed Chromite's chances. MacArthur originally designated the 5th Marine Regiment and 2nd Infantry Division for Operation Chromite. However, reverses on the peninsula necessitated their commitment to the front lines in late July. Similarly, the 1st Cavalry Division was committed to the peninsula as the North Koreans continued driving south (Appleman 1992). Notwith-standing these diversions, MacArthur continued to promote the landing.

The X Corps was assembled in Japan as the operational headquarters for Chromite in July. The staff was created from the best amphibious planners in the Far East Command. MacArthur reluctantly turned to the 7th Infantry Division, the last uncommitted US unit in Japan, but it was a division in name only. It had performed garrison duty in Japan and was not well trained. Further, it was only at half strength because it was stripped of soldiers to serve as replacements. MacArthur had the division rebuilt with nearly 8600 Korean augmentees and individual replace-ments culled from American units in the US. Chromite's other division was the hastily assembled 1st Marine Division (Appleman 1992). MacArthur's staff performed a Herculean effort and assembled supplies and nearly 230 ships to transport the invasion force. It at last appeared that the landing was going to happen.

The geography of Inchon

Relative location was Operation Chromite's most compelling strategic geographic consideration. MacArthur preferred Inchon because it is the port city of Seoul, which is only 18 miles inland. Although the North Korean Army had nearly over-run South Korea, it was dangling at the end of a very long, vulnerable logistical rope. A successful landing at Inchon followed by a rapid capture of Seoul would have far-reaching strategic repercussions. First, it would place a US corps astride the North Korean lines of communication with no significant reserves to retrieve the situation. Second, MacArthur was convinced that the psychological and political ramifications of retaking Seoul were powerful. He argued that this would capture the imagination of Asia and win support for the UN's cause (Appleman 1992). General MacArthur summed up Inchon's strategic geographic importance in his summary to the Joint Chiefs of Staff on 8 September 1950:

> The seizure of the heart of the enemy distributing system in the Seoul area will completely dislocate the logistical supply of his forces now operating in South Korea and therefore will ultimately result in their disintegration. This indeed, is the primary purpose of the movement ... the enemy cannot fail to be shattered.
>
> (Appleman 1992: 495).

Despite Inchon's strategic appeal, at the tactical level it manifested a dreadful collection of geographic problems. Inchon is located in the Yomha River estuary, a low-lying basin with a tidal range of nearly 32 feet. At low tide, the receding waters expose acres of mud. The harbor was connected to the Yellow Sea by Flying Fish Channel, a narrow, sinuous affair through which an invasion force of some 230 ships would have to pass. There were no real beaches at Inchon; instead, planners were faced with acres of mud flats exposed at low tide and a massive seawall that surrounded the city, and the landing beaches were backed by an urban area with a population of about 250,000 (Utz 1994). Finally, the harbor was split into inner and outer sections by Wolmi-Do [note: "Do" is the Korean term for island], which was occupied by North Korean troops (Appleman 1992).

Unquestionably, the tides were the most difficult problem, especially combined with the physical constraints of Flying Fish Channel. The draft of the landing craft and tidal range meant that the assaulting forces had only two hours to enter and leave the harbor. The largest of the landing craft, the Landing Ship Tank (LST), required a minimum of 29 feet of water, a condition that existed only once a month. The 15th of September was the only day with a maximum water depth of 31.2 feet over the mud flats, which satisfied the Navy (Appleman 1992). The 27th of September was marginal, but, once this window closed, the invasion would have to be delayed until 11–13 October when the spring tide again created a water depth of 30 feet (Utz 1994).

A tidal range this large means that a great deal of water must be exchanged as the tide ebbs and floods during the tidal cycle. Thus, ebb currents in the main boat channel exceeded the forward speed of the landing craft, and operations would have to be suspended. Low tide also exposed a vast mud flat stretching three miles out to sea. The only channel deep enough to allow the assault force into Inchon Harbor was littered with rocks, shoals, reefs, and islands. The combination of tidal currents and the difficult channel called for a daylight approach and a main landing during the late afternoon high tide (Center of Military History 1989).

Wolmi-Do made this problematical because of its prominent location in the harbor (see Figure 12.2). Invasion planners did not think it feasible that the invasion force could land without first securing Wolmi-Do (Weintraub 2000). However, the tidal and channel conditions did not allow a simultaneous landing on Wolmi-Do and the main beaches. Hence, a landing was planned on Wolmi-Do by the 3rd Battalion, 5th Marines, at 6:30 a.m., coincident with the morning high tide, with a very tricky approach in Flying Fish Channel during hours of darkness. During the intervening 12 hours, the battalion was essentially on its own until the fleet could return with the afternoon high tide (Appleman 1992).

Figure 12.2
Reconnaissance photographs of Inchon and its harbor. The upper image illustrates the built-up nature of the beaches and the seawall. The lower image demonstrates how Wolmi-Do dominates the approaches into the inner harbor. *Source*: US Army photograph.

Operation Chromite faced other difficult challenges as well. The 16-foot seawall that surrounded the city required planners to equip the assault forces with ladders (see Figure 12.3). Marines in the assault force would have to scale a difficult obstacle from bobbing landing craft, perhaps in the face of enemy fire (Utz 1994). Additionally, once ashore, the assault troops were involved immediately in an urban setting (see Figure 12.4). One of Chromite's important assumptions was that the X Corps could move quickly inland and seize Seoul, thus severing the North Korean lines of communications before they could recover (Appleman 1992). An urban battle could clearly upset that timetable. MacArthur paid little mind to the risk because his intelligence staff assured him that there were only 6500 poorly trained North Koreans in the area (Weintraub 2000).

Weather was also a critical factor because September is the transition monsoon season. Seas are typically calm during the summer period and higher seas dominate between October and March (Appleman 1992). Naval planners thought that conditions would remain adequate during the projected invasion time. However, September is the height of the typhoon season and a typhoon of any size could delay the invasion until October, which was deemed too late (Utz 1994). As it turned out, the invasion had two brushes with typhoons. The first, Typhoon Jane, struck Japan on 3 September while the invasion force was loading. It caused

Figure 12.3
Marines scale the seawall at Inchon. *Source*: US Marine Corps photograph.

Figure 12.4
Vertical aerial photograph taken of Inchon on 16 August 1950. The photograph illustrates the extent of the urban area behind the beaches. *Source*: US Army.

damage to some ships, but not enough to suspend the operation. The second, Typhoon Kezia, threatened the region on 13 September, but shifted direction at the last possible moment permitting the landing force to sail from Japan (Appleman 1992).

The landing controversy

The Joint Chiefs of Staff knew that MacArthur wanted to land at Inchon; however, they were concerned over its geographic challenges. The Navy's opposition to the plan centered largely on the difficult tidal conditions and the intricate timing required for the operation. The Marines were uneasy over the plan to leave a battalion isolated on Wolmi-Do for twelve hours and the difficult nature of the landing beaches. Both the Navy and Marines favored Kunsan as the objective for Chromite. Consequently, Army Chief of Staff, General Collins, and the Chief of Naval Operations, Admiral Sherman, met with MacArthur on 23 July to discuss the suitability of the Inchon plan. Also present was Rear Admiral J.H. Doyle, commander of the invasion fleet, who spoke for one hour and presented the landing's naval considerations. Doyle was pessimistic as he enumerated the formidable geographic obstacles and the intricate timing needed for the two-phase landing. Collins and Sherman asked many pointed questions and the plan was debated hotly by MacArthur's staff and the Pentagon representatives. Finally, Admiral Sherman asked Admiral Doyle for his appraisal. Doyle replied that, "The operation is not impossible, but I do not recommend it" (Appleman 1992: 493).

Thus, the fate of Operation Chromite was clearly uncertain, and Doyle, a veteran of the Pacific, did not give it a ringing endorsement. However, MacArthur interceded and gave all in attendance a 45-minute soliloquy on the strategic and tactical advantages of the Inchon plan. He reasoned that Kunsan was a good idea, but the wrong location. It was too close to the front lines and afforded the North Koreans interior lines. Furthermore, the turning movement was not deep enough to cause the North Korean front-line units to collapse (Weintraub 2000). He pointed out that the enemy had neglected his rear area and was at the end of an exposed logistical tail. North Korea committed practically all of its combat-ready formations against the Pusan Perimeter and no trained reserves were available. Hence, the ability for the enemy to disrupt the invasion was limited (Appleman 1992).

MacArthur understood the strategic impact of severing the North Korean lines of communications and the impact it would have on the battle. He pointed out that the amphibious operation was the most compelling strategic instrument available and, by using it decisively at Inchon, he could reverse the tide of the war. Clearly, as he saw it, the proper use of the amphibious attack was to strike deep and hard into the enemy rear. Kunsan was low risk, but it also promised a much smaller payoff and could not guarantee strategic reversal (Appleman 1992).

MacArthur called attention to the fact that everything indicated that the North Koreans considered a landing at Inchon to be geographically impossible and had devoted only minimum efforts to securing the harbor. Hence, surprise would be complete. The most important advantages of an amphibious operation were his to enjoy: mobility, surprise, and absolute, overwhelming firepower (Utz 1994).

Finally, MacArthur recalled his operations in World War II. He praised the Navy, which made his historic island-hopping campaign possible. He declared his conviction in the Inchon operation and that the Navy would be able to pull it off. He finished by saying that, "The Navy has never turned me down yet, and I know it will not now" (Appleman 1992: 494). He evidently convinced Chromite's doubters and won approval from the Joint Chiefs of Staff. It is important to note that, under ordinary circumstances, Inchon would likely not have happened: who but MacArthur could have swayed the Joint Chiefs of Staff, who were his military juniors? However, we cannot overlook the fact that Operation Chromite was skillfully designed and MacArthur was able to maintain an absolutely clear vision of its tactical requirements and strategic possibilities (Weintraub 2000).

Epilogue: victory at Inchon

The preliminary naval and air bombardment of Wolmi-Do and the Inchon beaches began in earnest on 13 September. The X Corps arrived offshore with nearly 70,000 troops on 15 September and the landing group took position off Wolmi-Do at 05:30. During the pre-dawn light the 3d Battalion, 5th Marines, landed at Green Beach on Wolmi-Do (see Figure 12.5). The landing was preceded by a short naval bombardment. The assault was a spectacular success and it was the first US amphibious assault since Okinawa (Appleman 1992). The fist two waves of assault troops were ashore by 06:45 and encountered little resistance. The reduction of the island was complete and it was declared secured at 07:50. The North Koreans were bewildered by the size and swiftness of the assault. The Marines captured nearly 400 prisoners, with only a few casualties (Appleman 1992).

Following the relatively effortless capture of Wolmi-Do came the long, anxious wait during the period of ebbing tide when all activity was suspended. The remainder of the 1st Marine Division boarded their landing craft at 15:30. Another short, violent bombardment blasted Red and Blue Beaches (see Figure 12.5) and the 5th and 1st Marines breasted the seawall at 17:33 (Appleman 1992). The North Koreans were fully alerted by now and the fighting once ashore was much heavier. Nonetheless, the Marines pushed inland quickly and their biggest obstacle after the seawall was the approaching night. The timing of the complex plan worked nearly to perfection (Utz 1994).

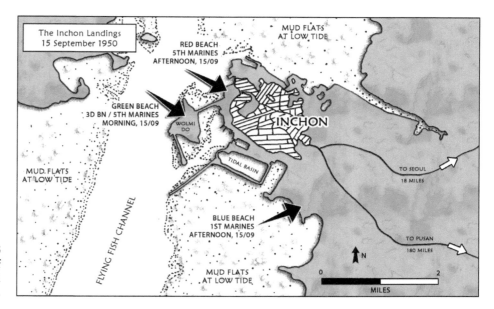

Figure 12.5
Map of the invasion of
Inchon. *Source*: adapted
from Knox (1985).

Conclusion

The North Korean invasion was defeated by a single devastating stroke. Why was Inchon chosen? General MacArthur made the decision to use Inchon because, in his words, "the very arguments you have made as to the [geographic] impracticalities involved will tend to ensure for me the element of surprise. For the enemy commander will reason that no one would be so brash as to make such an attempt" (Utz 1994: 23). The landing at Inchon was a success and the course of the Korean Conflict dramatically changed.

The geography of the Korea peninsula and Inchon drove operational and tactical planning for the invasion. Inchon's relative location made it the single decisive place for a turning movement. Likewise, Inchon's geographic characteristics made a landing there so unlikely that the North Koreans guarded the area with only weak forces. MacArthur was able to clearly "see the terrain" and employ the inherent advantages of amphibious operations in a single, devastating stroke against a decisive point.

Amphibious operations are perhaps the most difficult to plan and undertake because they take place in a very dynamic environment where three spheres converge. Small changes in weather patterns can alter wave height and direction, currents can rapidly shift, and the attacker must contend with tricky tidal conditions. The physical challenges are compounded by the fact that there are a finite number of suitable landing beaches and the enemy typically knows where they are as well. Consequently, military planners are challenged by daunting and complex physical parameters such as waves and tides, and the intricate tactical challenge of outwitting the enemy to insure that the invasion force has a reasonable chance of success.

Editor's note: This chapter is a revised and updated version of a public domain chapter previously published as Galgano, F. A. 2005. "Amphibious warfare: the turning movement at Inchon." In *Military geography: from peace to war*, E. J. Palka & F. A. Galgano (eds), 113–48. New York, NY: McGraw-Hill Custom Publishing.

References cited

Addington, L. H. 1984. *The patterns of war since the eighteenth century*. Bloomington, IN: University of Indiana Press.

Appleman, R. E. 1992. *South to the Naktong, north to the Yalu*. History of the United States Army in the Korean War. Center of Military History, Washington, DC: US Government Printing Office.

Brown, J. E. 1992. "Tarawa: the testing of an amphibious doctrine." In *Combined arms in battle since 1939*. ed. Spiller, R. J. Fort Leavenworth, KS: US Army Command and General Staff College Press.

Center of Military History. 1989. *Korea—1950*. Publication 21-1, Washington, DC: US Government Printing Office.

Costello, J. 1981. *The Pacific War*. New York, NY: Rawson, Wade Inc.

Department of the Army. 1993. FM 101-5-1, *Operational terms and graphics*. Washington, DC: US Government Printing Office.

Department of Defense. 1992. *Conduct of the Persian Gulf War*. Washington, DC: US Government Printing Office.

Fleet Marine Force. 1934. *Tentative manual of landing operations*. Washington, DC: US Government Printing Office.

Fleet Marine Force, Pacific. 1944. *Staff officer's field manual for amphibious operations*. Washington, DC: US Government Printing Office.

Galgano, F. A. 1993. "The landings at Anzio." *Military Review* 74(1): 69–73.

King, E. J. 1946. *The United States Navy at war, 1941–1945*. Official Reports to the Secretary of the Navy, Washington, DC: US Government Printing Office.

Knox, D. 1985. *The Korean War, an oral history, Pusan to the Chosin*. New York, NY: Harcourt, Brace & Jovanovich.

Miller, J. 1989. *Guadalcanal: the first offensive*. United States Army in World War II, the War in the Pacific. US Army Center of Military History, Washington, DC: US Government Printing Office.

Morrison, S. E. 1960. *Volume II: operations in North African waters, October 1942–June 1943, history of United States naval operations in World War I*. Washington, DC: US Government Printing Office.

——. 1963. *The two ocean war: a short history of the United States Navy in the Second World War*. Boston, MA: Little, Brown Inc.

Parker, W. D. 1970. "Advanced base expeditionary era, 1916–1941." In *A concise history of the United States Marine Corps, 1775–1969*. 45–58. US Marine Corps Historical Division, Washington, DC: US Government Printing Office.

Polmar, N and P. B. Mersky. 1988. *Amphibious warfare: an illustrated history*. New York, NY: Blanford Press.

Russ, M. 1975. *Line of departure: Tarawa*. Garden City, NY: Doubleday & Company, Inc.

Utz, C. A. 1994. *Assault from the sea, the amphibious landing at Inchon*. The US Navy in the Modern World, Publication No. 2, Naval Historical Center, Washington, Navy Yard, Washington, DC: US Government Printing Office.

Weigley, R. F. 1973. *The American way of war, a history of the United States military strategy and policy*. Bloomington, IN: Indiana University Press.

Weintraub, S. 2000. *MacArthur's war, Korea and the undoing of an American hero*. New York, NY: The Free Press.

Chapter thirteen

Bosnia and Herzegovina, 1992–5

Epitomizing Yugoslavia's bloody collapse

STEVEN OLUIĆ

Introduction

> The past is not dead. It is not even past.
>
> (William Faulkner)

THE CATASTROPHIC COLLAPSE OF YUGOSLAVIA in the 1990s was characterized by a ruthless and savage warfare unseen in Europe since World War II. From 1992 to 1995 Bosnia and Herzegovina was at the epicenter of this tragedy, pitting neighbors against one another based on identity, history, and religion. Bosnia's cultural and physical geography played a dominant role in setting the stage for civil war that was brilliantly manipulated by nationalist politicians.

Bosnia and Herzegovina's physical setting

Bosnia's physical geography is dominated by rugged mountains and valleys; in fact, the term Balkan is translated from the Turkish for mountain. The Dinaric Alps comprise almost 75 percent of Bosnia's landscape, trending southeast across most of the country (see Figure 13.1). The limestone and dolomite mountains are a barrier to travel from the coast to the interior because there are no natural passes. Sinkholes and caverns lace the limestone plateaus. Deep ravines, gorges, and valleys cut through the mountains, making movement and communication difficult under the best circumstances and virtually impossible during wartime, as many invaders have experienced. The region is sparsely populated and forestry and mining are the chief economic activities. Extensive forests cover much of Bosnia, with the exception of high and arid plateaus in the west and southwest, adding immensely to the difficulty of cross-country movement and remoteness of most places in Bosnia.

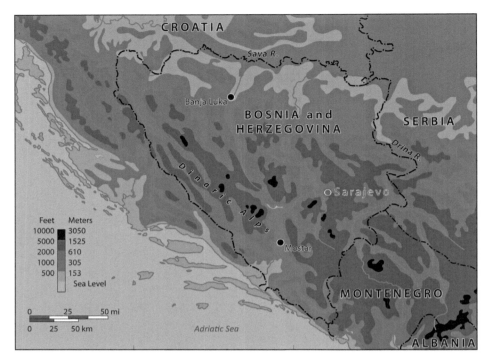

Figure 13.1
Map of Bosnia and Herzegovina.

Only along Bosnia's natural northern border with Croatia, the Sava River, does one find rolling fertile plains (see Figure 13.1). To the west, mountains form another natural boundary with Croatia and, to the east, the Drina is the historical boundary with Serbia. Both the Drina and Sava Rivers are formidable obstacles, crossed in very few places by substantial bridging. Although Bosnia possesses approximately five miles of coastline and the minor port of Neum along the Adriatic Sea, mountain barriers and lack of major roads from major cities and industries to the coast makes Bosnia and Herzegovina a virtually *landlocked state*.

The recent fighting in Bosnia was characterized by the combatants seizing and holding key terrain such as hilltops, ridgelines, and river valleys. Major road and rail networks follow river valleys. Bosnia's physical setting, when coupled with history, determined the settlement patterns and cultural development. Moreover, it inhibited the ability of rulers and invaders to assert control of Bosnia outside of urban areas.

Overwhelmed by the relics of history

Bosnia's earliest existence can be traced to the eleventh century. Prior to the Ottoman arrival and after the *Eastern Schism* of 1054, Bosnia was situated between the domains of the Western Latin Christian Church and the Eastern Byzantine Christian Church (White 2000). The Eastern Schism created two dominant churches: Catholicism centered in Rome and Eastern Orthodoxy centered in Constantinople. The ecclesiastic boundary cut across the Balkans. Once the Ottomans firmly established their presence in the fifteenth century, Islam spread across southeastern Europe. The Balkans became a frontier between the Habsburg and Ottoman Empires for several centuries until Islam was driven out during the 1912–13 Balkan Wars.

According to Fine (2002), the appearance of Muslims in Bosnia came from two sources: the first, from Muslim migrants traveling with the Sultan's armies and, the second, by far the largest component, from Christian converts. There was no wholesale conversion, but a gradual process in which converts came from all the Christian churches (Fine 2002; Malcolm 1994). The Christian *millets*, into which all Christian subjects of the Sultan fell, were second-class citizens while the Islamic *millet* had the most favored status (Fine 2002; Stavrianos 2000). Muslims controlled land through a feudal system, and many Bosnian Muslims were able to rise high in Turkish society and assume posts of importance within the Ottoman Empire (Pavlovich 1988). Bosnian and Ottoman Muslim elites developed in the towns and cities from which the Ottomans ruled Bosnia. The peasants, termed *rayah* (Turkish for cattle), worked the Muslim feudal estates, and were overwhelmingly drawn from the Christian *millet*.

Although frequently asserted by the media that Bosnia was a model of inter-ethnic tolerance and harmony, Christians were second-class citizens in the Ottoman Empire. Christians were oppressed; the record exists in the large-scale uprisings of the Serbs in the 1590s, 1640s, 1650s, and 1690s (Pavlovich 1988). As the Empire declined and became known as the "sick man of Europe," historical evidence indicates that Ottoman corruption, misrule, and oppression against the Christian *millet* was cruel, indifferent, and harsh (Gerolymatos 2002; Jelavich 1983; Pavlovich 1988; Stavrianos 1965). This legacy of Ottoman rule would cause immense suffering for the Bosnian Muslim population during the 1992–5 civil war, being used as grounds for avenging past grievances by Yugoslavia's Catholic and Orthodox communities.

The idea of an *ethnicity* came to Bosnia in the nineteenth century. Bosnian Christians began acquiring ethnic and national ideas from their co-brethren in neighboring Serbia and Croatia. Fine (2002) claims that this is the first time Serbs, as Orthodox Christians, and Croats, as Catholics, come to be known as separate nations within Bosnia. Until then, Fine (2002) writes that there was no internal ethnic or religious warfare, although the Muslims dominated Bosnia entirely.

The 1878 Treaty of Berlin allowed the Austro-Hungarian Empire to occupy and administer Bosnia, although it ostensibly remained part of the Ottoman Empire. This occurred with much consternation on the part of Bosnia's three religious groups. The Austrians imported a secular school system that found the Muslims worried that they would be compelled to convert to Catholicism—the religion of the Habsburg

Empire. The normally "loose fit" or more liberally practiced Islam was now seen as a quandary by educated Muslims. The Muslim elite involved themselves in affairs of the villages in an attempt to stave off threats to their religion. This resulted in rising tensions, where none existed before, between sophisticated elites of the urban centers and Muslims in rural regions, highlighting an *urban–rural divide* within the Muslim community. This moderate Islamic resurgence also strained the relations with Bosnia's Christian population, which had always viewed the Muslims skeptically.

During the late nineteenth century, the Habsburg Minister Benjamin von Kallay, Bosnia's administrator, attempted to weaken the predatory ideologies of Croat and Serb nationalism by advocating that all communities embrace the notion of *bošnjastvo*, or Bosniakdom (Malcolm 1994). This was an endeavor to supplant the growing disparate nationalisms by reviving the common notion of a Bosnianess, or *bošnjak,* which was inclusive of all (Magaš 2003). It was a complete failure among Bosnia's Christian population but did lay the seeds of a Bošniak identity among the Muslim elites (Glenny 1999).

Bosnia would be annexed by Austria in 1908, and remain under Habsburg control until the end of World War I. Sarajevo, Bosnia's largest town, served as the administrative center and capital of Austria's new province. It was a period in which Catholics received a favored position and Muslims would also be in the Emperor's grace. Orthodox Serbs, the vast majority of whom lived in the rural areas, remained second-class citizens. The 1914 assassination of Archduke Franz Ferdinand and his wife, by the Serb nationalist Gavrilo Princip, would lead to World War I and to widespread executions and massacres of Bosnia's Serb population.

The hatreds develop, 1918–45

The post-World War I Kingdom of Serbs, Croats, and Slovenes was in essence a Greater Serbia. Serbia had been a loyal ally to the British, French, and Americans, and suffered horrendously during the three years of Central Power occupation. The Serbian Karageorgević royal dynasty became the monarchy of the newly founded Kingdom, to be renamed the Kingdom of Yugoslavia in 1929, which would rule in some form until 1941. The most vociferous opponent to Belgrade was the Croatian population, and Hitler would play upon these animosities once World War II erupted.

German, Italian, Hungarian, and Bulgarian forces quickly overran Yugoslavia in April 1941. Shortly thereafter, Croatia was established as an independent fascist state with new boundaries incorporating most of Bosnia and a portion of Serbia (see Figure 13.2). As Bosnia only had a 20 percent Croat population, the new Croatian fascist or *Ustaše* leadership actively sought Muslim support in its plan to eradicate Serbs, Jews, and *Roma*. On 22 July 1941 Milan Budak, the Croatian Minister of Education, elucidated the state's plan for the Serbs when he announced that a third would be killed, a third converted, and a third expelled (Trifković 1998). The *Ustaše* campaign of terror provoked a Serb nationalist response, resulting in a vicious guerilla campaign against the Axis invaders, but also against the *Ustaše* and hapless Croat and Muslim civilians and villages. By the end of the war, it is estimated that between 350,000 and 700,000 Serbs were exterminated and 200,000–300,000 were converted to Catholicism (Ivanović 2002; Jelavich 1983). It is at this time that the ethnic element of World War II Bosnia assumed a religious dimension, creating intractable hatreds that linger to this day.

Bosnia became a scene of bizarre horrors as massacre and revenge massacres took place between the various national groups. The Yugoslav government-in-exile Royalist Movement, or *"Četniks"* under the leadership of General Draža Mihailović, a former Yugoslav officer, fought not only the *Ustaše* and Germans, but also the growing communist *Partisans*. Thus, a civil war within a world war was being waged in the former Yugoslavia.

Josip Broz Tito, the leader of the Communist Partisans, rose above the ethnic strife to serve as a *centripetal force* uniting all Yugoslav peoples against a common enemy (West 1942; Pavlovich 1992). He called the

Figure 13.2
Map of the Independent State of Croatia 1941–5. *Source*: Malcolm (1994).

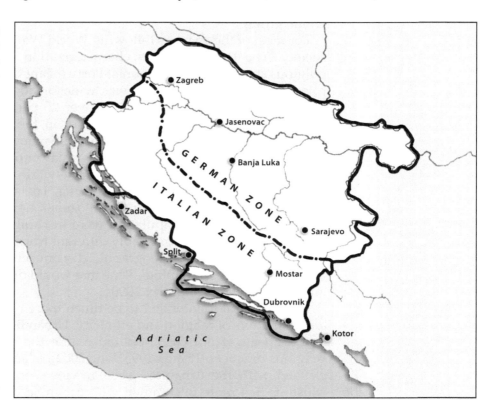

205

Yugoslavs together under the slogan of *"bratsvo i jedinstvo"* (brotherhood and unity). His Partisan cause included all ethnic groups in Yugoslavia, but it was the Serbs that were greatest in numbers. During the course of the war, Tito succeeded in leading Yugoslavia to liberation; however, the living memory of the nightmares experienced during World War II Yugoslavia would be rekindled with nationalism's rise in the 1980s.

Post-World War II communist Yugoslavia, 1945–91

In 1945, communist Yugoslavia consisted of six republics, each based on a dominant ethnic group. The only exception was Bosnia, which included Serb, Muslim, and Croat nationalities. Tito recognized that nationalism posed a constant threat to the new state and that strong adherence to one's religion correlated to a strong tie to one's national community, which could lead to separatist nationalism (Bringa 2002). Yugoslavia progressed well as a country, but a policy of decentralization over the years left increasing power in the hands of the Yugoslav republics. By 1968, Muslims, after realizing that they did not fit in as "Muslim Croats" or "Muslim Serbs," became an officially recognized *nation* in Yugoslavia. Their label, "Muslim" (*Musliman*), possessed a double meaning. Similar to the Jewish community, the new, officially declared Muslim was a member of a religious community and also an ethnic group.

For most of the 45 years following World War II, Bosnia was a secular society. The loose religious characterization coupled with an anti-religious stance of the Communist Party meant that religion played little role in Bosnia. Intermarriage was widespread, roughly 40 percent of urban marriages were mixed, and over 20 percent of urban Bosnians declared themselves Yugoslav or other in the years before civil war (Fine 2002). The 1991 census notes that of Sarajevo's 525,980 inhabitants, 16 percent identified themselves as Yugoslav or other. A certain harmony existed between ethnic groups, primarily within urban settings. Bosnia's five largest towns—Sarajevo, Banja Luka, Tuzla, Zenica, and Mostar—accounted for barely one-quarter of Bosnia's 4.4 million citizens in 1992. Three-quarters of the population were in rural or small-town settings where attitudes were remarkably different from those in the cities (Bose 2002). This points to a geographic disconnection in the identities of urban and rural communities—one that would dramatically affect Bosnia and Yugoslavia in the early 1990s.

Bosnian rural folk tended to be much more conservative in behavior and in matters of religion and ethnicity. Urban Bosnians saw themselves as European, if not cosmopolitan, while the villagers kept up their religious practices (Bringa 1995; Fine 2002). Islamic values and practices clashed with the urbanites' secular views on life. Moreover, urban Muslims had more in common with urban Serbs or Croats as opposed to the Muslim villager. In many, if not most, cases entire villages were made up of single ethnic communities. This important geographic disparity meant that the true secularism of the urban centers simply did not exist in the smaller towns and villages.

As Croatia and Slovenia seceded in 1991, Yugoslavia descended into chaos and ethnic tensions in Bosnia mounted. Serbia and Croatia, through their state-controlled media and propaganda, sought to sway their ethnic brethren in Bosnia to their side. During the 1990 Bosnian republic elections, three nationalist parties won. These were the Bosnian Muslim *Stranka Demokratska Akcija* (Muslim Party of Democratic Action or SDA), the Croat *Hrvatska Demokratska Zajednica* (Croatian Democratic Community or HDZ) and the Serb *Srpska Demokratska Stranka* (Serbian Democratic Party or SDS). According to some authors it was only the SDA, the Muslim Party of Alija Izetbegović, which called out to other groups to join their political party in the early days of the secession. The reasoning is simple: Izetbegović realized that the Muslims would not survive without the Serbs or the Croats as they were trapped between the stronger Croatia and what remained of Yugoslavia.

Moreover, Izetbegović always manifested Islamist tendencies, writing in his 1969 book *Izlamska Deklaracija* (The Islamic Declaration) that a modern, technological state could exist while keeping Islamic values. Indeed, in 1984 Izetbegović was tried and convicted with fellow co-conspirators of belonging to the Muslim nationalist political activists. Croat and Serb leaders stoked fears that an Islamic state was the goal of Izetbegović and his SDA. In 1991 and leading up to the independence referendum of 1992, an atmosphere was created that guaranteed Bosnian Serbs would not agree to Bosnian Muslim moves towards independence.

During the April 1992 referendum on Bosnian independence, the Muslims and Croats voted to secede from Yugoslavia whereas Serbs chose to boycott the referendum altogether. It is commonly misunderstood that Yugoslavia's Constitution permitted republics the right to secede—which it did—but only if the majority of each of a republic's constituent people voted for secession. This was not the case in Bosnia or Croatia, in which the Serb populations vehemently protested secession. Bosnian Serbs immediately began their rebellion with the support of the Yugoslav People's Army (JNA), which by now was primarily officered by Serbs.

Civil war comes to Bosnia

Beginning of the end

Ethnic fragmentation in Bosnia was well underway before the April 1992 referendum, and wars in Slovenia and Croatia polarized Bosnia's inhabitants. Bosnian Croats made no secret of their desire to affiliate with an independent Croatia, and the Serbs defiantly maintained their position of remaining in Yugoslavia. Izetbegović, the Bošniak President of the newly declared independent Bosnia, did not want the Bosnian Muslims left in a rump landlocked state between Croatia and Serbia (Nation 2003). Given the demographic reality of a higher Bosnian Muslim birth rate, Nation (2003) asserts that the Izetbegović administration aimed to hold together a unitary state in which the Bošniaks would eventually dominate.

During the early stages of the war, although clearly possessing an ethnic and religious component, military and police forces in the capital city of Sarajevo were multi-ethnic. A third of the defenders were Serb (Fine 2002; Nation 2003). However, given atrocities in the rural areas, the siege of Sarajevo, and the latent ethno-religious antagonisms, the fear of an Islamic component in Bosnia became a self-fulfilling prophecy. By the fall of 1993 Muslim nationalism had moved closer in character to the virulent Serb and Croatian versions. Muslim leadership, confronted with the efforts of international leaders to promote ethnic partition as part of the solution, began to embrace the notion of a Muslim *nation state* as a goal.

Moreover, with the various sanctions and weapons embargoes in place on former Yugoslav republics, the Bošniaks turned to their co-religionists in southwest Asia and the Middle East for *matériel*, financial, and moral support. The notion of a multi-ethnic Bosnia was quickly lost during the early fighting: it became an "us versus them" scenario within which religion and ethnicity became the key component. This was exacerbated by the Western media's trumpeting of atrocities and claims of genocide. Foreign Muslim fighters, or *mujahedeen*, were invited by Izetbegović to help the battered Bosnian Muslim army, forever changing the character of the war and Bosnian Muslims (Shrader 2003). Anywhere from 600 to 3000 foreign fighters were in Bosnian Muslim forces by the end of 1995, bringing their radical Islamic fanaticism with them (Oluić 2008).

The influx of rural Muslim refugees changed the character and political atmosphere of most Muslim towns and cities, especially Sarajevo. As the Muslim refugee population grew, it did so with an increasing rural constituency. Given their treatment at the hands of the Serbs and Croats, these Muslim refugees readily adopted an intolerant stance towards Bosnia's non-Muslims. Tensions developed between secular Sarajevans and these new refugees, and the character of Sarajevo was forever altered. Public offices, governmental administrations, and the army, once multi-ethnic, were now permeated with Islamic symbolism and beliefs.

Popular misperceptions portray the nature of the Bosnian civil war involving large numbers of insurgents operating in the mountains as part of a protracted guerilla war. The Bosnian War, however, involved conventional, positional warfare, more akin to World War I than Tito's Partisan struggles during World War II. Trench and bunker lines, fronted by extensive minefields, faced each other throughout Bosnia, across a no man's land that would have appeared familiar to soldiers of the 1914–18 war. Until late 1995, most combat operations were attempts to gain control of key roads, hills, and villages a few kilometers or meters from the front line, not rapid strikes deep into enemy territory (CIA 2002).

Muslim–Croat Fracture

The Muslim–Croat Federation was nominally a coalition against a militarily more powerful Serb force. However, by the summer of 1992 the Croats made clear their intent to create their own state of *Herceg-Bosna*, centered on Mostar. On 3 July 1992 the Croats seceded, declaring Herceg-Bosna a sovereign state. In fact the Bosnian Croat's military, the *Hrvatsko Vjece Odbrane* (Croatian Defense Council or HVO), was directly controlled by the Croatian Army (Nation 2003). Friction between these erstwhile allies was present since the war's beginning.

The complete breakdown of the Croat–Muslim alliance occurred in early 1993. Tensions between the two in the equity of weapon and supply distribution, disposition of forces, command and control between Croat and Muslim commanders for example, had been endemic early on. There were incidences of localized fighting between the two in late 1992 in central Bosnia (Nation 2003). By April 1993, the two allies became enemies as open fighting in Gornji Vakuf, Zenica, the Lašva Valley and in Mostar itself began in earnest (Nation 2003; Sells 2003; Shrader 2003). This infighting led to brutal massacres of Muslims in Ahmići (16 April 2004) and Stupni Do (October 1993) by the HVO. The Croat siege of the Muslim-controlled part of Mostar was in every way as horrendous as the Serb siege of Sarajevo; however, the siege never attracted the same level of international attention as did Sarajevo.

Given the Muslims' numerical superiority, military action in terrain favoring infantry operations would increasingly favor the Army of Bosnia and Herzegovina (ABH) as long as it could stave off defeat. By September 1993, the Croats were checked on the battlefield and the Muslims began to turn back HVO gains. Without any direct intervention by forces from Croatia, the HVO found itself in a standoff with the ABH. A truce in February 1994 brought an end to the "war within a war."

The outbreak of fighting between Croat and Muslim allies, and the internal war among the Muslims in the northwestern Bihać pocket, reveal a sequence of shifting alliances at regional levels (Nation 2003; Burg and Shoup 2000). On many occasions the Serbs would support Croat military efforts against the Muslims. There were numerous times during the civil war that it degenerated into a series of confused struggles for local control, alliances of convenience, and with no sense of a larger strategic purpose being present (Nation 2003).

As fighting erupted in Bosnia, Yugoslav military units were still withdrawing from Croatia into Bosnia under a UN-brokered ceasefire. These forces, in addition to those already stationed in Bosnia along with

JNA forces from Serbia proper, took part in this fight. Having inherited much of the JNA's arsenal before it left Bosnia, the *Vojska Republike Srpske* (Bosnian Serb Army or VRS) gained control of most of Bosnia by mid-1993 (see Figure 13.3). The Serbs made up for their lack of infantry with armor and artillery.

There were several efforts by the international community to end the war. The Lisbon Cutilheiro Plan, which fell apart in March 1992, the Vance–Owen Plan rejected by the Serbs in May 1993, and the Owen–Stoltenberg Plan rejected by the Muslims in September 1993 are the best known. Over eighty UN resolutions were passed on the former Yugoslavia, and indeed the only major action by the international community was to deploy UN Protection Forces (UNPROFOR), which grew from 1500 troops in 1992 to over 23,000 by 1995 (Nation 2003). Sanctions were in place on all of the warring parties in the former Yugoslavia, but, since the Serbs and Croats had the preponderance of war *matériel*, only the Muslims and the ABH suffered under them.

Given the public outcry over only Serb-perpetrated atrocities and ethnic cleansing, US policy in the region shifted towards assisting the

Figure 13.3
Map of approximate areas of control, May–June 1993. *Source*: Burg and Shoup (2000).

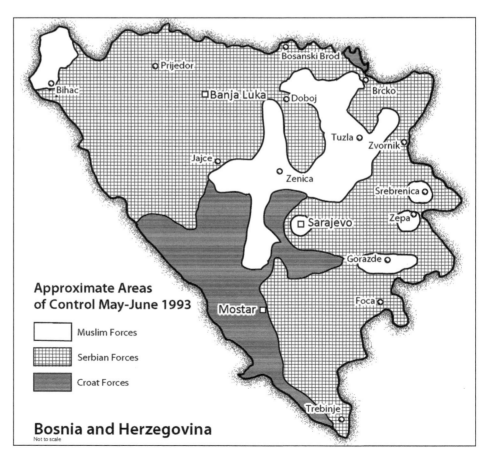

Approximate Areas
of Control May-June 1993

☐ Muslim Forces

▦ Serbian Forces

▨ Croat Forces

Bosnia and Herzegovina
Not to scale

Muslims. It must be noted that the media focus and sensationalism given Serb misdeeds were all but absent when atrocities were perpetrated by Croat and Muslim forces against the Serbs (Burg and Shoup 2000). In mid-May 1993, the Vance–Owen Plan's rejection was due in no small part to the Clinton Administration's proposed policy dubbed "Lift and Strike," i.e. lift the arms embargo against the Muslims and conduct selective NATO air strikes against the Serbs. Neither the Bush nor Clinton administrations were convinced of US vital interests in the region, and were indecisive in their resolve until 1994.

By June 1993, six UN safe havens were established in Bosnia: Sarajevo, Goražde, Srebrenica, Tuzla, Žepa, and Bihać. However, safe haven was a euphemism as enclaves that were encircled by the VRS, were used on many occasions to launch Muslim attacks against the Serbs as they were never demilitarized by the UN (Nation 2003; Burg and Shoup 2000). It is estimated that more than 3000 Serb civilians and soldiers were killed by Bošniaks operating from Srebrenica (Rohde 1997; CIA 2002).

The continuing humanitarian catastrophe and graphic imagery televised around the world led to greater Western initiatives to halt the fighting. The February 1994 *Markale* Market massacre in Sarajevo, in which 65 people were killed and over 200 wounded, allegedly by a Serb shell, helped to galvanize the West's resolve to end the conflict. NATO set an ultimatum for the Serb forces to withdraw all heavy weaponry from a 20 km "total exclusion zone" around Sarajevo (Nation 2003).

Serb encroachments on UN safe havens, such as Goražde, violation of UN imposed "no-fly zones," and incidents with UNPROFOR led to military action by NATO against the Serbs. The US became more involved in Bosnia as the US–NATO relationship, upcoming mid-term elections, reputation in the Muslim world, and America's stature as a global leader were questioned (Nation 2003).

Western intervention

Throughout 1994, a more assertive, US-dominated approach slowly affected events on the ground. The West hoped that accommodation could progress towards a negotiated peace and would be achieved by coupling diplomacy with military action. The year-long fighting between Croats and Muslims was ended by their Washington Agreement, settled in Petersberg, Germany. It allowed the SDA and HDZ to put aside their differences in order to concentrate on a common foe—the Bosnian Serb Army. However, the agreement did not give rise to common institutions or any meaningful commitment to co-habitation (Nation 2003).

Building on limited successes achieved under the agreement in forming the Federation of Croats and Muslims, efforts were made to reinvigorate international efforts with the establishment of the Contact Group in April 1994. This international body, composed of the US, the UK, France, Germany, and Russia, was used as a forum to collaborate and pursue peace initiatives. In reality, due to increasing US action, the

US wound up taking the international lead through the Contact Group (Nation 2003; Burg and Shoup 2000).

By the end of 1994 and into 1995 the ABH, to the dismay of its Croat members, were penetrated by Islamic extremists. As the war dragged on, and atrocities mounted, the influx of new fighters from the devastated Muslim regions coupled with foreign fighters led to the introduction of Islamic symbols and Koranic quotations in army units.

The Contact Group formulated a framework for a 51/49 percent territorial division between the Muslim–Croat Federation and the Serbs. Offered to the two sides in July 1994, it was eventually rejected by the Serbs, apparently not willing to surrender its territorial gains. The relationship between UNPROFOR, with its peacekeeping troops on the ground in Bosnia, and NATO, which favored direct military action via air strikes, grew tense.

The end of Bosnian Serb military dominance

As 1995 dawned, an eerie status quo existed in Bosnia. The Serbs held their gains, and the HVO and ABH were only capable of mounting local offensives (see Figure 13.4). The only force capable of engaging the Bosnian Serb Army was the US-trained and German-equipped Croatian Army (Nation 2003; Burg and Shoup 2000). The HVO would reassert control of western Croatia in spite of UNPROFOR's presence, driving tens of thousands of Serbs into Serb-held Bosnia and Serbia.

Antagonism between the Bosnian Serbs and the UN and NATO was exacerbated by the events around the UN safe havens of Srebrenica and Žepa in July of 1995. The Serbs overran the two towns in a matter of hours, pushing aside Dutch peacekeepers in Srebrenica and massacring thousands of male Muslim prisoners from both towns (Nation 2003; CIA 2002; Burg and Shoup 2000). Although provoked, as the safe havens were never demilitarized and were used as bases from which to launch attacks against the Serb villages, the massacre was unique due to the scale of horror perpetrated and the level of planning required to execute the operation. Indeed, *ethnic cleansing*, commonly associated with wars in the former Yugoslavia, was apparent in Srebrenica. Securing contested areas for one's own ethnic faction resulted in the destruction of the enemy's homes, churches or mosques, cemeteries and national structures—the removing of the historical footprint of the other ethnic group's presence. This phenomenon was practiced by all sides, and, by late summer 1993, the former Yugoslavia had over 4 million refugees and displaced persons (Nation 2003). Ethnic cleansing was a military operation with the goal of clearing territory of all the traces of its former inhabitants.

In July and August 1995, the Croatian Army would prepare and launch Operation Storm (*Oluja*) to regain control of the Serb *Krajina* region in Croatia. With tacit US approval and covert air support, the Serbs were

pushed out in a matter of days, again flooding Bosnia and Serbia with

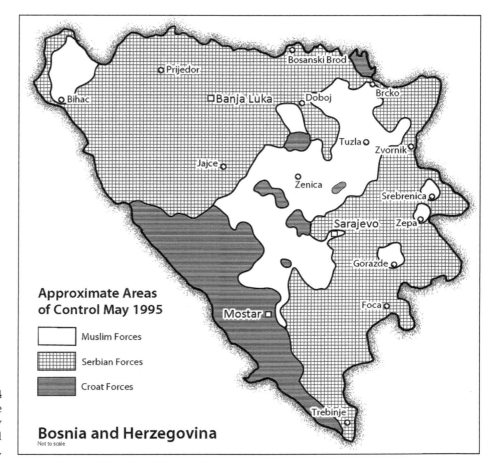

Figure 13.4
Map of approximate areas of control in May 1995. *Source*: Burg and Shoup (2000).

tens of thousands of refugees. This resulted in the largest ethnic cleansing of the Yugoslav wars, with upwards of 250,000 people becoming refugees (Nation 2003; Burg and Shoup 2000; Glenny 1996). The Bosnian Serb Army was unable to assist the Krajina Serbs as it was heavily engaged with Bosnian Croat and Muslim offensives that were launched in co-ordination with Operation Storm.

By the end of the offensive, the Serbs had lost significant territory. In addition to this disaster, another shelling incident in Sarajevo on 30 August gave NATO the pretext to conduct extensive air operations against the Serbs. The air raids were substantial and intended to break the siege of Sarajevo (Nation 2003). This resulted in accelerated Muslim–Croat advances and, with the increasing loss of Serb-held territory, the Contact Group's 51/49 percent territorial division was becoming a reality (see Figure 13.5). There was a real fear that the HVO and Federation forces would conquer even more Serb territory and, in order to halt these advances, the UN and NATO feigned military action to get them to heel (Silber and Little 1997; CIA 2002).

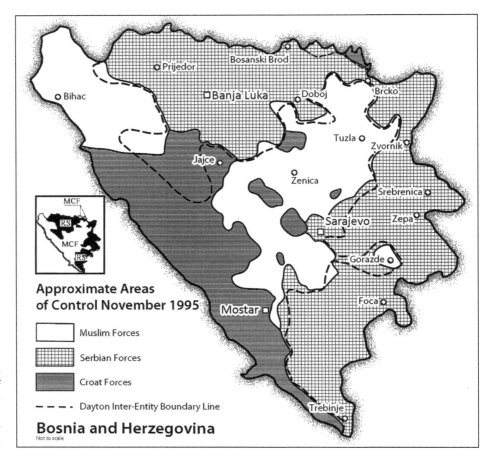

Figure 13.5
November 1995 areas of
control and the Inter-
Entity Boundary Line.
Source: Burg and Shoup
(2000).

Although the Bosnian Serb Army was not knocked out of the war, it could not engage Croatian and Bosnian Croat and Muslim forces along its entire front and roll back their territorial gains. The military balance of power dramatically changed to the detriment of the Serbs. Through diplomacy led by the US's Richard Holbrooke, a ceasefire was declared on 5 October 1995. The battlefield gains of the Croat–Muslim alliance would set the stage for peace negotiations and the resultant Dayton Peace Accords' territorial division of Bosnia into the *Republika Srpska* dominated by Serbs and the *Federacija* led by the Muslim–Croat allies.

Conclusion

The 1995 Dayton Peace Accords ended the fighting and established the new Bosnia and Herzegovina as a two-entity state. *Republika Srpska* and the Federation were separated by a 1400 km-long Inter-Entity Boundary Line, or IEBL, which in essence created two sub-state territories. The Serbs look to Banja Luka as their capital and oversee an entity now predominantly inhabited by Serbs. The Federation is further divided into cantons, these being dominated by either a *Bošniak* or Croat majority, with Sarajevo as the capital of not only the Federation but of Bosnia also. Mostar has become the *de facto* capital of the Federation's Croats.

The Dayton Peace Accords did not solve the historical grievances and the legacy of the civil war created even more—*rapprochement* is unachievable. It also established a weak state in which the real political power was vested in the entities, and control of the state vested in the Office of the High Representative (OHR) having veto authority over Bosnian legislation, hire-and-fire authority of public servants, and the ability to institute draconian measures to compel compliance of Bosnia's ethnic groups. Although NATO forces no longer perform peacekeeping operations, that role has been assumed by a small European Union police presence.

The cultural and physical geographic factors that provided the basis for Bosnia's bloody civil war are still present. The historical grievances, religious differences, neighbors with *irredentist* tendencies, and nationalist politics and rhetoric are still prevalent in public life. In fifteen years since the end of fighting, the very centripetal forces present before the war are present today and may instigate further conflict in the region.

References cited

Bose, S. 2002. *Bosnia after Dayton: nationalist partition and international intervention*. New York, NY: Oxford University Press.
Bringa, T. 1995. *Being Muslim the Bosnian way*. Princeton, NJ: Princeton University Press.
——. 2002. "Islam and the quest for identity in post-Communist Bosnia and Herzegovina." In *Islam and Bosnia: conflict resolution and foreign policy in multi-ethnic states*, Maya Shatzmiller (ed.), 24–34. Montreal: McGill-Queen's University Press.
Burg, S. & P. Shoup. 2000. *The War in Bosnia and Herzegovina: ethnic conflict and international intervention*. Armonk, NY: M. E. Sharpe.
Central Intelligence Agency (CIA). 2002. *Balkan battlegrounds: a military history of the Yugoslav conflict, 1990–1995 Volumes I & II*. Washington, DC: US Government Printing Office.
Fine, J. 2002. "The various faiths in the history of Bosnia: Middle Ages to the present." In *Islam and Bosnia: conflict resolution and foreign policy in multi-ethnic states*, Maya Shatzmiller (ed.). Montreal, Canada: McGill-Queen's University Press.
Gerolymatos, A. 2002. *The Balkan Wars*. New York, NY: Basic Books.
Glenny, Misha. 1996. *The fall of Yugoslavia: the Third Balkan War*. 3rd edn. New York: Penguin.
——. 1999. *The Balkans: nationalism, war and the Great Powers, 1804–1999*. New York, NY: Viking Press.
Ivanovic, I. 2002. *Witness to Jasenovac's hell*. Mt Pleasant, TX: Dallas Publishing Company.
Jelavich, B. 1983. *History of the Balkans: twentieth century*. New York, NY: Cambridge University Press.
Magaš, B. 2003. "On Bosnianness." *Nations and Nationalism* 9(1): 9–23.
Malcolm, N. 1994. *Bosnia: a short history*. London, UK: Macmillan.
Nation, C. 2003. *War in the Balkans, 1991–2002*. Carlisle, PA: US Army War College, Strategic Studies Institute.
Oluić, S. 2008. "Radical Islam on Europe's frontier: Bosnia & Herzegovina." *National Security and the Future* 1–2(9): 35–52.

Pavlovich, P. 1988. *The Serbians: the story of a people.* Ontario, Canada: Serbian Heritage Books.

Rohde, D. 1997. *End game: the betrayal and fall of Srebrenica, Europe's worst massacre since World War II.* Boulder, CO: Westview Press.

Sells, M. 2003. "Crosses of blood: sacred space, religion, and violence in Bosnia-Hercegovina." *Sociology of Religion* 64(3): 309–31.

Shrader, C. 2003. *The Muslim Croat civil war in central Bosnia: a military history, 1992–1994.* College Station, TX: Texas A&M University Press.

Silber, L. & A. Little. 1997. *Yugoslavia: death of a nation.* New York, NY: Penguin Books.

Stavrianos, L. S. 2000. *The Balkans since 1453.* New York, NY: New York University Press.

Trifković, S. 1998. *Ustaša: Croatian separatism and European politics, 1929–1945.* Aiken, SC: The Lord Byron Foundation for Balkan Studies.

West, R. 1995. *Tito and the rise and fall of Yugoslavia.* New York, NY: Carroll & Graf Publishers.

West, Rebecca. 1942. *Black lamb and grey falcon: a journey through Yugoslavia.* London: Macmillan.

White, G. 2000. *Nationalism and territory: constructing group identity in southeastern Europe.* Lanham, MA: Rowman & Littlefield, Inc.

Chapter fourteen
Afghanistan
Operation Enduring Freedom and military geographic challenges

EUGENE J. PALKA

Introduction

MILITARY GEOGRAPHY INVOLVES the application of geographic information, tools, and techniques to solve military problems across a spectrum from peace to war. Each operational scenario, regardless of where it occurs along this spectrum, presents a unique range of problems. Shortly after the September 11, 2001 terrorist attacks on the United States, the US Military embarked on *Operation Enduring Freedom (OEF)*, with the intentions of destroying Osama bin Laden's network of terrorist training camps, disassembling *al-Qaeda*'s infrastructure, and unseating the *Taliban* government. The operation was oriented on Afghanistan, a war-torn country located more than 11,000 kilometers away from New York's Twin Towers. What began as a high-intensity military operation within a wartime context, appeared to transition to a *stability and support operation (SASO)* within two years, and, shortly thereafter, the US Military and other coalition partners begin to undertake a number of peacetime missions within Afghanistan. Unfortunately, conditions have deteriorated over the past couple of years and, currently, the US is involved in *full-spectrum operations*. During his Senate confirmation hearings in June 2009, General Stanley McChrystal, commander of NATO's International Security Assistance Force (ISAF) and US Forces–Afghanistan, explained that the current scenario stems from a resilient *Taliban* insurgency, increasing levels of violence, lack of governance capability, persistent corruption, lack of development in key areas, illicit narcotics, and malign influences from other countries (French 2009). The synergistic effect of these factors is an extremely challenging operating environment within which US and NATO forces must conduct a holistic *counterinsurgency* campaign (French 2009).

Afghanistan, like Iraq, provides a previously unprecedented case where military operations are being conducted across the entire spectrum and within a context where both the physical and human geography pose fundamental challenges to coalition forces. The country's continental location and contiguity to the Himalaya Mountains contribute to climatic diversity and an assortment of severe meteorological events, while its location relative to plate boundaries results in intense seismic activity and extremely rugged physiography. Meanwhile, the country's history of conflict, ethnolinguistic diversity, political instability, poverty, and permeable borders produce a complex and dynamic cultural scenario.

This chapter examines the impact of Afghanistan's geography on military operations. I explain the challenges that stem from the country's location and discuss the potential effects of the natural environment on efforts to combat terrorism, stabilize the country, and provide humanitarian assistance. While the chapter focuses primarily on the difficulties posed by the natural environment, I briefly introduce the complex human geography, which in the long term presents even greater impediments to stability and economic development.

The impact of location

The geographic center of Afghanistan lies at approximately 33° North latitude and 65° East longitude. To a soldier deploying from Fort Bragg, North Carolina, to Bagram, Afghanistan, a change in absolute location translates to a distance of about 11,500 kilometers, or about thirteen hours of travel time by air and a difference of nine and a half time zones.

Afghanistan is a landlocked Central Asian country that is bordered by Turkmenistan, Uzbekistan, and Tajikistan to the north, China to the east, Pakistan to the east and south, and Iran to the west (see Figure 14.1). The country is only slightly smaller in size than the state of Texas, but finds itself at the crossroads of Western Asia.

Afghanistan's location has had a direct impact on military operations during Operation Enduring Freedom. First, the country is located half way around the world relative to the US, making it expensive, time consuming, and challenging to transport soldiers and equipment. Second, the country's *landlocked* location within Central Asia makes it inaccessible other than by air. These two conditions have placed a significant drain on air resources. Third, Afghanistan is surrounded by countries that have not had any long-term political or military relationships with the US. Consequently, the use of airspace and support bases was almost unprecedented and required extensive negotiations at the outset of the campaign. Since 2001, political maneuvering, infrastructure upgrades, and inflated financial compensation have been necessary to sustain the use of key bases like Manas Air Base in Kyrgyzstan. The US has been less successful with Karshi-Kanabad (K2), a strategic airfield and logistics hub that had been leased from

Figure 14.1
Afghanistan in a Central
Asian context.

Uzbekistan from the outset of Operation Enduring Freedom until the host country ordered the US withdrawal in 2005. Thus, a continuing challenge for the US Military stems from Afghanistan's distant location, as well as its inaccessibility within the context of Central Asia.

The physical setting

Afghanistan's physical geography is diverse. Changes in elevation are extreme, and climate, soils, and vegetation vary considerably from place to place. Despite the popular perceptions about the inhospitable nature of its natural environment, cultures have been rooted in the space of this present-day country for several thousand years (Palka 2001). Comprehending the physical setting is a first step towards anticipating the impacts on military operations, as well as understanding the lifestyles of the inhabitants of the country.

Topography

Afghanistan's dynamic physical landscape is continually shaped by the forces of nature and dominated by mountainous terrain. The Hindu Kush Mountains form a barrier between the northern provinces and the remainder of the country. The range divides Afghanistan into three distinct geographic regions: the Central Highlands, the Northern Plains, and the Southwestern Plateau.

The Central Highlands comprise about 70 percent of the country's territory and consist primarily of the Hindu Kush Mountains, a rugged, snowbound highland often described as one of the most impenetrable regions in the world. The Hindu Kush Mountains form the western extremity of the Himalayas and extend for about 1000 kilometers in a southwesterly direction from the Vakhan Corridor in the northeast almost to the border with Iran in the west (see Figure 14.2). The Northern Plains comprise about 15 percent of the country and consist of foothills and plains through which the Amu Darya River flows. The average elevation is about 600 meters above sea level ("Land and Resources," Microsoft "Encarta" Online Encyclopedia 2001). The Southwestern Plateau region is made up of sandy deserts and high plateaus. Elevation

Figure 14.2
Afghanistan's relief featuring the rugged Hindu Kush mountains.

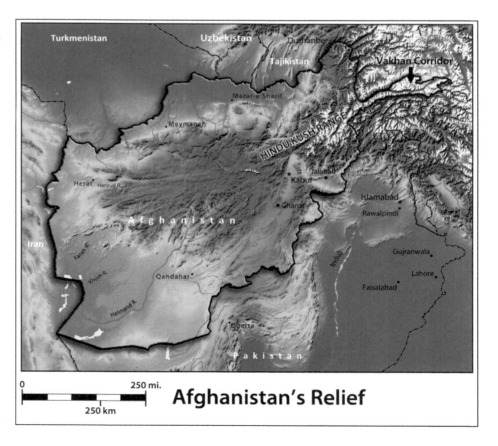

averages about 900 meters ("Land and Resources," Microsoft "Encarta" Online Encyclopedia 2001).

Afghanistan's topography has affected military operations in numerous ways. The rugged mountains and high elevations have posed significant challenges to troop movement, re-supply, communications, and equipment and weapons functionality. Few roads penetrate the Central Highlands, where most military activities have occurred during Operation Enduring Freedom, and those which do are extremely restrictive (see Figure 14.3). Soldiers are routinely positioned via helicopters since overland movement is slow and canalized, and often treacherous because of landmine hazards. At elevations in excess of 8000 feet, however, the Army's standard assault helicopters experience degraded lift capabilities. Consequently, Chinook helicopters (normally used for logistics re-supply) are routinely employed to transport and reposition soldiers. Communications are often degraded because some systems rely on "line of sight" relationships to be effective. Equipment of all kinds is occasionally inoperable because of extreme cold, ice, or snow, which occur at high elevations. Finally, the effects of certain weapons systems (like artillery howitzers) are negated because of the need to employ high-angle fire due to the steepness of the terrain. Repositioning artillery is equally troublesome over short or long distances based on the need to use helicopters to support the displacements.

Figure 14.3
A US-improved and paved road east of Kabul contrasts significantly with the rugged and austere landscape.
Source: Eugene J. Palka.

Caves

The Hindu Kush Mountains are largely comprised of granites and schist that were uplifted between 70 and 5 million years ago. Limestone, shale, and clays overlie these bedrock materials. The latter serve to create ideal conditions for caves. The Central Highlands constitutes an expansive area of cave formation, spreading out laterally to cover an areal extent of about two-thirds the size of Texas, while also boasting a significant vertical range of relief.

The US Geological Survey (USGS) estimates there are more than 10,000 caves in the eastern half of the country. Some underground networks traverse several miles and have dozens of branches. Most are still unexplored, despite the fact that they have provided shelter, if not residence, for some of the country's current and previous inhabitants for hundreds of years. Caves are naturally occurring, but many have been continually developed over time to suit the specific needs of goat herders, refugees, and even terrorists (Palka 2008).

Al-Qaeda and the *Taliban* once considered caves as safe havens. Caches of weapons, ammunitions, equipment, supplies, and even underground laboratories serve as testament to the utility and importance of the underground formations (Palka 2008). It has been challenging for US forces to locate caves and ascertain that the latter were being used for wartime or terrorist purposes. Once identified, it is still a complicated matter to target particular caves with the appropriate ordnance and delivery system, and employ soldiers within the complexes to conduct sensitive site exploitation (see Figure 14.4). Throughout Operation Anaconda and since, US forces have captured or destroyed enemy materials in caves and have rendered the complexes unusable when possible (Palka 2008). These activities, however, have been dangerous, time consuming, and extremely difficult to accomplish, given the ability of some caves to withstand conventional ordnance.

Soil

Afghanistan has a range of soils that correspond with its physiographic regions. The Northern Plains constitutes the most fertile region of the country, and comprises about 15 percent of the land area. The South-western Plateau region exhibits soil that is generally infertile, except along the rivers. The soils within the Central Highlands vary considerably with elevation. Valley floors are most fertile, while increasing elevations display rocky, thin soils consistent with highland undifferentiated climates.

Afghanistan's soil types and characteristics impact on military operations in a couple of fashions. First, regardless of particle size or composition, blowing sand and dust is a nuisance to soldiers and reduces visibility. Second, dust storms and associated "brown-out" conditions make flying conditions extremely hazardous for helicopters and

Figure 14.4
A soldier from the 82nd
Airborne Division
searches a cave in the
Baghni Valley of
Afghanistan while
participating in
Operation Enduring
Freedom.
Source: US Army photo
by SGT Vernell Hall.

complicate pick-ups and landings. Third, blowing sand has an abrasive effect on aircraft components, weapons systems, and communications equipment. Fourth, dust degrades optical capabilities of weapons systems and intelligence-gathering devices, and impedes target acquisition. Finally, dust clouds are generated during helicopter landings and take-offs, creating signatures that can be seen for many miles, which makes it difficult to maintain operational security.

Earthquakes

The northeast region of Afghanistan is one of the most seismically active areas in the world. This area is bisected by a transform boundary between the Eurasian and Indo-Australian plates. The two plates slide past one another, producing frequent seismic activity (Hudson and Espenshade 2000). Recent catastrophic earthquakes include one in Takhar province on 4 February 1998, about 50 kilometers from the border with Tajikistan. The earthquake (magnitude 6.1 on the Richter scale) affected twenty-eight villages, killed about 4000 people, and left another 20,000 without shelter ("Thousands reported killed in Afghanistan quake" 1998). Just three and a half months later, on 30 May, a magnitude 6.9 quake occurred along the boundary of Badakshan and Takhar provinces, again in the northeast. Approximately 4000 people

223

were killed, and as many as 70,000 people in seventy villages were affected ("Impact of the earthquake" 1998).

Shortly after the commencement of Operation Enduring Freedom, three major earthquakes occurred in the area north of Kabul. The first occurred on 3 March 2002, with the epicenter located less than 150 miles from Bagram, the command post and base of operations for coalition forces. More than 100 people were killed. Two additional quakes occurred on 25 and 26 March within only 50 miles of Bagram. One measured only 5.9 on the Richter scale, but the shallow nature of the quake produced extensive damage and an estimated 1800 dead.

In these mountainous areas, earthquakes typically trigger devastating landslides. Heavy rain that precedes quakes can exacerbate matters by prompting mudslides that can cause immense destruction and render roads impassable. Sun-baked mud dwellings perched on the mountainsides can be simply swept away. Landslides can also destroy water sources by collapsing wells and springs ("Impact of the earthquake" 1998). Each of these impacts occurred during the earthquakes of spring 2002. In the midst of Operation Anaconda, a massive relief effort launched by US forces helped to provide food, medical care, water, shelter, and building supplies to minimize some of the effects of the devastation. The humanitarian relief effort was a noble cause, but diverted critical resources from what was at that time America's longest ground war since Vietnam.

Climate

Afghanistan's climate exhibits subtropical to mid-latitude steppe in most areas and drier subtropical deserts in other places (see Figure 14.5). The country has hot summers and cool winters, although winters in the highlands are more extreme. Summertime high temperatures frequently exceed 38°C, particularly in the southwest, while wintertime lows can drop below −25°C (AFCCC 1995). High mountains influence local climates by decreasing temperatures at high altitudes and affecting precipitation regimes. The majority of precipitation occurs in winter and early spring, where conditions in areas such as Kabul are cloudy, foggy, and snowy.

The Hindu Kush Mountains play a dominant role in determining local climate. The increased precipitation due to orographic lifting and cooler temperatures results in unexpected climates for the region. Variability in altitude, slope aspect, and prevailing winds make the central highlands of Afghanistan difficult to characterize (Pannell 2004). As such, the latter are labeled as Undifferentiated Highlands (H). Extreme conditions are the norm and severe events such as heavy snowfall can render roads and trails impassable for weeks or months. It is common for the high passes to be closed from November through late March and snow pack is permanent for elevations above 3655 meters (AFCCC 1995).

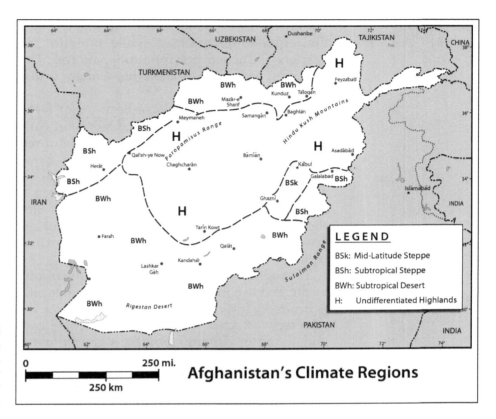

Figure 14.5
Regional climate patterns
based on station data.
Source: Data from *Air
Force Combat Climatology
Center*, OCDS, 1995.

The northern region around Mazar-I-Sharif is classified as a sub-tropical desert (BWh). The infrequent precipitation peaks in the early spring and is highly irregular, depending on the strength of the Siberian high (Pannell 2004). The region is surrounded by areas of variable rainfall that may be classified as subtropical steppes (BSh).

The southern region of the Rigestan is the country's largest expanse of desert. The area around Khandahar, Bust, and Farah is dominated by the subtropical high throughout the year and is extremely dry. The mountain ranges to the north protect it in winter from the effects of the northeast monsoon, resulting in dry conditions, although temperatures may fall below freezing. Summers are extremely hot with temperatures exceeding 45°C in July (AFCCC 1995).

Finally, in the eastern steppe areas around Kabul and Jalalabad, conditions are cooler and moister, particularly in winter. Both Jalalabad and Khowst experience subtropical steppe (BSh) climates. There is a climate gradient, however, as elevations increase to the west. Both Kabul and Ghazni are at considerably higher elevations and average monthly temperatures in winter are below freezing, resulting in mid-latitude steppes (BSk).

Climate controls such as altitude and *continentality* significantly affect the temperature regimes, while pressure systems and topographic barriers influence precipitation patterns. The result is a climate of extremes: hot summers and bitter winters, arid deserts and snow-packed highlands.

Climate and weather have been major factors affecting virtually all coalition plans and operations. Operation Anaconda (February–March 2002), for example, was postponed for three days because of poor weather conditions in the objective areas. Low ceilings, dense fog, and blowing snow or freezing rain, are common occurrences during winter months and often reduce visibility or even ground several types of aircraft. In spring and summer months, dust storms can routinely plague flight operations. Air Force airlift, tactical air, and reconnaissance planes are all ineffective during some periods of extreme weather, as are Army helicopters.

Throughout the country, logistics re-supply is conducted primarily by air, and to a limited degree by ground. In either case, logistics support is routinely interrupted by adverse weather. Ground movement can be adversely affected by heavy snow, which can close mountain passes, and flying or driving conditions can be unfavorable because of dust storms that may last for days.

High temperatures and wind also have adverse impacts on military operations. Both conditions serve to degrade the capabilities of *unmanned aerial vehicles (UAVs)*, which continue to be used extensively during combat operations.

Not to be forgotten are the problems associated with water. Water availability and quality is a persistent concern throughout the arid regions of Afghanistan and the rugged terrain and lack of adequate roads make transporting the critical resource to deficit areas even more problematic.

Vegetation

Two-thirds of Afghanistan is mountainous and supports little or no vegetation; one-sixth of the country is desert; and one-sixth of the land is pasture and farmland (Saba 2001; see Figure 14.6). Three percent of Afghanistan's land is forested and is concentrated in the eastern portion of the Central Highlands. The location of forested land coincides with the western edge of summer monsoon rains.

Most of the Central Highlands are classified as subtropical desert and mid-latitude grassland–steppe. Grasses and small, herbaceous forbs tend to be widely spaced. The vegetation may be more dense and continuous in sheltered sites, along waterways and other moist locations (Anderson 2004). In general, vegetation is sparse in highland deserts and steppe regions.

The Southwestern Plateau is a 50,000 square mile region of poor soils (with *Aridisols* being most common) and sparse vegetation. Many plants

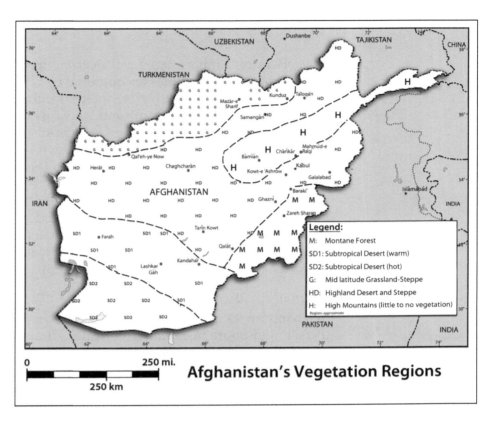

Figure 14.6
Vegetation patterns in
Afghanistan. *Source*:
Anderson (2004).

are xerophytes or ephemerals, but, in the hottest areas of the southwest, the landscape is barren.

The vegetation of the Northern Plains is classified as mid-latitude grassland–steppe. This 40,000 square mile region includes Afghanistan's most fertile soils and favorable climate (Saba 2001). Plants that are common include short grasses and herbaceous forbs on moist sites and bunch grasses and dry shrubs on drier sites (Anderson 2004).

Vegetation affords concealment for military personnel, equipment, weapons systems, and some activities. The sparse nature of the country's vegetative regimes means that adequate concealment is generally difficult to acquire. The result is enhanced observation and target acquisition capabilities, generally a good news story for US troops and bad news for *al-Qaeda* and *Taliban* forces. One particular problem concerns the location of Afghanistan's montane forest astride the boundary with Pakistan. In this particular area, the forest cover serves to enhance the permeability of the border by concealing trails and movement activities of *al-Qaeda* and *Taliban* forces between Afghanistan and Pakistan's Federally Administrative Tribal Areas and Waziristan.

The human environment

The effect of Afghanistan's physical environment addresses only a fraction of the complexities encountered by US and coalition forces (see Figure 14.7). Extreme poverty, internal cultural conflict, continuing political unrest, a war-torn cultural landscape, and the complete lack of infrastructure, serve as "drivers of instability" and hinder humanitarian relief and nation-building efforts that have been ongoing throughout most of Operation Enduring Freedom (see *Economist* 2001; Kaplan 2000; Lahood 2004; Lohman 2004; Malinowski 2004). By most measures, Afghanistan has one of the lowest quality of life ratings of any country in the world. Few citizens benefit from an adequate income, stable diet, medical care, education, access to clean water, and personal freedoms, which collectively contribute to a survivalist mentality among the majority of the population (see Figure 14.8).

Cultural complexity

Afghanistan's location between the former empire states of Central Asia, Persia, and South Asia has historically attracted invaders and settlers alike. But the area's rugged terrain facilitated isolation, while hindering the processes of acculturation or transculturation. Estimates identify forty-five languages within the country (*Ethnologue* 2001). Certain languages are generally associated with particular ethnic groups (see Figure 14.9). It is noteworthy, however, that none of Afghanistan's ethnic groups is Arab, and Arabic is only spoken by a few thousand people outside of religious services (Malinowski 2004).

Figure 14.7
A US Army soldier with the Jalalabad Provincial Reconstruction Team talks to Afghan children during a humanitarian aid mission held for nearly 100 displaced families living on the outskirts of Jalalabad in November 2004. *Source*: US Army photograph.

Figure 14.8
A young girl retrieves
water for her family on
the outskirts of Kabul.
Source: W. Chris King.

Figure 14.9
Ethnolinguistic groups.
Source: *Central
Intelligence Agency, 1997*

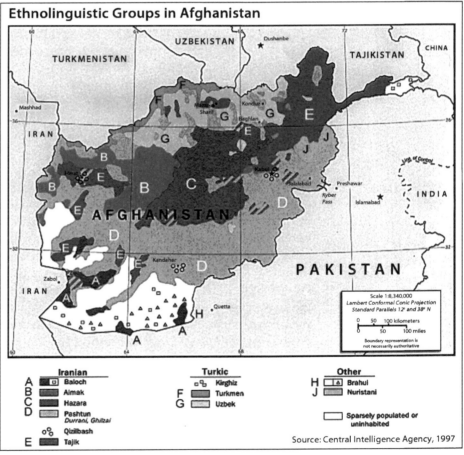

229

Islam is the most fundamental culture trait shared by virtually all ethnic groups. Although the overwhelming majority of Afghanis are Muslims (about 80 percent Sunni and 18 percent Shi'a), tribal norms, different sects, and varying degrees of fundamentalism preclude any sense of religious uniformity. Pre-Islamic beliefs and tribal customs contribute to variations in the practice of Islam from place to place.

Afghanistan's ethnic ties extend to Iran and the Middle East, the newly independent Central Asia republics, and to Pakistan and India, but absent is any notion of Afghan nationalism. For centuries, ethnic Pashtuns have generally dominated the country and successfully repelled invaders. Currently accounting for about 40 percent of the population, they occupy the southern half of Afghanistan, along with the eastern border region, and extend into Pakistan.

Culture traits vary considerably among tribes and from place to place. For example, Pashtunwali (or "the way of the Pashtun") is the tribal code that provides Pashtuns with a collective identity, as well as a set of rigid social norms. Key tenets of Pashtunwali include: nang (honor), badal (revenge), melmastia (hospitality), nanawatay (seeking forgiveness), and hamsaya ("one who shares the same shadow"). One cannot hope to understand the Pashtun and their way of life without comprehending the impacts of these tenets and their collective effect as a code of honor. Tribal structures and codes provide the keys to appreciating Afghanistan's cultural diversity and recognizing the significant differences among its culture groups.

Political instability

With over 5529 km (3317 miles) of boundaries, Afghanistan shares borders with six other states (China 76 km, Iran 936 km, Pakistan 2430 km, Tajikistan 1206 km, Turkmenistan 744 km, and Uzbekistan 137 km) (CIA 2001*a*). Although drawn by British and Russian representatives in the nineteenth century, the boundaries have proven relatively stable, despite dividing several nations of people and creating a country out of a heterogeneous mixture of ethnolinguistic groups. The complex cultural geography and difficult physical landscape have prompted some to describe Afghanistan's internal political situation as "ungovernable" (Weisbrode 2001). Matters have become increasingly complicated by massive migrations of displaced people, as a result of warfare over the past thirty years. Since the outset of Operation Enduring Freedom, the Afghanistan–Pakistan border region has been particularly problematic for coalition forces. Insurgents have moved freely back and forth across the porous border, hindering coalition efforts to stabilize the region.

More generally, political turbulence has made it extremely difficult for US forces to negotiate and co-ordinate relief efforts, security, and nation-building assistance. Although the presidential election in October of 2004 was an unprecedented event, the long-term implications are still uncertain and the transition to democracy is far from complete. The subsequent presidential election in August 2009 was another decisive event for the country's struggling democracy. Although it appears that President Hamid Karzai has garnered a sufficient percentage of votes to gain re-election, a number of controversies have emerged and the results are still being contested at this time.

Economic conditions

During the 1980s, the war with the Soviets severely damaged Afghanistan's physical infrastructure. The conflict also prompted 6 million people to flee the country. These conditions, coupled with internal regional power struggles spanning the 1990s, have seriously disrupted an already underdeveloped economy. Estimates indicate that from 67–85 percent of Afghanis are engaged in subsistence and commercial farming, but only 12 percent of the land is arable (Afghanistan Online 2001, CIA 2001*b*, Jackson et al. 2001). Given that most of the rural population lives on or adjacent to farmable land, this equates to an unfavorable physiological density of roughly 250 people per sq km in some places (see Figure 14.10).

Afghanistan's transportation network is also woefully inadequate. At the outset of Operation Enduring Freedom, there were only 21,000 km of roads within the country, most of which were characterized as unimproved surfaces and trails, while only 2793 km are paved and

Figure 14.10
Rural villages east of Kabul reveal the distinct architecture of Afghan family and extended-family dwellings, and exhibit typical land-use patterns in arable regions of the country. *Source*: Eugene J. Palka

capable of supporting limited commercial vehicles (CIA 2001*b*). Coalition forces have since invested significant resources to improving the primary road network, at least between major cities. The railroad system is also woefully inadequate for stimulating the economy, consisting of 24.6 km of track. And, of the ten airports with paved runways, only three are over 3000 meters and capable of accommodating large commercial aircraft. The lack of infrastructure poses fundamental challenges to distributing food, building materials, and equipment during humanitarian assistance efforts (see Figure 14.11). The greatest boost to the country's economy has come from foreign monetary aid and direct contracts awarded by the US Military to small businesses and laborers who cater to major military installations or nation-building projects that are scattered about the country.

The impact of landmines

More than thirty years of warfare have littered Afghanistan's landscape with millions of landmines and a wide range of *unexploded ordnance (UXO)*. Current estimates range from fewer than 1 million to more than 40 million landmines (although most surveys estimate between 7 and 10 million mines) in over fifty different varieties (Palka 2007). Civilian casualty figures also vary considerably, but a reasonable estimate would suggest nearly 15,000 killed and more than 800,000 injured from mines or UXO since the Soviet incursion in 1979 (Palka 2007). Landmines and UXO have also rendered fertile lands unusable and continue to plague development efforts. A concerted effort has been underway for many years to rid the country of its landmine and UXO hazard, but,

Figure 14.11
US soldiers deliver food to a village elder during a food distribution mission in Zabol province, Afghanistan, October 2004. *Source*: US Army photograph.

unfortunately, continuing warfare and the recent introduction and widespread use of *improvised explosive devices (IEDs)* have impeded progress. The ongoing insurgency is likely to exacerbate the problem.

Conclusion

This chapter has sought to examine the complexity of Afghanistan's physical geography and assess the impact on military operations during the course of Operation Enduring Freedom. The country's human geography is equally complicated, and, now, securing the population and separating them from the insurgents is perhaps the most significant challenge confronting US and NATO forces (French 2009). Meanwhile, continuing violence, a rudimentary infrastructure, and a war-torn cultural landscape continue to hinder coalition efforts.

Currently, US and NATO forces are involved in full-spectrum operations, a scenario so demanding that 21,000 additional troops are expected to deploy to Afghanistan by October 2009 (French 2009). Ongoing and future military operations will undoubtedly serve as major catalysts for change, but as the NATO ISAF commander, General McChrystal, warned, "Success will not be quick or easy" (French 2009). Additionally, there is a long history of cultural, political, and economic interaction across the political boundaries of the state, so it is difficult to project the country's future within a larger Central Asian context, especially given the recent increase in violence between the *Taliban* and Pakistani Army in Waziristan and the Federally Administered Tribal Areas of Pakistan.

Afghanistan's inaccessible location, rugged terrain, harsh climate, cultural complexity, political chaos, and poor infrastructure have limited the success of combat operations to a degree, but, perhaps more important, these same attributes have combined to hinder stability, peace operations, and *nation-building*. The current demand for full-spectrum operations presents a monumental task to US and NATO forces within this distant, austere, physically and culturally diverse, volatile country.

Editor's note: This chapter is a revised and updated version of a public domain chapter previously published as Palka, E. J. 2005. "Operation Enduring Freedom: the military geographic challenges of Afghanistan." In *Military geography: from peace to war*, E. J. Palka & F. A. Galgano (eds), 321–42. New York, NY: McGraw-Hill Custom Publishing.

References cited
Afghanistan Online 2001. *The state of the Afghan economy*. Office of the UN Co-ordinator for Afghanistan. www.afghan-web.com/economy/econstate.html [accessed 30 April 2010].
Air Force Combat Climatology Center. 1995. *Operational climatic data summary for Afghanistan, 1995*. www2.afccc.af.mil/cgi-bin/index_mil.pl?aafccc _info/products. html [accessed 1 October 2001].

Anderson, Peter G. 2004. "Biogeography." In *Geographic perspectives: Afghanistan*, Eugene J. Palka (ed.). New York: McGraw-Hill/Dushkin Publications.

Central Intelligence Agency (CIA). 2001a. *CIA world factbook*. Washington, DC: Government Printing Office.

——. 2001b. *The world factbook 2001*. Washington, DC: The Library of Congress. www.odci.gov/cia/publications/factbook/index.html [accessed 1 October 2001].

Economist. 2001. "The Afghan iconoclasts." *Economist* (8 March).

Energy Information Administration. 2001. *Afghanistan*. www.eia.doe.gov/emeu/cabs/afghan.html [accessed 25 September 2001].

Ethnologue. 2000. *Ethnologue: Volume 1 languages of the world, 14th edition*. Barbara F. Grimes, ed. Dallas, TX: Summer Institute of Linguistics.

French, Mary Blake. 2009. "News call: Afghanistan update: 'counterinsurgency takes time.'" *Army Magazine* 59(7): 8.

Hudson, J. & E. Espenshade, Jr. (eds). 2000. *Goode's world atlas*. 20th edn. New York: Rand McNally.

"Impact of the earthquake." 1998. www.oxfam.org.uk/atwork/emerg/afghan0698.htm [accessed 30 September 2001].

Jackson, B., Christina Surowiec, Julie Zhu, et al. 2001. *Country watch—Afghanistan 2001–2002*. Houston: CountryWatch.com.

Kaplan, Robert D. 2000. "The lawless frontier." *Atlantic Monthly* (September): 66–80.

Lahood, Albert A. 2004. "Economic geography." In *Geographic perspectives: Afghanistan*, Eugene J. Palka (ed.), 57–64. New York: McGraw-Hill/Dushkin Publications.

"Land and resources." 2001. www.afghan-web.com/geography/lr.html [accessed 30 April 2010].

Lohman, Andrew D. 2004. "Political geography." In *Geographic perspectives: Afghanistan*, Eugene J. Palka (ed.), 49–56. New York: McGraw-Hill/Dushkin Publications.

Malinowski, Jon C. 2004. "Cultural geography." In *Geographic perspectives: Afghanistan*, Eugene J. Palka (ed.), 39–47. New York: McGraw-Hill/Dushkin Publications.

Palka, Eugene J. 2001. "The physical setting of Afghanistan." *Post-Soviet Geography and Economics* 42(8): 561–70.

——. 2007. "Afghanistan's landmine tragedy: chronic repercussions and challenges." Paper presented at the 7th International Conference on Military Geology & Geography, 18–21 June, Quebec, Canada.

——. 2008. "Military operations in caves: observations from Afghanistan." In *Military geology and geography: history and technology*, C. P. Nathanail, R. J. Abrahart, & R. P. Bradshaw (eds), 268–77. Nottingham, UK: Land Quality Press.

Pannell, Richard P. 2004. "Climatology." In *Geographic perspectives: Afghanistan*, Eugene J. Palka (ed.), 17–24. New York: McGraw-Hill/Dushkin Publications.

Saba, D. 2001. "Geography: Land and Resources." www.afghanweb.com/geography/environment.html [accessed 1 October 2001].

"Thousands reported killed in Afghanistan quake," CNN, 6 February 1998. www10.cnn.com/WORLD/9802/06/afghanistan.quake/ [accessed 30 September 2001].

Weisbrode, Kenneth, 2001. *Central Eurasia: prize or quicksand? Contending views of instability in Karabakh, Ferghana, and Afghanistan*. International Institute for Strategic Studies. Adelphi Paper 338. New York: Oxford University Press.

Chapter fifteen
Iraq and Operation Iraqi Freedom
A military geography

EUGENE J. PALKA, FRANCIS A.
GALGANO, AND MARK W. CORSON

Introduction

THIS CHAPTER PROVIDES A geographic analysis of Iraq and Operation Iraqi Freedom (OIF). We begin with a brief, contemporary history of the country and then focus on the impacts of physical and human geography on the conduct of OIF. Iraq's physical geography is described in terms of the country's location, size, physiography, hydrology, climate, and weather, while its human geography is discussed in terms of culture, ethnicity, politics, and urban development. The final section of the chapter addresses relevant geographic technologies, including remote sensing, digital cartography, geographic information systems, and global positioning systems; it also offers a brief assessment of the importance of these technologies to modern military operations. Like other military geographies, this perspective draws from a range of geographic subfields, tools, and techniques to better understand Iraq's complex military operating environment.

Historical background

Following World War I, Great Britain and France became influential in the region that included present-day Iraq. The British and French subdivided the Middle East, and the territory that would become Iraq fell under British control. The British assembled Iraq out of three Ottoman provinces: Basra, Baghdad, and Mosul (Dalton 2004). While this may have appeared to be a geographically integrated region on a map, the creation consolidated three different major ethnic groups (and several minor ones) into one political entity. After a decade of direct occupation and continual dissidence, the British installed King Faisal on the throne of the new country (Ochsenwald and Fisher 2004).

Notwithstanding the installation of a new king, Iraq continued to experience instability and, from 1932 through 1979, it endured a series of coups. In 1958, a group of army officers led by General Qassem overthrew the monarchy and massacred the king, his family, and his ministers. Qassem's main support came from the communists, while his main rivals stemmed from an Arab nationalist political movement called the *Ba'ath Party*. In 1963, a group of Ba'ath Party officers overthrew Qassem, and their violent practices of mass arrest, torture, and executions resulted in a counter-coup that nearly destroyed the Party. It was during this period when Saddam Hussein emerged as a clever and ruthless operative within the Ba'ath Party.

The Israeli victory during the 1967 Six-Day War demoralized Arab regimes as they watched Israel defeat the armies of Egypt, Syria, and Jordan in a brief campaign. Although Iraq's involvement in the war was limited, the defeat afforded the Ba'athist regime an opportunity, and, thus, in July 1968 they took power under Ahmad Hassan al-Bakr, and once again purged their opponents through torture and execution. During this period, Saddam Hussein became head of the Iraqi secret police, began to extend his influence, and consolidated his power. In 1979, al-Bakr stepped aside so that Saddam Hussein could assume power, and he immediately purged 66 senior Ba'athist party members by having their surviving colleagues serve as the firing squad (Murray and Scales 2003).

The Saddam Hussein era

As Saddam was consolidating power in 1979, the Shah of Iran was overthrown by fundamentalist militants and a theocracy was established under the leadership of the Ayatollah Khomeini. Iraqi resentment of the Persian Iranians dates back to the domination of Mesopotamia by Persian kings. Saddam distrusted the *Shi'a* and the new Iranian theocratic regime, and he considered Iran vulnerable while in the midst of their revolution (Swearingen 1988). Thus, in September 1980, he initiated what would be a futile and destructive war with Iran. While initially successful, the conflict devolved into an eight-year stalemate. By the time the two sides agreed to peace in 1988, nearly 1 million Iraqis and Iranians had died, Iraq was nearly bankrupt, and no territory changed hands (Tibi 1998).

Having been frustrated in Iran, two years later Saddam turned his focus to his former benefactors in Kuwait, whom he accused of stealing his oil. Furthermore, he also considered Kuwait to be Iraq's historic nineteenth province. Consequently, in August 1990, Iraq invaded Kuwait and secured the country in only three days. Saddam then massed his forces on the Saudi Arabian border, threatening Saudi oilfields and roughly a quarter of the world's proven oil reserves (Clark 2004). The US responded by assembling an international Coalition to protect Saudi Arabia, in what came to be known as Operation Desert Shield. With UN backing and a Security Council resolution calling for Iraq to leave Kuwait, the Coalition eventually launched Operation Desert Storm in February 1991. The US-led ground force drove the Iraqis from Kuwait and seized southern Iraq in only 100 hours of ground combat. Not having a mandate to change the regime, Coalition forces withdrew from Iraq having accomplished their mission of liberating Kuwait, but leaving Saddam in power (DoD 1992).

The effects of the war lingered, however, and for the next decade Iraqi citizens would suffer under UN sanctions that caused severe shortages. To ease the burden on the Iraqi people, the UN initiated the now infamous and highly corrupt *Oil for Food Program.* This program was designed to allow Iraq to sell enough oil to buy food and medicine. Saddam, however, allegedly skimmed nearly a third of the revenues to rebuild his military forces and was suspected of also trying to reconstitute his chemical, biological, and nuclear weapons (Woodward 2008).

On September 11, 2001, the destruction of the World Trade Center in New York and the attack on the Pentagon by *al-Qaeda* terrorists were the hostile acts that initiated the *Global War on Terrorism.* While President George W. Bush focused his attention on Afghanistan, he identified three countries (Iraq, Iran, and North Korea) as the *Axis of Evil* and the stage was set for further conflict with Iraq. Throughout late 2002 and early 2003 the Bush Administration made its case against Iraq and sought to build a UN-sanctioned Coalition to use military force against the rogue country (Palka et al. 2005). When Russia, France, and Germany thwarted his efforts in the UN, President Bush unilaterally launched OIF on 20 March 2003 (Murray and Scales 2003; Clark 2004).

Operation Iraqi Freedom

On March 21, 2003, Secretary of Defense Rumsfeld and the Chairman of the Joint Chiefs of Staff, General Myers, held a press conference to articulate the objectives of OIF. The specific objectives included: 1) ending Saddam Hussein's regime; 2) identifying, isolating, and eliminating Iraq's weapons of mass destruction; 3) capturing and driving out terrorists harbored in Iraq; 4) collecting intelligence related to terrorist networks in Iraq and beyond; 5) delivering humanitarian relief to Iraqi citizens; 6) securing Iraq's oil fields and resources; and 7) helping the Iraqi people to create a representative self-government (Palka et al. 2005).

Unlike the situation during the Gulf War in 1991, when the US-led Coalition massed nearly a half-million troops in Saudi Arabia, the political situation was much different in 2003, as the Saudis did not allow their territory to be used as a staging base. Consequently, Kuwait became the key staging area and the US established major transportation operations there because its excellent infrastructure proved capable of handling the influx of troops and equipment. The sparsely populated northern portion of the country (bordering Iraq) hosted a number of camps that supported the build-up. The US-led Coalition was comprised of troops from thirty-one countries. Most of these were small (but politically important) contingents, with the notable exceptions of the UK and Australia, which provided substantial forces. The main US forces were the Vth US Corps (V Corps) and 1st Marine Expeditionary Force (I MEF) (Murray and Scales 2003).

V Corps had the equivalent of three *divisions* and launched its attack from Kuwait towards Baghdad, but remained west of the Euphrates River, moving rapidly through the desert and bypassing most of the populated areas (see Figure 15.1). Simultaneously, the I MEF (which included the 1st Marine Division and the British 1st Armored Division) attacked from Kuwait through the heartland of Iraq. Eventually the US 3rd Infantry Division (V Corps) would attack Baghdad from the west while the I MEF attacked Baghdad from the east (Murray and Scales 2003). The British 1st Armored Division secured southern Iraq by seizing the port cities of Basra and Umm Qasr, thus protecting the flank of the Americans (UK MOD 2003) (see Figure 15.1).

Allied special operations forces entered Iraq from Jordan to eliminate the *SCUD* threat against Israel. Even though the Turkish Government refused to allow the US 4th Infantry Division to attack Iraq from its soil, it permitted the Coalition to deploy Special Forces into northern Iraq. These Special Forces troops linked up with Kurdish *Peshmerga*, and, supported by the airdropped US 173rd Airborne Brigade, they secured northern Iraq and preoccupied a substantial number of Iraqi forces (see Figure 15.1).

This time, too, the ground war was short and decisive, and on May 1, 2003 President Bush declared an end to major combat operations in Iraq. It seemed to many that the mission was complete and the Coalition could bring the troops home as it had done in the first Gulf War (Woodward 2008). Iraq, however, had no functioning government and its infrastructure was badly damaged so the Coalition was compelled to establish itself as an occupation force. In October 2003, the UN authorized the occupation while calling for an early transfer of sovereignty to the Iraqis. A massive rebuilding effort was undertaken to restore critical services and to address the even greater damage from thirty years of Saddam's neglect, and the post-war looting of the country by Iraqis (Palka et al. 2005).

By June 2003, a growing insurgency was evident as multiple groups with varying agendas found common cause in challenging the Coalition occupation (Clark 2004). In the *Sunni Triangle* in the center of the country, a combination of Ba'athist Saddam supporters, Iraqi nationalists, and foreign terrorist elements launched bloody attacks against US forces. The insurgents proved to be resourceful and adaptable, and began using the massive amounts of leftover munitions to create *improvised explosive*

Figure 15.1
Major operations at the outset of OIF. *Source*: Adapted from Palka, Galgano, and Corson (2005).

devices *(IEDs)* that they planted as remotely detonated roadside bombs. In Shi'a areas to the south, a radical Islamic cleric, Moqtada al-Sadr, launched an insurgency to dispel the Coalition and put himself in a position of power. The opportunity to fight the Americans drew many foreign fighters and a virtual underground railroad of Jihadists developed, attracting opportunists from all over the region. Many of these fighters joined the ranks of the Jordanian militant and *al-Qaeda* commander, Abu Mussab al-Zarqawi, who was later killed during a US airstrike on 7 June 2006 (Woodward 2008).

The Coalition reacted to the insurgency with military force and political maneuvering. By mid-2004 Iraqi security forces were being rebuilt, an Iraqi interim government under Prime Minister Iyad Allawi was installed in June 2004, and plans were made for nationwide elections of a new government on 30 January 2005. In the meantime, various insurgent groups and foreign terrorists launched campaigns of intimidation and murder to derail the elections, and destroy the emerging Iraqi civil society (Palka et al. 2005).

239

Despite successful democratic elections in 2005, the multifaceted insurgency gained momentum throughout Iraq. During 2006 and 2007, the increased instability caused by multiple insurgent groups and sectarian violence was addressed via a "surge" of US ground forces and a comprehensive counter-insurgency campaign (Woodward 2008). US units operated from *forward operating bases (FOBs)* throughout the country and conducted daily patrols and various missions into its most populated areas in an effort to protect the civilian population while continuing the nation-building effort. The increased military presence, continual reconstruction, persistent support to Iraqi political and military institutions, and a range of economic development projects yielded dramatic improvements throughout the country during 2008 and 2009. However, the national elections in January 2010, unresolved Kurd–Arab tensions over disputed territories, sectarian violence, and the US commitment to troop withdrawals throughout 2010, present uncertainties during the final stages of OIF.

Iraq's military operating environment

There is a fundamental link between geography and warfare, and each location manifests a unique array of geographic characteristics that interact to produce a distinctive environment. The *military operating environment* is a construct composed of all factors of the natural and cultural landscape that shape and control the ebb and flow of battle. Herein, we have elected to examine fundamental aspects of Iraq's physical and human geography, which contribute to its unique operating environment.

Physical geography

When they invaded Iraq, Coalition forces faced essentially the same physical environment and challenges that they did during Operation Desert Storm, more than a decade earlier. However, the effects of Iraq's physical landscape must be reassessed in light of more recently developed military doctrine, tactics, and technological advances.

LOCATION AND SIZE

To understand adequately Iraq's military geography, it is essential to examine first its location and territorial extent. Iraq's geographic center lies at about 33° north latitude and 44° east longitude, which is about the same latitude as Tennessee (Thompson 2004). Iraq is a nearly landlocked state about the size of California; it is bordered by Iran to the east, Turkey to the north, Syria and Jordan to the west, and Saudi Arabia and Kuwait to the south (see Figure 15.2).

Strategic distance was an important consideration during the war because Iraq is far from the US: about 9500 km (≈ 5900 miles) from the

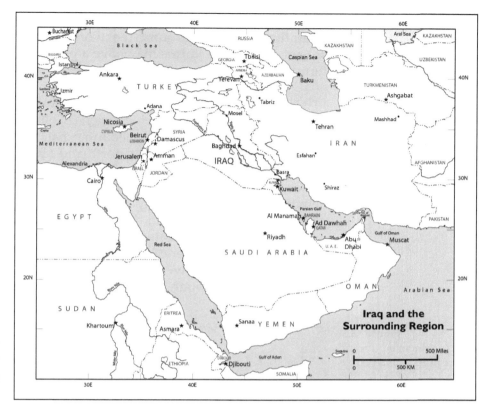

East Coast and approximately 11,000 km (≈ 6800 miles) from the West Coast by air. Thus, a non-stop aerial deployment from the US requires about 12 to 12.5 hours with numerous aerial re-fuelling. This distance is taxing on soldiers and airmen, as well as airframes (Corson 2001).

Distance and location are problematic in terms of a maritime deployment as well. From the US East Coast, ships must cross the Atlantic, then transit one or more of the world's critical maritime choke points. Using the northernmost route, ships must negotiate the Straits of Gibraltar, Sicilian Straits, Suez Canal, Bab el Mandeb, and Straits of Hormuz. The southern route, which is twice as long, requires ships to navigate the Cape of Good Hope, Mozambique Channel, and Straits of Hormuz. From the West Coast, ships must transit the very congested Straits of Malacca and Lombok, followed by passage through the western Indian Ocean and Straits of Hormuz (Peele 1997). These deployments are time consuming, requiring approximately 23 days from the East Coast and 14 days from the West (Corson 2001).

The travel times and distances mentioned above place a strain on sealift assets, which must deliver much of the heavy equipment and supplies needed to conduct and sustain military operations. Shortages in *roll-on/roll-off* craft, *break-bulk* craft capable of handling large, outsized cargo, and self-sustaining craft exacerbate the challenge of sustaining military operations halfway around the world (Collins 2003). Furthermore, seasonal maritime storms may have a profound influence on the short-term viability of sea lanes.

PHYSIOGRAPHY, HYDROLOGY, AND GEOGRAPHIC REGIONS

Iraq has three major geographic regions (Collins 2003) with two principal rivers (see Figure 15.3). The country has high mountains along its boundaries with Turkey in the north and Iran in the east. The center of the country is dominated by the fertile Tigris and Euphrates River basin, which includes the majority of the population and its agricultural activity. Finally, the landscape transitions to the barren, rocky desert—called the *an Nafud*—which extends southwest into Saudi Arabia.

The Tigris and Euphrates Rivers rise in the uplands of Turkey and flow through the center of the country, bringing fertile soils and water for agriculture. Both rivers are exotic in that they are formed in a humid area, then flow through an arid region. The rivers form a huge *alluvial*

Figure 15.3
Iraq's principal physical regions. *Source*: After Collins (2003).

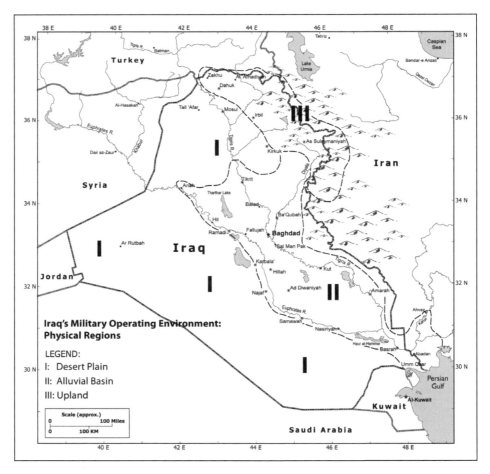

basin, which extends from the region north of Baghdad to the Persian Gulf, and this river basin includes nearly 75 percent of Iraq's population and infrastructure (Nyrop and Smith 1979). The rivers join at the Shat El Arab near the Persian Gulf, forming a large marsh region that has been home to the "Marsh Arabs" for thousands of years.

Region I (see Figure 15.3) consists of a flat, barren desert plain that extends from the Persian Gulf and northern Saudi Arabia almost to the Mediterranean Sea. There is little relief, although the area includes many *wadis* and a few small escarpments (Nyrop and Smith 1979). Region I includes three varieties of deserts: *erg, reg,* and *hamada*. The *erg* is the classic sea of sand, which is small in spatial extent, and found in small pockets near the border with Saudi Arabia. The predominant desert type is the *reg*, which includes a gravel surface and offers perhaps the best mobility for military units. The *hamada* is a region of exposed bedrock on the surface, and this type of desert is limited to the most northerly segment of Region I. *Wadis* indicate the orientation of drainage patterns and are of great concern because of flooding during the infrequent, but intense, rainstorms. These features can be quite deep and may represent major obstacles to vehicular movement (US Army 1992; Collins 2003) (see Figure 15.4).

Region II (see Figure 15.3) is the central alluvial basin that correlates to the region of ancient Mesopotamia (Collins 2003). The region is bounded on the east by the Tigris River and on the west by the Euphrates. The rivers form a common delta near Basra and an immense

Figure 15.4
Wadis dissect the region to the northwest of Tikrit, impeding mobility and maneuverability by track and wheeled vehicles. *Source*: Eugene J. Palka.

marsh called the *Hawr al Hammar*, then meander southward to the Persian Gulf as the Shat al Arab. The region includes numerous swamps, mud flats, lakes, canals, drainage ditches, and dikes. Thus, the streams and the marshy lower course present difficult obstacles to maneuver and require bridging operations for mechanized units (US Army 1992). Although the region includes a great deal of water, much of it is polluted and undrinkable. Furthermore, the area is a breeding ground for mosquitoes and flies, which spread a number of diseases, such as *malaria* and *Rift Valley Fever*. These health hazards are problematic because the alluvial basin includes nearly 75 percent of Iraq's population (Gamez and Watson 2004).

Within Region III (see Figure 15.3), elevations increase from south to north from the uplands near Kirkuk and Erbil to mountains along the Turkish and Iranian borders. Mountains rising to 3600 meters (11,000 feet) are found in this region. Geologically, Iraq and Iran converge at the boundary of the continental–continental convergent plate boundary between the Arabian and Eurasian tectonic plates, resulting in complex folded and faulted mountains. This geology produces the region's numerous earthquakes and vast petroleum deposits (Sampson 2004).

CLIMATE

At a macro-scale, the climate in Iraq is characterized by hot, dry summers and milder winters with little precipitation, although there are many local variations from this pattern. Summer (i.e. June–September) and winter (i.e. November–April) constitute the two seasons, with a one-month transition period between each. Temperatures typically exceed 43°C ($\approx$ 110°F) in the summer and seldom drop below freezing during the winter, except in the higher elevations (US Army 1992). Average annual precipitation is less than 12.5 cm ($\approx$ 5 inches), and some locations receive no rain for years at a time. Skies are usually clear throughout the year because of pervasive atmospheric stability, although cloud cover can increase during the winter months. Visibility is generally best in the winter and poorest in the summer because of suspended dust. The pervasive aridity, lack of vegetation, and prevailing winds, combined with exposed, fine-grained surface materials produce *shamals* (dust storms), which occur primarily during the winter months.

Iraq has three climate zones: subtropical desert, subtropical steppe, and Mediterranean (see Figure 15.5). Iraq's location between 39° and 37° north latitude means it is influenced strongly by subtropical high pressure. Pervasive *anticyclonic* activity generates subsiding air, which means that the region will remain dry throughout the year. Subsiding air also means that the skies will remain cloudless, thus producing a net surplus of solar radiation, which is manifested as high average annual temperatures. Altitude associated with the mountainous terrain in northern Iraq generates cooler temperatures and a slight increase in precipitation through orographic lifting (Nyrop and Smith 1979; Pannell 2004).

Figure 15.5
Iraq's climatic regions.
Source: adapted from
Pannell (2004).

The region between southwestern Iraq and the Persian Gulf (i.e. more than half the country) has a subtropical desert climate (BWh) (see Figure 15.5). It is extremely hot in the summer, sometimes exceeding 54°C (≈ 130°F), and milder in the winter; however, average winter temperatures never drop below freezing. There is little precipitation, but, when it does rain, it can generate flash floods, especially in *wadis* or built-up areas with poor drainage. Southern Iraq has little natural vegetation; however, riparian vegetation along the Tigris and Euphrates flourishes (Palka et al. 2005).

The region extending north of Baghdad to Kirkuk is a subtropical steppe or grassland climate (BSh) (see Figure 15.5). This region has cooler temperatures and receives slightly more winter rainfall from the sporadic passage of fronts during winter months. The availability of moisture and slightly cooler temperatures generate conditions that support grasses and broadleaf evergreen shrubs and, thus, this region is far greener than southern Iraq (Pannell 2004).

The higher elevations of northern Iraq make it much wetter and cooler due to altitude. Orographic lifting generates increased rainfall in the region (see Figure 15.6). The mountains get very cold in the winter and snow is common above 1000 m (3300 ft). The climate and weather of Iraq generate three major natural hazards: drought, flooding, and sandstorms. Flooding and sandstorms had significant effects on operations during the early stages of OIF [*Editor's note*: for a complete description of this event refer to Chapter 17].

Physical geography and military operations

Physical geography had a considerable influence on military operations in Iraq. Iraq's relatively large size causes military units to maneuver over long distances, with equally long and vulnerable supply lines. Problems of distance were compounded by the nature of the terrain and climate in Iraq. Much of Iraq is a flat, featureless desert with little permanent vegetation outside areas nourished by the Tigris and Euphrates Rivers. This operating environment poses four fundamental challenges to military operations: navigation and concealment, pervasive dust, the effect of temperature and aridity, and the impact of fluvial features.

In many ways, the featureless desert is the most challenging problem in Iraq because navigation in a region without readily identifiable landmarks is inherently difficult. In practice, however, this generally proved to be a problem that US forces could overcome by using a *Global*

Figure 15.6
Vegetation in the northern Iraqi province of Dohuk is indicative of its Mediterranean climate. *Source*: Eugene J. Palka.

Positioning System (GPS). Far more serious for contemporary military operations is the fact that the apparently featureless nature of the Iraqi desert can be deceptive. Although the near absence of vegetation and seemingly flat terrain permits extended visibility, the region exhibits a great deal of *microterrain.* This microterrain, which includes *wadis* and *intervisibility lines*, is of little value in terms of concealing large, modern forces. However, small, fast-moving insurgent forces can find adequate concealment throughout the region (Hoffman 2004).

Microterrain, combined with the expansive desert, enhanced insurgent operations, especially in western Iraq. US forces, initially configured and equipped to detect and fight large, mechanized forces in the open desert, were compelled to reorganize and adopt new methods for employing available technology to defeat this unforeseen enemy advantage (Hoffman 2004). Aerial surveillance platforms, the use of unmanned aerial vehicles, and electronic signature-detection systems are examples of readily available technology designed to enhance intelligence gathering and target detection in such austere places. Insurgents in western al-Anbar Province, however, benefited from the remote nature of the terrain to infiltrate into urban and periurban areas of Iraq (Hoffman 2004).

The poorly developed, dry soils in the Iraqi desert are inherently dusty. This is especially problematic for a mechanized force because dust is damaging to engines, necessitating specialized air filters and more frequent maintenance stops during operations. Iraq's desert soils are unique in that they contain abundant amounts of carbonates, sulfates, and chlorides, along with silt- and clay-sized particles. This type of dust, when mixed with various lubricants, forms sand-sized aggregates and proved to be particularly damaging to rifles and machine guns (McDonald and Caldwell 2005). Thus, soldiers were required to maintain their weapons in ways far different from those mandated for more temperate environments. Helicopters needed specialized rotor blades in order to operate safely in an environment with highly abrasive dust (Palka et al. 2005).

Pervasive dust is a fact of daily life in the Iraqi desert and had a debilitating effect on soldiers. The surface material in southern Iraq is fine clay with the consistency of talcum powder. This "sand" gets into everything and had an adverse impact on troop morale, air and ground operations, and equipment operability. Because of experiences during the first Gulf War, most US equipment was resistant to dust, but its performance was degraded nonetheless. Despite improvements to engine air-filter systems, the pervasive, fine dust caused motors to run at higher temperatures, thus accelerating wear on components and degrading fuel efficiency. Additionally, blowing desert particles are by nature abrasive and caused scratches in optics, reducing their efficiency regardless of protective measures. Finally, dusty conditions interfered with lasers, degrading guided munitions and range finders (Fontenot et al. 2005).

US planners knew that heat would be a major consideration. Thus, OIF was launched just prior to the transition from winter to summer, when temperatures begin to warm, with the hope of ending operations before the summer (Fontenot et al. 2005). However, operations continued into the summer period, and by August the temperature made even simple, day-to-day activities difficult. Because of the perceived threat of chemical weapons, coalition soldiers initially wore heavy chemical-protective suits, which made heat-related illnesses and injuries a constant threat (Palka et al. 2005). The suits cause soldiers to nearly double their water intake; however, the nature of the protective gear makes drinking very difficult. Thus, soldiers are frequently susceptible to heat exhaustion and can suffer from dizziness and restricted vision, which can cause vertigo or disorientation. These conditions are not life threatening, but they do lower efficiency and slow routine operations considerably (Fontenot et al. 2005).

Aridity and high temperatures are necessary planning considerations in desert environments. The most obvious is the combined effects of aridity and heat on soldiers. Gradual acclimatization to conditions and sufficient levels of hydration are extremely important to long-term mitigation of these heat-related impacts. The accepted acclimatization period for the summer period is about three weeks (Gamez and Watson 2004). The need for a supply of clean drinking water is self-evident. The less obvious effects of aridity and heat are their physiological effects on soldiers because human tolerance for climatic variation is actually quite limited. Temperature variations of more than 5° above or below 21°C will impair performance, and a 9°C increase in temperature above 21°C will cause the average body to respire more rapidly. Finally, an 18°C increase will establish conditions for heat exhaustion and, potentially, heatstroke (Palka et al. 2005). In Iraq, these circumstances were exacerbated by the extreme aridity, which caused soldiers to dehydrate more quickly. Other physiological conditions attendant to this hot, dry, and dusty climate included eye infections, severe chapping, sun blindness, and a host of other problems. Individually, these afflictions are generally considered minor, but for soldiers operating in austere environments their combined effects can be debilitating.

Ironically, for a desert war, fluvial features played a surprisingly critical role. Because coalition forces expected the Iraqis to destroy bridges to slow their advance, US forces practiced river-crossing operations before the outbreak of fighting and brought with them a tremendous amount of bridging equipment. However, initial planning for the 2003 attack established that the V Corps would be required to conduct nearly 800 individual water-crossing operations, an effort that would have required more bridging equipment than was available in the Army inventory. This geographic analysis led to alteration of the plan, and the V Corps made its drive across the desert, east of Samawah and Najaf to the Hillah gap.

Human geography

While Iraq's physical geography varies from one part of the country to the next, the pattern and conditions in each of these places are relatively constant from year to year. Its human geography, however, changes continually over time, and the cultural landscape is always evolving. When examining the human components of the operating environment, military planners usually consider various subfields of geography to assemble an integrated snapshot of the human landscape. The result is an appraisal of the region's population, culture groups, cultural institutions, settlement patterns, land use, economic activities, and networks (e.g. transportation and communication). While Iraq's physical landscape presented a plethora of challenges to military operations, most were predictable. Human activities, however, are much more dynamic, and, therefore, complicate matters more.

Cultural patterns

Iraq is a culturally fragmented country with three major ethnic/religious groups that share a long history of conflict, which seriously influences the political geography of the country (see Figure 15.7). While most Iraqis are Muslims, they are divided along both ethnic and religious lines. Ethnically, the country is divided between Arabs and Kurds (and includes smaller percentages of other ethnic groups, such as Yazedis and Turkomen), while the religious cleavage occurs between *Shi'a* and *Sunni* Muslims (and to a lesser degree between Muslims and Christians, Mandaeans, and Jews).

Shi'a Iraqis constitute the majority with about 60 percent of the population and are concentrated in the south and east of the country. Iran to the east is a Shi'a theocracy and has close cultural and religious ties with some elements of the Iraqi Shi'a. Historically, Shi'a were brutally suppressed by the Iraqi Sunni population, and Saddam Hussein continued this oppression. Traditionally, the Shi'a lived in the rural countryside or smaller peripheral cities. Basra, in southern Iraq, is a major Shi'a city, and the cities of Karbala and Najaf house their most important religious sites. The Shi'a have their own form of *Hadj* that draws tens of thousands of pilgrims to trek from Najaf to Karbala; however, Saddam forbade the Shi'a to conduct this pilgrimage for three decades. The Shi'a, however, resumed the practice with his downfall in 2003. Shi'a clerics play an important role in directing their society and have the ability to incite their followers to rebel, or to persuade them to co-operate and participate in political processes.

Iraqi Sunnis are a minority—20 percent of the population—but historically they have been the ruling element of Iraq. When the British created Iraq, they installed a Sunni monarch and it was the Sunnis who lived in and around Baghdad, and dominated political and economic

Figure 15.7
Map of major culture groups. *Source*: adapted from Malinowski (2004).

life. Saddam Hussein was a Sunni from Tikrit. He feared both the Shi'a and the Kurds, and brutally suppressed both groups during his regime.

The Kurds are Muslims, but they are culturally distinct from the Shi'a and Sunni Arabs. The Kurds have their own language and practice their own brand of Sunni Islam. The Kurds and their kinsmen also occupy parts of Syria, Turkey, and Iran. Kirkuk is the main, yet most contested, city of the Kurdish north. The Kurds are a classic *stateless nation*, meaning they are a culturally homogenous group that self-identify as a nation, but have no political state of their own. Historically, some Kurds aspired to create a state of Kurdistan from parts of Iraq, Iran, Turkey, and Syria. This desire bred an active insurgency in each country. Saddam brutally suppressed the Kurds for decades and killed thousands of them with chemical weapons during his infamous al-Anfal Campaigns. The Kurdish north also has a substantial minority of Turkomen and other ethnic groups clustered in and around Kirkuk. The Kurds have a reputation for being warlike and there is a traditional hostility between the Kurds and the lowland Iraqi Sunnis to the south (Malinowski 2004).

Currently, the Iraqi constitution recognizes the historical claims of the Kurds and enables them to occupy and govern a semi-autonomous territory within the northern third of the country, including territories within the provinces of Dohuk, Erbil, Sulaimaniya, Kirkuk, Diyala, and Nineveh. Disputed areas (including the symbolic city of Kirkuk), however, are far from resolved, and occur along the "Green Line" that separates Iraqi Kurdistan from the remainder of the country.

Iraqi society is a juxtaposition of the old and the new. At the national level, Iraq has had a secular government, various administrative districts, and provincial governors and councils. However, the tribal system at the local and regional levels influences virtually all aspects of life. Tribal sheiks wield great influence in local affairs and tribal membership plays an important role in determining political power. Saddam surrounded himself with his family and tribal members from his home city of Tikrit. Any effort to reform Iraq must take into account both the policy of the official national government and the viewpoints of the unofficial tribal and religious authorities. While nationalism may be the ultimate goal, relationships in Iraq begin with the family and evolve to the extended family, clan, tribe, and tribal confederation.

Political geography

Cultural differences between Sunnis, Shi'as, and Kurds have a considerable influence on Iraq's political geography. Politically, Iraq has been a monarchy and a military dictatorship beset by coups. Saddam ruled for thirty years through violence and intimidation, suppressing the political aspirations of both the Shi'as and the Kurds, and any Sunnis who might pose a challenge. Iraq has never known democracy and, with Saddam deposed, it was ruled by an occupation authority for a short time and then by an interim government. Thus, 2005 was the beginning of a new political era for Iraq. National elections were conducted in early January, with an estimated 58 percent voter turnout. The Iraqi people ratified a permanent constitution in October, and national elections were conducted in December to elect the first government under the new constitution. With a 77 percent voter participation rate, the national election of December 2005 was hailed as an unprecedented success and a historic milestone. The provincial council elections (held in fourteen of eighteen provinces) of 31 January 2009 included more than 14,000 candidates, of which some 4000 were women (Besheer 2009). The efforts of Prime Minister Nuri al-Maliki and President Jalal Talabani have been noteworthy, if not remarkable, but expectations appear to be higher as Iraq approaches the elections of 2010 and sectarian challenges remain.

The Shi'a community has the most to gain from elections where each adult can vote. With their 60 percent majority, the 2005 election was their grand opportunity to take political power after centuries of repression. Despite Prime Minister Maliki's efforts, the Shi'as, however, are still not unified. Rivalries persist, making it difficult for them to consolidate their power. The most powerful Shi'a cleric, the Grand Ayatollah Ali al-Sistani, has proven to be relatively moderate in his view of the Coalition occupation, the security agreement, and the political process. The other central Shi'a figure is the 35-year-old cleric Moqtada al-Sadr, who has been a violent opponent of the Coalition occupation, has instigated terrorist acts against Coalition soldiers and Iraqi civilians who supported the interim government, and who continues to be at odds with the current regime. Al-Sadr appeals to the masses of young, poorly educated, and angry urban Shi'a youth who have few economic prospects or career opportunities (Palka et al. 2005).

Sunnis remain relatively fragmented in their attitudes towards the forthcoming election. Many Sunnis suffered under Saddam and were glad to see him overthrown, but they remain bitter about losing their former status in society. Some opted to participate in the 2005 elections to gain at least a share of power in order to protect their interests. Many more, however, elected to boycott the elections, and, as a result, lost a significant voice in the government. The 2009 provincial elections witnessed a far greater participation among Sunnis as they hoped to regain some of their political power. Yet, as of this writing, there are still a number of competing groups within the Sunni minority, each with its own agenda and willingness to use violence to undermine the country's political process and stability.

The Kurds enjoyed a degree of autonomy in northern Iraq ever since the 1991 Gulf War. Protected by their *Peshmerga* fighters and a Coalition "No-Fly Zone," Saddam was forced to let them run their own affairs. The Kurds are staunch supporters of the Coalition and participated in the elections in order to ensure local control of the four provinces they dominate. The main Kurdish agenda is to ensure that a future Iraq is federal or decentralized in nature and that they continue to enjoy substantial autonomy in local affairs. If their autonomy is threatened, or if the national elections fail and there is civil war, the Kurds will presumably fight for their independence. This would have major political implications for Kurds in Iran, Syria, and Turkey, as well as for strategic relations between the US and the Arab world.

The political future of Iraq has regional and international implications as well. The best-case scenario is that the January 2010 elections succeed. The Obama Administration hopes that other countries in the region will follow Iraq, undertake democratic reforms, and modernize their societies and economies, thus removing the underlying causes of Islamic terrorism. A worst-case scenario is that the elections either fail or result in a radical Shi'a government unacceptable to the Sunnis and Kurds, prompting a civil war and the devolution of the country. Such instability would also be disastrous to the world economy should it prompt dramatic spikes in oil prices or interruptions in supply.

Urban geography and infrastructure

Iraq is an urbanized country with three cities of over a million, eight cities of over 500,000, and numerous smaller settlements. Even the 5 million Iraqis in the rural countryside tend to live in nucleated settlements (see Figure 15.8). This urbanized geography had serious implications for military operations in Iraq as the necessity to fight in cities became unavoidable.

Baghdad, Iraq's capital, is a sprawling city on the Tigris River with a population of 5.6 million people (PRB 2005). It is a mix of Sunni and Shi'a, with numerous other minorities. It is also the *primate city* and core of the country. Mosul is the second largest city with 1.74 million people. It has a large population of Kurds but also a substantial Sunni population. Basra lies only about 10 miles from the Gulf and is Iraq's major seaport city. It is home to 1.3 million mostly Shi'a Iraqis and is a major oil center (PRB 2005).

Traditionally, military forces avoid fighting in cities, but the international trend towards urbanization and the fact that cities are key terrain make it essential to bring them under control (Krulak 1999). The US Marine Corps and US Army have developed and refined urban combat doctrine during the course of OIF, and several key battles have occurred in urban settings. The seizure of Saddam's palaces in Baghdad in April 2003 broke the regime's resistance and precluded a long siege. The battle against Sadr's forces in Najaf, Karbala, and Sadr City

Figure 15.8
A nucleated village like this one southeast of Mosul is typical of Iraq's rural settlement pattern.
Source: Eugene J. Palka.

253

(Baghdad) forced him into the political arena, and the fight for Fallujah was a tactical victory that deprived the insurgents of a safe haven.

A number of lessons were learned from these battles. First, it takes a large force of well-trained troops to fight effectively in the urban environment. Distances are reduced, communication is difficult, and junior leaders with small groups of soldiers must use initiative and routinely operate in a decentralized fashion. Secondly, precision firepower is essential to prevent excessive collateral damage. Third, non-lethal force often provides the best insurance against incurring civilian casualties, generating collateral damage, or alienating the local populace. Finally, insurgents generally like to fight in cities because it affords them an opportunity to take refuge among the civilian population, and, in some respects, the built environment negates the Coalition's technological advantage (Fontenot et al. 2005).

Historically, armored vehicles had limitations when operating in cities, as they were vulnerable to being canalized or ambushed from the top and rear. In the battle for Baghdad, the 2nd Brigade of the 3rd Infantry Division launched an audacious armored thrust at high speed, straight into the city center where they seized Saddam Hussein's palace. This attack broke the regime's resistance and demonstrated that armored forces could operate in urban terrain. Key factors, however, were the nature of the city (relatively open and modern) and the enemy (equipped with older equipment and mostly rifles and rocket-propelled grenades). In Najaf, the Marines found they were taking unacceptably heavy casualties despite their advanced urban combat training. The arrival of Abrams tanks and Bradley Fighting Vehicles brought the armor-protected firepower they needed to overcome the insurgents.

There are different types of urban environments ranging from the modern open construction of central Baghdad to the narrow streets and densely packed buildings of older cities (see Figure 15.9). Different areas of the same city will have different types of buildings and street patterns whether they are old or new, commercial, residential, or industrial. Good intelligence and maps, as well as an understanding of layout and construction of the urban area, are essential knowledge for combat leaders in urban environments.

Often overlooked but of critical importance to successful military operations are the logistics functions of supply, transportation, maintenance, and medical care. These logistics functions utilize the infrastructure of urban areas, roads and highways, railroads, airports, and seaports. Central Iraq had a limited but well-constructed road system that enabled the Coalition to rapidly advance to Baghdad. Major towns were generally connected by well-constructed, two-lane roads that facilitated military movement.

Saddam Hussein International Airport on the west side of Baghdad was seized as early as possible during OIF. The airport had not

functioned since 1991 when Coalition forces cratered the runway and

Figure 15.9
Unit movements are
often restricted by the
narrow streets and
alleys, such as in
the "Old Town"
section of Mosul.
Source: Eugene J. Palka.

UN sanctions restricted air travel. The Coalition used a long taxiway to
reopen the airport to military transport aircraft and eventually repaired
the runway. Civil air traffic resumed for the first time in over a decade,
but the threat of shoulder-fired surface-to-air missiles makes travel into
the renamed Baghdad International Airport dangerous. The Coalition
also rapidly reopened the civilian airports at Basra and Kirkuk.

The port facilities at Basra and nearby Umm Qasr were in disrepair
after a decade of sanctions, the Iran–Iraq War, and the first Gulf War.

Mines were an ever-present danger so the ports played little role early in the war. Coalition forces led by the British worked diligently to de-mine the waterways and repair the port infrastructure. This was essential both for Iraqi economic development and for potential military use that could take some of the pressure off the heavily used Kuwaiti port of Ash Shuibah.

Geotechnology

Geographers invented, perfected, and use a number of tools that are invaluable during military operations. From the early use of maps for navigation and planning, to the use of aerial photographs and other remotely sensed imagery, to the exploitation of geographic information systems and global positioning systems, the geo-techniques have proven essential. The elements of the so-called Revolution in Military Affairs including long-range precision strikes, dominant *battlespace* awareness, and space warfare are all predicated on geographic technologies (Corson and Palka 2004).

Maps have always been critical tools for soldiers. The challenge has always been to produce accurate maps at appropriate scales that can be quickly distributed to troops. The US and other NATO armies now have the capability to update and rapidly produce maps in mobile units. An Air Force program called *Falcon View* provides a digital map of all of Iraq that can zoom in and out to change scales. The classified version enables users to zoom in to see satellite imagery of an area at very high resolution. Users can customize their maps and print them out as needed. The integration of digital maps into systems such as the Military Tracking System (MTS) coupled digital mapping with a global posi-tioning system. MTS provides a digital map display with icons that show one's location and the location of other MTS-equipped units. MTS also facilitates text messaging via satellite and thus is an excellent long-range communications system.

Since the first use of kites and balloons with cameras, remote sensing has been a tool for the soldier. Satellite imagery and data from other sensors was important in locating enemy forces. Applications in OIF included the use of *unmanned aerial vehicles (UAVs)* by tactical units to determine what was over the next hill or the next village. The use of small UAVs has extended technologies to individual soldiers who carry a small UAV that they can fling into the air and image either the next terrain feature or the next street within an urban area.

Global Positioning Systems (GPS) were developed by the Department of Defense and its military applications have evolved. GPS is still a useful navigation system to provide one's location, but its integration with digital maps into systems such as MTS now shows one's location on the map and enables one to make navigational calculations. This technology has proven important to logisticians by enabling them to maintain in-transit visibility of convoys and cargos. Another evolution in the use of GPS was for targeting purposes. Cruise missiles that formerly relied on terrain following radar now use GPS to become extraordinarily accurate, and an inexpensive kit turns an old, unguided bomb into a GPS precision-guided Joint Direct Attack Munition (JDAM).

A *Geographic Information System (GIS)* is a computer-based system that collects, stores, analyzes, and displays spatial information to solve problems. A convergence of GIS, using digital maps and fed real-time information via remote sensing, and GPS-equipped units is creating a new generation of digital command and control systems. These systems enable US and Coalition commanders to know the locations and activities of friendly and enemy units, and to achieve dominant battle-space awareness. Systems such as Blue Force Tracker show the location of friendly and enemy units on a digital map display. Commanders can more effectively maneuver their forces, engage targets with greater precision, and minimize fratricide. Logisticians use the Joint Deployment Logistics Network to track and control the distribution of supplies to the force. Systems such as these increase efficiency dramatically (Corson and Palka 2004).

While providing a significant technological advantage, all of these systems have their limitations. Nevertheless, the evolution of these geographic-based technologies is proving revolutionary and enables military forces to be more efficient, more lethal, and more precise in the application of force to reduce civilian casualties and unintended damage.

Conclusion

This chapter examined the military geography of Iraq and OIF. In terms of physical geography, Iraq is a country the size of California and has three major physiographic regions ranging from marshlands and deserts to mountains, and two major rivers that are the lifeblood of the country. It is an arid country with desert and steppe environments in the south and central regions, and a mountainous region with a Mediterranean climate in the north. Heat, dust, and rain pose challenges, and hazards such as sandstorms and flooding can severely affect military operations (Malinowski 2004).

Iraq's human geography is even more complex. Although most Iraqis are ethnically Arab, 80 percent speak Arabic, and the great majority are Muslim, the cultural/political divide between the Shi'a majority and the Sunni and Kurd minorities is great. These cultural differences translate into a complex political geography where a newly democratic Iraq finds itself facing a second round of national elections in 2010. The Shi'a majority and Kurds support the elections as do most Sunnis, but a small and violent minority have alternative agendas and ambitions to derail the political process so that they may impose their version of a new Iraqi state, whether that be an Islamic fundamentalist theocracy or a return to Ba'athist authoritarian rule. This drama is played out in an urbanized landscape where most Iraqis live in large cities that make complex battlefields.

Iraq stands at a crossroads. As of this writing, the political process continues and national elections are scheduled for January of 2010, but their successful execution and outcome are not assured. Time will tell whether Iraq becomes the stable, democratic, and prosperous country envisioned previously by the Bush Administration and currently by President Obama; or a failed state that devolves into civil war, destabilizing the region and becoming a spawning ground for Islamic terrorist attacks against the US and the West. In either case, knowledge of the physical and human geography of Iraq or any other place is essential if one is to be successful in warfare, nation building, and peacemaking.

Editor's note: This chapter is a significantly revised and updated version of a chapter previously published in: Palka, E. J. & F. A. Galgano. 2005. *The scope of military geography.* New York, NY: McGraw Hill; and Palka, E. J., F. A. Galgano, & M. W. Corson. 2005. "Operation Iraqi Freedom: a military geographical perspective." *Geographical Review* 95(3): 373–99.

References cited

Besheer, M. 2009. "UN envoy: Iraq: provincial elections 'historic.'" Voice of America News (3 February). www.voanews.com/english/index.cfm [accessed 30 April 2010].

Clark, W. K. 2004. *Winning modern wars: Iraq, terrorism and the American empire.* New York, NY: PublicAffairs.

Collins, J. M. 2003. "Military geography of Iraq." *U.S. Naval Institute Proceedings* (May). www.usni.org/Proceedings/Articles03/proCollinsIraq3.htm [accessed 15 March 2005].

Corson, M. W. 2001. "Strategic mobility in the 21st century: projecting national power in a MOOTW environment." In *The scope of military geography*, E. J. Palka & F. A. Galgano (eds). New York, NY: McGraw-Hill, Inc.

Corson, M. W. & E. J. Palka. 2004. "Geotechnology, the U.S. military, and war." In *Geography and technology*, S. D. Brunn, S. L. Cutter, & J. W. Harrington (eds). Dordrecht, Netherlands: Kluwer Academic Publishers.

Dalton, J. B. 2004. "Historical geography." In *Geographic perspectives: Iraq*, J. C. Malinowski (ed.). New York, NY: McGraw-Hill/Duskin.

Department of Defense (DoD). 1992. *Conduct of the Persian Gulf War: final report to Congress.* Washington, DC: US Government Printing Office.

Fontenot, G., E. Degan, & D. Tohn. 2003. *On point: the United States Army in Operation Iraqi Freedom.* Leavenworth, KS: Center for Army Lessons Learned.

Gamez, A. & R. F. Watson. 2004. *Combat health support (CHS) rehearsals.* Fort Leavenworth, KS: US Army Combined Arms Center, Center for Army Lessons Learned.

Hoffman, B. 2004. *Insurgency and counterinsurgency in Iraq.* Santa Monica, CA: RAND, National Security Research Division.

Krulak, C. C. 1999. "The strategic corporal: leadership in the three block war." *Marines Magazine* (January): 1–7.

McDonald, E. V. & T. G. Caldwell. 2005. "Geochemical characteristics of Iraqi dust and soil samples and related impacts to weapon malfunctions." In *Proceedings of the 6th*

International Conference on Military Geology and Geography. University of Nottingham, Nottingham, England, 19–22 June.

Malinowski, J. C. 2004. *Geographic perspectives: Iraq*. New York, NY: McGraw-Hill/Duskin.

Murray, W. & R. H. Scales. 2003. *The Iraq War: a military history*. Cambridge, MA: Belknap Press of Harvard University Press.

Nyrop, R. F. & H. H. Smith. 1979. *Iraq: a country study*. Washington, DC: US Government Printing Office.

Ochsenwald, W. & S. N. Fisher. 2004. *The Middle East: a history*. Boston, MA: McGraw-Hill, Inc.

Palka, E. J., F. A. Galgano, & M. W. Corson. 2005. "Operation Iraqi Freedom: a military geographical perspective." *Geographical Review* 95(3): 373–99.

Pannell, R. P. 2004. "Climate." In *Geographic perspectives: Iraq*, J. C. Malinowski (ed.). New York, NY: McGraw-Hill/Dushkin.

Peele, R. B. 1997. "The importance of maritime chokepoints." *Parameters* 27(2): 61–74.

Population Reference Bureau (PRB). 2005. *World population data sheet 2005*. Washington, DC: Population Reference Bureau. www.prb.org/pdf05/05WorldDataSheet_Eng.pdf [accessed 30 April 2010].

Sampson, M. R. 2004. "Geomorphology." In *Geographic perspectives: Iraq*, J.C. Malinowski (ed.). New York, NY: McGraw-Hill/Dushkin.

Swearingen, W. D. 1988. "Geopolitical origins of the Iran–Iraq war." *Geographical Review* 78(4): 405–16.

Thompson, W. C. 2004. "Location." In *Geographic perspectives: Iraq*, J. C. Malinowski (ed.). New York, NY: McGraw-Hill/Dushkin.

Tibi, B. 1998. *Conflict and war in the Middle East: from interstate war to new security*. New York, NY: St Martin's Press.

UK MOD. 2003. *Operations in Iraq: first reflections*. London, UK: Ministry of Defence.

US Army. 1992. *ST 101-8: Southwest Asia staff planning book*. Fort Leavenworth, KS: US Army Command and General Staff College.

Woodward, B. 2008. *The war within*. New York, NY: Simon & Schuster.

PART III

Applied military geography

THE EVOLUTION OF THE GLOBAL strategic environment following the end of the Cold War stimulated a completely new approach to global security interests and the field of military geography. The *de facto* strategic partitioning of the world during the Cold War era restricted regional conflicts, or at least ensured that sufficient control was exerted on surrogate regimes to preclude most conflicts from escalating into major wars—such as we saw during the Israeli–Arab conflicts. Ethnic violence, disaster relief missions, peacekeeping operations, and other humanitarian missions were concerns that were usually relegated to the UN, or other non-governmental organizations. The evolving contemporary situation required military geographers to be aware of the breadth and depth of the new strategic reality that necessitated better insight into these complex issues and an ever-shifting strategic setting. However, following World War II, military geographers were mainly focused on the rather limited strategic realities of the Cold War, and military and academic thinking stagnated.

Clearly, all that changed following the end of the Cold War. With the devolution of former Eastern Bloc regimes, the effects of globalization, the rise of Islamo-terrorists, the proliferation of ungoverned space, and the absence of superpower control, smoldering regional, ethnic, and religious enmities erupted into violent regional conflicts that challenged international management. Thus, new missions and strategic realities also demanded an adept understanding of the dynamic factors that have ignited long-smoldering divisions into violent, open warfare. In view of this new operational reality, military geographers have changed their focus in order to anticipate and respond effectively to the uncertainties of a changing technological, social, political, and economic world.

Consequently, the last decade of the twentieth century and the early years of this one have witnessed a rapid evolution of military geography in response to requirements that were formally never considered by military forces, or at least certainly never during the forty-five years following World War II. Clearly, the nature of modern conflict is not new: insurgency, ethnic clashes, and civil war are ancient forms of warfare. We claim, however, that we have witnessed an increase in the frequency of these conflicts during the past twenty years. Certainly, the end of the Cold War generated an entirely new approach to viewing the relationship between military forces and a broader variety of potential missions; military geographers unquestionably have had a critical role in providing cogent analyses to support this paradigm shift. With Somalia, Bosnia, Rwanda, and Kosovo as the precedent, the use of military forces to address the humanitarian dimensions of regional conflict has been now well established. Conflict with clear environmental, humanitarian, and ethnic dimensions, such as those in Darfur have increased the pressure on political leaders, as well as the Department of Defense to commit military units to humanitarian and peacekeeping missions. Accordingly, this section of the book examines the nexus between a broad range of contemporary military problems, geography, and military forces—all from the important vantage point of the military geographer.

In *Chapter 16*, Bill Doe examines the perplexing problem of providing training analogs for US forces. This is important because US forces are expected to deploy anywhere in the world; hence, the DoD has to locate places that can replicate numerous operational environments so that it may properly train units and test equipment to meet the challenges of those environments. One such forbidding environment is the desert, and, in *Chapter 17*, Joseph Henderson uses the 1980 Iranian Hostage rescue mission and Operation Iraqi Freedom to illustrate the considerable operational constraints and challenges imposed by arid regions.

Since Hurricane Andrew in 1992, US forces have been used to respond to a number of natural disasters at home and abroad. So, too, did US forces provide important and timely relief following the Indian Ocean Tsunami in 2004, and they stabilized a deteriorating situation in New Orleans following Hurricane Katrina in 2005. Given that reality, Wiley Thompson offers a timely and insightful perspective of planning requirements for an anticipated catastrophic event along the Oregon coast in *Chapter 18*. In *Chapter 19*, we shift our focus to the profound and debilitating effect that military operations have on ecosystems. The evolution of military conflict has witnessed changes in the size of military forces and weapons technology—armies have become larger and weapons have become more potent. With this in mind, in *Chapter 19*, Joseph P. Hupy examines the effect of military operations on the landscape following the siege at Khe Sanh, Vietnam. In this chapter, he demonstrates how changes in land use following that war have slowed the recovery of the ecosystem.

Operations in Afghanistan and Iraq have demonstrated that who controls the land is a very important piece of geographic data during counter-insurgency operations. In *Chapter 20*, Doug Batson employs a modern version of Napoleon's cadastral system of land analysis to demonstrate how counter-insurgency operations can benefit from this methodology. This chapter is followed by Sarah Meharg's perceptive analysis of the modern trend of identicide, which has become a central component of ethnic conflict, especially in the Balkans. In *Chapter 21*, she examines the burning of the National University and Library in Bosnia, and how Serb forces perpetrated this event to, in part, wipe away very important Bosnian historical records and, thus, eliminate their identity and claims to the land.

In the final two chapters, Clifton Pannell and Frank Galgano examine two very intriguing contemporary military issues facing the US. In *Chapter 22*, Clifton Pannell explores China's rapidly expanding strategic claims within its region and its profound impact on regional and global stability. In *Chapter 23*, Frank Galgano presents an analysis of the perplexing problem of ungoverned space and the reconstitution of the *Taliban* and *al-Qaeda* in western Pakistan. This region has become the epicenter of the Global War on Terror, and the West must contend with violent non-state actors who are essentially operating a parallel government within the Tribal Lands of western Pakistan with the tacit acceptance of the Pakistani government.

The chapters of this section collectively represent an interesting and significant cross-section of some of the captivating contemporary problems being examined by military geographers. They demonstrate many of the seminal issues of regional and global security related to globalization, the devolving governance in many of the world's developing states, and the proliferation of ethnic and sub-national tensions that threaten warfare. Collectively, they demonstrate the very power of geography and the clear relevance of military geography in the modern world.

Chapter sixteen

Military lands as spatial analogs for a twenty-first-century Army

Natural environments for testing and training

WILLIAM W. DOE III

Introduction

US MILITARY INSTALLATIONS COMPRISE approximately 30 million acres of the federal land management system. While these lands quantitatively represent only 7 percent of the total federal lands, and less than 1 percent of the total acreage of the fifty states, they are critical to the Department of Defense (DoD) for training military personnel and testing military equipment. In a spatial sense, these lands are distributed throughout a variety of geomorphic provinces and climatic regimes, thus enabling soldiers and equipment to be exposed to those conditions they may find in operational environments worldwide. Essentially, these military lands represent analogs to other places in the world where US forces may operate (Doe and Bailey 2007). The US Army manages almost two-thirds ($\approx$ 18 million acres) of the DoD acreage. There is a direct geographic relationship between where the Army trains soldiers and tests equipment and where it will deploy its forces. Military geography provides ample evidence that understanding and adapting to the physical environment is a prerequisite for operational success.

Presently, Army units are deployed in more than 120 countries, across six continents, to support a wide range of missions, including combat operations, peacekeeping, stability, and humanitarian response. The vast geographic regions in which US forces operate contain a spectrum of natural environments that present unique and varied operational challenges to soldiers and equipment. As shown in Figures 16.1 and 16.2 these forces are deployed under the direction of six regional *Combatant Commands* (see Figure 2.1, Chapter 2). As the Combatant Commanders consider the deployment of their forces against a wide and emerging array of threats to national security, each must fully consider the

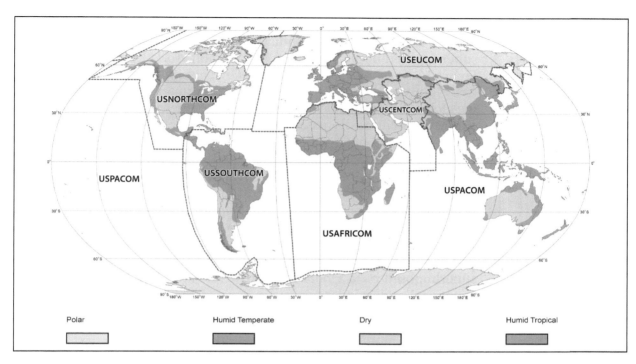

Figure 16.1
World climatic regions—Combatant Commanders' Areas of Responsibility.

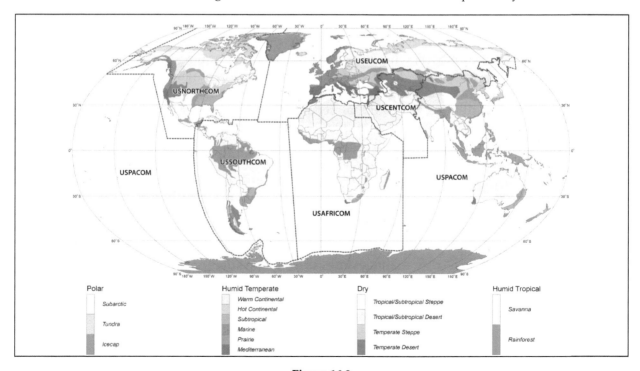

Figure 16.2
MOEs—Combatant Commanders' Areas of Responsibility.

environmental factors that will be encountered their Area of Responsibility (AOR). Regional boundaries of the Combatant Commands are superimposed upon a map of four common *World Climatic Regions* (see Figure 16.1) and fifteen common *Military Operating Environments (MOEs)* (see Figure 16.2), delineating physical and climatic environments across the globe. The derivation and applications of the World Climatic Regions and MOEs will be discussed further in this chapter.

Emerging and potential threats from transnational actors, regional and emerging global competitors, and failed states present a complex and multi-dimensional array of adversaries and challenges across the globe, and US forces must adapt to face each unique scenario. In his visionary book, *The Pentagon's New Map,* Thomas Barnett (2004) defines a global region, the Non-Integrating Gap, where the majority of conflicts, disasters, and military deployments have occurred during the past fifteen years. As demonstrated in Figure 16.3 these conflict areas are superimposed on a global map of MOEs, and principally include the equatorial and mid-latitudinal regions of the Caribbean Rim, Africa, the Balkans, the Caucasus, Central Asia, the Middle East, Southwest Asia, and Southeast Asia. The Non-Integrated Gap region lies outside what Barnett defines as the Functioning Core—the regions of North America, Europe, East Asia, and Australia. The Gap region is characterized by diverse natural settings where environmental conditions—disease, famine, and poverty induced by natural disasters and resource exploitation—often contribute to or trigger violent conflict. These regions are largely composed of desert and tropical regions in developing countries, where the exploitation of natural resources, combined with a wide range of natural disasters and climate change, are causing increased internal conflict and population migrations. Several recent reports address the national security implications of these evolving conflicts (CNA 2007; Palka 2008). Furthermore, emerging concerns about the availability of oil and other fossil fuel reserves have raised the stakes in the Middle East, Southwest Asia, and the former Soviet republics.

Thus, it is increasingly important that Army forces are able to train in a variety of physical and climatic environments at their home installations in the US (Doe et al. 1999; Shaw et al. 2000). Figure 16.4 depicts the spatial distribution and approximate size of forty of the Army's major installations in the fifty States and territories. While the Army manages hundreds of installations, these forty represent the diversity and scale of its land inventory. The installation boundaries in Figure 16.4 are superimposed on a map of the MOEs found within the geographic boundaries of the US. All of the MOEs, except tundra, are at least minimally represented by the Army's land inventory. However, as will be discussed further in this chapter there are critical shortages in the Army's inventory for several critical MOEs, given expected strategic challenges.

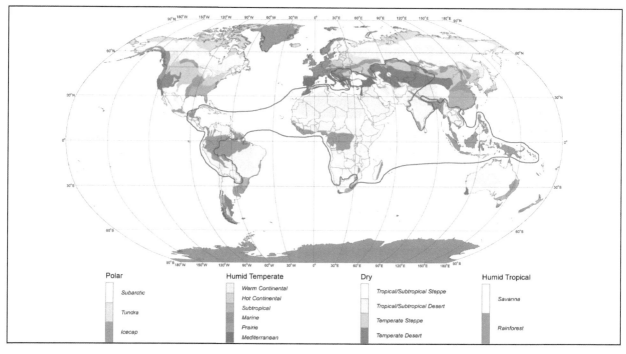

Figure 16.3
MOEs—Non-Integrating Gap Region.

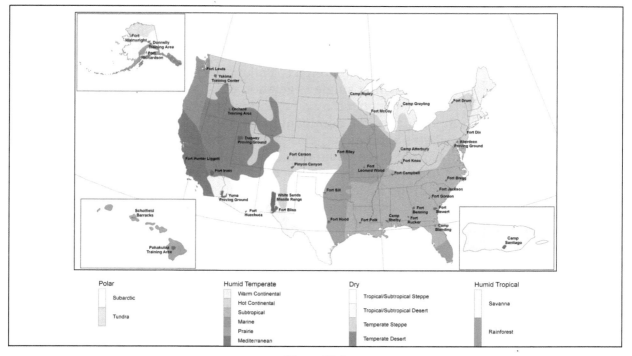

Figure 16.4
MOEs—major US Army installation analogs.

Bailey's ecoregional framework

The MOE framework was developed by a panel of civilian scientists and Army planners to better understand the importance of existing military lands and their analog relationships to operational environments (Doe and Bailey 2007; King et al. 1998, 2004, 2009). This framework is derived from the hierarchical ecosystem classification system designed by Dr R. G. Bailey of the US Forest Service, and hence known as Bailey's ecoregional classification system (Bailey 1998*a*, 1998*b*, 2005). This system is used extensively by federal, state, and regional agencies for environmental planning, research, and analysis.

The primary factor used in Bailey's *ecoregion* classification system is the climatic regime, defined as the seasonality of temperature and precipitation. The global distribution and patterns of climatically similar environments depend broadly upon large-scale climate controls. These controls include: latitude, continental position, global atmospheric patterns, and oceanic circulation patterns. The presence of major mountain ranges further modifies these patterns and their geographic distribution.

Bailey's ecoregions are large, regional-scale ecosystems. Climatic parameters are used to establish ecoregional differences. However, no attempt is made to use the climatic parameters to establish specific ecoregional boundaries. Rather, climatic differences are inferred where discontinuities appear in physiography (e.g. where flat plains change to mountains) and/or vegetation physiognomy (e.g. where tall-grass prairie changes to short-grass steppe or savanna). In other instances, geological boundaries are used because different types of geology override the climatic effect (Bailey 2005). Generally each climate is associated with a single vegetation class (such as broadleaf deciduous forest), characterized by a broad uniformity both in appearance and in composition of the dominant plant species.

Bailey's ecoregional classification system divides the earth's land surface into three different hierarchical classes, increasing in specificity, and called Domains, Divisions, and Provinces. Each category of the classification system can be mapped at different geospatial scales based on specific environmental criteria. Depending on the geospatial scale, the classes are designed to exhibit similar patterns in: (1) climate, (2) vegetation, (3) topography and landform, (4) hydrologic function, and (5) soils. At the Province level, the macro-features of associated plant formations are used to further distinguish climatic differences. At both the Division and Province levels, mountainous regions are distinguished from their surrounding lowland classification because mountain climates are vertically differentiated based upon the temperature and precipitation changes that occur with altitude (Bailey 1998*a*). As an example of this altitudinal zonation at an equatorial latitude, a high mountain range (e.g. 4000 meters elevation) may exhibit several climatic zones from its base to its peak, with associated vegetation types, ranging from tropical to subarctic.

Domains constitute the four principal sub-continental regions of closely related climatic zones. These macro-environments comprise land areas of related climates that are characterized by broad differences in latitudinally controlled annual temperature, precipitation, and evapotranspiration. Three domains are humid and differentiated based on their thermal character: Polar with no warm season; Humid Temperate, rainy with mild to severe winters; and Humid Tropical, rainy with no winter season. The fourth Domain, Dry, is defined solely based on moisture and transects the otherwise humid climates.

Divisions are the second-order classes recognized based on the seasonality of precipitation or degree of dryness or cold. Bailey identifies fifteen Divisions worldwide. The Divisions correspond to groups of specific climate as determined by regions of vegetative similarity (e.g. rainforest, tundra) within the same zones of regional climate. The climate is not uniform within each Division. For example, there is a wide range of aridity within dry climates, ranging from very dry deserts through areas with transitional levels of moisture in the direction of the adjacent moist areas. Climatic and vegetation criteria that are representative of each of the Divisions are given in Table 16.1.

Table 16.1: Criteria for Bailey's divisional classification system

Divisional name	Criteria
Icecap	All months below 0°C (32°F); perpetual snow and ice
Tundra	All months below 10°C (50°F). Vegetation physiognomy: tundra
Subarctic	Up to 3 months over 10°C (50°F). Vegetation physiognomy: dense coniferous forest dominant
Warm continental	Same as hot continental, warmest below 22°C (71°F)
Hot continental	4–7 months over 10°C (50°F), coldest month below 0°C, warmest above 22°C (71°F)
Subtropical	Same as Mediterranean, no dry season
Marine	4–7 months above 10°C (50°F), coldest month over 0°C (32°F)
Prairie	Sub-humid. Vegetation physiognomy: grasslands
Mediterranean	8 months over 10°C (50°F), coldest below 18°C (64.4°F), dry summer
Tropical/subtropical steppe	Semi-arid: all months above 0°C (32°F)
Tropical/subtropical desert	Arid: half precipitation of steppes, all months above 0°C (32°F)
Temperate steppe	Semi-arid: cold month below 0°C (32°F)
Temperate desert	Arid: all months dry, cold month below 0°C (32°F)
Savanna	Same as rainforest, with 2 months dry in winter
Rainforest	Wet: no dry season

In adopting Bailey's ecoregional system for Army use, the four Domains are renamed *World Climatic Regions* and the fifteen Divisions are renamed as *MOEs*. These levels of classification best define and characterize the operational levels of natural environments in which Army operations may occur (Doe and Bailey 2007).

Three MOEs are defined within the Polar World Climatic Region: icecap, dominated by permanent ice sheets (e.g. Greenland and Antarctica); tundra, where the average annual temperature of the warmest month lies between 0 and 10°C (32–50°F), and subarctic, where only one month each year has an average temperature above 10°C (50°F). The Humid Temperate World Climatic Region is divided into six MOEs based on distinct combinations of winter and summer temperatures. The Warm Continental is characterized by cold, snowy winters and warm summers, the Hot Continental regions have cold winters and hot summers, and Subtropical regions are rainy and characterized by mild winters and hot summers. The prairie is classified as a sub-humid area that is transitional between dry and humid climates. The Mediterranean classification has dry, hot summers and rainy, warm winters, whereas the marine environment is characterized by rainy, mild winters and warm summers. The Dry World Climatic Region can be partitioned into arid areas (deserts) and semi-arid areas (steppes) that separate arid regions from humid climate regions. Four MOEs are defined as the tropical/subtropical steppe: a large semi-arid zone with tropical deserts to the north and south; the temperate steppe is characterized by a semi-arid continental climate with cold winters and warm to hot summers; the tropical/subtropical desert is characterized by extremely arid conditions with high air and soil temperatures; and the temperate desert is arid with hot summers and cold winters. In the Humid Tropical World Climatic Region, which contains two MOEs, there is no winter season and each month has an average temperature above 18°C (64°F). The Savanna has distinct wet and dry seasons that lead to the development of tall grasslands that manifest drought-tolerant shrubs and trees. The Rainforest is located astride the Equator, ranging between 10°N and 10°S latitude and has a wet, equatorial climate with no distinct dry season. Figure 16.6 illustrates the percentage distribution of the fifteen MOEs and four World Climatic Regions.

Figures 16.5 and 16.6 illustrate the percentage distribution of World Climatic Regions and MOEs within each of the major AORs. These pie charts are useful as planning tools to quickly discern the types and amounts of natural environments present within each military region.

Because of altitudinal zonation, whereby ecoregional patterns change with increasing elevation at a given location, mountainous regions present unique environments that must be considered within each of the fifteen MOEs. Within the MOE system, mountainous regions have

Table 16.2: Distribution of world acreage by MOE and World Climatic Region

MOE category	% world acreage by MOE	% world acreage by World Climatic Region
Icecap	10%	27% Polar
Tundra	4%	
Subarctic	13%	
Warm continental	2%	16% Humid Temperate
Hot continental	2%	
Subtropical	4%	
Marine	2%	
Prairie	4%	
Mediterranean	2%	
Tropical/subtropical steppe	10%	30% Dry
Tropical/subtropical desert	14%	
Temperate steppe	2%	
Temperate desert	4%	
Savanna	17%	27% Humid Tropical
Rainforest	10%	

been incorporated into the corresponding adjacent 'lowland' category for this level of analysis. However, it is useful from an operational perspective to understand where mountain environments exist, regardless of their discrete latitude or continent. Figure 16.7 depicts the mountainous regions of the world as defined by Bailey's system. As shown in Figure 16.7, mountainous ecoregions are distributed across each continent, and represent approximately 22 percent of the world's land surface (Bailey 1998*a*).

Figure 16.5
Distribution of
Combatant Commands
by World Climatic
Region.

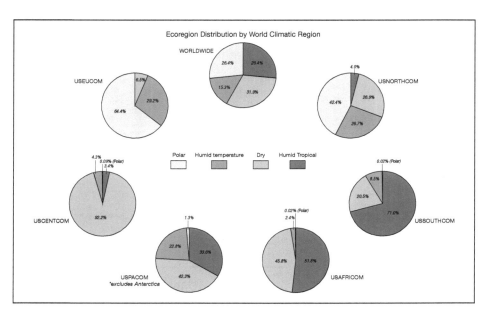

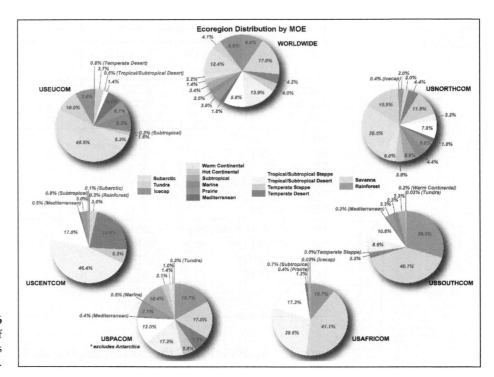

Figure 16.6
Distribution of Combatant Commands by MOE.

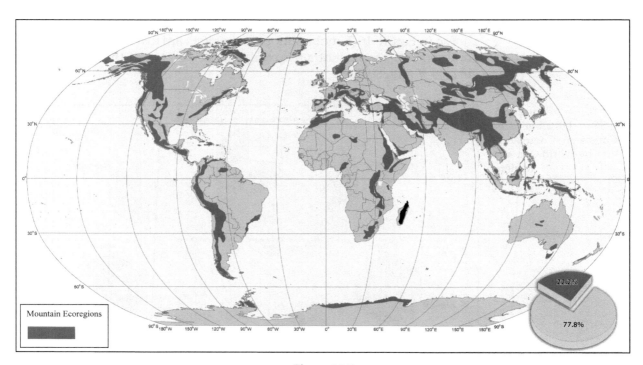

Figure 16.7
MOEs—mountain classification.

The Army's installations as analogs

The US Army manages a diverse inventory of installations in the US and at forward basing areas to train its forces and test equipment prior to deployment (Shaw et al. 2000; Doe et al. 1999). The ability to conduct pre-deployment activities in similar natural environments and settings is critical to mission success. The Army's National Training Center (NTC) in the Mojave Desert of California, and the Yuma Proving Ground (YPG) in the southwestern desert region of Arizona, have been essential resources to prepare and test units and equipment for extended operations in similar arid environments during Operation Desert Storm and Operation Iraqi Freedom (OIF) (King et al. 2004). Similarly, Army installations in Alaska and Hawaii provide training and testing capabilities in preparation for deployments to mountainous, cold regions and tropical environments, respectively, which are found on other continents (Doe 2009; Harmon et al. 2008; King et al. 2009). For example, US forces deployed to Afghanistan have participated in major campaigns during Operation Enduring Freedom (OEF) in the Hindu Kush mountain range and Central Highlands of northeastern Afghanistan along the Pakistan border, with the need for specialized conditioning and equipment associated with high-altitude environments. Army forces participating in humanitarian relief missions in Southeast Asia and Indonesia have experienced tropical environmental conditions, including the need for training in disease and vector control, water sanitation, and typhoon response. Future conflict and potential disaster areas may differ significantly from current operations in terms of climate, physiography, and other environmental parameters. Therefore, the Army must continue to assess its land inventory to provide a variety of training and testing environments. Figure 16.8 illustrates this analog relationship for three Army installations in the tropical/subtropical MOE of the desert southwest.

Table 16.3 displays the locations of forty major US Army installations (given in Figure 16.4) and their corresponding MOEs. Table 16.4 identifies major strategic regions of US deployment abroad. It is evident from spatial distribution of these illustrations that there are many Army installations that reside within the hot continental and subtropical climates, and hence are similar in their physical characteristics to potential deployment areas (i.e. Russia, Kazakhstan, Georgia, Turkey, Afghanistan, China, Korea, etc.). As shown in Table 16.4, geographic areas of tropical/subtropical desert and temperate desert (i.e. Iraq, Iran, Sudan, Egypt, Algeria), locations where many conflicts are occurring, are also well represented by Army installations. However, this comparison also reveals a significant lack of adequate land resources that represent potential conflict areas in the Mediterranean, savanna, and tropical rainforest MOEs. This is important and ironic because, in the late 1990s, the US returned existing tropical training and testing areas in Panama

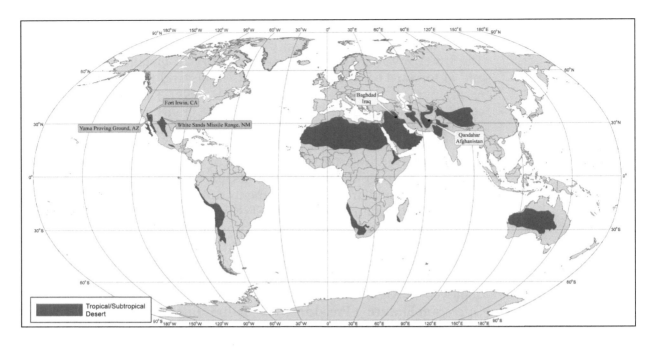

to the Panamanian government, eliminating the US Jungle Warfare School that was used to train soldiers since the early days of the Vietnam Conflict. Existing training and testing areas in tropical ecoregions in Hawaii and Puerto Rico are lacking in tropical characteristics, and are limited by other factors (King et al. 1998, 2009).

Conclusion

Army installations and their associated military lands are important natural assets to the Army's strategic readiness. As a comprehensive federal land inventory, allocated specifically for the training and testing of military forces and equipment, these installations represent spatially distributed geographic analogs to current and potential deployment areas abroad. In order to fully understand these analog relationships, the use of Bailey's ecoregional classification system was adopted to compare forty of the Army's major installations with current and potential deployment areas. This system defines four World Climatic Regions and fifteen Military Operating Environments. This comparison illustrates that the Army's land inventory is well suited to meet operational demands, although critical land shortfalls exist in both tropical and savanna landscapes. The Army must continue to assess its land requirements for training and testing as strategic threats and new strategic objectives emerge.

Table 16.3: MOE distribution of forty major US Army installations

MOEs	Major Army installation analogs									
Subarctic	Fort Wainwright, AK	Fort Richardson, TA, AK	Donnelly TA, AK							
Warm continental	Camp Grayling, MI									
Hot continental	Fort Knox, KY	Fort Leonard Wood, MO	Fort Campbell, KY	Fort Drum, NY	Camp Ripley, MN	Fort McCoy, WI	Fort Dix, NJ	Camp Atterbury, IN		
Subtropical	Aberdeen Proving Ground, MD	Fort Benning, GA	Fort Bragg, NC	Fort Stewart, GA	Fort Polk, LA	Fort Rucker, AL	Fort Jackson, SC	Fort Gordon, GA	Camp Blanding, FL	Camp Shelby, MS
Marine	Fort Lewis, WA									
Prairie	Fort Riley, KS	Fort Hood, TX								
Mediterranean	Fort Hunter Liggett, CA									
Tropical/ subtropical steppe	Fort Sill, OK									
Tropical/ subtropical desert	Fort Irwin, CA	Fort Bliss, TX	Fort Huachuca, AZ	White Sands Missile Range, NM	Yuma Proving Ground, AZ					
Temperate steppe	Fort Carson, CO	Pinon Canyon Maneuver Site, CO								
Temperate desert	Yakima Training Center, WA	Dugway Proving Ground, UT	Orchard Training Area, ID							
Savanna	Camp Santiago, Puerto Rico	Pohakuloa Training Area, HI								
Rainforest	Schofield Barracks, HI									

Table 16.4: Worldwide deployment areas of US Army by MOE

Potential deployment areas	MOE	Army installation analogs
Iraq, Kuwait, Saudi Arabia (Southwest Asia), Afghanistan	Tropical/subtropical desert	Fort Irwin, CA; Fort Bliss, TX; Yuma Proving Ground, AZ; White Sands Missile Range, NM; Fort Huachuca, AZ
Iran, Somalia	Tropical/subtropical steppe	Fort Hood, TX; Fort Sill, OK
Korea	Hot continental	Fort Campbell, KY; Fort Knox, KY; Fort Drum, NY; Fort Leonard Wood, MO
Haiti	Savanna, rainforest	None
Panama, Nicaragua (Latin America)	Savanna, rainforest	None
Rwanda, Ivory Coast (Africa)	Savanna, rainforest	None
Philippines, Indonesia	Savanna, rainforest	None
Bosnia, Kosovo	Mediterranean	None

Acknowledgements

The author would like to thank Dr Robert G. Bailey, USDA-Forest Service, Fort Collins, Colorado, for his collegial and scientific contributions towards adopting his ecoregions classification framework for the US Army as the MOE system. The author also acknowledges the leadership and funding support of Mr Graham Stullenbarger, formerly Chief, Natural Environments Test Office (NETO), US Army Yuma Proving Ground (YPG), Yuma, AZ, who was instrumental in initiating many of the studies referenced in this chapter. Finally, the author acknowledges the technical mapping and graphics support of Shannon Voggesser and Tracy Wager, both of the Center for Environmental Management of Military Lands (CEMML), Warner College of Natural Resources, Colorado State University.

References cited

Bailey, Robert G. 1998*a*. *Ecoregions: the ecosystem geography of the oceans and continents.* New York: Springer-Verlag, p. 176.

——. 1998*b*. *Ecoregions map of North America (explanatory note)* US Department of Agriculture, US Forest Service Miscellaneous Publication 1548, p. 10.

——. 2005. "Identifying ecoregion boundaries." *Environmental management* 34(Supp 1): S14–26.

Barnett, Thomas P.M. 2004. *The Pentagon's new map: war and peace in the twenty-first century.* New York: G.P. Putnam's Sons, p. 435.

Center for Naval Analyses (CNA) Corporation 2007. *National security and the threat of climate change.* Alexandria, VA, http://SecurityandClimate.cna.org [accessed 30 April 2010], p. 63.

Doe, W. W. 2009. "Cold regions and mountain testing and training areas in the U.S." Proceedings, 8th International Conference on Military Geosciences, 15–19 June, Vienna, Austria.

Doe, William W. & Robert G. Bailey 2007. *Military operating environments: an ecoregions framework to characterize U.S. Army testing and training lands as operational analogs*. Interim Contract Report, Center for Environmental Management of Military Lands, Colorado State University, p. 56.

Doe, W. W., R. S. Shaw, R. G. Bailey, D. S. Jones, & T. E. Macia. 1999. "Locations and environments of U.S. Army training and testing lands." *Federal Facilities Environmental Journal* (autumn): 9–26.

Harmon, R. S., E. J. Palka, C. Collins, W. Doe, E. McDonald, K. Redmond, C. Ryerson, S. Shoop, L. Spears, & M. Sturm. 2008. *Scientific characterization of cold region environments for Army testing of materiel and systems and a technical analysis of interior Alaska*. West Point, NY: Center for Environmental and Geographic Sciences, US Military Academy, p. 80.

King, W. C., E. J. Palka, J. Juvik, R. Harmon, Jan M. H. Hendrickx, S. Fleming, & W. W. Doe. 2009. *A technical analysis of locations for tropical testing of Army materiel and opportunities for tropical training of Army personnel*. West Point, NY: Center for Environmental and Geographic Sciences, US Military Academy, p. 107.

King, W. C., D. Gilewitch, R. S. Harmon, E. McDonald, K. Redmond, J. Gillies, W. Doe, S. Warren, V. Morrill, G. Stullenbarger, & L. Havrilo. 2004. *Scientific characterization of desert environments for military testing, training and operations*. Army Research Office Report, April, p. 111.

King, W. C., R. S. Harmon, T. Bullard, W. Dement, W. Doe, J. Evans, M. C. Larsen, W. Lawrence, K. McDonald, & V. Morrill. 1998. *A technical analysis to identify ideal geographic locations for tropical testing of Army materiel and systems*. Army Research Office Report, July, p. 47.

Palka, E. J. 2008. "Potential effects of climate change on the U.S. Army, regional instability, and war." In *Climatic change and variation: a primer for teachers*, William A. Dando (ed.), 175–9. Washington, DC: National Council for Geographic Education (NCGE).

Shaw, R. S., W. W. Doe, E. J. Palka, & T. E. Macia. 2000. "Sustaining Army lands for readiness in the 21st century." *Military Review* (Sept–Oct): 68–77.

Chapter seventeen
Aeolian processes and military operations

JOSEPH P. HENDERSON

Introduction

A EOLIAN PROCESSES, PARTICULARLY THE entrainment and transport of dust, can have a significant effect on military operations in arid regions. For military forces, dust storms have been a particular hindrance during desert operations throughout history. During the twentieth century, the two World Wars, with extensive campaigns in the Middle East and North Africa, demonstrated that dust could be a formidable adversary. More recently, a dust storm in March 2003 slowed the advance of Coalition forces toward Baghdad during Operation Iraqi Freedom (OIF). Not only does dust cause maintenance problems and slow offensive operations on the ground, but also these events can substantially disrupt air operations. This chapter uses two historical vignettes to illustrate the effect of dust storms. The first is the Iran Hostage rescue attempt in 1980, also known as Operation Eagle Claw, and the second is the large dust storm of March 2003 that substantially slowed a major offensive during OIF.

General overview of aeolian processes

The term *aeolian* refers to the geomorphic processes associated with wind action. These processes are most effective in arid regions where vegetative cover, moisture, and other forms of protection for fine, unconsolidated surface sediments are scant. Consequently, the effects of aeolian processes on military operations are most pronounced in arid regions. The processes of sediment entrainment and transport by wind are rather complex; therefore, a brief introduction is warranted.

Physical mechanisms of dust erosion and transportation

Erosion and transport are the two processes responsible for the develop-ment of windborne dust particles. The erosional process is *deflation*, where fine, unconsolidated sediments at the surface are lifted into the

278

air by local turbulence at the surface (Leet et al. 1978). Three conditions must exist in order for fine sediments to become entrained by wind. First, the surface must be generally devoid of vegetative cover that holds sediments in place. Second, the surface must be dry, as moisture adds weight and cohesion to individual soil particles. Third, wind speeds must be moderate to high; a general rule of thumb is that wind speeds must exceed 15 knots ($\approx$ 17 m.p.h.) in order to mobilize dust and produce turbulent eddies at the ground level (COMET 2003; El-Baz 1994). Sudden downdrafts in air movement such as those created by thunderstorms are often responsible for the deflation of sediments that would be otherwise undisturbed in the thin layer of calm air near the surface (Leet et al. 1978).

Transportation processes include *creep* (sliding or rolling), *saltation* (bouncing along the surface), and *suspension*. Suspension, where fine particles float high in the air because of turbulent eddies, is the primary transportation mechanism during dust storms. In major news coverage, dust storms are often erroneously referred to as "sand storms," but the processes that form dust events and their characteristics are dissimilar to those of sand storms. Whereas sand storms, consisting of heavier particles, are limited to about 3–6 m ($\approx$ 10–20 ft) above the ground and primarily involve saltation, dust storms extend hundreds of meters into the atmosphere because of the suspension of silt and clay-sized particles.

Bagnold (1941) distinguished the upper limit of dust particle size as approximately 0.2 mm, where the terminal velocity of fall becomes less than the upward eddy currents. The terminal velocity of fall is defined as the constant rate of fall of a particle when the acceleration due to gravity is balanced by the resistance of the air through which the particle falls (Leet et al. 1978). Once entrained by the wind, dust particles can remain aloft much longer than larger, heavier sand-sized sediment. Consequently, dust particles can move over great horizontal distances in excess of 1600 km ($\approx$ 1000 miles) (McKnight and Hess 2005). As this chapter contains vignettes that involve dust storm events, a more in-depth look at dust storms is necessary.

Types of dust storms

Dust storms are events resulting from turbulent wind systems entraining particles of dust into the air, so that visibility is reduced to less than 1000 m ($\approx$ 3280 ft) (Middleton et al. 1986). The extreme reduction in visibility distinguishes dust storms from other aeolian dust events, and dust storms are typically classified by the type of meteorological conditions that form them. The two types of dust storms discussed in this chapter are the *haboob*, generated by thunderstorms, and the synoptically forced or *frontal dust storms* produced by wave cyclones. Although not dust storms in the classic sense, dust clouds generated by helicopter rotor wash will also be introduced, as their effects on rotary-wing aircraft are significant.

THE HABOOB

The term *haboob* is derived from the Arabic word *"Habb,"* meaning wind (Pye 1987). This term is used in the Sudan and Iran to describe dust storms of any origin, and "downdraught *haboob*" is applied more specifically to dust storms generated by the outflow of cool air from cumulonimbus clouds in thunderstorms and maintained by horizontal density gradients (Lawson 1971). Similar phenomena occur in the southwestern US and are referred to as "American *haboobs*" (Idso et al. 1972). Solid walls of dust form at the leading edge of these thunderstorm-generated dust clouds, which have the shape of a density current head. The head of cold air flows along the ground in front of the main belt of hail and rain, and the dust is entrained by shear and pressure fluctuations associated with the nose of the current head. The head may develop a lobed structure due to parcels of warm air becoming trapped beneath the advancing cold-air current (Lawson 1971).

Compared to other types of dust storms, *haboobs* are spatially small and temporally short. They occur within 90–150 km ($\approx$ 55–95 miles) of a collapsing thunderstorm, their average height extends from 2400–4200 m ($\approx$ 7500–13,700 ft), and they are maintained by turbulent mixing in and behind the density head (Idso 1976; Reusse 2002). Winds within a *haboob* may reach 90 km/hr ($\approx$ 55 m.p.h.), and dust particle sizes are normally quite small, ranging from 10–50 micrometers (Edgell 2006). The horizontal extent of a *haboob* averages around 95–145 km ($\approx$ 60–90 miles) (COMET 2003). While the average duration is three hours, visibility usually begins to gradually improve within an hour (Reusse 2002). However, if the trailing thunderstorm does not arrive or the rain evaporates before reaching the ground, the dust may linger for days (Idso 1976). *Haboobs* are normally seasonal events. For example, they are most frequent in the Arabian Desert during the late Northeast Monsoon and the April–May transition period when thunderstorm activity is at its peak (Reusse 2002).

FRONTAL DUST STORMS

In contrast to *haboobs*, frontal dust storms are much larger and may easily exceed 1000 km ($\approx$ 600 miles) in aerial extent. Frontal storms are associated with low-pressure systems influenced by the polar and subtropical jet streams. In the Middle East, these types of dust storms are prevalent in the winter and early spring when the jet stream exerts its greatest influence on the region. The northwesterly winds of the *Shamal* (Arabic for north) produce some of the most hazardous weather in the region (COMET 2003). Maximum sustained winds average around 55 km/hr ($\approx$ 34–45 m.p.h.) with gusts up to 74 km/hr ($\approx$ 45 m.p.h.) (Edgell 2006). Frontal dust storms are much longer in duration compared with *haboobs*, lasting days, rather than hours, and, because of the transitory nature of wave cyclones, the winter *shamal* usually lasts for 3–5 days. Summer *shamals* also occur in parts of the Middle East, but this wind is monsoonal in nature and not associated with wave cyclones. Consequently, the summer *shamal* is much more persistent, lasting for several weeks in many instances (Edgell 2006).

Dust storm source areas

The regions of the world with the most persistent dust storm activity include the Sahara, the Middle East, Southwest Asia, and Mongolia (see Figure 17.1). Besides large-scale and local wind phenomena described above, each of these regions contain areas with fine-grained sediments required for the formation of dust storms. Locally, these areas of silt- and clay-rich soils are typically found in fluvial deposits (Bagnold 1941). Alluvium from floodplains, playas, and dry lakebeds is the major source of sediments entrained in dust storms. Extensive alluvial deposits are found in both Iran and Iraq, where the historical examples in this chapter occurred. Other local sources of fine-grained sediments may be found in areas where extensive maneuver damage of desert pavement has exposed the finer materials just below the protective layer of close-fitting rocks (Gilewitch 2003).

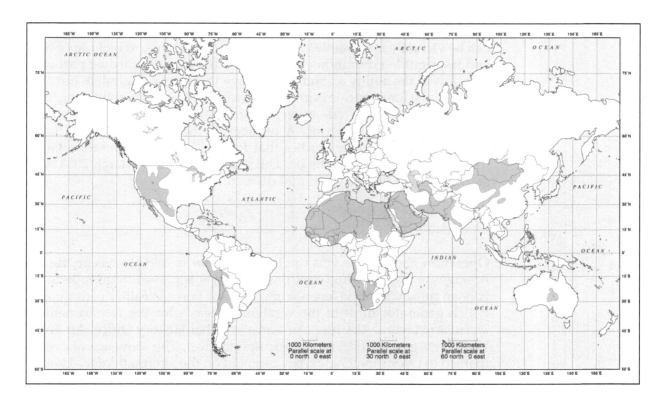

Figure 17.1
Global dust-producing regions. Worldwide, most global airborne dust production occurs in arid regions. Aeolian operations are most effective where dry soils and lack of vegetative cover allow the entrainment of fine surficial materials. The majority of dust storms occur in the Sahara, Middle East, Southwest Asia, and Mongolia. *Source*: USGS.

Effects on military operations

Having examined the physical processes involved in dust storm formation, what follows is a brief discussion of general effects of aeolian processes on military operations, followed by case studies that highlight the profound effect of two discrete events. Aeolian processes place great demands on equipment maintenance, adversely affect soldier health, and influence tactical operations by reducing visibility. Maintaining equipment becomes much more difficult because of the effects of abrasion on exposed surfaces such as rotor blades, decreased performance, and damage to engines and electrical systems, and weapons jamming (Scales 1994). Soldier health is a major concern from the inhalation of airborne particles and pathogens that can lead to respiratory and other illnesses. Moreover, the mere presence of persistent airborne dust can have a negative effect on morale.

Reduced visibility can play havoc on military operations. Air operations can be curtailed or suspended altogether, depending on the capability of the particular aircraft system. Likewise, ground operations can grind to a halt, as occurred during the early phase of OIF. Without sophisticated navigation systems such as GPS, when visibility reaches zero-zero, navigation and command and control during a dust storm can be virtually impossible. Various weapon systems, to include optical and laser-guided munitions, can be degraded by airborne dust particles. Not only is the ability to find and engage the enemy degraded, but also the potential for fratricide is greatly increased. Finally, the ability to gather intelligence is hindered, especially for satellite and reconnaissance aircraft collection platforms. A number of these adverse effects were evident in the two case studies that follow. The first, Operation Eagle Claw, was affected by a *haboob*. The second, the 25–27 March 2003 dust storm during OIF, was a frontal dust storm event.

Operation Eagle Claw

Operation Eagle Claw was the failed attempt in 1980 to rescue the US hostages in Iran. The role environmental events played in this operation is often misunderstood, even within the Air Force Weather community, which generates most of the weather forecasts for the Department of Defense (Moyers, A., Chief, Air Force Weather History Office, Air Force Weather Agency, 2003, email correspondence). The sequence of events that led to Operation Eagle Claw centered on the aftermath of the change of power in Iran that replaced a pro-US regime with a radical Islamic leader who wanted to eliminate all US influence in the state.

A general uprising in Iran in January 1979 forced Shah Mohammed Pahlavi, a staunch US supporter, into exile. Later, the Ayatollah Ruhollah Khomeini, a fundamentalist Shiite cleric, came to power and instituted a radical regime based on a fundamentalist Islamic perspective (Kreisher 1999). In November 1979, with the approval of the regime, thousands of Iranian "students" attacked the US Embassy in Tehran and held fifty-three US diplomats hostage for fourteen months. On 11 April, President Jimmy Carter gave permission to launch a rescue mission, code named Eagle Claw, with a target date of 24–25 April 1980.

The rescue plan

During Eagle Claw, the personnel most affected by the dust event were helicopter crewmembers, with the mission to transport the hostages from Tehran to an extraction airfield southwest of the city. The plan called for eight US Navy *RH-53s* (see Figure 17.2) to depart from the aircraft carrier *Nimitz* about 100 km (≈ 60 miles) off the coast of Iran and fly to a predetermined refueling site called Desert One, about 430 km (≈ 270 miles) southeast of Tehran (see Figure 17.3). At Desert One, the helicopters would be refueled from fuel bladders transported to the site by C-130 airplanes. The C-130s, based out of Oman, would precede the helicopters to the refueling site at Desert One. After departing Desert One, the helicopters would continue toward Tehran, leaving a Delta Force team in a secure area southeast of the city. The Delta Force team would be transported by truck to the Embassy, and, once the hostages were freed, the team and hostages would link up with the helicopters in a nearby stadium. From that point, the helicopters would fly to an airstrip southwest of Tehran, where the hostages and military personnel would board C-141 airplanes for evacuation to Egypt (Cogan 2003).

Figure 17.2
US Navy RH-53 Sea Stallion helicopter takes off from aircraft carrier during Operation Eagle Claw. *Source*: US Navy photograph.

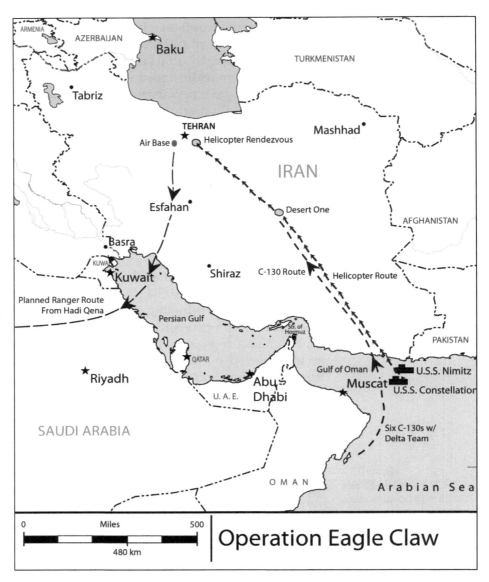

Figure 17.3
Map of Operation
Eagle Claw.

Pre-mission: weather forecasting and mission planning

WEATHER FORECASTING

A team of Air Force weather personnel formed in November 1979, led by Air Force Captain Don Buchanan, the Joint Task Force Environmental Officer. Upon assignment, Buchanan and his team immediately began collecting climatological surveys of Iran and determining available weather reporting stations and satellite coverage for making forecast data (Kyle 1990).

    In their analysis of climate and weather data from the operation area, the team specifically focused on weather hazards that helicopters might encounter *en route* (DoD 1980). The weather team was well aware of the significant weather hazards, including dust/sand hazards, and the frequency and location of suspended dust phenomena were specifically cited in the operation plan weather annex (DoD 1980; Snellman et al. 1980).

Although senior leaders had knowledge that dust hazards might occur in the operations area, the pilots apparently were never briefed, or never saw the weather annex due to reasons of operational security (Ryan 1985). In fact, the weather team had no direct contact with the aircrews, and the pilots received their weather briefings from the intelligence section. Although secrecy was paramount to the success of the operation, the severing of the traditional relationship between pilots and weather forecasters was a flaw that led to critical hazard information not being communicated (DoD 1980). Without knowledge of the hazard, the pilots were ill prepared to react and make tactical decisions once they became engulfed in dust.

Another reason why the pilots were unaware of the possibility of a dust event was that it was not mentioned in the forecast. In fact, the restricted visibility in two regions along the helicopter route was the only weather element in the 24–25 April forecast that did not verify for the entire Middle East region (DAF 1980, Snellman et al. 1980). Along the flight route, the forecast called for nearly clear-sky conditions with good visibility, and the thunderstorms to the west were accurately predicted (US Joint Chiefs of Staff 1980). The clear weather conditions for the flight route were actually a mission requirement levied by the planners and had prompted the final decision to execute (Kyle 1990).

MISSION PLANNING

Because of the high reliance on a clear weather forecast, the mission preparation and training did not appear to take into account the likelihood of a dust storm hazard. Although the pilot training (primarily at Yuma, Arizona) was designed to duplicate as closely as possible the mission profile, to include refueling and ground operations at night (US Joint Chiefs of Staff 1980), the post-mission investigation revealed the pilots were not prepared for the protracted instrument flying encountered (Ryan 1985). In terms of long-range navigation equipment, the RH-53's OMEGA and its inertial navigation systems were state-of-the-art electronic equipment. However, according to the Holloway report, the pilots received only limited training in these systems and were not confident in their ability to employ the equipment (DoD 1980).

Mission execution and the dust encounter

Just after dark on 24 April, the helicopters began their 960 km ($\approx$ 600 miles) flight toward Desert One, flying at altitudes of 30–60 m ($\approx$ 100–200 ft) above the ground. About two hours after takeoff, one of the helicopters received a main rotor blade failure light, and the crew landed, abandoning the aircraft. Shortly after the halfway point—about three hours into the flight—the helicopters entered suspended dust conditions (DAF 1980).

The pilots knew it was suspended dust because they did not experience the noise or abrasion associated with sand, but, instead, felt a powder-like sensation in their mouths (DAF 1980). The pilots described the air as being opaque, like dark milk (US Joints Chiefs of Staff 1980). The cockpit temperatures also increased to about 34°C ($\approx$ 93°C) (Ryan 1985). Consequently, the helicopter formation became somewhat disorganized, but they regrouped when they broke out into a clear area.

Within an hour, however, the helicopters encountered another region of reduced visibility, larger and denser than the first. The pilots estimated the horizontal extent was some 320 km ($\approx$ 200 miles) along the route of flight to an altitude of 1830 m ($\approx$ 6000 ft) (Ryan 1985). The pilots reported no gusty winds within those areas, and the air was stable and smooth. Visibility during this leg of the flight was usually less than 8 km ($\approx$ 5 miles) (DAF 1980). At this point, the dust event began to have a problematical effect on the mission and a second helicopter experienced mechanical failure, this time affecting several critical navigation instruments, and returned to the *Nimitz*. However, the helicopter crews were unaware that, at the time they turned back, they were only 25 minutes from exiting the dust, which was another manifestation of this event. Virtually all the crews experienced vertigo from flying with night vision goggles in extremely low visibility.

The mentally and physically taxing mission of flying 960 km ($\approx$ 600 miles) non-stop wearing full-face night vision goggles was exacerbated by flying through dust during one-third of the route. Some of the Marine pilots stated that flying in the dust cloud was worse than any flying condition they had encountered, including combat missions in Vietnam (Kreisher 1999). Nevertheless, the pilots continued flying at low level for fear of losing contact with terrain features on their maps and to avoid radar detection (Kyle 1990). Sick (1985) described the pilots' failure to rely on on-board navigation equipment as a profoundly human response to technological uncertainty.

The remaining six helicopters were able to continue through the dust, breaking into the clear about 55 km ($\approx$ 35 miles) from the refueling site (i.e. Desert One). Because of the effect of the severe dust on the helicopters and crews, they were behind schedule; when yet another helicopter was grounded due to a partial hydraulic failure, the mission was aborted because the minimum number of helicopters required for the mission was six. Thus, the *haboob* had a decisive effect on the mission: it had reduced the number of available aircraft below the minimum needed, placed the various elements of the rescue team hopelessly behind schedule, and, finally, the flying conditions caused severe fatigue among the air crew—these factors were about to have a disastrous effect. During the subsequent refueling and repositioning operations at Desert

One, an RH-53 collided with a parked C-130 refueling aircraft and eight servicemen were killed in the accident. Dust clouds generated by the rotor wash of the RH-53 produced brownout conditions, which contributed to the mishap. All the helicopters were abandoned, and all personnel departed in the remaining C-130s.

The Haboob

Based on the available evidence, the dust cloud that troubled the pilots was most likely a *haboob* that was generated by thunderstorm activity over the Zagros Mountains to the west of the route. During the period of maximum daytime heating, meteorological satellite imagery showed towering cumulus activity over the Zagros range. The next meteorological satellite coverage showed isolated thunderstorms moving eastward with associated cirrus blow-off over the easternmost ridge of the central Zagros Range (DAF 1980). An upper-level disturbance formed over southwest Iran and caused thunderstorm activity to continue and increase over the Zagros Mountain area (DAF 1980). Although skies over central Iran were cloudy, skies in southeastern Iran were clear in the area of the dissipating southern portion of the frontal system (DAF 1980).

Two separate reviews by the Air Weather Service and a team of civilian weather experts concluded that there was a good probability that gust fronts (or downdrafts) from the thunderstorms over the mountains about 80 km ($\approx$ 50 km) to the west had moved into the valley and raised the dust (Snellman et al. 1980). The turbulence could have caused the fine dust to be suspended in the air for hours (DAF 1980). A meteorological officer in US Marine Forces Central Command who is very familiar with the weather in Iran also speculated that the increase in temperature experienced by the pilots was likely the result of adiabatic warming of the air as it flowed down the mountain into the desert valley (Reusse 2002).

Post-mission analysis

Based on known spatial and temporal weather patterns, there was a reasonable expectation that the pilots might encounter a dust event during the mission. The fatal geographic flaw in the overall plan was the lack of preparation for this contingency. Clearly, the pilots were not adequately prepared for low-visibility conditions that would preclude terrain-following using their night vision goggles. That not a single aircraft crashed when flying in almost zero visibility near mountainous terrain is astonishing and a credit to the skill and determination of the pilots. The stress and fatigue of the long flight mission (seven hours in the cockpit), coupled with limited visibility, placed tremendous demands on the helicopter crews, and these conditions directly affected mission execution. In the refueling accident, the extreme fatigue of the pilots, exacerbated by the dust encountered *en route*, contributed to the refueling disaster at Desert One.

Given the state of the art of forecasting at that time, could the localized weather conditions have been anticipated? The special weather review teams concluded that the forecasters could not have predicted this mesoscale event with the degree of skill necessary for use during the operation (Snellman et al. 1980; DAF 1980). The forecast was as accurate as the data available and the state of the art of meteorology permitted (Snellman et al. 1980; DAF 1980). For example, weather satellites, in the 1980s at least, were not capable of producing accurate and timely imagery of dust clouds (Ryan 1985).

That the forecast was very accurate except for the dust events is remarkable considering that there were no active reporting stations along the route of flight, and Iran is considered a sparse weather data area (DAF 1980). Ironically, there were two automatic weather stations along the flight path that might have provided useful information; however, they had broken down during the Khomeini regime and not been repaired (Sick 1985).

The rescue team's reliance on clear weather as a mission prerequisite was a major oversight, and perhaps unrealistic. There was enough confidence in the forecaster's ability that alternative means to visual flight conditions were not pursued (DoD 1980). This mindset kept leadership from focusing on the worst-case scenario and developing plans to mitigate any weather hazards that might be encountered. The Holloway report observed that years of observations are necessary to reliably predict weather patterns, and the mission planners should have been more aggressive in their pursuit of contingencies that would reduce uncertainties with regard to the mission (DoD 1980).

Post-operation equipment and training improvements

Operation Eagle Claw was the subject of intense investigation, particularly within the Special Operations and Air Force weather communities. While the debate continues on whether or not the dust storm resulted in the failure of the mission, all sides recognize that it was not forecasted, the pilots were ill prepared to deal with the hazard, and the dust significantly hampered the mission.

Within the Special Operations aviation community, the Army developed an elite helicopter unit, known as Task Force 160, which trains extensively on long-range, low-level flying with night vision goggles. To more effectively bring together the Special Operations capabilities of all the armed forces, Congress mandated the Special Operations Command in 1986. The current state of US Special Operations is vastly improved from 1980, and the forces are trained and ready to rapidly react to contingencies in a wide range of terrain and weather conditions.

For the Air Force weather community, the lesson learned was they needed to improve the ability to forecast sand and/or dust events. One of the improvements was the development of the Relocatable Window Model (RWM), a numerical weather prediction capability specifically designed to capture sand/dust storms in the desert. The newest development is the Dust Transport Application (DTA), which can forecast the spatial and temporal extent of a dust storm for days in advance (Kuchera 2003). This new forecasting capability was employed for the first time during combat operations in OIF.

Operation Iraqi Freedom, 25–27 March 2003

It did not take long for aeolian processes to have a significant effect on military operations during OIF. Less than a week into the invasion of Iraq, a massive dust storm engulfed advancing US forces and disrupted operations for over two days. Compared with the dust storm that affected Operation Eagle Claw, this event was much broader in extent and lasted much longer. These qualities are characteristic of a major frontal dust storm such as the *shamal*.

At the time the dust storm struck on 25 March, elements of the 3rd Infantry Division and the 101st Airborne Division were advancing rapidly toward Baghdad from the south. The dust storm halted the 3rd Infantry Division halfway between Najaf and Karbala, within 150 km ($\approx$ 93 miles) of Baghdad. Helicopter operations by the 101st Division, in support of 3rd Infantry Division's attack, were stopped for three days. The 1st Marine Division had advanced northward as well toward Nasiriyah in the center of the country. The dust storm caused logistical problems as even ground vehicle traffic was suspended for a period, and it also provided concealment that permitted Iraqi forces to close with US units—something they had been unable to do previously.

The "mother of all dust storms"

The fine dust that smothered Iraqi and US forces was stirred up by a large wave cyclone with an accompanying cold front that moved eastward off the Mediterranean Sea (see Figures 17.4 and 17.5). The dust storm was of the prefrontal type and was labeled a *shamal* by US forces, but it may have been more aptly named a *turab* since the anomalously strong winds were largely southwesterly early on rather than northerly. In any case, the storm will be called a *shamal* in this chapter as it most resembles the winter *shamal* described in the literature (Anderson 2004). The dust was highly concentrated up to 1.5 km ($\approx$ 1 mile) aloft, and dust particles reached well into the troposphere as high as 10 km ($\approx$ 6 miles), and an analysis of available weather data indicates that this was likely a once-in-a-decade type of event (Grumm 2009). Winds were strong and sustained, reaching 50 knots ($\approx$ 60 m.p.h.) or greater at the surface (Atkinson 2004). On the morning of 27 March, the dust finally cleared from the area of operations as high pressure moved into the region.

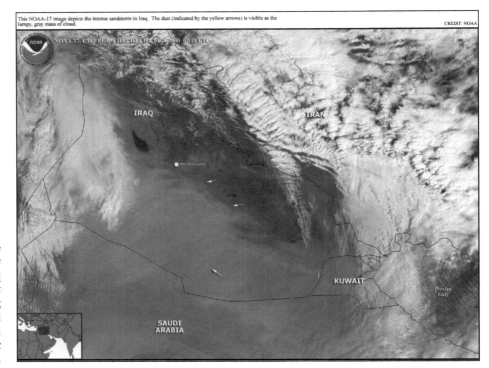

Figure 17.4
NOAA 17 satellite image
of dust storm over Iraq
on 26 March 2003. Light
arrows indicate blowing
dust. *Source*: National
Oceanic and
Atmospheric
Administration.

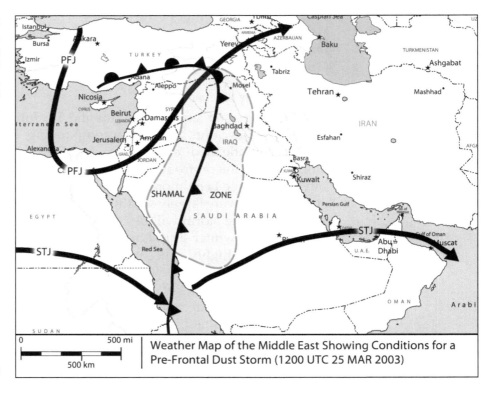

Figure 17.5
Weather map for 25
March 2003 showing the
cold front and position of
the polar and subtropical
jets. *Source*: Air Force
Weather Agency.

Unlike the *haboob* that affected the Iran hostage rescue attempt, this storm was well forecasted up to five days out (Anderson 2004). Numerical weather prediction models as well as the latest advances such as DTA were employed with a high degree of skill. Commanders took full advantage of the forecast to tailor battle plans and implement measures to prepare for the weather conditions. For example, the early warning of the impending storm allowed planners to front-load air tasking orders with additional sorties prior to the onset of the bad weather. Furthermore, planned weapons loads for fighter-bombers were shifted in favor of GPS-guided munitions (Anderson 2004).

Effects of the dust storm

Despite efforts to prepare for the dust storm, its effects were significant, although it was essentially an inconvenience that did not turn the tide of the war. Yet, the *shamal* was able to halt the advance of a powerful, well-equipped military force. The blowing sand and dust resembled brown talc that coated equipment and soldiers, forcing them to use all means available to cover themselves and their equipment (Atkinson 2004). Sunlight refracting through the heavy dust particles in the lower atmosphere gave the air an orange to crimson hue. Raindrops were incorporated in the driving dust, which gave the soldiers the impression that mud was raining from the skies (Atkinson 2004) (see Figure 17.6).

Figure 17.6
Army aviator from 3rd Squadron, 7th Cavalry, 3rd Infantry Division during dust storms in March 2003. Note the raindrop splatter on the windshield of the OH-58D Kiowa Warrior. *Source*: CW3 Mitch Carver, 3rd Infantry Division.

In some areas, soldiers were unable to read maps, wear glasses, or employ their night vision goggles in the dusty conditions (Fontenot et al. 2004). Vehicle operations all but ceased during the height of the storm because of severe visibility issues, and this adversely affected resupply, so that 3rd Division became dangerously low on food and water (Atkinson 2004). Dust interfered with optical, audio, and laser sensing of targets, increasing the chances of fratricide. Thermal sights, however, continued to work relatively well despite the thick dusty haze (Anderson 2004).

Amazingly, fighting continued in some areas, albeit slowly, as in An Najaf where 3rd Infantry Division units engaged Iraqi forces at close range. Because of the reduced visibility, Iraqis were able to approach within a few feet of US forces before they were positively identified, and engagements were often at point blank range (Fontenot et al. 2004). Fighting at close range occurred between 3rd Infantry Division cavalry units and Iraqi paramilitary fighters in *technical vehicles* and on foot armed with small arms, *RPGs*, and mortars (Fontenot et al. 2004).

Understandably, helicopters were grounded during most of the storm, and air operations over the entire area of operations were affected, to include naval air operations in the North Arabian Gulf. In fact, during the period 25–27 March, the aircraft carriers *Kitty Hawk*, *Abraham Lincoln*, and *Constellation* reduced their sortie production by 20 percent (Anderson 2004). The dust storm did not, however, preclude many of the US Air Force aircraft, such as the *B-1*, from continuing to attack targets on the ground by flying above the dust and employing GPS-guided munitions. The ability to make accurate battle damage assessments of these air strikes was interfered with because of the reduced capability of satellites and reconnaissance planes to see through the blinding dust (Atkinson 2004).

Continued efforts to mitigate the effects of dust

As the example in OIF indicates, efforts to forecast and overcome the effects of dust storms and blowing dust have improved since the debacle in Operation Eagle Claw. Better forecasting using the US Air Force DTA and the US Navy's Aerosol Analysis and Prediction System (NAAPS) are two examples of new developments in computer models by the DoD for forecasting dust storms, both of which are being employed in OIF and in Afghanistan.

To reduce the possibility of helicopter brownout and vehicle-generated dust in both field conditions and on US military installations, a number of measures have been implemented. An array of dirt sealants can be used as a temporary surface covering that forms an almost instantly waterproof hard pavement in refueling areas and transportation routes. For more permanent sites, cobbles and other rock material are spread on the surface, dramatically reducing airborne dust production. On military installations, the US Army Environmental Command has helped to implement dust control by providing field guides on dust control guidance and technology. Dust monitoring stations on US military arid lands help to track the efficiency of these efforts to combat airborne dust.

Conclusion

Military operations in arid lands are always affected by aeolian processes, in spite of the latest technologies in forecasting, navigation, and targeting. When measures are not taken to reduce the effects of airborne dust, disastrous consequences can ensue, as occurred during Operation Eagle Claw. Commanders and pilots planned for a clear-weather operation, and they encountered nothing of the sort. Clearly, the worst-case flying hazard, a *haboob*, was not factored into the planning or execution of Operation Eagle Claw, even though the weather experts had identified the hazard. Out of the ashes of this failed mission, the US military made substantial improvements in weather forecasting and mission preparation, and these advancements paid dividends decades later during OIF in 2003. The "mother of all dust storms" of the frontal type was predicted days in advance, and commanders made efforts to mitigate its effects. Nonetheless, the march toward Baghdad was halted for the better part of four days, and soldiers on the ground suffered in the miserable environmental conditions. Clearly, military commanders and planners will continue to be challenged in future operations by the bane of the desert, wind-blown dust.

References cited

Anderson, J. 2004. *An analysis of a dust storm impacting Operation Iraqi Freedom, 25–27 March 2003.* Master's thesis. Naval Postgraduate School, Monterey, California.

Atkinson, R. 2004. *In the company of soldiers: a chronicle of combat.* New York, NY: Henry Holt & Company.

Bagnold, R. A. 1941. *The physics of blown sand and desert dunes.* London, UK: Methuen & Co., Ltd.

Cogan, C.G. 2003. Desert One and its disorders. *Journal of Military History* 67: 201–16.

COMET program 2003. *Forecasting dust storms.* University Corporation for Atmospheric Research. National Center for Atmospheric Research. Online training program retrieved from: http://meted.ucar.edu/mesoprim/dust [accessed April 2010].

Department of the Air Force (DAF). 1980. *Mission environmental support.* Air Weather Service White Paper. 2 May.

Department of Defense (DoD). 1980. "Rescue mission report" (Holloway Report). August. (D5.2:R31/2).

Edgell, S. 2006. *Arabian deserts: nature, origin, and evolution.* Dordrecht, The Netherlands: Springer.

El-Baz, F. 1994. "Gulf War disruption of the desert surface in Kuwait." In *The Gulf War and the environment*, F. El-Baz & R.M. Makharita (eds). Amsterdam: Gordon Breach Science Publishers.

Fontenot, G., E. J. Degen, & D. Tohn. 2004. *On point: U.S. Army in Operation Iraqi Freedom.* Office of the Chief of Staff, US Army. Fort Leavenworth, KS: Combat Studies Institute Press.

Gilewitch, D. 2003. *Military geography: the interaction of desert geomorphology and military operations.* Doctoral dissertation. Arizona State University, Tempe, Arizona.

Grumm, R. H. 2009. *Southwest Asian dust storm of 25–27 March 2003.* National Weather Service, State College Pennsylvania, unpublished manuscript.

Idso, S. B. 1976. "Dust storms." *Scientific American* 235(4): 108–14.

Idso, S. B., R. S. Ingram, & J. M. Pritchard. 1972. "An American haboob." *American Meteorological Society Bulletin* 53: 930–95.

Kreisher, O. 1999. "Desert One." *Air Force Magazine* 82(1): 1–10.

Kuchera, E. 2003. "DTA Predicts Dust Storms During OIF." Air Force Weather Observer. https://afweather.afwa.af.mil/observer/JUN_2003/dta_predicts_dust.html [accessed 15 July 2009].

Kyle, J. H. 1990. *The guts to try.* New York, NY: Orion Books.

Lawson, T. J. 1971. "Haboob structure at Khartoum." *Weather* 26: 105–12.

Leet, D., S. Judson, & M. E. Kauffman 1978. *Physical geology.* Englewood Cliffs, NJ: Prentice Hall, Inc.

McKnight, T. L. & D. Hess. 2005. *Physical geography: a landscape appreciation.* Upper Saddle River, NJ: Pearson Education, Inc.

Middleton, N. J., A. S. Goudie, & G. L. Wells. 1986. "The frequency and source areas of dust storms." In *Aeolian geomorphology*, W.G. Nickling (ed.). New York, NY: Allen & Unwin.

Pye, K. 1987. *Aeolian dust and dust deposits.* London, UK: Academic Press.

Reusse, J. R. 2002. *Meteorological impacts on Operation Eagle Claw.* Unpublished Information Paper. United States Marine Forces Central Command (MARCENT) G2 Meteorology and Oceanography (METOC) Officer.

Ryan, P. B. 1985. *The Iranian rescue mission.* Annapolis, MD: Naval Institute Press.

Scales, R. H. 1994. *Certain victory: the US Army in the Gulf War.* Fort Leavenworth, KS: US Army Command and General Staff College Press.

Sick, G. 1985. *All fall down.* New York, NY: Random House.

Snellman, Leonard, Vincent J. Oliver, & Robert E. Beck. 1980. "Special evaluation of weather support to attempted hostage rescue mission." Requested by Office of the Joint Chiefs of Staff, 21 May.

US Joint Chiefs of Staff. 1980. David C. Jones. "Report on rescue mission" (Jones Report). Office of Chairman, Joint Chiefs of Staff, 6 May.

Chapter eighteen

Infrastructure vulnerability in a catastrophic CSZ event and implications on disaster response for the Oregon coast

WILEY C. THOMPSON

Introduction

EVIDENCE OF THE LAST GREAT Cascadia Subduction Zone (CSZ) rupture and similar events during the Indian Ocean Tsunami of 2004 suggests that significant portions of Oregon's Willamette Valley and coastal community populations, facilities, and infrastructure are vulnerable to a future *subduction zone* rupture (Wang and Clark 1999). The most recent great seismic event occurred on 27 January 1700 (Satake et al. 1996; Ludwin et al. 2005), resulting in a 9.1 earthquake and a large tsunami that spread its destructive effects across the Pacific Basin. Other earthquakes have occurred in the past in Cascadia (Atwater et al. 1995). Many of these earthquakes have been large and have produced significant effects to include shaking, *subsidence*, uplift, and *tsunami*. Following a CSZ rupture, likely hazards associated with an earthquake and tsunami include: ground shaking, *liquefaction*, subsidence, landslides, flooding, and damaging wave impact. These hazards present a threat to vulnerable populations and infrastructure along the Oregon coast. As many in-state disaster response resources will be degraded or engaged in post-hazard activities in the more populous Willamette Valley, significant contributions from federal and possibly international resources will be required to carry out an ensuing large-scale disaster response.

This chapter examines the role of the military geographer in preparing for and responding to a large-scale disaster. It does so by exploring the integration of military resources in humanitarian assistance operations following a large-scale natural hazard event, tracing the contributions a military geographer can make to disaster preparedness and then proposing a real-world, large-scale disaster response plan to a known, impending natural hazard.

Geography, military geographers and disaster response

Geography has a definitive role in the study of hazards and disasters. Alexander (2000: 30) notes that the main schools of thought contributing to the study of disasters are "geography, anthropology, sociology, development studies, medicine and epidemiology, and the scientific and technical disciplines such as volcanology, seismology and engineering." Geography is a discipline uniquely suited to form the core of disaster studies. It does, by its nature, accommodate an interdisciplinary approach to problem solving. Many disasters are results of natural hazards (e.g. earthquakes, volcanoes, hurricanes, floods, tornadoes). Such hazards have an observable spatial component and can be studied and even forecasted to a limited extent by examining spatial and temporal data. Furthermore, a hazard only becomes a disaster when its effects intersect with something, be it a living thing, or vulnerable resource.

Complex problems, such as disasters, manifest their effects throughout a large space and require the synchronization of resources across that space, and, thus, are problems uniquely suited for military geographers. While very knowledgeable of local resources and capabilities, county-level emergency planners may lack the perspective to see how their plans fit into a larger-scale state or regional disaster response effort. The same may be said for state planners. Although they may have better visibility of regional and federal assets and capabilities, they too may lack the large-scale contingency planning expertise to develop a comprehensive response plan, which incorporates local, state, federal, and perhaps international assets. Although lacking specific emergency-management training and experience, the military geographer, in the role of disaster response planner, can contribute to disaster preparation by incorporating an understanding of the scope and scale of natural hazards an area faces and the knowledge of how to use geographic tools to develop a regional response plan. The military geographer employs knowledge of the effects of terrain and weather on air, sea, and land operations—key factors that may affect a response operation. Military geographers can employ differing scales of analysis to define the disaster space and estimate the scope of impact. Both steps are necessary to develop supporting plans at multiple levels. The military geographer's understanding of the effects of natural hazards enables him or her to estimate the potential vulnerability of existing response assets and capitalizes on resources that will survive while supplementing degraded capacity with outside capabilities.

In addition to requiring knowledge of the hazard, co-ordinating the response to a large-scale disaster demands the ability to visualize complex operations across the affected area. When planning and co-ordinating the activities of many participants in a large operation, spatial information is invaluable, and a familiar tool of the military geographer.

Military geographers are familiar with map products at virtually any scale, as well as other geographic tools such as geographic information systems (GIS). These systems enable planners to see beyond the limits of their physical senses and immediate geographic understanding. Thus, GIS plays a fundamental role in hazard assessment and disaster response.

In practice, military geographers played key roles as planners in the humanitarian response to the 2005 South Asian (Kashmir) earthquake (Thompson and Halter 2006). However, this was not the first use of military forces or military geographers in large-scale humanitarian efforts (Walker 1992; Gaydos and Luz 1994; DoD 2001; Palka 2005). Following the onset of a hazard, military resources may be called upon to supplement existing capabilities. Military resources will most often be employed during the early phases of the *Emergency Management Cycle* (see Figure 18.1). This has elsewhere been called the Emergency Response Cycle (Cutter 2003) or simply the Disaster Cycle (Alexander 2000). The model conceptualizes the full cycle of activities from the hazard event through response and mitigation back to an enhanced state of rebuilt structures and systems that are better prepared to resist future events.

US Department of Defense (DoD) *Joint Publication 3-07.6* defines foreign humanitarian assistance (FHA), a military term synonymous with disaster response, as operations that are intended to "relieve or reduce the results of natural or man-made disasters or other endemic conditions such as human suffering, disease, or privation that might present a serious threat to life or that can result in great damage to or loss of property" (DoD 2001: I-1). US military forces will typically find themselves involved in the Rescue, Relief, and to a lesser extent, the Recovery phase of this cycle. These phases reside in the Response portion of the Emergency Management Cycle (see Figure 18.1). Response is defined in scholarly literature as "the provision of emergency relief and

Figure 18.1
Emergency Management
Cycle. Modified from
Cutter (2003) with image
by author. Used with
permission, 2008.

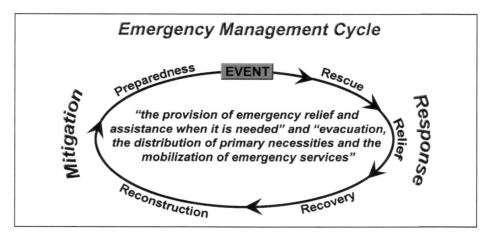

297

assistance when it is needed" and as the "evacuation, the distribution of primary necessities and the mobilization of emergency services" (Alexander 1999: 407). Military geographers have examined the role of military resources in responding to disasters and continue to contribute a better understanding of that role through teaching and publication (Palka 2005). As demonstrated in this chapter, military geographers can also make significant contributions in mitigating the long-term impact of a natural hazard, and thus reducing the scale of the ensuing disaster.

Recent events: a basis for planning

Recent seismic events, such as the 2004 Indian Ocean earthquake and tsunami, and the 2005 South Asian earthquake, demonstrate the large impact a disruption in lifelines can have on an affected population. These events also challenged the abilities of disaster responders to provide timely rescue and relief (Hicks and Pappas 2006; Ozerdem 2006). A military geographer can both analyze events and estimate the complexity of a CSZ rupture in the Pacific Northwest and its potential impact on the local population and rescuers (see Figure 18.2).

The 2004 Indian Ocean earthquake and tsunami resulted in a great loss of life and significant damage to lifelines (Ballantyne 2006). The implications of damage over a great distance are that outside help may have to come from resources situated much farther than originally expected and that neighboring communities with mutual response partnerships may in fact be struggling to support their own affected populations. The seismic zone along the Java Trench that triggered the

Figure 18.2
Area of interest depicting the Cascadia Subduction Zone. Map by author.

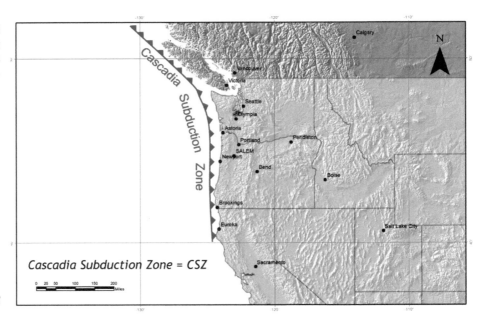

Cascadia Subduction Zone = CSZ

2004 earthquake and tsunami is geologically similar to the structure created by the subduction of the Juan de Fuca plate beneath the North American plate in the Pacific Northwest. The subduction zone in Cascadia, which runs approximately from the Mendocino Fracture zone to the south to the Explorer Ridge in the north, has produced large earthquakes and tsunamis in the past.

On Saturday morning, 8 October 2005, the Kashmir region in northern Pakistan and India was struck by a moment magnitude (M_w) 7.6 earthquake. Although Khattri (1999) had previously suggested the high probability of a large earthquake killing many hundreds of thousands of South Asians and resulting in vast economic devastation, this earthquake nonetheless took Pakistan by surprise. The surprise may be a result of the fact that there had not been an event of this magnitude in the area for approximately 450–500 years (Bilham and Hough 2006; Thakur 2006). This earthquake, striking a very mountainous area of Pakistan and India, triggered many landslides, which segmented the north–south road network and severely hampered the ground flow of rescue teams and relief supplies into the region (see Figure 18.3). Many bridges were unusable, and telephone lines were knocked down. The disruption to these lifelines resulted in many valleys and numerous villages being isolated or cutoff from disaster response assets, both physically and in an information sense.

Figure 18.3
Landslides in Kashmir disrupted ground lifelines and interrupted the flow of rescue teams and relief supplies.
Source: Image by author.

Kashmir's mountainous terrain is very similar to the Coast Range Mountains in Oregon. Many of the roads, power lines, and telephone lines that connect the more populous Willamette Valley with communities along the Oregon Coast run along valley floors that are flanked by steeply rising terrain (see Figure 18.4). Similarly, the Pacific Coast Highway (i.e. Highway 101), which provides the north–south connectivity along the coast, hugs the sides of steeply rising terrain and relies upon bridges to span resistant basalt headlands. The potential to disrupt both the north–south and east–west lifelines in this region is great. In fact, even without seismic shaking, many roads are rendered temporarily unusable from mass wasting events aided by heavy precipitation during winter storms.

Lifelines

Lifelines are essential components of daily life and economic viability for communities, but can be of even greater importance following a disaster. Lifelines are "systems or networks which provide for the circulation of people, goods, services, and information upon which health, safety, comfort, and economic activity depend" (Platt 1991: 173). Lifelines and supporting infrastructure include: roads and bridges, rail lines, airports, port facilities, electrical power transmission, water and

Figure 18.4
The Coast Range Mountains in Oregon. Mass wasting events often block roads and numerous events could isolate communities. A large earthquake will trigger many landslides in this region. The effects of human activity, like the road cut pictured, could exacerbate the situation. *Source*: Image by author.

waste water systems, petroleum and natural gas pipelines, and communications systems. During a disaster scenario, lifelines connect affected areas with the world outside; hence, when a disaster disrupts lifelines, responders are challenged to bring response assets and resources to those in need. Lifeline degradation also adversely affects the ability of communities to transmit their specific needs to responders. While not undertaken as a component of this research, systemic approaches to assessing seismic effects on lifelines do exist (Menoni et al. 2002) and, if completed, would serve to complement this research.

Disaster response planning to a major coastal hazard scenario has a temporal component as well. Should a catastrophic CSZ event occur during summer months, local emergency managers and relief decision-makers must account for the needs of a much greater population than would be indicated by census data, resulting from a sizable transient tourist population. A winter CSZ relief scenario would bring about its own unique set of planning requirements. While the affected population would better reflect census data, the ability for that population to survive when exposed to winter conditions is greatly diminished compared with conditions during other seasons. Additional considerations for winter disaster response must include the potential loss of overland routes from snow and icy roads, and occasional loss of air lifelines from low ceilings and visibility. Many of the arteries from the less-affected interior transit through the Coast Range Mountains. When moisture-laden soils are subjected to shaking, the potential for slope failure and landslides is very high. Landslides in the Coast Range may block east–west overland lifelines for an extended period.

With ground lifelines blocked and fleet vessels and port infrastructure capability diminished, disaster response planners would likely turn to aviation assets to create an air bridge over the Coast Range. Aviation assets employed in this air bridge would likely deliver relief supplies and *matériel* to the affected areas, and evacuate any casualties that exceed local or on-site treatment capacity.

Anticipated damage and lifeline viability, PNW CSZ

While both the Willamette Valley and Oregon Coast are at risk from potential devastation from a catastrophic CSZ, coastal areas would incur additional damage as they are also at risk from a resulting tsunami. Statewide damage estimates from the earthquake alone approach 8000 casualties, 30,000 buildings destroyed, and over $12 million in economic losses (Wang and Clark 1999). Studies also suggest that only 65 percent of police, fire stations, and emergency operations centers, along with 66 percent of schools, 82 percent of bridges, and 71 percent of broadcasting stations, will be usable the day after the earthquake (Wang and Clark 1999). When emergency managers add losses from the resulting tsunami, the problems for coastal communities will increase greatly.

The city of Newport, Oregon, the county seat for Lincoln County, is situated on the Central Oregon Coast (see Figure 18.5). The population of Newport is 9532 (2000 US Census); however, summertime tourist and seasonal-employ populations result in an additional 6500 people at risk from an extreme event. The addition of at-risk individuals has planning and resource implications for emergency planners. Lincoln County emergency managers estimate number of deaths from a great CSZ event to be near 5000 (Hawley 2008). Current estimates indicate that the Newport hospital and airport will remain functional, although in a degraded sense. A qualitative assessment of lifelines is given below.

WATER AND WASTE WATER

Potable water will be disrupted by pipe breakages. Wells near the coast may experience salt-water intrusion, rendering them unusable. Waste-water transmission and treatment systems, to include septic systems, will also be disrupted and could pose a serious health risk if they contaminate water sources.

COMMUNICATIONS

Degradation to communications will result from the loss of broadcast and reception towers, transmission lines, and loss of power. This will limit the ability of affected communities to get out information regarding

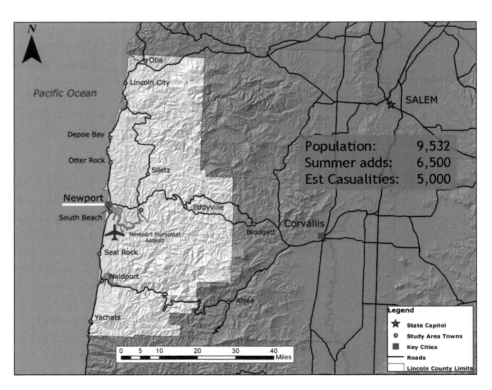

Figure 18.5
Lincoln County, Oregon.
Source: map by author.

their needs, and challenge responders to assess aid requirements and prioritize their effort. However, it is of interest to note that, following the 2004 Indian Ocean tsunami, cellular service was quickly restored, supplementing the loss of landlines (Ballantyne 2006).

FUEL DISTRIBUTION SYSTEMS

The earthquake and tsunami will severely damage fuel delivery and distribution systems. Storage facilities will also be damaged, if not in terms of their storage capacity then in their ability to dispense fuel. A fuel shortage will severely affect the ability of systems (i.e. vehicles, generators, and heaters) to support the relief effort.

ROADS

The primary ground lifelines into Lincoln County from the Willamette Valley are Highways 18/22 from Salem to Lincoln City, Highway 20 from Corvallis to Newport, and Highway 34 from Corvallis to Waldport. Highway 101 interconnects the coastal cities. Landslides in the Coast Range triggered by earthquakes, road surface rupture from shaking and displacement, and loss from liquefaction will create temporary disruptions to road traffic. Professional estimates suggest that the Yaquina Bay Bridge will be destroyed, if not by earthquake shaking then by scour from the tsunami (Wang and Clark 1999; Wood and Good 2004). Other, smaller bridges may experience similar effects. Planners should anticipate that all roads will be unusable or at best segmented.

RAIL

During the 2004 Indian Ocean earthquake and tsunami, railroad tracks were twisted like pipe cleaners (Ballantyne 2006). Similarly, rail systems to the coast will most likely be unusable for an extended period. However, the flat beds upon which the tracks are built may provide an overland route for vehicles if the rail bridges are not badly damaged and slope failures have not rendered them unusable.

AIRPORTS

Newport Municipal Airport is situated upon an elevated Pleistocene terrace at approximately 160 feet above sea level. The stability and composition of the subsurface decreases the potential for liquefaction, and the fact that it is above predicted tsunami inundation zones suggests that the airport will be usable after a CSZ event, although in a degraded capacity. The control tower and navigational aides will likely be destroyed, but the runway should remain viable. With runways of 5400 feet and 3000 feet the airport will be able to accommodate *C-17 Globemaster* (3500 feet minimum), *C-130 Hercules* (3000 feet minimum), and *C-27J Spartan* (1800 feet minimum) military aircraft.

PORT FACILITIES

GIS analysis (Wood and Good 2004) indicates that either an earthquake or subsequent tsunami will destroy most port facilities along Bay Street in Newport, to include docks, fuel, cold storage, power, marine repairs, and marine supplies. Main-channel depth reductions from bank slumping and debris could render it unusable to fishing fleet craft. Beach-launchable boats not moored during the tsunami would still be usable.

The air bridge concept

After conducting interviews with the Lincoln County emergency manager, Jim Hawley (Hawley 2008) and State officials, the author discovered that, while Lincoln County has a proactive plan to shelter affected individuals in place, there was no large-scale plan to supplement or reconnect lifelines to Newport or other coastal communities. Subsequently, using data collected during site surveys and interviews, reviewing academic literature of past disaster response efforts, and integrating operational large-scale disaster response experience, the author developed a recommendation for providing a comprehensive response plan, which utilizes inter- and extra-regional assets to restore lifelines to an isolated coastal zone.

Following a large CSZ rupture, the immediate impediment to a large-scale response effort to coastal communities in Oregon may be the loss of communication lifelines. Accurate information flow is essential to co-ordinate the response to a disaster. Without accurate reporting on actual damage, those executing the disaster response must rely on previously derived estimates of damage until reports can verify actual losses. Communications will not just be hampered by loss of infrastructure along the coast, but may also be hampered from degradation to facilities and infrastructure in the more populous Willamette Valley.

Further compounding damage assessment and response efforts will be loss of use of the east–west roads connecting the Willamette Valley through the Coast Range Mountains to coastal communities. Research and past observations suggest that seismically induced mass wasting or rupture will disrupt these ground lifelines. Both requirements— understanding the situation on the ground and the immediate rescue requirements that exceed local capacity—leave initial responders reliant upon an air bridge response plan.

Ground and air response assets to a large event will most likely come from less affected areas in Eastern Oregon or even from outside of the state. As these assets flow into the affected area, the tendency to stop and render aid in the more populated Willamette Valley will be difficult to overcome; in fact, these actions would be a logical first step. The Willamette Valley is the center of population and government in Oregon and arguably the critical link to restoring functional capacity and economic viability. Therefore, to ensure greatest effectiveness and efficiency of relief, large-scale relief planners must commit early on for a western Oregon response plan that supports near and deep response simultaneously. Response planners must create an *air bridge*, stipulating that some aviation assets will have to deliberately bypass relief requirements in the Willamette Valley and direct their efforts and resources beyond the Coast Range Mountains to coastal communities. As the Newport Airport is the largest and least vulnerable aero-facility on the coast, if intact, it should be designated as a forward staging area and advanced functional node around which responders can begin to cluster relief activities.

In the case of a great CSZ rupture and subsequent tsunami, an air bridge response would be executed in three phases. Phase one would consist of initial rescue, assessment of damage along the coast, and staging of rescue and relief assets. Phase two would consist of continued rescue activities, the provision of relief, and building capacity to continue these activities. The final stage would consist of activities focused on relief, recovery, and preparation for reconstruction. Each phase has assumptions, which are necessary planning requirements and represent a best estimate of expected conditions based on experience and empirical evidence in other similar disasters.

Phase one tasks would consist of initial rescue, assessment of damage along the coast, and staging of rescue and relief assets (see Figure 18.6).

Figure 18.6
Map depicting actions during phase one of the air bridge concept. *Source*: map by author.

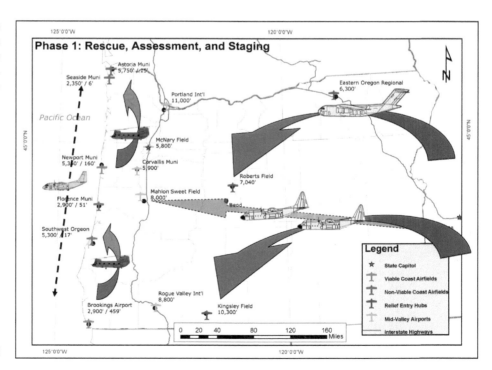

Activities conducted by aircrews will include each of these tasks. For example, as a helicopter moves forward into the affected coastal zone, it will be loaded with relief supplies to be dropped off at staging bases. *En route* and while stopping at destinations, the aircrew will observe the conditions and also gather damage assessments and support requests from people on the ground. Prior to departing from the coast, the aircraft would collect as many critically injured persons as possible, and evacuate them to a medical facility. Assumptions made for this phase were: relief entry hub airfields are viable; one mid-valley airfield can accept short take-off and landing (STOL) aircraft; Oregon National Guard *CH-47s* Chinooks can forward deploy from their airfield in Pendleton, Oregon; strategic airlift and cargo will come from outside of the Pacific Northwest; ground movement to and between coastal communities does not exist or is extremely limited.

Much like the Emergency Management Cycle, tasks performed during a large-scale disaster response are not discrete, sequential efforts, but often overlapping, near-simultaneous events. However, in some instances, certain actions, such as forward basing of aircraft, can only occur once critical conditions are met or capabilities are achieved. If US Coast Guard rotary-wing assets can be repositioned between the shaking and the subsequent tsunami, they can provide immediate rescue to affected communities. Additionally, these aircraft can collect and forward information regarding damage.

In order to cover quickly, get an assessment of airfield viability along the entire coast, and assess damage, fixed-wing aircraft must be utilized. Fixed-wing aircraft can originate from viable Willamette Valley airfields, airfields east of the Cascade Range, or from outside the region. Due to the great distances involved, CH-47s from the Oregon National Guard must be used to confirm fixed-wing reconnaissance, deliver priority relief supplies such as fuel, food, water, and medical supplies, and evacuate urgent casualities. These same aircraft can emplace forward liaison teams at forward staging areas. The forward liaison teams will collect relief requirements and forward this information to disaster support staging areas for future resourcing. As CH-47s continue to fly rescue missions, relief supplies and capability can be built up in staging areas. If airfields at Newport and Brookings are able to accept fixed-wing aircraft, rescuers can deliver bulk relief supplies and evacuate greater numbers of the critically injured. In areas that cannot accept fixed-wing aircraft, responders can employ container delivery system (CDS) or bundle drops (see Figure 18.7) to increase the volume of relief supplies.

In phase two rescue efforts continue, but one will most likely see a shift in priorities toward increased relief and building capacity (see Figure 18.8). Planners must also make key assumptions during this phase. Among them are the assumptions that two of the mid-valley airfields could accept fixed-wing traffic and two of the coastal airfields are viable, with one, most likely either Newport or Brookings, being able to accept

Figure 18.7
Methods of aerial re-supply. Left: AC-130 delivers supplies via container delivery systems (DoD image). Right: A CH-47 Chinook in Afghanistan conducts a slingload operation with 500 gallon "blivets" of fuel. *Source*: image by author.

STOL aircraft. As fuel availability and life support capacity should be increasing, Oregon National Guard CH-47s can forward deploy from Pendleton to mid-valley locations. This would greatly decrease the distances over which they would have to fly to get to the disaster area and thus would increase their loiter time and cargo capacity.

Figure 18.8
Map depicting actions during phase two of the air bridge concept. *Source*: map by author.

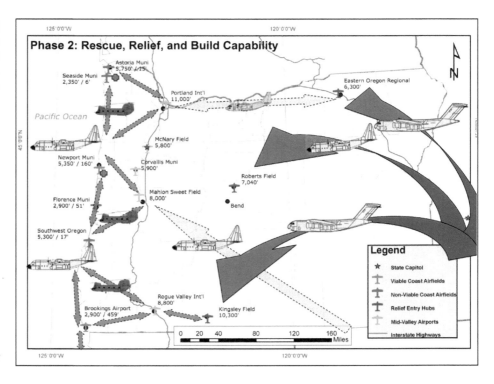

As capacity increases and logistical systems mature in the coastal area, responders can begin to establish forward medical treatment facilities on the coast. One of these facilities should be located at Newport because of its central position and the potential survivability of the airport. Another factor driving the location may be the quantity and nature of casualties. As crews open overland routes to the mid-Willamette Valley and make temporary repairs to airports, logisticians can increase bulk fuel capacity. Increases in fuel storage and dispensing capacity should also be occurring at key forward logistical bases along the coast. With the forward deployment of CH-47s, aircrews can begin to execute a series of "ring routes" from mid-valley to coast to deliver relief and evacuate casualties. With shorter route segments and forward availability of fuel, aircrews can expand their reconnaissance efforts to include more rural areas of coast range. As aircrews identify requirements, responders can continue to use CDS drops to bring relief supplies to isolated communities. The key task needed to transition from phase two to phase three is a readiness to jump robust capabilities forward into bases along the coast. Planners should expect that this would occur approximately five to six days after the earthquake.

Phase three includes a transition as responders place less emphasis on rescue and more on relief while they prepare for and set conditions for recovery and reconstitution (see Figure 18.9). Typically, military assets will begin to phase out as relief operations end. During this phase, planners should expect that four mid-valley airfields can accept fixed-wing traffic, and that two coastal airfields can accept STOL aircraft, and have bulk fuel available. Routine medical care should be available at forward hospitals in the coast, and mid-valley hospitals can meet all theater medical requirements. After emplacing temporary repairs and clearing debris, Interstates 5 and 84 can accommodate commercial trucking so that bulk aid, recovery, and reconstruction materials can move by surface into the region. With a decreased emphasis on rescue and increased availability of fuel, road-clearing crews have been able to provide limited road access from the Willamette Valley to the coast. Correspondingly, sections of Highway 101 are usable and are only blocked by very large mass-wasting events or damaged bridges.

During phase three disaster responders will co-ordinate with logisticians to move main logistics and operations staging areas from eastern Oregon to Willamette Valley locations. Operational airfields on the coast will see the large build-up of forward logistical bases. Inter-theater airlift will be greatly diminished and used on an as-needed basis, as intra-theater airlift should be able to meet most operational, medical, and logistical needs. As lifeline restoration continues, CH-47s continue flying coastal ring routes while being supplemented by C-27 Sherpas. This phase is complete when relief operations are nearly absent and the focus shifts to recovery and reconstruction.

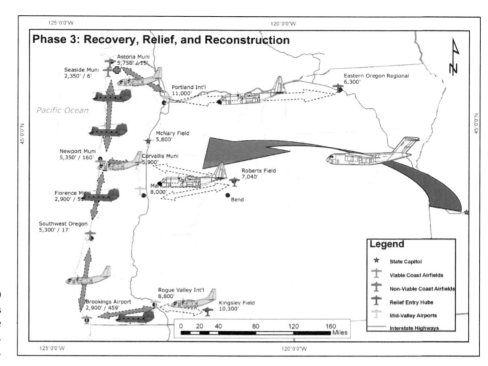

Figure 18.9
Map depicting actions
during phase three of the
air bridge concept.
Source: map by author.

Regarding implementation

The scenario as described above is based on an understanding of the geography of natural hazards and their secondary effects, knowledge of the disaster space, and real-world operational experience of planning and executing a response to a similar hazard of corresponding magnitude. However, the plan is just that, a plan. Plans like the one described above must be scrutinized and validated by potential participants. While large-scale rehearsals are expensive in terms of time and money, planners can use tabletop or map exercises or simulations to allow all actors to see themselves and the actions of others, and to co-ordinate and de-conflict activities by time and space. These exercises are essential to successful implementation and help avoid the paper-plan syndrome, which is the tendency to believe that, if a written plan exists, then a community is in an enhanced state of disaster preparedness (Auf der Heide 1989).

As a great CSZ earthquake will result in many communities being isolated, local preparedness and self-sufficiency is vital. Additionally, any large-scale response plan will be much more successful if measures are taken to enhance preparedness at the community level. Many of the most effective, high-payoff measures are also low cost. Individual households should create home emergency kits. Neighborhoods should hold disaster preparedness meetings during which they identify special-needs people and those with unique capabilities (medical, electrical skills, engineering, etc.) or critical resources (generators or chainsaws). Neighborhood leadership can also discuss or rehearse movement to the closest disaster shelter. Community leaders must have redundant communications systems with higher and adjacent jurisdictions. Key personnel and community members must exercise their disaster plans. Emergency managers must note plan deficiencies and implement fixes, if not on the spot then quickly thereafter.

It has been 310 years since the last great Cascadia Subduction Zone rupture. Data suggests that the recurrence interval is between 200 and 1000 years, with 500 years being the average (CREW 2005). The clock is ticking on preparedness. It is past time to begin to prepare and having a comprehensive, rehearsed response plan is a good first step.

References cited

Alexander, D. 1999. *Natural disasters*. Dordrecht, Netherlands: Kluwer Academic Publishers.

——. 2000. *Confronting catastrophe*. Hertfordshire, UK: Terra Publishing.

Atwater, B., A. Nelson, J. Clague, G. Carver, D. Yamaguchi, P. Bobrowsky, J. Bourgeois, M. Darienzo, W. Grant, E. Hemphill-Haley, H. Kelsey, G. Jacoby, S. Nishenko, S. Palmer, C. Peterson, & M. Reinhart. 1995. "Summary of coastal geologic evidence for past great earthquakes at the Cascadia subduction zone." *Earthquake Spectra* 11(1): 1–18.

Auf Der Heide, E. 1989. *Disaster response: principles of preparation and coordination*. St Louis, MO: C. V. Mosby Company.

Ballantyne, D. 2006. "Lifelines—summary report on the great Sumatra earthquakes and Indian Ocean tsunamis of 26 December 2004 and 28 March 2005." *Earthquake Spectra* 22: 46–52.

Bilham, R. & S. Hough. 2006. "Future earthquakes on the Indian Subcontinent: inevitable hazard, preventable risk." *South Asian Journal* 12: 1–9.

CREW. 2005. *Cascadia subduction zone earthquakes: a magnitude 9.0 earthquake scenario*. Seattle, WA: Cascadia Region Earthquake Workgroup.

Cutter, S. 2003. "GI science, disasters, and emergency management." *Transactions in GIS* 7(4): 439–45.

Department of Defense (DoD). 2001. *Joint publication 3-07.6 joint tactics, techniques and procedures for foreign humanitarian assistance*. Washington, DC: US Government Printing Office.

——. 2006. *Joint publication 3-0 joint operations*. Washington, DC: US Government Printing Office.

Gaydos, J. & G. Luz. 1994. "Military participation in emergency humanitarian assistance." *Disasters* 18(1): 49–57.

Hawley, J. 2008. Personal communication with Jim Hawley, Lincoln County Emergency Manager. 9 February.

Hicks, E. & G. Pappas. 2006. "Coordinating disaster relief after the South Asia earthquake." *Society* 43(5): 42–50.

Khattri, K. 1999. "Probabilities of occurrence of great earthquakes in the Himalaya." *Proceedings of the Indian Academy of Science* 108(2): 87–92.

Ludwin, R., C. Thrush, K. James, D. Buerge, C. Jonientz-Trisler, J. Rasmussen, K. Troost, & A. de los Angeles. 2005. "Serpent spirit-power stories along the Seattle fault." *Seismological Research Letters* 76(4): 426–31.

Menoni, S., F. Perganlani, M. Boni, & V. Petrini. 2002. "Lifelines earthquake vulnerability assessment: a systemic approach." *Soil Dynamics and Earthquake Engineering* 22: 1199–1208.

Ozerdem, A. 2006. "The mountain tsunami: afterthoughts on the Kashmir earthquake." *Third World Quarterly* 27(3): 397–419.

Palka, E. 2005. "Decades of instability and uncertainty: mission diversity in the SASO environment." In *Military geography: from peace to war*, E. Palka and F. Galgano (eds). New York, NY: McGraw Hill.

Platt, R. 1991. "Lifelines: an emergency management priority for the United States in the 1990s." *Disasters* 15(2): 172–6.

Satake, K., K. Shimazaki, Y. Tsuji, & U. Kazue. 1996. "Time and size of a giant earthquake in Cascadia inferred from Japanese tsunami records of January 1700." *Nature* 379: 246–9.

Thakur, V. 2006. "Lessons learnt from the 8 October 2005 Muzaffarabad earthquake and need for some initiatives." *Current Science* 91(5): 566.

Thompson, W. & S. Halter. 2006. "Aviation warfighters excel during disaster assistance operations in Pakistan." *Army Aviation* 55(2): 40–3.

Walker, P. 1992. "Foreign military resources for disaster relief: an NGO perspective." *Disasters* 16(2): 152–9.

Wang, Y. & J. Clark. 1999. *Earthquake damage in Oregon: preliminary estimates of future earthquake losses*. Oregon Department of Geology and Mineral Industries Special Paper 29.

Wood, N. & J. Good. 2004. "Vulnerability of port and harbor communities to earthquake and tsunami hazards: the use of GIS in community hazard planning." *Coastal Management* 32: 243–69.

Chapter nineteen

Khe Sanh, Vietnam

Examining the long-term impacts of warfare on the physical landscape

JOSEPH P. HUPY

Introduction

NO ACCOUNT OF A BATTLE IS complete without an analysis of its nexus with geography and a description of the physical environment in which it took place. Such narratives are replete with stories of unprepared armies and poorly informed commanders being defeated by elements of the natural and human landscape. For example, powerful armies have been defeated by severe winter conditions, fleets have been destroyed by maritime storms, unforgiving terrain has thwarted well-planned maneuvers, and disease has crippled the ability of states to keep soldiers in the field. History demonstrates that these types of geographically enabled military disasters were fostered by poor geographic awareness and sometimes by neglect and leader incompetence. These accounts are not lacking; throughout history, warfare and the environment have indeed shared a close and interconnected relationship. Thus, the outcomes of many battles and campaigns have been influenced, or even pre-empted, by the effects of geography (Winters et al. 1998).

Clearly, the study of military geography would not be complete without a focus on the effects of the physical environment on battles and military campaigns. While it is important to examine how the physical environment has influenced past military operations, and to recognize how to cope with the physical environment in future military campaigns, it is also important to examine the converse, i.e. how and where military operations have adversely affected the landscape (Hupy 2008). An extended examination of this relationship—between battle and the environment—has the potential to expand military geography into new and exciting directions.

Researching the impact of military activities on the natural landscape is a topic that requires considerable attention because of current circumstances surrounding the Department of Defense (DoD) and its relationship with the public. An increasing sense of environmental awareness exists within the US population and proper management of military lands is no exception. The DoD is expected to maintain a high level of environmental stewardship during its activities in peacetime and war. The DoD land estate constitutes only 3 percent of public land holdings and the amount of training facilities is a limited, finite resource. These holdings are being eroded further by civilian encroachment on military training areas at a time when advances in technology require an increasing amount of space. Regardless, the DoD is expected to implement plans and conditions for the proper environmental management of military lands. In recent years, the DoD has done an excellent job managing its existing training facilities and a number of studies have examined the effects of military training on the landscape. Indeed, recent studies have suggested that biodiversity, a sign of good environmental stewardship, is higher on military lands than on most federal land holdings (Cablk 2009).

While proper management of DoD lands remains an important issue, clearly a need exists to go beyond studies of landscape disturbance as a consequence of routine training activities. By coincidence, there are many twentieth-century battlefields from which we can draw cogent examinations of landscape disturbance (King 2001). These battlefields exist around the world in a variety of geographic settings and manifest the scars of war.

With the onset of the twenty-first century, the DoD has been presented with a new form of warfare. In this new era, military operations are commonly not aimed at the state, but often at specific groups within a particular state such as rogue governments, terrorist groups, or insurgent movements. This form of warfare typically places military forces in situations where they are fighting small enemy units on foreign soil, surrounded by an otherwise friendly population. This is important because war-related environmental degradation can erode the local population's morale and may lead to a loss of support. In addition, extensive environmental damage presents the DoD with the potential task (and cost) of cleaning up after the combat phase of an operation or campaign has ended. Thus, it is important to limit the level of environmental damage when military action is taken.

This chapter will focus on the effects of warfare on the physical and, to a limited extent, human environment. I will begin with a brief discussion of the various impacts of warfare. This discussion is then followed by a case study that examines the Khe Sanh, Vietnam, battlefield. Khe Sanh is an excellent case study for this chapter because it not only exemplifies a typical modern warfare disturbance, but also illustrates how human land use patterns shape the recovery of landscapes impacted by conflict.

Environmental impacts of warfare

Environmental disturbance associated with warfare occurs when armies intentionally eliminate the cover or resource base of an enemy, or, more commonly, as an unintentional consequence associated with the war effort. Based on these premises, environmental disturbances associated with war can historically be placed into three general categories (Hupy 2008): environmental disturbance and destruction from weaponry; direct consumption of resources such as timber, water, and food to support armies; and indirect consumption of resources by military industrial complexes that supply the war effort.

The common thread among each of these disturbance categories is that, when viewed from ancient times up until the present, the scope of environmental disturbance has continually and significantly increased in magnitude (Hupy and Schaetzl 2006). Technological innovations have not only enabled humans to increasingly inflict harm upon the enemy, but also on the environment. Every aspect of modern war, certainly in terms of weapons power, is of greater magnitude than that of warfare prior to the industrial age: armies and battlefields are larger, munitions are more powerful, and the disturbances are more widespread. However, the remarkable improvements in accuracy have done much to limit the areal extent of war-related environmental damage. With few exceptions damage to the environment has been incidental. That is, the damage inflicted upon the environment in warfare occurred because the enemy happened to be in that particular area, and it was the enemy who was targeted, not the natural environment. Whether incidental or deliberate, this chapter will focus on the direct impacts of battle on the immediate environment.

Pre-modern warfare and the advent of gunpowder

In today's world, which is so influenced by images portrayed by the media, it is easy to imagine that warfare was always a highly destructive epic event capable of widespread destruction. Images rendered by modern cinema that conjure up displays of exploding cannon rounds in nineteenth-century warfare—dislodging fountains of earth, blasting soldiers and trees skyward—inaccurately describe the technological capabilities of warfare at the time. For hundreds of years gunpowder, or *black powder*, was simply too primitive to be deployed as anything but a propellant of solid objects from the barrel of a gun. Projectiles differed little from the stones thrown from mechanical catapults that had been used previously. The mass of the cannon ball was used to destroy or disrupt the target and its use as an explosive munition was limited (Partington 1960). Additionally, individuals manning the artillery piece considered explosive munitions unreliable and dangerous. Consequently, solid shot was delivered from a smoothbore artillery device, employed along the front lines and fired at flat trajectories so the round would take erratic bounces into massed troop formations (Bailey 2004). Hence, environmental disturbances were limited to divots and burrows. From an environmental perspective, the introduction of black powder did little to alter the destructive effects associated with military weaponry, that is, until smokeless gunpowder was introduced during the late nineteenth century (Hupy 2008).

The introduction of smokeless gunpowder

It was not until Alfred Nobel introduced the world to smokeless gunpowder during the late nineteenth century that the world benefited from blasting caps and a new 'safer' form of explosive called trinitro-toluene, commonly known as TNT. Shortly after this development, the French introduced high-explosive (HE) munitions in 1899. This artillery shell was filled with explosive cordite and fired from a rifled, breech-loading gun. The British soon followed with melanite, and through the use of chemistry the world came to know the possibilities of ever larger and more powerful HE rounds (Hogg 1985, 1987). These explosives, combined with increased industrial production, ushered in a new era of warfare capable of leveling forests and cratering landscapes beyond recognition.

Several wars at the turn of the century (e.g. the Franco-Prussian, Russo-Japanese, and Spanish–American) enabled armies to test and develop munitions, but it was not until World War I that these developments were fully implemented. Instead of armies that numbered in the thousands, states fielded armies in the millions, equipped with thousands of cannon, and a state required a robust infrastructure and massive industrial complex to support these large armies. For example, during the early months of World War I, it was realized that indus-trialized productivity would provide a state with a distinct advantage over a less capable enemy. Commanders also realized that the days of dashing cavalry charges and brightly colored uniforms were over and new tactics needed to be implemented (Keegan 1976, 1998).

The longer range of rifled infantry weapons and rate of fire of the machine gun forced commanders to take artillery off the front lines after devastating losses during the opening phase of World War I. Thus, artillery took up positions in the rear and perfected the art of indirect fire. Furthermore, expenditures of ammunition increased dramatically during the war. Artillery commanders soon learned that massive amounts of firepower were needed to achieve gains on the battlefield. Bombardments lasting for several days were not uncommon during the first years of the war. For example, the British preceded their attack at the Somme in 1916 with a seven-day bombardment that used 1.7 million shells (Keegan 1976). However, these massive multi-day bombardments did not last for the duration of the war; by the end of the war in 1918, influenced by tactical changes implemented by German forces, bombardments became shorter and more focused.

This type of warfare had severe environmental consequences: forests were obliterated and the landscape was significantly cratered, thus creating wide swaths of destruction, limited only by the range of artillery shells. Perhaps the best-known example of this swath of destruction is the trench system of the Western Front. The strip of devastated land adjacent to the front averaged 20 km wide and stretched from the English Channel to the Swiss border (see Figure 19.1). Although the footprint of the battlefield had increased significantly from previous wars, the disturbance was still confined to the fairly predictable linear dimensions of the battlefield (Hupy and Schaetzl 2008). World War I was unique, however, because, for the first time, humankind realized that technological advances in weaponry were capable of rendering destruction far beyond the scope of previous wars.

The destruction produced in World War I was not overlooked by the scientific community. Foresters were some of the first in the scientific community to take note of the environmental disturbance brought about by war. By the end of World War I, European and US foresters began to assess the toll exacted on the environment. This assessment was accomplished primarily by determining forest damage in terms of board feet of lumber lost by: outright destruction; damage due to shrapnel impregnation; and harvest to support the war effort. Researchers estimated that 2.5 billion board feet of lumber in French forests had been destroyed during the course of the war. One forester attached to the US Army reported that not only did artillery reduce forests to splinters along

Figure 19.1
Craters cover modern-day Verdun, France. This World War I battlefield on Europe's Western Front was particularly devastated by artillery in World War I. *Source*: Joseph P. Hupy, May 2003.

the Western Front, but it also created a cratered landscape and reduced the stable soil ecosystem into mounds of loose, unconsolidated sediment that was hardly worth calling soil.

Unfortunately, however, World War I only set the stage for World War II and, barely 20 years later, the world plunged into another round of warfare. However, damage to the *soilscape* was to be more limited (Hupy 2008). Even though technological innovations produced more powerful weapons, the toll exacted on the landscape was minimized due to the fluidity of the front lines and increased accuracy, which obviated the needed for massed bombardments. In addition, the majority of aerial bombardments of World War II were concentrated in urban areas, unlike World War I, where stalemate conditions took place in relatively unpopulated areas.

Disturbances during the Second Indochina War

Following World War II, military theorists believed that widespread destruction associated with the two world wars was a relic of the past. Warfare was believed to be approaching a new age: one of rapid movement with urban areas as key military objectives (likely, over the eastern plains of Europe). If, by chance, stalemate conditions did occur, military planners believed the culmination would be mutual nuclear devastation. History proves that these predictions fell far short of the mark, and many 'hot wars' were fought during the Cold War.

This was certainly the case in Southeast Asia, which was a region that was particularly contested during the Cold War and, subsequently, was involved in a series of conflicts from the late 1940s up until the early 1980s. The US became militarily involved with Southeast Asia following the Communist victory over French colonial forces in 1954, when they found themselves trying to prevent South Vietnam from falling under Communist control. The common view among US military experts was that they could win because they had the ability to use more advanced weapons and tactics by which they could defeat the North Vietnamese.

The National Vietnamese Army (NVA) regular army and the National Liberation Front (NLF) guerilla insurgency knew that they could not fight a conventional pitched battle against the technologically superior US forces, and therefore took advantage of the dense forest canopy cover in the region. Because the enemy sought refuge in forests, the landscape suffered greatly throughout the American involvement in SE Asia. As has been shown, damage inflicted on forests and soilscape is common in warfare, yet incidental, in that the damage was a side effect of the intention to eliminate enemy forces. Environmental disturbances in the Vietnam War were mainly incidental—munitions were aimed at the enemy, not forests or soilscape. However, the Vietnam War differed from previous wars because, during this war, the destruction of key components of the physical environment was a deliberate component of military strategy (Lewallen 1971). Deforestation of the dense, tropical *selva* was performed to eliminate cover for enemy troops, provide bases of operation, and establish helicopter landing zones (LZs) (Westing 1976). For example, an entire US Air Force wing of C-130 Cargo Planes, equipped with advanced crop sprayer technology, was established to eliminate the tropical canopy providing cover to the enemy forces. Playing on the slogan established by the US Forest Service, this unit established a motto that read "Only You Can Prevent Forests."

Whether intentional or incidental, Vietnam's physical landscape was mainly disturbed by three military activities: explosive munitions; dioxin-based herbicides (Agent Orange); and land-clearing operations from specialized bulldozers called *Rome plows* (Westing 1976). Although artillery bombardments were used during this war, aerial bombardments inflicted damage to the forests at a scale never before accomplished. Unlike World War I, where the damage was confined to a static and linear front, the damage inflicted on Vietnam, Laos, and Cambodia was spatially more widespread. Additionally, the sheer number of munitions dropped on the region exceeds that of any previous wars. Conservative estimates suggest that over 8 million tons of bombs were dropped in Indochina between 1965 and 1972. That is more than twice as much expended by the Allied armies during World War II. Specifically, roughly 250 million craters with a 3-meter diameter covered an area the size of California by the time the US began to leave the region in 1972. Much of the damage inflicted on the forests was the same as seen during previous wars, except that it was accomplished with larger and more powerful bombs, typically dropped from B-52 bomber formations. This *carpet-bombing* did several things: it destroyed vegetation outright, damaged millions of trees with shrapnel, and left trees and the soil impregnated with residual toxic constituents. Air Force bombers routinely used carpet-bombing in which formations of B-52 bombers blanketed an area with bombs. This type of bombing left wide swaths of disturbance, dotting the Vietnamese landscape with millions of craters. Typically, these bombing runs consisted of three to twelve aircraft, each carrying 108 500 lb bombs. The swath of disturbance created by such missions saturated an area with bombs approximately half a kilometer wide and over 1000 meters long. Conservative estimates place the number of craters generated by carpet-bombing missions at approximately 26 million (Orians and Pfeiffer 1970; Pfeiffer 1969). In certain areas, the craters from these bombing missions can still be seen on the Vietnamese landscape (see Figure 19.2).

Not surprisingly, many of the same tactics employed by the US Army to destroy forests were used to destroy enemy agriculture. Herbicides were dumped on large expanses of rice paddies while Rome plows were used to destroy the dikes associated with rice production (Westing and Pfeiffer 1972; Westing and Stockholm International Peace Research Institute 1984). Similar to the efforts in Europe following World War I, scientists examined Vietnamese forests to assess the extent of

Figure 19.2
Remnants of 500 lb bomb craters dot a ridgeline on the Khe Sanh Battlefield. The craters were likely formed during a B-52 bombing run during the 1968 battle. *Source*: J.P. Hupy, May 2009.

disturbance. After flying over many areas subjected to an aerial bombardment, foresters reported a landscape that resembled the surface of the moon. It was estimated that 1.65 million hectares of forest had been completely destroyed. In addition, foresters estimated that 4.0 percent of the forests were so impregnated with shrapnel they had no lumber value (Flamm and Cravens 1971).

In addition to forest damage, the impact of the war on soils was also widespread, though much less studied. However, researchers proposed a less than accurate theory that, after the soil loses its protective forest cover, it may undergo *laterization*—a process that turns exposed soils into dry, rock-like laterite (Westing and Pfeiffer 1972). They also proposed that soil disturbance had implications for the way vegetation and soils respond to changes in local water table conditions. Indeed, previous studies by this author have demonstrated that, in some instances, impermeable bedrock and soil layers are breached by cratering, depriving the vegetation of its former source of water (Hupy 2006). In other instances, cratering exposes the water table and inhibits deep rooting of vegetation, limiting subsequent reforestation (Hupy 2005). Disturbances of this nature can lead to divergent paths in the evolution of a soilscape. These theories are applied to the Khe Sanh case study, which follows, hypothesizing that the recovery and subsequent evolution of the soilscape was dramatically altered by explosive munitions and herbicides.

Case study: disturbance and recovery patterns at Khe Sanh

The Khe Sanh battlefield is located in Vietnam's central highlands and is characteristically rugged, covered with a tropical-monsoon climate forest canopy. Khe Sanh is situated on a small plateau at approximately 450 m above sea level (see Figure 19.3). The plateau is part of a larger mountain range, the Annamese Cordillera, which extends 2700 km from Laos to southern Vietnam (Prados and Stubbe 1991). Although most of Vietnam is known for its monsoonal climate, Khe Sanh lies within central Vietnam, which has no dry season because of the upslope movement of moisture-laden winds from the South China Sea. For that reason, pre-war vegetation in Khe Sanh is especially dense, consisting of tropical rainforest, buffalo grass, and bamboo forest. Copious precipitation within this tropical rainforest, and the stable upland plateau-like setting, created conditions that lead to the development of *oxisols* (Winters et al. 1998). Oxisols are heavily leached and nutrient deficient, and their nutrient deficiencies and high clay content led many scientists to propose, at that time (i.e. 1968), that following disturbance the soils would bake into hard clay, and no vegetation would return to the area. The devastation they witnessed, and the limited knowledge of tropical soils at the time, led to these erroneous conclusions.

Figure 19.3
Khe Sanh battlefield.
Hills and other elevation
high points in the
Vietnam War were
named according to their
height above sea level.
Hills 881N, 881S, and 861
were particularly
contested areas, and
therefore were subjected
to considerable amounts
of bombing and artillery
fire. *Source*: map
compiled by Jonathan
Laager, University of
Wisconsin—Eau Claire.

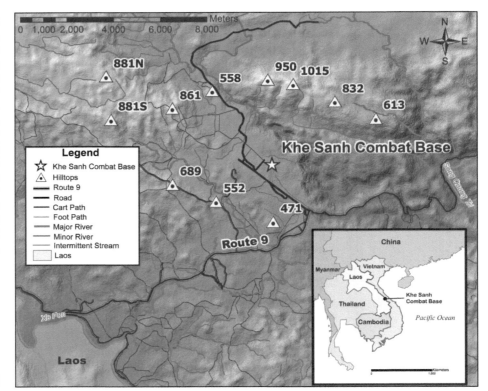

Although many areas in Indochina were devastated by war, the Khe Sanh battlefield stands out in particular. Khe Sanh was the site of an offensive launched by the NVA against US Marines at that remote outpost. The NVA offensive became bogged down into a prolonged siege operation against the base. While the Marines were well established on the hilltops surrounding the base, all roads into the area were controlled by the enemy, and fire support was provided by air power and artillery (see Figure 19.3). Between February and April 1968, aircraft delivered 98,721 tons of munitions to the Khe Sanh battlefield—more than all the tonnage delivered by Allied forces in the Pacific Theatre during World War II (Littauer and Uphoff 1972; Page-Demroese et al. 2000; Prados and Stubbe 1991). The combined effect of thousands of artillery rounds and aerial bombs produced a scarred landscape at Khe Sanh (see Figure 19.4).

Marine accounts used words such as hell, inferno, moonscape, or another world to describe the area after prolonged bombardments. The images of destruction still reside in the minds of the contemporary world, with blame for a lack of reforestation linked to US bombings and use of defoliants. Contemporary literature and documentary movies make note of the distinct war-related patterns left on the landscape (Webster 1996). Indeed, this author was influenced by those accounts and expected this pattern when visiting the battlefield, but these notions proved to be wrong. The battlefield's modern landscape is far from a

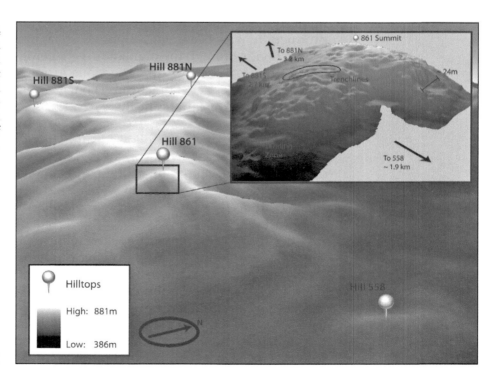

Figure 19.4
Oblique view of terrain on Khe Sanh battlefield with detail of current microtopography of hill 861 summit. *Source*: map compiled by Tom Koehler, University of Wisconsin—Eau Claire.

moonscape, although it is quite different from the one that existed before the Second Indochina War. Recent findings by this author point to a landscape whose long-term re-vegetation patterns are a consequence of economic and human activity, and not the latent effects of munitions and herbicides associated with the battle of Khe Sanh.

To gain a better perspective of landscape recovery patterns at Khe Sanh, one must understand the region's history, which is a story of diverse land-use activities following the war. This case study is based on written historical accounts (Lamb 2002), interviews with indigenous people, NVA soldiers, and US veterans.

The Khe Sanh plateau is home to many indigenous groups such as the *Bru*, *Hmong*, and *T'ai*. Many of these groups did not support the North Vietnamese, and instead fought with the French, and later the Americans. At Khe Sanh region the *Bru* served with the US forces and, unfortunately, they fought for the losing side. Consequently, following the war they were highly marginalized, to the point of persecution. When Vietnam was reunified in 1975, party members and those who fought for the North were given large plots of land in valley bottoms. Much of this land originally belonged to the indigenous groups, but now became to be considered People's Land. These groups—and among them the *Bru*—were forced into the surrounding highlands. Indigenous groups at first took advantage of land already cleared by US bombings and (unfortunately) herbicides. This land was not fertile as in the valleys, and was prone to erosion. Because of low soil fertility, the groups needed to constantly rotate their crops, and soon resorted to illegal logging in order to remove trees for more farmland. Meanwhile, in the valleys, rice production was occurring, along with a limited amount of coffee production. Although the highlands were being removed of their triple-canopy rainforest cover by indigenous groups, widespread landscape disturbance was not yet practiced. Then, in 1989, the Vietnamese government, following a famine in the early 1980s, noticed how well China was doing after allowing free enterprise to take place within the economic sector, and soon followed suit. Thus, party members with land in the valleys began widespread production of coffee and ranching operations. This activity pushed the indigenous groups into even more marginal lands, and opened up widespread land-clearing operations in valley bottoms that, in 1968, were completely covered with triple-canopy rainforest.

Other forms of economic development, such as dam construction to supply power to the rapidly growing economy, converted other areas that were once forest. Photographs taken by veterans in 1968 compared with a view of the landscape today illustrate how these post-war practices by the Vietnamese actually deforested large segments of the landscape, not explosive munitions or defoliants (see Figure 19.5).

The modern Khe Sanh landscape manifests many different land-use patterns: the steepest slopes are forested, the steep slopes are grazed by

Figure 19.5
Images taken from same location on summit of Hill 558 looking east towards hill 950 in the background. The left image is from 1968 and the image on the right was taken in May 2009. Note how steep slopes deforested from bombing and defoliants in 1968 are now back in forest, while the 1968 forested valley is now rice fields, or deforested. *Source*: images courtesy of Tom Ford, USMC veteran of Khe Sanh. Image rendered by Thomas Koehler, University of Wisconsin—Eau Claire.

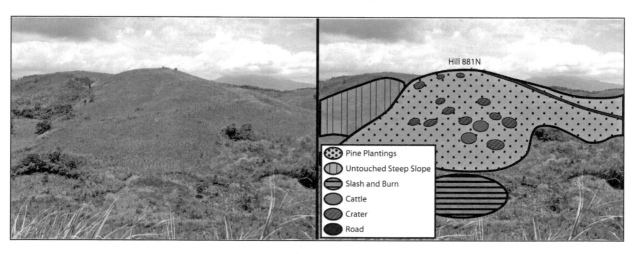

Figure 19.6
Hill 881S image from May 2007 looking north to 881N (left). The right side highlights the land coverage for the same hill. It is important to note that the war may not have changed this landscape from a dense forest to what it is today, but likely a combination of the disturbances from the Second Indochina War and the *resulting* changes in land use.
Source: Joseph P. Hupy, May 2007.

Figure 19.7
Thick vegetation covers the bottom of a 700 lb bomb crater on the Khe Sanh battlefield. This particular crater was likely reworked into a defensive position, and was later excavated by the local populace for shards of shrapnel, to be sold on the market as scrap metal. Source: Joseph P. Hupy, May 2009.

cattle, and the gentle slopes to flat highland areas are mainly used for coffee production (see Figure 19.6). Today, heavily cratered hilltops support intensive cattle-grazing efforts, and crater bottoms support some of the thickest, most lush vegetation (see Figure 19.7).

It is in these crater bottoms where woody vegetation is taking hold, protected from grazing cattle and the high winds that buffet the summits. Not surprisingly, in a country roughly the size of California, with over 6 million people, with some of the highest rural population densities in the world, people will make economic use of the land as allowed. Hence, a lack of reforestation on this battlefield is not a result of explosives and their lingering constituents, or herbicides. Instead, it was caused by post-war economic activity. A quick glance at the economic growth figures for Vietnam illustrate how much their economy has grown since the introduction of a free-market system, but those numbers do nothing to describe changes rendered upon the landscape associated with this shift in policy. Subsequent publications associated with this research at Khe Sanh will help refine some of the theories associated with the long-term impacts of warfare on the environment.

Conclusions

The Khe Sanh case study offers an important perspective as to why the nexus between warfare and its influence on the environment should be studied. As we have seen, from the beginnings of warfare, the environment has suffered, both incidentally and intentionally. Activities associated with military operations—maneuver training, practice firing, and warfare—have a pervasive and sometimes insidious effect on the landscape. Thus, military geographers need to extend their traditional research beyond the examination of operational environments, and begin to explore the expanded scenario—the effects of military operations *upon* the environment. This research theme has the potential to open many avenues of research within a broader arena of geography. Consequently, military geography can expand into branches of academic geography that will promote the advancement of scientific theories concerning landscape recovery following disturbance (such as military training grounds).

Finally, in studying the impact of warfare on the environment, as the case study on Khe Sanh shows, one must also keep an open mind to multiple hypotheses. While the war may have acted as a catalyst for these changes, the resulting landscape patterns are much more related to human activity, and not from warfare itself. These findings should serve as a reminder to the reader that military geography is more than just an analysis of the physical landscape; it is an analysis that links that all too important element to the physical realm—ourselves.

References cited

Bailey, J. B. A. 2004. *Field artillery and firepower*. Annapolis, MD: Naval Institute Press.

Cablk, M. E. 2009. "Experiencing nature in militarized landscapes: if a bomb drops in the desert do we still call it wilderness?" Association of American Geographers Annual Meeting, Las Vegas, Nevada.

Flamm, B. R. & J. H. Cravens. 1971. "The effects of war damage on the forest resources of South Vietnam." *Journal of Forestry* 69(11): 784–9.

Hogg, I. V. 1985. *The illustrated history of ammunition*. Secaucus, NJ: Chartwell Books.

——. 1987. *The illustrated encyclopedia of artillery*. Secaucus, NJ: Chartwell Books.

Hupy, J. P. 2005. "Verdun, France: examining the effects of warfare on the natural landscape." In *Military geography from peace to war*, E. Palka & F. A. Galgano (eds). New York, NY: McGraw Hill.

——. 2006. "The long-term effects of explosive munitions on the WWI battlefield surface of Verdun, France." *Scottish Geographical Journal* 122(3): 167–84.

—— 2008. "The environmental footprint of war." *Environment and history* 14: 405–21.

Hupy, J. P. & R. J Schaetzl. 2006. "Introducing 'bombturbation': a singular type of soil disturbance and mixing." *Soil Science* 171(11): 823–36.

——. 2008. "Soil development on the WWI battlefield of Verdun, France." *Geoderma* 145(1–2): 37–49.

Keegan, J. 1976. *The face of battle*. New York, NY: Penguin Books.

——. 1998. *The First World War*. New York, NY: Vintage Books.

King, W. C. 2001. Forward. In *The environmental legacy of military operations*, J. Ehlen & R. S. Harmon (eds). Boulder, CO: Geological Society of America Reviews in Engineering Geology.

Lamb, D. 2002. *Vietnam now: a reporter returns*. New York, NY: Public Affairs.

Lewallen, J. 1971. *Ecology of devastation: Indochina*. Baltimore, MD: Penguin Books.

Littauer, R. & N. Uphoff. 1972. *The air war in Indochina*. Boston, MA: Beacon Books.

Orians, G. H. & E. W. Pfeiffer. 1970. "Ecological effects of the war in Vietnam." *Science* 168(3931): 544–54.

Page-Demroese, D., M. Jurgensen, W. Elliot, T. Rice, J. Nesser, T. Collins, & R. Meurisse. 2000. "Soil quality standards and guidelines for forest sustainability in northwestern North America." *Forest Ecology and Management* 138: 445–62.

Partington, J. R. 1960. *A history of Greek fire and gunpowder.* Cambridge, UK: W. Heffer.

Pfeiffer, E. W. 1969. "Ecological effects of the Vietnam War." *Science Journal* 5(2): 33–8.

Prados, J. & R. W. Stubbe. 1991. *Valley of decision.* New York, NY: Dell Publishing.

Webster, D. 1996. *Aftermath: the remnants of war.* New York, NY: Pantheon Books.

Westing, A. H. 1976. *Ecological consequences of the Second Indochina War.* Stockholm, Sweden: Almqvist & Wiksell International.

Westing, A. H. & E. W. Pfeiffer. 1972. "The cratering of Indochina." *Scientific American* 226(5): 20–9.

Westing, A. H. and Stockholm International Peace Research Institute. 1984. *Herbicides in war: the long-term ecological and human consequences.* London, UK, and Philadelphia: Taylor & Francis.

Winters, H. A., G. E. Galloway, W. J. Reynolds, & D. W. Rhyne. 1998. *Battling the elements: weather and terrain in the conduct of war.* Baltimore, MD: Johns Hopkins University Press.

Chapter twenty
Napoleonic know-how for stability operations

DOUGLAS E. BATSON

Introduction

IN POST-CONFLICT AFGHANISTAN and Iraq competing land claims have impaired *stability operations (SO)* and thwarted hopes of a lasting peace. While carrying out a myriad of SO missions under fire, US military forces in those countries have been cast in the unenviable role of land dispute arbiters. This situation will occur more frequently in SO until US foreign policy, development programs, and civil–military reconstruction efforts appreciate relationships between people and their land, information typically registered in a *cadastre*. Napoleon Bonaparte, renowned for his military genius, also moved decisively to improve post-conflict governance and called his cadastre the greatest achievement of his civil code.

This chapter posits that geography matters at the parcel level for soldiers and civilians conducting SO. Moreover, it establishes why shared goals for reconstructing a shattered nation—stability, development, peace, and effective local sovereignty—cannot be realized without *land administration* (Manwaring 2006). Finally, this chapter introduces a new tool, the Land Administration Domain Model (LADM). With the potential to geo-locate, describe, and register *land tenure* across cultures and international boundaries, the LADM can enable a new discipline, cadastral analysis, by which US civilian development/aid organizations and US military forces, as well as the US and NATO partners, can co-operatively achieve whole-of-government and whole-of-alliance mission success.

The soldier may ask what this tiresome subject of cadastres and land administration has to do with his job, with warfare. The answer is "nothing"—unless he wants to find and fix an elusive enemy; unless it is important to the soldier to establish conditions after combat that will allow him to go home; unless he thinks it important to keep insurgencies from forming so that his presence in those difficult environments is not necessary; or unless he would prefer there to be fewer places where terrorists are bred and sponsored.

(Demarest 2008: 352)

The "who" question in stability operations

Following the Cold War, the US Department of Defense (DoD) reduced its force structure and prepared to reap the benefits of a so-called peace dividend that was never realized. In the decade after the fall of the Berlin Wall, US forces participated in more than fifteen SO, intervening in places such as Haiti, Liberia, Somalia, and the Balkans. Many of these efforts continued into the new century, and incursions into Afghanistan and Iraq revealed a disturbing trend throughout the world: the collapse of established governments, the rise of international criminal and terrorist networks, and unending humanitarian crises (Department of the Army 2008). In his foreword to Field Manual 3-07 (*Stability Operations*), LTG William B. Caldwell IV notes that SO will address the fundamental causes of conflict among the disenfranchised people (Department of the Army 2008). Whether or not a conflict is about control over, or access to, land resources, McGill University geography professor Jon Unruh remarks how land issues plague the peace process.

> An end to armed conflict, especially a prolonged one, prompts the affected population to begin to seek access, or solidify claims, to land resources. Often, large rural populations have been displaced. As a result, local land tenure and property rights issues can emerge quickly, over large geographic areas, for considerable numbers of people. Complex histories of property, land, and territory lead to conflict scenarios. Likewise, the postwar re-establishment of ownership, use, and access rights will also be complex. Left unattended, they promote renewed confrontation.
>
> (Unruh 2002: 337)

Military commanders have demanded, and receive from a sprawling intelligence apparatus, answers to "what" (i.e. opposing forces' order of battle) and "where" (i.e. grid co-ordinates of enemy dispositions) questions. The US, however, has invested little in collecting or creating land-related information that can potentially answer the "who" questions that vex commanders conducting people-centric SO: Who is behind poppy cultivation, ethnic cleansing, or attacks on United Nations (UN) peacekeepers? Intelligence collection has not sought to associate a personal name with a property. Yet, as depicted in Figure 20.1, an intervening military force, emergency humanitarian aid, and long-term nation-building all require an understanding of whose land interests have been affected by natural disasters or warring factions.

Figure 20.1
US military assists displaced persons in the wake of a Central American natural disaster. *Source*: Department of Defense.

Today's adversaries are not conventional armies that, once defeated, disband and desist. Rather, they are nameless, tenacious, and adaptive individuals who trump superior US military power "by refusing to mass together and by submerging themselves in urban seas" (Peters 2007) where no current Geographic Information Systems (GIS) layers can trace them. The 1807–14 Peninsular War in Spain was marked by Napoleon's swift military victory over Spanish forces followed by a protracted and draining guerilla war, hence the term's Spanish origin, waged by unknown partisans against French occupiers. US Marine Corps LTC George W. Smith, Jr. describes a historical parallel between Napoleonic and contemporary post-conflict scenarios with a peptic effect too similar to ignore:

> Napoleon's "Spanish ulcer," as he described the Spanish response to his occupation, provides a myriad of timeless lessons for strategic and operational planners. The strategic gap that developed between Napoleon's rapid conventional military victory and the immediate requirement to influence positively the population as part of stabilization operations highlights the limits of conventional military power in post-conflict operations and the perils of forgetting "the people" in the initial and ongoing strategic calculus. Unfortunately, nations and militaries around the globe have been forced to relearn that lesson many times in the ensuing 200 years.
>
> (Smith 2004: 22)

Attorney and former military attaché officer, Geoffrey Demarest (2004, 2008), submits that contemporary terrorists, insurgents, crime bosses, narco-traffickers, and slumlords well understand the power ungoverned territory offers for the taking. Shielded by anonymity and impunity, these purveyors of instability hide in unregistered properties, and use their hidden wealth in those properties to fund illicit activities. They decide who gets what by imposing their own property ownership regimes on the local populace; they offer services to offended claimants, create loyalties and obligations, and sow fear (Demarest 2008).

For the SO commander, cadastral data offers an unparalleled glimpse into a society's human terrain, that is, it allows the commander to identify power brokers on the ground whose support or obstruction may determine mission success. By tying a name to a place, a cadastre can answer the difficult "who" question, i.e. who is impeding road construction or a minority group's access to a health clinic? Additionally, analysis of cadastral data has the potential to identify a group's ideologies and economic pillars. Thus, for the intelligence analyst, spikes in property transactions, inexplicable from market forces alone, can indicate escalating ethnic tensions or criminal activity. "Early in this decade Colombian police found it impossible to serve a legal warrant in the slums of Medellin. The streets and shacks were so irregular that violent actors could confuse [police regarding their] addresses and identities" (Demarest 2008: 264). In this manner, cadastral information also aids forensic work and law enforcement. For these reasons, cadastres threaten those who want to maintain a status quo that cements their prestige, power, and profit. Not only nefarious characters, but also host nation government officials, and their well-placed relatives, can have ulterior motives to resist formalization of property regimes.

> Slum organizers, political bosses, and tribal chiefs can often view tenure regularization as eroding their privileged social and economic position. Municipal officials and ministries that exhibited near absolute power over land decisions do not easily give up control. Political sympathy for squatters is frequently low. Change, which improves the situation for some, will necessarily erode political, cultural, and/or economic power for others. For all these reasons and more, the process is often complicated, political and violent.
>
> (Durand-Lasserve and Royston 2002: 241).

Demarest (2008) reminds an SO commander, perplexed that new roads and clinics have done little to win hearts and minds, that only when the purveyors of instability lose anonymity and impunity will the local populace be less likely to support them. He concludes, "the consequence is obvious and advises industrial-level GIS cadastral projects for countries of special interest" (Demarest 2004: 1). What Demarest advised just a few years ago is now, for the first time in cadastral history, feasible: a standard for analyzing cadastres across cultures and international borders.

Send money, guns, lawyers

Incessant and costly guerilla warfare in Spain prevented Napoleon from consolidating his military victory there. His *Grand Armée*, weakened by the catastrophe in Russia, was eventually pushed off the Iberian Peninsula. However, where Napoleon was able to consolidate his hold in Europe, the Low Countries, Italy, and some German states, he implemented commercial, transportation, and legal reforms that far outlasted his reign. It is no coincidence that uniform weights, measures, coinage, property registration, and taxation—coupled with internal improvements such as construction of bridges, roads, and canals; and civil code and judicial reforms—fueled the prosperity of these emergent nineteenth-century nation states. Napoleon also moved to improve governance in his Grand Empire and nowhere is this more evident than in his cadastre. By employing statistical analyses, he improved government planning and efficiency. His cadastre created a universal type of property right; its perennial representation would eliminate civil strife caused by boundary disputes and facilitate uniform taxation. Robert Burtch (2006), Professor of Surveying Engineering at Ferris State University, notes that Napoleon's 1808 cadastre, still evident today in *continental law*, was not the singular result of an expanding empire; instead, he notes that, "It also reflected societal changes, both in structure and in character, that were happening at this time. This effort by Napoleon is very significant in light of information technology and public administration" (Burtch 2006: 6). Indeed, it is phenomenal that, by the end of the nineteenth century, former Napoleonic satellites in present-day Belgium, Italy, and Germany so rapidly developed their political and economic bases, that they could compete with long-established seafaring nations of Europe in the race for overseas colonies and dominions.

Two centuries after Napoleon's cadastre, there still has never been an accepted standard or method for evaluating land administration across international borders. "Each land system reflects the unique cultural and social context of the country in which it operates" (Steudler, Rajabifard, and Williamson 2004: 4), which is why deed- or title-based land registries have been unworkable in *informal settlements*, *customary tenure*, and post-conflict situations, all replete with competing land claims. The resettlement and reintegration into society of 4.7 million Afghan refugees since 2002, depicted in Figure 20.2, plus the 3 million currently under pressure from Pakistan and Iran to return home, has been a decades' long humanitarian effort unprecedented in its scale.

Conor Foley (2003), a consultant to human rights and refugee organizations, notes the implication for SO in Afghanistan:

> Continued fighting and human rights violations mean that many other Afghans remain internally displaced, often occupying other

people's lands The looting ´and destruction caused by war was recently compounded by severe drought, which devastated much of the countryside over a four-year period. Disputes over land and property remain a significant cause of internal tension in Afghan society. The inability of the courts to deal with these problems is also having an extremely destabilizing effect. A recent report by the independent Afghanistan Research and Evaluation Unit described land disputes as the "number one source of conflict" in Afghanistan.

(Foley 2003: 2)

The numbers of refugees from Iraq are also distressing: since 2003, 2 million Iraqis have left their country. Additionally, another 2.3 million Iraqi internally displaced persons (IDP) have fled their homes in refugee-like circumstances (International Organization for Migration in Iraq 2007). Iraqi refugee and IDP problems are legion, and the human drama there greatly impairs SO. Resolution and settlement of displaced persons' land-related claims are more hopeful in Iraq, however, due to a Napoleonic legacy. Major Dan E. Stigall, a US Army Judge Advocate (JAG) trained in continental civil law at Louisiana State University, deployed to Iraq in 2003, and has published widely on Iraqi civil law since that time. Stigall (2008) notes that Iraqi property law is derived primarily from Continental European civil law but also contains elements of Ottoman and Islamic land law. Though there is still a great need to increase the administrative capacity of the judiciary, Iraq has been and remains capable of sound land administration (Stigall 2008).

In Afghanistan, sadly, this is not the case; thus, building the capacity of land administration and the judiciary in that shattered nation will take decades. When prescribing remedies for the international community to untangle the forty-year impact that tribalism, communism, Islamic theocracy, and now the lure of a free-market economy has successively had on land and property in Afghanistan, Foley rightly concludes, "send money, guns, and lawyers" (Foley 2008: 177). The US is sending money and guns to Afghanistan, but very little in the way of land administration because land administration tools and expertise in the ranks of the US military members and civilian development/aid workers is paltry.

The Land Administration Domain Model

Modeling the world's varied and complex interrelationships between persons and geographic places is far more difficult in post-conflict environments where masses of people have been displaced. Yet restoring those people to the land is a key part of any serious effort to reconstruct the country. Reconstruction attracts people from a variety of viewpoints. There are various competing theories on cadastres and how to rectify a nation's defective, fragmented, or non-existent land administration system.

Figure 20.3
Complexities and conflicts resulting from different types of tenure. *Source*: Food and Agriculture Organization of the United Nations (FAO).

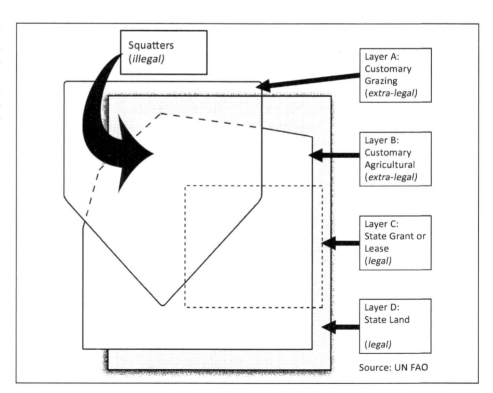

Imagine Figure 20.3 to be a well-watered valley in a developing country. Every year a family of herders do what their ancestors have done for centuries—bring their flocks to pasture in the valley every spring (see Layer A, Figure 20.3). In that same valley there are farmers practicing their ancestral livelihood (Layer B, Figure 20.3), who, honoring a longstanding verbal agreement, allow the herders water rights every spring. Recently, a major drought forced a related ethnic group from a neighboring country to migrate to the valley. The government does not enjoy friendly relations with the neighboring country and considers these new arrivals as illegal squatters. Decades ago, unbeknownst to either the herders or the farmers, the newly emergent government laid claim to the entire valley as state domain (Layer D, Figure 20.3). The government never attempted to develop the land until now, when a foreign mineral company notified the government of a valuable resource in part of the valley, and negotiated a lease (Layer C, Figure 20.3). For each of these four layers, and the squatters as a quasi-fifth layer, a different land right is at work. Now imagine a SO commander charged with keeping peace in the valley following a civil war. The negotiated settlement would have involved only the four recognized parties (i.e. Layers A–D). The illegal squatters in the valley, excluded from the settlement, are angry at not receiving legal refugee status and, thus, they immeasurably complicate the commander's mission.

As Demarest (2004) stated, for the SO commander to sort out such disorder, an industrial-strength GIS cadastre is not only advisable, it is indispensable as the primary source of information about the broad spectrum of formal and informal rights and interests in land. Such information includes (FIG, the International Federation of Surveyors 1995):

- people who have interests in parcels of land
- interests in the land, e.g. nature and duration of rights, restrictions and responsibilities
- basic details about the parcel, e.g. location, size, improvements, value.

European development and aid agencies have long included property formalization in their agenda for foreign aid, democratization, and human rights. By instituting transparent cadastres in areas of the world where land administration was weak or non-existent, unsung civilians from NATO member states have, perhaps unwittingly, swept scores of malignant non-state actors from the field with Napoleonic gallantry. Even if cadastral surveyors were awarded the *Légion d'honneur*, created by Napoleon in 1802 for civilian as well as military merit, this award, France's highest decoration, would only recognize a fraction of the valor that has improved countless livelihoods, established the rule of law, and saved billions of dollars in police and military expenditures.

The urgency of multiplying the positive effects of cadastres across the developing world perhaps can be demographically quantified. By 2050, a staggering 3 billion people, of an estimated world population of 9 billion, will live in informal settlements without formal property registries (UN-HABITAT 2001), making for an unstable world. To meet this challenge, the ability to measure, compare, and analyze the world's various cadastral systems is forthcoming. In the late 1990s, Juerg Kaufmann and Daniel Steudler co-authored Cadastre 2014, a pioneering approach to model the cadastral domain based not on parcels, but on legal land objects. Kaufmann notes that a cadastre, with its traditional role of documenting land rights, restrictions, and responsibilities, can be viewed as a bookkeeping or accounting system for land issues, ultimately supporting a post-conflict reconstruction period through the transition to sustainable development (Kaufmann, 2000). A research group at the Department of Geomatics of the University of Melbourne has developed a cadastral template that can link the operational aspects of a country's land administration systems with its land policy (Williamson et al. 2009). The side-by-side country comparisons and statistics are already useful for analysis. For example, self-reports from forty-two nations indicate that 72 percent have title-based cadastral systems, 21 percent deed-based, and the remaining 7 percent a mix of the two.

Cadastre 2014 is a fine starting point but is highly abstract and years away from any implementation. Only now, for the first time in history, is the systematic recording of non-title-based land rights and interests feasible with the Land Administration Domain Model (LADM), a new conceptual approach to land administration. The LADM, with spatial and legal/administrative components, possesses the needed flexibility to geo-locate, describe, and record the customary socio-tenures and even claims with no apparent legal basis. The LADM's designers, Dutch cadastral experts Christiaan Lemmen, Peter van Oosterom, and Paul van der Molen, and Nairobi-based Clarissa Augustinus, chief of the Land Tenure Unit at UN-HABITAT, have made the LADM compelling. It makes explicit the various types of land rights, restrictions, or responsibilities. It is flexible enough to record land tenure types that are not based on the traditional cadastral parcel, that is, customary, informal land rights such as occupancy, *usufruct*, lease, or *traverse*. Still in development and undergoing field testing, the LADM has garnered support from standardization and professional bodies such as the International Federation of Surveyors (FIG), Open GIS Consortium (OGC), UN-HABITAT, and the Infrastructure for Spatial Information in Europe (EU-INSPIRE) (van Oosterom et al. 2006). In 2008, the International Standards Organization (ISO/TC211), the body responsible for determining all international standards, accepted the LADM as New Work Item Proposal 1954. At this writing, the working draft has progressed to a committee draft, and by the end of 2009 the LADM, as ISO 19152, is poised to become a Draft International Standard. The timeline suggests that, by

335

2011, the LADM could become the world's first international standard for cadastre (Lemmen et al. 2009).

The LADM would be an invaluable tool in the scenario discussed in Figure 20.3 because it has reduced the complex database models that underlie title-based cadastres to a simple principle: that a relationship (i.e. rights, socio-tenure) always exists between land (i.e. spatial objects) and people. No matter how messy or difficult the world's land disputes, nothing falls outside this basic principle. The LADM then translates these three categories into *Unified Modeling Language (UML)* to establish three classes for its cadastre: Person–Right–Spatial Object, in that order. The LADM enables registration and maintenance of "relationships between people and land irrespective of the nature of the country's jurisprudence; this ability offers opportunities for the integration of statutory, customary, and informal arrangements within conventional land administration systems" (Lemmen et al. 2007: 7). Because the LADM should be able to accommodate any legal framework, it allows tremendous flexibility in describing the persons and places involved and in systematically recording rights that are not title-based legal rights. The LADM can merge formal and informal land tenure systems, and urban and rural cadastres, into one data environment. It covers all basic information-related components of land administration (Lemmen et al. 2009: 4–5):

- an abstract, conceptual schema with five basic packages, related to people and organizations (*parties* in LADM terminology), parcels (spatial units in LADM terminology), property rights (rights, responsibilities, and restrictions in LADM terminology), surveying, and geometry and topology
- simplified terminology for land administration, based on various national and international systems; the terminology can describe different practices and procedures from various jurisdictions
- a basis for national and regional land use profiles
- a coherent synthesis of land administration information from different sources.

Operationally, the LADM links spatial data from very different systems. In the past, this linking has been problematic for land information, in part because of the database structure. Registering human landscapes with a myriad of land tenures requires one to link disparate data, and this is where the LADM excels. LADM is less a database than a word processor. Anything, even photographs, hand-drawn sketches, and oral testimony, can be put into the document as long as it records evidence relevant to a property and the rights various people claim on it. Thus, LADM is especially suited to recording deeds. Furthermore, the LADM promises the following features (Lemmen et al. 2007):

- formal and informal tenure systems can be held in one data environment
- the computer-based system is reversible to and from a paper-based one
- spatial information can be represented in existing geodetic networks and in new spatial frameworks
- spatial data can be linked to other systems
- the environment is distributed and decentralized, simultaneously processed on multiple computers linked over a network, making it usable centrally and locally
- source data can be of disparate types, with different geospatial accuracies
- different tenures can overlap
- places can be identified by a range of identifiers—geo-referenced parcels, unreferenced parcels, lines, and points
- conflicts can be recorded
- women's rights to land can be recorded, and therefore preserved
- highly complex relationships can be described.

Ideally, land administration should serve decision-makers at national, regional, and local levels, and it should promote decentralized decision-making. This is the basic concept behind the LADM: to produce and provide land registration (the administrative/legal component) and geo-referenced cadastral mapping (the spatial component) for those who are locally administering land where there is decentralized or ineffective governance. The model will allow better vertical co-ordination, between "bottom up" local/community interests and "top down" information and policy guidance. National land policies, once developed, can be harmonized with local tenure formalization programs (Lemmen et al. 2007). Thus, LADM facilitates the rehabilitation of both local and central governance. The LADM can support SO by recording all forms of land rights (and even claims), all types of rights holders, and all kinds of land and property objects (spatial units) regardless of the level of formality. It focuses on land and property rights that neither have been registered nor are registerable, as well as on overlapping claims over the "who," the "where," and the "what right" for a given piece of land.

While some foreign aid projects have modernized property regimes in developing countries, these have not insisted on a product in the form of transparent, digital property data (Demarest 2008). How can this approach promote sustainable development? Only analyzable cadastral data can support law enforcement and guide effective post-conflict reconstruction. Napoleon recognized how a good cadastre reduces civil strife, strengthens economic development, and institutes the rule of law, all of which are key end-state goals of SO.

The only way to sort out the confusion in the field of general land records is to proceed with the surveying and evaluation of each individual land parcel in all the communities of the Empire. A good cadastre will constitute a complement of my [civil] Code as far as land possession is concerned. The maps must be sufficiently precise and complete so that they could determine the boundaries between individual properties and prevent litigations.

(Napoleon Bonaparte, in Burtch 2006: 6)

Conclusion

In SO there are tensions, both domestically, between military and civilian entities, and internationally, between the US and other NATO members. The resource imbalance between the US Department of Defense versus the US State Department and the US Agency for International Development (USAID) is an irritant to the overtaxed civilian agencies that impedes interagency co-operation. Internationally, the brawny and agile US military outperforms NATO partners in deployment and logistical capacities, in Intelligence, Surveillance, and Reconnaissance assets for counter-insurgency operations, and in legal freedoms to operate. The LADM can be a unifying instrument both domestically and internationally.

At the domestic level, the US Federal Geographic Data Committee (FGDC), an interagency committee that promotes the co-ordinated development, use, sharing, and dissemination of geospatial data on a national basis, should examine the LADM for the needs of both US military and civilian organizations. For learning global land administration, the playing field is level; neither the military services nor civilian agencies have any inherent advantage over the other. By incorporating cadastral analysis into their planning and decision-making, military and civilian officials would both learn some startling facts with which to markedly improve their respective spheres of SO.

First, underdeveloped countries remain underdeveloped, even following massive infusions of foreign aid because landless people have little incentive to engage in productive economic behavior (Frye 2004). In sum, property rights anchor economic development and civil society. Foreign aid, in the absence thereof, is a waste of much time and money (Demarest 2004).

Second, transparent cadastres shape geographies for effective intelligence against non-state actors. In other words, geophysical aspects are only half the puzzle; not interpreting the human terrain via property data is tantamount to not understanding a society (Demarest 2008).

At the international level, Napoleon's cadastre stands to become more influential than his battlefield tactics, should NATO partners impart their foremost asset for SO—their cadastral expertise! Land administration is a professional discipline in Europe, much like Geomatics is in Australia and Canada. Whereas only one single course in global land administration can be found in the US, at the University of Florida, many European nations boast entire graduate degree programs in this discipline, many of them taught in English! By implementing Napoleonic know-how into US foreign policy, development programs, and civil–military reconstruction efforts, cadastral analysis can become the active ingredient for *conflict transformation* and a unifying element for whole-of-government and whole-of-alliance SO.

References cited

Burtch, R. 2006. Ferris State University lecture notes for surveying engineering SURE 325. www.ferris.edu/htmls/academics/course.offerings/burtchr/sure325/notes/land_information_systems.pdf [accessed 30 April 2010].

Demarest, G. 2004. "Cadastres (land registries) and global security". *2004 ESRI users conference proceedings.* http://proceedings.esri.com/library/userconf/proc04/abstracts/a2177.html [accessed 30 April 2010].

——. 2008. *Property and peace: insurgency, strategy, and the statute of frauds.* Fort Leavenworth, KS: Foreign Military Studies Office.

Department of the Army. 2008. *Stability operations. Field manual (FM) 3-07.* https://rdl.train.army.mil/soldierPortal/atia/adlsc/view/public/9630-1/fm/3-07/TOC.HTM [accessed 30 April 2010].

Durand-Lasserve, A. & L. Royston. 2002. *Holding their ground: secure land tenure for the urban poor in developing countries.* London, UK: Earthscan Publications Ltd.

Fédération Internationale des Géomètres (FIG)/The International Federation of Surveyors, Commission 7, Cadastre and Land Management. 1995. *The FIG statement on the cadastre.* Copenhagen, Denmark: The Surveyors House. www.fig.net/commission7/reports/cadastre/statement_on_cadastre_summary.html [accessed 30 April 2010].

Foley, C. 2003. "Afghanistan: the search for peace." *Minority rights group international.* November. www.minorityrights.org/download.php?id=45 [accessed 30 April 2010].

——. 2008. "Housing, land, and property restitution rights in Afghanistan." In *Housing, land, and property rights in post-conflict United Nations and other peace operations,* S. Leckie (ed.), Cambridge, UK: Cambridge University Press.

Frye, T. 2004. "Credible commitment and property rights: evidence from Russia." *American Political Science Review* 98(3): 453–66.

International Organization for Migration in Iraq. 2007. www.iom-iraq.net/idp.html [accessed 10 July 2009].

Kaufmann, J. 2000. "Future cadastres: the bookkeeping systems for land administration supporting sustainable development." 1st International Seminar on Cadastral System, Land Administration and Sustainable Development, 3–5 May. Bogota, Colombia.

Lemmen, C., C. Augustinus, P. van Oosterom, & P. van der Molen. 2007. *The social tenure domain model—design of a first draft model.* FIG Working Week, 13–17 May. Hong Kong, SAR, China. www.fig.net/pub/fig2007/papers/ts_1a/TS01A_01_lemmen_augustinus_oosterom_molen_1373.pdf [accessed 30 April 2010].

Lemmen, C., P. van Oosterom, H. Uitermark, R. Thompson, & J. Hespanha. 2009. "Transforming the land administration domain model (LADM) into an ISO standard (ISO19152)." FIG Working Week, 3–8 May. Tel Aviv, Israel. www.fig.net/pub/fig2009/papers/ts06a/ts06a_lemmen_oosterom_etal_3282.pdf [accessed 30 April 2010].

Manwaring, M. G. 2006. *Defense, development, and diplomacy (3D): Canadian and U.S. military perspectives.* Strategic Studies Institute, Carlisle, PA: US Army War College Press. www.strategicstudiesinstitute.army.mil/pubs/display.cfm?pubID=732 [accessed 30 April 2010].

Peters, R. 2007. "Out-thought by the enemy." *New York Post.* www.nypost.com/seven/06012007/postopinion/opedcolumnists/out_thought_by_the_enemy_opedcolumnists_ralph_peters.htm [accessed 30 April 2010].

Smith, G. 2004. *Avoiding a Napoleonic ulcer: bridging the gap of cultural intelligence (or, have we focused on the wrong transformation?).* Washington, DC: National Defense University Press.

Steudler, D., A. Rajabifard, & I. Williamson. 2004. "Evaluation of land administration systems." *Land Use Policy* 21: 371–80.

Stigall, D. E. 2008. *Refugees and legal reform in Iraq: the Iraqi civil code, international standards for the treatment of displaced persons, and the art of attainable solutions.* Social Science Research Network. http://papers.ssrn.com/sol3/papers.cfm?abstract_id=1157449. [accessed 30 April 2010].

United Nations Human Settlements Programme (UN-HABITAT). 2001. *Millennium development goals/overview.* www.unhabitat.org/content.asp?cid=2799&catid=312&typeid=24&subMenuId=0 [accessed 30 April 2010].

Unruh, J. 2002. "Local land tenure in the peace process." *Peace Review* 14: 3.

Van Oosterom, P., C. Lemmen, T. Ingvarsson, P. van der Molen, H. Ploeger, W. Quak, J. Stoter, & J. Zevenbergen. 2006. "The core cadastral domain model." *ScienceDirect: Computers, Environments and Urban Systems* 30: 629.

Williamson, I., A. Rajabifard, D. Steudler, & S. Enemark. 2009. *Cadastral template: a worldwide comparison of cadastral systems.* University of Melbourne, Australia. www.cadastraltemplate.org [accessed 30 April 2010].

Chapter twenty-one

Identicide in Sarajevo

The destruction of the National
and University Library of
Bosnia and Herzegovina

SARAH JANE MEHARG

Introduction

> For thousands of years, the library represented a fortress of closely guarded
> knowledge, a private citadel of information that its builders viewed as both
> precious and dangerous. Among the foremost targets of a conquering army
> would be a great city's library—to be either carried away as booty or put
> to the torch, in an effort to tear the heart from an alien civilization.
> (Donald 2001: 1).

THE NATIONAL AND UNIVERSITY Library of Bosnia and Herzegovina
(NUB) in Sarajevo was shelled and destroyed during the *Siege of
Sarajevo* in 1992. Although the burning of archives and libraries was
thought to be a tactic of bygone times, it was revived once again as a
method of erasing the existence of a marginalized people. The intentional
act of attacking the cultural heart of Sarajevo using siege tactics suggests
a broader strategy was in use by the belligerent forces. *Identicide*, the
intentional targeting and destruction of places, people, and practices
representative of group identity, frames this broader strategy and offers
a logic to the culture wars meted out in the former Yugoslavia from 1990
to 1995.

The old library, which housed multicultural and multiethnic collections, was a famous building called the *Vijecnica*. Its intentional targeting
and destruction was used against the Bosnian Muslim civilians of
Sarajevo as a tactic to weaken group identity (both present and future)
and to rid the area of an important symbol representing an entire cultural
history of a people. The destroyed library is an example of military
geography explained through the theory of identicide and tactics of
culture wars made infamous in the 1990s. The effects of military activities
on cultural places are worthy of examination as they can alter identities
and incite additional destructive acts, which can forever change the
human landscape in which people live and work. The military operation

that sought to destroy the Vijecnica through the Siege of Sarajevo is the focus of this chapter.

Understanding people and their places

People are strongly connected to places because it is in place that routinized, even ritualized, quotidian practices construct distinctive identities. Identity, derived from *identitas*, and from *idem,* meaning same, is the quality or condition of being a specified person or thing. It refers to the state of being, or relating to, the same substance, nature, and qualities that can determine one's role in relation to society. Identity begins with the individual and his or her understanding and sense of self, positioned upon a group history/heritage, collective memory, and upon experience. In so far as identity refers to the characteristics shared by individuals and groups, it refers to both the material conditions that constitute place, and the behavior, beliefs, actions, symbols, and rituals that are materialized in such places. That is, identity is space-bound: it refers to the specific places created by people sharing a way of life, as well as contributing to the particular experience of life in such landscapes.

People cannot be separated from this spatial world because they are physically born into it and continue creating it by expressing cultural values and beliefs through it, and, so, create places. Through the creation of such places we build identities that allow us to orientate ourselves and make sense out of the world, and ensure cultural continuity (Connerton 1989; Osborne 2002).

Place becomes unique and particular because it is where a series of events happen, both real and imagined. This sense of place is a synthesis of nature and culture based on histories recalled by individual and collective memories. As elements of symbolism and meaning create a particularity of place, they also act as narratives of collective memory that underpin the cohesion and identity of groups (Halbwachs 1992; Connerton 1989; Fentress and Wickham 1992; Hutton 1993; Gillis 1994; Nora 1996). This particularity of place reinforces ethnicity, culture, and identity. Some places have great value to the cultural groups that subscribe to them, and the markers that suggest heritage, sacredness, and a collective past assist people to remember and to give meaning to their lives (Sack 1997). Places, with their defining material elements, become a part of the mythology of cultures and are building blocks of identity. As elements of culture materialize in the landscape, there is but little choice for those who live in these landscapes to identify with these particular places (Mitchell 2001).

Experts suggest that elements of group identity including histories, heritages, libraries, monuments, art, music, gender, language, religion, rituals, economies, politics, collective memories, and cultural landscapes, amongst others, are potent representational symbols of a people, as much as existence itself (Shirinian, 2000; Kaiser 2000; Osborne, 2002). Moreover, the notion of place as a factor of identity is significant because of the sense of relatedness between people and their places, which in turn modify cultural practices and behaviors. This sense of connection creates a kind of empathy between people and their places. Identities are entrenched in place because people define community through them, commune in them, and to them.

War practices

Identity is among the most salient of social factors and can provoke the greatest degree of ambivalence and conflict between peoples (Herb and Kaplan 1999). Some societies have gone to great lengths to target cultural places and practices, forcefully disperse contested groups, and deliberately and systematically destroy an entire people. Such strategies of warfare that denigrate and destroy people and their places are not new, and, before the nineteenth century, international rules of warfare were not standardized; although there existed so-called traditional war practices, war was unregulated and the actions of warring parties unlimited (Jote 1994).

Taking *spoils of war*, rape, abuse, burning libraries, archives, and museums, and toppling famous architecture have been effective tactics of war through the ages (Nicholas, quoted in Simpson 1997) and became part of the culture of soldiering. Part of a soldier's payment was to plunder the goods of a vanquished group after the battle was over; such permissible behavior made cultural objects targets of appropriation that could become trophies of conquest (Jote 1994) and a means to undermine a vanquished group by attacking its symbols of identity.

Although the targeting of strategic military points, such as munitions factories, transportation routes, and communication lines, is still an effective war tactic, there is an increased awareness of the impact that the destruction of symbols, people, places, and practices can have on contested civilian populations. These tactics are some of the most effective war tools and have been revived in recent years. Contemporary armed warfare is symbolized by brutalities reminiscent of another age, meted out on civilians by insurgent forces, militias, and rebels, with, surprisingly, regular forces obliged to comply with the laws of armed conflict.

This is most apparent when prevailing hierarchies of power in the form of political regimes are repulsed by contested peoples, places, and their practices. Often, strategies to destroy places and cultural practices ensue as a way to rid an area of a marginalized or openly contested group, which can become a highly territorial form of nationalism (Kaplan 1993; Cigar 1995; Wood 2001). Typically, this is achieved through the manipulation and control of symbols and, thereby, the territorialization of the collective space in which they are embedded. Political movements

343

that seek to gain control over the social production of space, place, and landscape to manipulate citizens have been witnessed in the politically contrived ethnic wars of the 1990s (Cigar 1995; Allcock 2000; Glenny 2000; Mitchell 2001). For example, on 2 July 1998, Protestant arsonists set fire to ten Roman Catholic churches in Northern Ireland, three of which were destroyed. Cited as a form of sectarian madness by David Trimble, leader of the Ulster Unionist Party, and as criminal acts by Reverend Ian Paisley, no stranger to anti-Catholicism, both warring factions agreed on the absurdity of targeting culturally significant civilian sites. Between 1991 and 1994, sixteen mosques and eleven Roman Catholic churches and monasteries were destroyed in Banja Luka, Bosnia and Herzegovina (most were systematically dynamited and bulldozed), though there was no actual fighting in the city, which was under Serb national control throughout the war. The destruction made historical reconstruction impossible. According to Dodds (1994: 48), "a national newspaper quoted Bosnian Serb officials as saying that 'the leveled site [of the Pasina mosque] would make an excellent parking lot.'" The heightened use of this culturally destructive strategy reflects the increased recognition of the significance of symbols as the key to group identity. Perpetrators think that targeting the symbols of a culture reduces the transfer of memory and identity to future generations and, in effect, erases the existence of a group.

Identicide

The intentional annihilation of a group's identity through the destruction of places, people, and practices are the underpinnings of *genocide*. Identicide, in a military context, is a strategy of warfare that deliberately targets and destroys cultural elements through a variety of means in order to contribute to eventual acculturation, removal, and/or total destruction of a particular identity group, including its contested signs, symbols, behaviors, values, heritages, places, and performances (Meharg 1999). Identicide is distinct from ethnic cleansing in a few ways. Ethnic cleansing is both a euphemism and a policy referring to the persecution, mass expulsion, rape, and murder of an ethnic minority by an ethnic majority in a particular region within the former Yugoslavia in order to achieve ethnic homogeneity in majority-controlled territory. It is a direct attack against people. In this way, ethnic cleansing is an activity that is similar to genocide. Comparatively, identicide is the attack against places and their people, and the negotiated outcomes of cultural identity. It derives its meaning from the collocation of identity with the epithet - *cide*. Taken literally, identicide refers to the intentional killing of that which is subsumed under the term identity. Significant in the meaning of identicide is, therefore, what is to be understood in the concept of identity, and what is destroyed in the act of killing identity. Identicide offers a way to describe the precursor to genocide as something in and of itself, with effects of its own.

Identicide, in a military context, is the killing of the relatedness between people and place, and eliminates the bond that underpins individual, community, and national identity. The method to destroy people and their places is most obvious when applied through military means, yet the strategy can also be employed beyond the realm of guns and bombs through economic, social, political, and religious warfare, amongst others. Typically, as a strategy of warfare, identicide is used against the material landscape in which people claim their own and is the destruction of places that bear no military importance yet are strategically targeted in an attempt to erase identity. Identicide has a meaning of its own, rather than being incidental to, or an outcome of, contemporary armed warfare.

Strategic decisions to target and destroy elements of identity are intentional, yet such destruction is veiled as unintentional *collateral damage*. However, recent examples of the elimination of the Bridge of Mostar (Bosnia), the Bamiyan Buddhas (Afghanistan), and the World Trade Towers suggest that these places were high-value targets with extensive 'symbolic footprints' that went far beyond their material value to further any war efforts. As one journalist suggested, cultural casualties of war are not "accidental occurrences of hostilities. It has been one of the main objectives of . . . war to destroy . . . identity. You can do this in a number of ways: you take people's lives; you can humiliate them, rape them, expel them from their homes; and you can destroy the physical and historical identity of a place" (Dodds 1994: 52). Identicide takes many forms, but serves a single function: to lead to the decimation of a people, their places, and practices.

Claims to one's past are incited by the destruction or endangering of that particular past, especially the symbols and signs that create it. Even the possibility of threat can incite a group to great lengths to preserve something from the past. Elements of architecture, oral and written history, landscapes, industry, and the symbols that represent them, can be violently protected by those claiming identity through their existence. Targeted groups may regroup, repatriate, and reinvigorate those symbols that were the focus of the destruction (Clout 1996). These targeted groups maintain identities through the sharing of language, song, symbols, heritage, folklore—in fact, strengthening their identity through collective remembering despite the intent to eliminate their symbolic footprint (Shirinian 2000).

By looking at the nature of destruction implied in identicide, it is possible to identify a logic of destruction that defines its purposes. In light of recent systematic attacks upon significant cultural properties during conflict, the strategy of identicide emerges as a commonly employed element in contemporary warfare by both regular and irregular forces. Yet, many Western regular forces think that such tactics

345

are the remit of irregular forces; however, countries with regular armies, some having signed the Geneva and Hague Conventions, have used the strategy of identicide. For example, during the Boer War, the British Army destroyed the material elements of culture such as farms and homes; and the Japanese used it against the Chinese in Nanking by waging war against the culture of "honor" of the people, raping and defiling women, children, and sacred material elements. When potent cultural symbols are intentionally targeted and destroyed, the resulting phenomenon forever changes identities and becomes another lens through which to understand military geographies.

Burning libraries: a military geography perspective

A library is more than a building of books. It is the collective memory of a people, written through the ages, in different languages, with different methods, and with different views. As a body of work, it is the culmination of thought and progress over a period. A library is a mnemonic device because it holds the memory, heritage, and history of a culture; a library is indeed a *Memory Palace* (Donald 2001).

Both van der Hoeven (1996) and Yushkiavitshus (2000) argue that political upheavals and armed conflict have caused intense situations for libraries as new regimes feel obliged to take measures to protect their own ideologies and set out to destroy threatening histories. Indeed, most attempts to eradicate pluralism have been accompanied by the burning of books (Riedlmayer 1995). Donald argues that:

> the apparent power of these [libraries]—especially their ability to cause a very large agglomeration of people to function as a unity—meant that they were, from the start, intertwined with priestly magic, imperial ritual, privilege, and elitism; thus it was not surprising that conquerors always made the destruction of libraries one of their first priorities.
>
> (Donald 2001: 5)

Although it was not feasible to destroy all books during these upheavals, the burning of libraries quickly became a pattern of warfare for those vying for domination. In the twentieth century, millions of books have been lost to extreme censorship exemplified by nationalistic pathologies, particularly noted during the two World Wars. As well, untold volumes have been destroyed in the communist revolution of China and the Khmer Rouge regime in Cambodia, including recent reports of the libraries destroyed in Kabul during the *Taliban*'s infamous regime. Even libraries within neutral states have been affected during warfare, as was the case for the Catholic University of Louvain, Belgium and its library. It was burned to the ground by German troops in 1914, rebuilt, and then burned again in World War II by the Nazis.

International organizations declared the destruction of libraries and archives as systematic and deliberate, which constitutes a crime against humanity as defined by international law and the Geneva (1949) and Hague (1954) Conventions (Riedlmayer 1995; Blazina 1996). Furthermore, the last century of peace activism and the work of international organizations have not successfully eliminated library burning as a *modus operandi* to eliminate contested cultures. It is easy to identify a *logic* behind this war strategy, because, when a library is destroyed, memory is also destroyed. When memory of a culture is destroyed, people forget, and the intent of the burning is achieved because it is as if the contested culture never existed. Books can become the enemy along with people in an effort to eliminate evidence of pluralistic heritages. When a culture is forced to experience the destruction of their mnemonic devices perpetuating their history, they undergo a terrible cultural amnesia: Who are we? Where did we come from? Such problematic queries caused by the destruction of one's identity, heritage, and memory have emerged at the forefront of concerns of the international heritage community.

Sarajevo and the National and University Library of Bosnia and Herzegovina

Sarajevo is the capital city and the economic, political, and cultural center of Bosnia and Herzegovina (see Figure 21.1). According to the pre-conflict census statistics released in 1991, 49 percent of the population was Muslim, 29 percent Serb, 6 percent Croat, 11 percent Yugoslav, and 4 percent other. The city occupies a long, narrow valley on the banks of the Miljacka River. Steep mountain slopes and ridges, once covered by forests, dominate the valley. Sarajevo consists of a dense urban core, surrounded by a number of quarters with the old Turkish quarter at one end, the Austro-Hungarian remnants in the centre, and the socialist housing and outskirts at the other end in more open ground (UNSC 1994).

The National and University Library of Bosnia and Herzegovina (NUB) was housed in the Vijecnica—the Serbo-Croatian word for town hall—a graceful Moorish Revival-style building constructed in the heart of the city during the days of the Austro-Hungarian administration and inaugurated in 1896. Throughout its 106-year history, it was used as the seat of the Austro-Hungarian administration, the Bosnian parliament building, the Sarajevo Town Hall, and, finally, Tito's government assigned the building to house the National and University Library. The building is situated on the banks of the Miljacka River facing the hills to the south (see Figure 21.2).

The Vijecnica was Sarajevo's most emblematic building. According to architecture experts, the Moorish–Spanish style that the Austro-Hungarian authorities created as a commemoration to their Ottoman predecessors is largely inaccurate and does not resemble known

Figure 21.1
Situation map: Sarajevo,
Bosnia and Herzegovina.
Source: University of
Texas Map Collection,
2009.

architecture in any way (Barry 1999). Nevertheless, it has been claimed
that the Vijecnica's mix of imposing architectural frivolity captured the
city's pre-war personality (Schork 1992). Prior to the war, Islamic critics
were known to denounce the eclectic architecture of the large triangular
building, with its octagonal atrium supported by its famous marble
pillars.

As an institution, the National and University Library was the most
important source of scientific information for the country's research
community, as well as the heart of the cultural and intellectual life of
Sarajevo and Bosnia and Herzegovina. It contained the university's
348   collections and the country's national archives of newspapers and

Figure 21.2
The Vijecnica, 1936.
Source: http://
i164.photobucket.com/
albums/u35/milan_sc/
Sarajevo_Tramvaj_
Vijecnica_1936_A.
jpg, 2009.

periodicals. The NUB had multicultural and multiethnic holdings that were designed as an ethnically and culturally diverse collection representing the people and history of Yugoslavia. Historical circumstances made the country a crossroads of different cultures and the collections reflected this. They contained works of *Bosniaca*, Croatian, and Serbian, as well as works in Latin, English, Russian, Arabic, German, Italian, Spanish, Turkish, Hebrew, Persian, and other languages. Interestingly, many books in the library had been salvaged from library collections damaged during World War II (Abid, quoted in van der Hoeven and van Albada 1996).

Bosniaca is defined as all documents in any format written or published about Bosnia and Herzegovina in every territory or in any language regardless of the author's origin. Works pertaining to the Ottoman Empire in Bosnia are also considered *Bosniaca*. Most significant in the collection were some of the *Bosniaca* holdings. The collection of 155,000 rare Ottoman manuscripts and books, some handwritten, was the only comprehensive *Bosniaca* collection of its kind in the world. Although the magnitude of the *Bosniaca* holdings was unparalleled, it was not over-representative in comparison with the library's Serb or Croat holdings, as the intention of the library was to be a national and university institution useful to all parts of the former Yugoslavia.

A large representation of the cultural heritage of the Bosnian people was codified in the unique collections of manuscripts and books, libraries, and archival institutions in the country. Some of these collections were original in nature and only minimally reproduced or existing outside the country.

The Siege of Sarajevo

Intrastate conflict began in 1991 when Bosnia and Herzegovina decided to secede from Yugoslavia and declare itself an independent nation state. Serbian factions of the local government did not want independence and were against the separation. Through a series of events, conflict erupted in the heart of the region. The old Yugoslav military regime, predicated on a decentralized system of both trained soldiers and weapons caches, directed the type and level of fighting in Bosnia and Herzegovina. Clashes involved armed civilians, police, and paramilitaries of all nationalities, and the conflict intensified and became widespread after the March 1991 referendum on independence. The president, Alija Izetbegovic, declared a state of emergency and mobilized territorial defense units. In early April, violence eventually escalated to a full-scale war (UNSC 1994).

Beginning in April 1992, Serbian nationalists attacked Bosnian cities and towns, and deliberately targeted national libraries, museums, and archives. They succeeded in wiping out nearly the entire written record of Bosnia's history. Such destruction did not go unnoticed by the international community witnessing the atrocities in Bosnia and Herzegovina. In May 1992, two UNESCO Executive Board members representing Turkey and Egypt suggested:

> It is evident that, unless steps are taken to dissuade the military forces which assault Bosnia-Herzegovina, the world will continue to witness further tragic devastation of mankind's cultural heritage and educational institutions there.
>
> (UNESCO 1992: 2).

However, no international efforts were taken to dismantle the Yugoslav army, nor the leaders who continued to foment the pathologies of ethnic nationalism. The Battle of Sarajevo began in April 1992 at a time when the Yugoslav National Army (JNA) still had troops stationed in barracks in Sarajevo. Due to the adoption of a new constitution for the Republic of Yugoslavia (FRY), all members of the JNA who were nationals of the newly proclaimed FRY were to leave Bosnia and Herzegovina within fifteen days. The fighting in Sarajevo involved both JNA forces and Bosnian-Serb forces (BSA), which surrounded the city. The besiegers were formed into nine brigades based and sent to their original territorial units. The brigades on the front of the siege line had a territorial affinity and had previously occupied such offensive/defensive positions (UNSC 1994). Serbian forces divided Bosnia and Herzegovina into five areas: the northwest (the so-called Muslim Triangle); the northeast; central (Sarajevo area); Srebrenica; and the south. The commander of the Socialist Republic of Bosnia and Herzegovina (former Yugoslavian State) (SRBiH) was General Ratko Mladic, a former JNA Brigadier General and former commander of the JNA's 9th Corps headquartered at Knin. The Sarajevo Romanija Corps was the Bosnian Serb force of the Bosnian Serbian Army (BSA). The Romanija Corps had surrounded the city of Sarajevo since the beginning of the siege in 1992. The BSA forces concentrated their efforts on weakening the city through constant bombardment from the surrounding hills (UNSC 1994). By July 1993, the strategic situation was such that the Serb forces continued to dominate the hills surrounding the city, creating a nearly impermeable perimeter.

From the beginning of the siege, the 1st Corps Sarajevo served as the Bosnia and Herzegovina defensive force in and around Sarajevo. According to reports, the 1st Corps had superior infantry numbers to the besieging forces but deficient firepower, and could not effectively break the siege. The Croat Army (HVO) was also stationed in Sarajevo and fought against the BSA. Due to extenuating military circumstances, the operations in Sarajevo developed into a classic siege with neither side being in possession of either the will or the military might to force a conclusion (UNSC 1994).

General Mladic was reported to have issued explicit orders to bombard non-Serbian civilian targets within Sarajevo. Such targets included the main hospital, mosques, churches, archives, museums, libraries, and other civilian targets. Local commanders had full freedom to use their unit's heavy weapons and the unit determined the scale and target of destruction.

The areas of strategic concern were the high ground along the steep ridges surrounding the city, and the open ground at the west end between the airport and the nearby mountain positions (UNSC 1994). This area eventually became known as Sniper's Alley. Due to the constant sniper fire in the city, key crossroads were shielded to facilitate pedestrian and vehicular movement. The BSA depended on their artillery and fought, virtually, at point blank range within the city. Most lines of fire were direct due to occupation on the high ground and there were ample weapons caches *in situ* to facilitate the destruction of key landmarks within the city.

According to the UNSC (1994) report on the Battle of Sarajevo there was some evidence to suggest that Bosnia and Herzegovina forces stationed or positioned their weapons either directly in, or in close proximity to, structures of *cultural property*. However, the destruction of such cultural properties in Sarajevo does not account for the sheer volume of fire directed at them (UNSC 1994). National and international media coverage illustrated the intentions of the Yugoslav army as they enacted a strategy to decimate the morale of the people of Sarajevo. It became clear that the express purpose of the siege was to terrorize the besieged civilian population. Some of the shelling of populated quarters of the city may well have had *bona fide* military objectives, but the sheer weight of fire precluded any discussion of proportionality, which is the relationship between sites destroyed and sites considered to be military objectives. There were many allegations of civilians being targeted at schools, parks, sports fields, water and food distribution points, hospitals, and cemeteries (UNSC 1994). Even holy and sacred sites were not free from the terror inflicted upon the civilians.

The aim of the siege was to terrorize people—humiliate them, and force them to surrender or leave, and, indeed, the cultural richness and complexity of the urban centers were themselves under attack (Riedlmayer 1995). Such blatant destruction and defilement clearly indicated a disregard for the resolutions set out in both the Geneva Conventions of 1949 and the Hague Conventions of 1954 by which the seceding states from the former Yugoslavia were bound.

During the conflict, there was a high level of destruction inflicted by the Serbian Army. The Siege of Sarajevo resulted in damage or complete destruction of major cultural centers, as well as of all infrastructure and residential areas. Most notable, however, was the destruction of the National Museum of Bosnia and Herzegovina, the Historical Archive of Sarajevo, the Oriental Institute of Sarajevo, the Historical Institute of Sarajevo, the Gazi Husrev-Beg Library, the Historical Museum of Bosnia and Herzegovina, the Museum of the City of Sarajevo, the National Art Gallery of Bosnia-Herzegovina, the Institute of Medicine of the University of Sarajevo, and the School of Music. The Oriental Institute in Sarajevo had a valuable collection of 5300 codices (20,000 titles) of mainly Ottoman origin. The entire contents were completely destroyed in 1992, including all card catalogues and inventory lists. The library alone was targeted; adjacent buildings stand intact to this day (Riedlmayer 1995).

The Vijecnica was in a similar position and was an easy target for Serb artillery (Riedlmayer 1995). The Vijecnica was shelled and destroyed with incendiary grenades from 25–26 August 1992. According to eyewitnesses, while the building blazed, some brave librarians and citizens of Sarajevo attempted to save what written history they could:

> Crowding in from the surrounding streets and alleys in total disregard of danger, half of Sarajevo—starved and misery-stricken people, exhausted by a long and cruel siege—rushed to save the soul of their city
>
> (Lovrenovic 1994: 1).

Human chains were formed and books heaved along the long lines of civilians and staff. The fire department also loaned their expertise to the efforts. Serbian artillery in the hills overlooking the city kept up a constant barrage from machine guns and mortars to block access to the burning books. Only a few of the more precious and rare books were saved because the blazing fire was too powerful and the enemy snipers too deadly (see Figure 21.3).

Figure 21.3
The Vijecnica burns.
Source: Friends of Bosnia,
metropolismag.com/
html/content_0699.
ju99phow.htm [accessed
2 September 2009], 1999.

The beautiful "Soul of Sarajevo" was a torch in the night and black billowing smoke poured out of the delicately ornate stone filigree windows along the top floor of the building. The library holdings were soon in ashes and Sarajevans remarked that, for days afterward, it rained ashes from the burned books and manuscripts. The Final Report of the United Nations Commission of Experts unequivocally states that it was apparent that the NUB structure had been deliberately destroyed by Serb artillery from the nearby hills. The interior of the library was gutted, yet several surrounding buildings were completely untouched (UNSC 1994).

During the siege, the BSA was capable of terrorizing Sarajevo in its geographic entirety with heavy weapons, but could not force the fall of the city from a military point of view. In contrast, the Bosnia and Herzegovina forces denied the urban terrain to the BSA but could not break the siege that was destroying the social fabric of the city and terrorizing its citizens:

353

The destruction of the building is very important in a different way [than the collections]. The destruction of cultural heritage is the creation of a new landscape. It's the creation of new cities, or new rural landscapes. And Vijecnica is a landmark, it is not only a library, but also a city hall. It had various political functions in the history of Bosnia as well, and it is a notable, recognizable, important landmark in the town. You're hitting something different when you target such a site.

> (Kaiser, Colin. Personal communication via
> telephone. UNESCO Chef de Bureau Sarajevo.
> 15 October 2002)

Eventually the international community realized that civilians and their cultural properties were the key target in this contemporary war.

Colin Kaiser, UNESCO Chef de Bureau Sarajevo, suggests that the library holdings were in fact a military objective, the destruction of which was part of a well-devised plan of destroying an entire realm of memory:

> The actual destruction of things, or the destruction of an object is not so interesting—specialists will jump and all that—but it's far more worrying to historians the destruction of archives. It's infinitely more serious or devastating than the destruction of a building, from an objective point of view. An archive that is burned that nobody looked at, is gone.

> (Kaiser, Colin. Personal communication via
> telephone. UNESCO Chef de Bureau Sarajevo.
> 15 October 2002)

Experts agree that the destruction of the Vijecnica was "an attempt by Serb forces to obliterate symbols and evidence of the country's multicultural roots—its Muslim heritage, in particular" (Bollag 1995: 2). Riedlmayer (1995) echoes this sentiment by arguing:

> Throughout Bosnia, libraries, archives, museums and cultural institutions were targeted for destruction, in an attempt to eliminate the material evidence that could remind future generations that people of different ethnic and religious traditions once shared a common heritage in Bosnia. In towns and villages of occupied Bosnia, the communal records of over 800 Muslim and Bosnian Croat communities were torched by Serb nationalist forces as part of ethnic cleansing campaigns.

> (Riedlmayer 1995: 2)

The emotive response to the destruction of the Vijecnica reached un-precedented proportions (see Figure 21.4). Federico Mayor, UNESCO's

Figure 21.4
Only the architectural
shell remains of the
Vijecnica. *Source*:
Meharg, 2001.

Director-General, called the devastation of Bosnian cultural heritage
and collective memory an act of barbarism perpetrated in the context
of a whole series of assaults on the national heritage. Moreover,
he called for the immediate reconstruction of the Library of Sarajevo
(Mayor 1994).

Conclusion

Although there are international standards, codes, and norms regarding
the rules of engagement and the protection of cultural property during
times of peace and war, it remains challenging to protect such places
when belligerents seek to dominate their so-called enemies by targeting
the people, places, and practices that represent a contested culture and
identity. The burning of the famous library and its collections was an
act of identicide perpetrated by belligerent forces against the people of
Sarajevo. Sarajevans had a strong bond with this famous place, and they
shared a collective memory of its symbolism throughout their collective
history. The physical geography of Sarajevo allowed for ideal siege
conditions so that the BSA could maintain military dominance of the
civilian population of Sarajevo. By positioning themselves in the hills
surrounding the city, the BSA was easily able to target and destroy what
they considered to be contested Bosnian–Muslim cultural property.
Reports suggest, though, that such contested cultural property had been
appropriated as multiethnic and multicultural by the Sarajevans. To
them, the library was not a Bosnian Muslim or Ottoman symbol.

The destruction of the library forever changed Sarajevans' interpretation, meaning, and identification with this place. Never again would the library serve public education and knowledge as it once did, and never again—even if reconstructed—could a new Vijecnica retain its meaning to the people who felt this place represented their identities. Yet, the symbolism of the Vijecnica awaits reconstruction. The smashed dome, the melted marble pillars, and the smoke stained shell of Sarajevo's National Library are marked with a small sign that urges: "Do not forget. Remember and warn."

References cited

Allcock, J. B. 2000. *Explaining Yugoslavia*. New York, NY: Columbia University Press.

Barry, E. 1999. "All the sympathy in the world hasn't rebuilt the Sarajevo Library." MetropolisMag.com online feature. June. metropolismag.com/html/content_0699/ju99howt.htm [accessed 30 April 2010].

Blazina, V. 1996. "Memoricide ou la parification culturelle: la guerre contre les bibliotheques de Croatie et de Bosnie-Herzegovine." *Documentation et bibliotheques* 42: 149–64.

Bollag, B. 1995. "Bosnia's universities see hope as academic year begins." *Chronicle of Higher Education* 6 (10 June).

Cigar, N. 1995. *Genocide in Bosnia: the policy of ethnic cleansing*. College Station, TX: Texas A&M University Press.

Clout, H. 1996. *After the ruins: restoring the countryside of northern France after the Great War*. Exeter, UK: University of Exeter Press.

Connerton, P. 1989. *How societies remember*. Cambridge, UK: Cambridge University Press.

Dodds, J. D. 1994. "Bulldozing sacred sites." *Archaeology* 51: 52.

Donald, M. 2001. "Memory palaces: the revolutionary function of libraries." *Queen's-Quarterly* 108(4): 558–73.

Fentress, J. & C. Wickam. 1992. *Social memory: new perspectives on the past*. Oxford, UK: Blackwell Publishers.

Gillis, J. (ed.). 1994. *Commemorations: the politics of national identity*. Princeton, NJ: Princeton University Press.

Glenny, M. 2000. *The Balkans: nationalism, war and the great powers 1804–1999*. New York, NY: Penguin Books.

Halbwachs, M. 1992. *On collective memory*. Lewis A. Coser (ed. and trans.). Chicago, IL: University of Chicago Press.

Herb, G. & D. Kaplan (eds). 1999. *Nested identities: nationalism, territory and scale*. Lanham, MA: Rowman & Littlefield.

Hutton, P. H. 1993. *History as an art of memory*. Hanover, NH: University Press of New England.

Jote, K. 1994. *International legal protection of cultural heritage*. Stockholm, Sweden: Juristforlaget.

Kaiser, C. 2000. "Crimes against culture." *UNESCO Courier* (September). www.unesco.org/courier/2000_09/uk/signe2.htm [accessed 30 April 2010].

Kaplan, R. 1993. *Balkan ghosts: a journey through history*. New York, NY: St Martin's Press.

Lovrenovic, I. 1994. "The hatred of memory: in Sarajevo, burned books and murdered pictures." *New York Times* (28 May).

Mayor, F. 1994. "UNESCO appeal launched: 13 April 1994." *The burning books of Sarajevo*. www.indexnthings.com/THE%20BURNING%20BOOKS%20OF%20SARAJEVO.pdf [accessed 30 April 2010].

Meharg, S. Jane. 1999. *Making it, breaking it, and making it again: the destruction and reconstruction of war-torn societies*. Master's thesis. Kingston, Canada: Royal Military College of Canada.

Mitchell, D. 2001. "The lure of the local: landscape at the end of a troubled century." *Progress in Human Geography* 25(1): 269–81.

Nora, P. 1996. *Realms of memory: the construction of the French past. I: Conflicts and divisions.* New York, NY: Columbia University Press.

Osborne, B. 2000. "Erasing memories of war: reconstructing France after the 'Great War.'" In *Canadian military history since the 17th century*, Yves Tremblay (ed.), 513–22. Proceedings of the Canadian Military History Conference, Ottawa, 5–9 May.

———. 2002. "The place of memory and identity." *Canadian Diversity* 1(1): 9–13.

Riedlmayer, A. 1994. "It has been done before! Reconstituting war-ravaged libraries." An introduction to a talk given by Enes Kujundzic. Boston Public Library. 21 October. www.kakarigi.net/manu/preced.htm [accessed 30 April 2010].

———. 1995. "National library." *Zones of separation: the struggle for a multiethnic Bosnia.* A documentary film. www2.crocker.com/~fob/zones/images/Images_10.htm [accessed 30 April 2010].

———. 1995. *Killing memory: the targeting of Bosnia's cultural heritage.* Testimony presented at a hearing of the Commission on Security and Cooperation in Europe.

———. 2001. "*Convivencia* under fire: genocide and book burning in Bosnia." In *The Holocaust and the book*, Jonathan Rose (ed.). Amherst, MA: University of Massachusetts Press.

Sack, R. 1997. *Homo geographicus: a framework for action, awareness, and moral concern.* Cambridge, MA: Cambridge University Press.

Schork, K. 1992. "Sarajevo's much-loved old town hall ablaze." *Reuters Library Report* (26 August).

Shirinian, L. 2000. *Writing memory.* Kingston, ON: Blue Heron Press.

Simpson, E. (ed.). 1997. *The spoils of war: World War II and its aftermath: the loss, reappearance, and recovery of cultural property.* Hong Kong: Harry N. Abrams, Inc.

UNESCO Executive Board. 1992. "The situation of the cultural and architectural heritage as well as educational and cultural institutions in Bosnia-Herzegovina." *139th Session: item 7.5 of the provisional agenda, 139 EX/33.* 18 May. Paris, France: UNESCO.

United Nations Security Council. 1994. *Annex VI.B: the battle of Sarajevo and the law of armed conflict.* S/1994/674/Add.2 (Vol. I). 28 December.

van der Hoeven, H. & Joan van Albada. 1996. *Memory of the world: lost memory—libraries and archives destroyed in the twentieth century.* Prepared for UNESCO on behalf of IFLA, Paris: UNESCO.

Wood, W. B. 2001. "Geographic aspects of genocide: a comparison of Bosnia and Rwanda." *Transactions of the Institute of British Geographers* 26(1): 57–75.

Yushkiavitshus, H. 2000. *Libraries and intellectual freedom.* Paris, France: UNESCO. www.unesco.org/webworld/points_of_views/yushkiavitshus.shtml [accessed 30 April 2010].

Chapter twenty-two
Geopolitics and the dragon's advance
An exploration of the strategy and reality of China's growing economic and military power and its effect upon Taiwan

CLIFTON W. PANNELL

China pursues a national defense policy which is purely defensive in nature. China's national defense policy for the new stage in the new century basically includes upholding national security and unity, and ensuring the interests of national development; achieving the all-round, coordinated and sustainable development of China's national defense and armed force; enhancing the performance of the armed forces with informationization as the major measuring criterion; implementing the military strategy of active defense; pursuing a self-defensive nuclear strategy.

(Information Office of the State Council of the People's Republic of China (PRC) 2009: 7)

CHINA'S LONG HISTORY OF CULTURAL achievements parallels an equally long and intriguing story of the ebb and flow of political expansion and military contest and conquest. A key part of this story derives from China's geography—its location on the southeastern margins of the Eurasian landmass facing the western Pacific Ocean on its east and southeast flanks. The country is vast, and its landforms and water systems are among the most spectacular found anywhere. While these biophysical systems have been a great blessing for China, they have also historically provided a major challenge to the spatial integration of the country—overcoming the friction of distance among major regions and places (Fairbank 1992; Veeck et al. 2007).

For many centuries, contesting states fought among themselves, and central power waxed and waned around the early core location (the *Zhong Yuan* or Central Plain) of north China (see Figure 22.1). Finally, the great unification of China occurred in 221 BC, and the state has been a unified and unitary system ever since, despite the shifting dynasties, expansions, and contractions of the state territory during these varying periods.

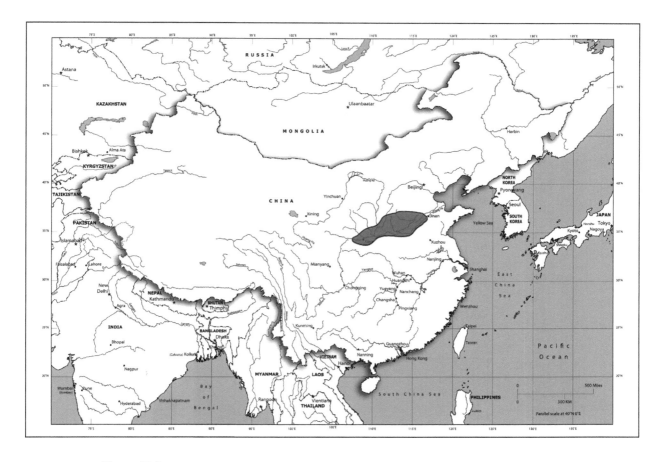

Figure 22.1
The *Zhong Yuan* or Central Plain. This region is the original core region of north China out of which the Chinese central state developed and grew.

Geography alone, however, does not tell the whole story, for the role of man has been notable in determining the trajectory of state power, its growth, and in the use and manipulation of the environment and huge territory of the Chinese state system. Traditionally, wealth and power in China were derived from land and the ability to produce food. More land meant more food and more food could support more people. The ability of the central state, assisted through regional and local officials, to manage and improve public works such as effective irrigation systems and canals to transport food and other products were key to ensuring the wellbeing of the population. Such effective management led to a surplus from which the central state could draw to support its civil and military apparatus, enabling it to provide effective domestic governance while maintaining sufficient military force to deter external enemies and invaders. It also facilitated territorial expansion in those regions that offered opportunities for China.

China, owing to the forces and realities of its geographic setting, and reinforced by the nature of its culture, was for most of its history a land-based power preoccupied with its own domestic stability and concerned with protecting itself from potential invaders from the north and west.

The adjacent seas on the east and southeast afforded protection, as did the very high and rugged mountains along its southern and southwestern frontiers. Consequently, its rulers for the most part looked inward and were concerned with domestic stability and prosperity.

Despite this traditional posture, there were episodes, for example during the early Ming Period (1368–1644), when a great naval armada was launched and China's maritime influence reached the coast of East Africa. Moreover, Arab traders arrived along China's southern coast as early as the twelfth century, and Chinese fishermen were coasting the waters of nearby Southeast Asia. While these episodes of external contacts appear uncommon, nonetheless they are useful as we seek to understand the manner in which China's traditional military thinkers viewed their own country and the world around them, while also helping us analyze the context in which contemporary grand and military strategy are unfolding. China has long had a special interest in the South and East China Seas. Today it continues to lay territorial claims to these adjacent maritime regions (Samuels 1982; DoD Report 2009) (see Figure 22.2).

Figure 22.2
Chinese claims to extensive adjacent maritime and economic zones in the South and East China Seas. These claims are contested by neighboring states as well as other nations who see these as international waters.

Maritime Areas & Economic Zones Claimed by China

Chinese Claims in East & South China Seas

A framework for strategy

China's classical thinking and writing about war and strategy is found in parallel with the great classical philosophical writings and those about statecraft. Yet the writings on strategy and war are few in comparison with the large number of classical essays that comprise the Confucian and related canonical writings. There is a fundamental paradox and contradiction in these early classical writings, for the Confucians and their intellectual allies disdained warfare and concepts of military strategy. We may surmise this was a reaction to the history of frequent conflict and strife that dominated the centuries of the Shang and Zhou Dynasties, especially in the Spring and Autumn (721–480 BC) and Warring States (403–221 BC) periods. Such thought also reflected the conventional interpretations of Confucianism that stressed the ideal of virtue for the true Confucian leader or gentleman, with a desirable goal of harmony in all social relations.

Nevertheless, war and its strategy and tactics were seen as too important to the short- and long-term viability of rulers and states, and various generals or other statesmen wrote on the subject and offered different views on how warfare should be conceived as well as how it should be conducted (Griffith 1963; Sawyer 1993). One of the most intriguing dimensions of these writings is the emphasis on strategy and the use of deception to avoid direct military confrontation. Such thinking or conceptualizing of strategy focused on analyzing the enemy and assessing enemy weaknesses to seek victory through means other than direct application of force or military engagement. For example, the writings of the famous general Sun Tzu, which date back to the Warring States period, emphasize the necessity of formulating a grand strategy that will ensure victory. Victory will be based on the full support of a prosperous and contented population while engaging in strategic diplomacy in step with military preparations. Secret maneuverings and intrigue to deceive the enemy and weaken his position may lead to success and victory without the need for armed combat. The goal was to conquer the enemy by various strategies and tactics that leave military conquest as the last resort. According to Sun, military combat should be the last resort to be employed only when the local and larger conditions for fighting were clearly in your favor to ensure victory (Sawyer 1993).

These writings illustrate, however, a fundamental contradiction that endures to the present as we strive to understand the various and sometimes seemingly inconsistent ways in which the Chinese approach diplomacy and statecraft, and how the use of force or military action may be applied. Yet the early writings of Sun Tzu and others such as T'ai Kung reflect the close linkage between critical thinking about warfare and the preservation of the state and its territory. Given the importance then of the strategy of warfare and its support of the security of the central state, we may conclude such grand strategy is a significant if small part of the classical canon of Chinese literature. Its importance to contemporary Chinese grand strategy should not be underestimated (Scobell and Kirby 2003). At the same time, Shambaugh (2000) has noted there are three enduring principles of Chinese state rule over the last century: modernize the economy; transform the society, and defend China against foreign aggressors.

David M. Lampton (2007) has written recently in assessing current Chinese strategic thinking about power and global relations that they view power from several perspectives—coercive power, economic power, and intellectual power. Coercive power, according to Lampton, refers to might or force and relates to military and related means to enforce one country's will on another. Economic power is the effective use of economic resources, production, and productivity to exercise power over others, while intellectual power refers to the power of intellect and ideas along with culture and spiritual values to influence others and control outcomes. In any analysis of Chinese grand strategy and concepts of power, we must consider these three categories of power and how the Chinese may use them over time and space.

Perhaps the best way to think about the uses of power in the modern or Communist period in China is to examine Chinese behavior over time. During the Maoist period from the mid-twentieth century, China applied coercive power based on Mao's vision of a revolutionary China. It fought limited wars with several of its neighbors as well as US and UN forces during the Korean War. Mao was also quite willing to apply force within the country to ensure that his vision of domestic revolution continued as in the violence that accompanied the Great Proletarian Cultural Revolution.

Following Mao's death in 1976 and the ascendancy of Deng Xiaoping as China's Supreme Leader, a more cautious and prudent policy was followed in which the emphasis was on economic development. The conventional view is that Deng wished to see China develop its economy rapidly while maintaining amicable relations with other countries including the US (Lampton 2007; DoD 2009). After the economy had grown and matured, more resources could later be transferred to military and nuclear forces. In this way, China's rise based on its growing economic power would not be seen as threatening to other major powers, and its economic growth could proceed with few constraints from outside. This is summed up in the quotation that is attributed to Deng from the early 1990s, "observe calmly, secure our position; cope with affairs calmly; hide our capacities and bide our time; be good at maintaining a low profile; and never claim leadership" (Pannell 2006; DoD 2009: 1).

The new generation of Chinese leaders, which took over in 2005, with Hu Jintao as President and CCP General Secretary, has continued a generally low-key approach, but as China's economic power has grown, and when counterpoised against the recent severe economic difficulties in the US and the European Union, China has become more assertive. Most analysts suggest that the current grand strategy of the PRC indicates a continuation of the high economic growth strategy for the next decade. According to this scenario, by 2020 China's military strength will have developed to the point where it may be more inclined to use coercive power. This appears to be based on material the Chinese have provided in which they recognize a far-reaching global *Revolution in Military Affairs (RMA)* that has provided strong impetus for modernizing the armed forces of the PRC. In their 2009 report, for example, they state they have formed "strategic plans for national defense and armed forces building and strategies for the development of the services and arms, according to which it will lay a solid foundation by 2010, basically accomplish mechanization and make major progress toward informationization by 2020" (Information Office of the State Council of the PRC 2009: 7.)

The salience of Taiwan

In considering China's behavior over the past three decades there are examples, however, where it has indicated a willingness to use coercive power or the application of brute force (Lampton 2007). Most prominent among these has been its attitude toward Taiwan. It is an article of faith and frequently repeated mantra of all PRC officials that Taiwan is inalienable territory of the Chinese state, and its return to the motherland is inevitable even if this requires the use of military force. Taiwan is seen in the same context as Hong Kong and Macao, a part of greater China (*Da Zhonghua*) (Harding 1993). This uncompromising stand and commitment has been the leading obstacle to closer relations between China and the US.

In normalizing diplomatic relations with the PRC in 1979, the US affirmed that it too recognized that there is only one China. However, the Joint Communiqué on the Establishment of Diplomatic Relations (*Shanghai Communiqué*) that established official relations with China signed on 1 January 1979 was soon followed by the *Taiwan Relations Act*. This new law allowed the US to establish unofficial relations with Taiwan and permitted the sale of defensive military equipment to enable Taiwan to defend itself in the event of attack (US Department of State 2009). China has never recognized the legitimacy of the Taiwan Relations Act and has strenuously protested the sale of US military equipment to Taiwan. Thus, continued US support for Taiwan to enable it to determine its own relations and timetable for dealing with China has persisted as an irritant in the bilateral relations between China and the US (Information Office of the State Council of the PRC 2009). With the 2008 election of Taiwan's new President Ma Ying-jeou, who has followed a more conciliatory policy toward China and improved economic ties and communications links with the mainland, the Taiwan issue has quieted down. Nevertheless, this prickly cause of disagreement continues to simmer and will no doubt emerge again as a flashpoint.

363

In 1995 and 1996, China twice tried to influence the outcome of elections in Taiwan by sending missiles into the East China Sea off the north coast of Taiwan and threatening naval activity in the adjacent seas. Only after President Clinton dispatched substantial US naval forces to the area did China back off its threatening behavior. During the ensuing thirteen years, China's naval, air, ground, and missile forces arrayed in the Fujian theatre across the Taiwan Strait have grown substantially. China's ability to challenge Taiwan's security and potential US forces dispatched to defend Taiwan has increased markedly to the point that, over time, this threat becomes overwhelming (Shambaugh 2003). However, Taiwan has also quietly continued to modernize its forces and recently reported a substantial build-up of its cruise missile forces to counter any potential attack from China (Strategic Forecasting 2008).

Taiwan is a nettlesome and continuing political dilemma for China and the US. China's leaders, for domestic political reasons, must present a strong and united posture that allows no compromise on the inevitable return of Taiwan to China. For the US, on the other hand, this is a matter for those on Taiwan to decide as to how they wish to establish their relations with China (DoD 2009). What the US does not want is for force or military action to be involved in resolving this dilemma. Given the US history of supporting the *Guomindang* and its retreat to Taiwan during the 1940s and 1950s, and its long political support for the island, a case can be made that Taiwan was a client state of the US. This implies the notion of a US moral obligation to ensure the security of the island, an idea that remains a continuing principle among certain political groups in the US (Lampton 2007).

Changing military goals and doctrine

The People's Liberation Army (PLA) has traditionally been a ground force. During the Maoist period before and after the success of the communist revolution, the PLA was primarily a force to defend the homeland in what Chairman Mao often described as people's war. The chief threats were seen as coming from China's neighbors such as the Soviet Union, Japan, and India, as well as the US and Taiwan. Ground forces were to be the key elements in defending China, although China did pursue strategic weapons and exploded its first atomic bomb in 1964. Doctrine was focused on defending China's territory and was defensive in nature. This was seen at its zenith during the Vietnam War when Mao argued for the relocation of strategic industries into the deep interior of the country behind what was called the "third line" (*san xian*).

The idea of a people's war continues, but it has been redefined in the context of the revolution in military affairs (RMA) and the modernization of China's armed forces under conditions of *"informationization"* (Information Office of the State Council of the PRC 2009). As China's economic growth advanced during the 1980s, conditions for a shift in military thinking and doctrine emerged. Several events conspired to accelerate this shift. First was the remarkable and quick success of US and UN forces in Operation Desert Storm, the first Iraq War in 1991. The use of all kinds of new and advanced weapons and munitions, as well as the integrated use of combined forces based on satellite communications and electronic networks, came as something of a shock to the Chinese military.

The early annihilation of Iraq's command and control systems that involved air, naval, and ground-based missiles and planes followed by a rapid and overwhelming ground assault apparently caused consternation among military leaders (DoD Report 2009). They quickly recognized that a new era of warfare based on high technology and information networks that involved satellite communications and navigational system had arrived. This was soon followed by co-ordinated air strikes of NATO forces in the attacks on Yugoslavia over Kosovo and Bosnia, and the Chinese again witnessed the remarkable effects of airpower and missiles launched from distant locations in determining the outcome of the conflict. We have already noted the arrival of US naval forces in the form of two carrier groups when China threatened military action and set off missiles against Taiwan in 1995 and 1996. These carriers and supporting ships exposed at the time the relative weakness of Chinese naval forces.

These events, coupled with rapid economic growth in China, provided the galvanizing impetus for a fundamental transformation of China's military. The goals were clear. China would seek to build a modern military that would employ new and advanced weapons, and would streamline, educate, and upgrade its military personnel throughout. The size of the military would be reduced, but quality would be increased. It would also be a comprehensive approach to build a modern military that would include new developments and advances in army, navy, air and missile, and nuclear forces. A rapid increase in the military budget would be necessary, and this was soon forthcoming. Continuing the fast economic growth of the previous decade enabled the overall national budget to grow, and it was this growth that has enabled a rapid growth in military expenditures while also maintaining growth in other critical goals of the state. The strategy that Deng Xiaoping laid out following the reforms of the late 1970s had indeed succeeded, and it continues to be a guidepost for continuing development of China's growing military power (DoD Report 2009).

In step with the new and modern transformation of military forces came a shift in doctrine that can only be described as more assertive. We have already discussed the salience and sensitivity of Taiwan as a strategic issue, but other priorities were also emerging. As China's economy has grown, the search for and dependence on foreign sources of fossil fuels and other mineral resources became more urgent. Associated with this was the importance of ensuring the reliability and security of shipping lanes from the Middle East and other locations.

Geographic factors that are not only domestic but also now, in fact, global in nature come into play, as China flexes its economic muscle in the search for and transit of new resources to fuel its growing industrial machine. For example, China now imports more than 50 percent of its petroleum, most from the Middle East, and this share will likely increase in the years ahead as the domestic auto industry grows. Ensuring the reliability of passage for tankers through the Strait of Malacca or other strategic choke points is a priority that will require more naval forces (see Figure 22.3). It also highlights the need for a modern economy to be able to project power beyond its borders in order to protect its strategic interests and security (DoD Report 2009).

Figure 22.3
China's critical sea lanes. China is increasingly dependent on surface shipping for imports of petroleum and other vital raw materials. Protecting these important sea lanes is vital for China's long-term security interests.

China increasingly has viewed the development of a modern navy as a priority for its military modernization that will support its more assertive strategic doctrine and will allow it to project power beyond its traditional spheres of interest. An example of this is seen in the new attention given to the western Pacific that extends far to the east of the South and East China Seas, the traditional zone of China's strategic concerns (Samuels 1982). The recent DoD report (2009) on China's

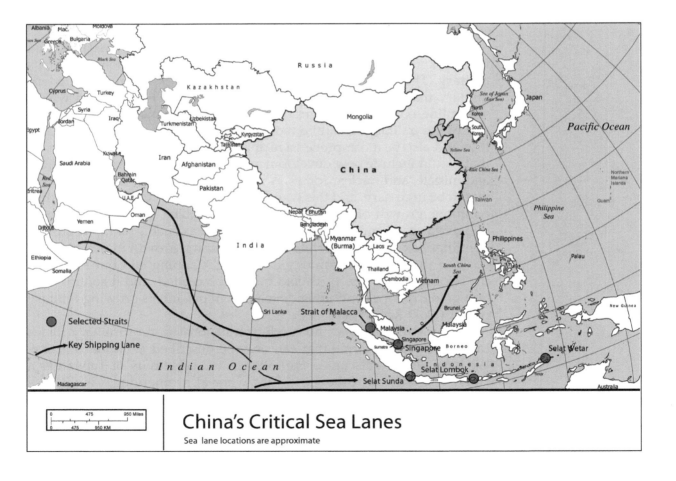

China's Critical Sea Lanes
Sea lane locations are approximate

military power includes a map that indicates two zones of influence or what are described as China's maritime defensive perimeter (see Figure 22.4). The first includes the East and South China Seas and Taiwan, which should be seen as China's more traditional maritime peripheral zone of interest.

The second outer line, called the *Second Island Chain*, extends from east of the Tokyo Bay area in a wide sweeping arc all the way to Guam and western New Guinea, and includes within its sphere the Philippines and the northern sweep of the Indonesian archipelago. While the PRC position and strategy continues to emphasize the defensive nature of Chinese military posture and doctrine, the reality of a rapidly increasing economy and a growing and more assertive foreign policy argues for a more aggressive military posture. As shall be seen below, the extraordinary growth in the military budget over the past fifteen years supports this assertion.

Rapid growth in military expenditures

The rapid growth of China's economy in recent years, which has averaged almost 10 percent/annum, has been followed by an even more

Figure 22.4
China's view of the First and Second Island Chains. Current strategic doctrine has extended China's maritime defensive perimeter far beyond its zone of traditional interest in the South and East China Seas.

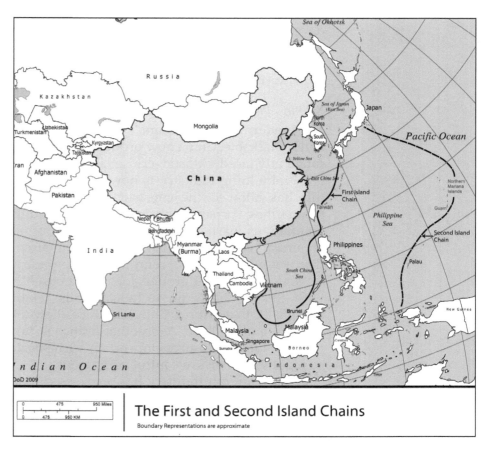

The First and Second Island Chains

Boundary Representations are approximate

rapid increase in military expenditures. The past decade of growth in military expenditures was estimated at approximately 13 percent/annum. During the past twenty years (except for 2003–5), according to official Chinese sources, there have been double-digit increases in military expenditures over previous years, which have produced exponential growth in funds available for force modernization and improvement. While official budget figures indicate considerable growth in military spending, the real figures are no doubt substantially higher owing to the Chinese habit of disguising various forms of spending for defense and military purposes (Information Office of the State Council of the PRC 2009; DoD Report 2009). This is also consistent with the penchant for secrecy that has always been a hallmark of the PLA and Chinese Communist Party.

The DoD Report (2009) indicated China's military budget was doubling about every five years from 1989 to the present. In early 2008, the official figure stood at $60 billion. DoD (2009) estimates the true figure for China's total defense expenditures to be between $105 and $150 billion based on 2007 prices and exchange rates. Rapid increases in defense spending have enabled China to expand its own defense industries in both size and sophistication. Dual-use technologies that may involve far-reaching military applications have also benefited in their development and growth. As China continues to increase the size, scope, and sophistication of its domestic defense industries, its need for outside sources of weapons and military technology lessens, and it too becomes a major source and competitor in the global arms trade.

Military forces and force structure modernization

The modernization of China's military forces has been comprehensive and remarkable. China now produces a full array of short- and medium-range advanced ballistic, cruise, air-to-air, and surface-to-air missiles. Its shipbuilding industry is now the second largest in the world, and this has allowed the construction of a number of naval vessels—submarines, surface combatants, support and transport ships including amphibious warfare vessels, naval aviation including an initiative for an aircraft carrier and the purchase of an aircraft carrier from Ukraine that is now undergoing refitting and upgrade at the Dalian shipyard.

Modernization of ground forces is focused on upgrading personnel with the emphasis on technical skills relating to the information battlefield. In addition, China produces new tanks, armored personnel carriers, and artillery. As in other branches, however, China continues to rely on foreign sources for certain sophisticated technical pieces such as night vision or fire control equipment.

China's aircraft industry has progressed steadily to the point where it can produce advanced jet fighters and a variety of other models often based on Soviet and Russian designs. While China has developed or imported high-technology precision machinery to enable it to fashion aircraft parts and advance its aircraft industry, it continues to rely on foreign sources for aircraft engines and avionics, a reality that inhibits its ability to expand aircraft production rapidly in case of military exigency.

The clear message here is that China is using its rapid economic growth to improve dramatically its basic and applied research that is quickly being extended into its military force modernization. The country has a plan that emphasizes research on material design, aeronautics and astronautics, information technology, and nanotechnology. More effort will also be given to advanced manufacturing, advanced energy technologies, marine technologies, laser and aerospace technologies. It is seeking to develop and build those areas of basic and applied technology where it is weak or lacking and will continue to develop in all high-tech areas where it has significant capacity. China will buy or lease technologies where available, and it will use all means possible, both legal and illegal, to obtain the information and technology it requires to advance its economy, technology, and military forces (DoD 2009).

Force disposition and the Taiwan factor

China has for more than half a century focused much of its military attention and activity toward Taiwan and the 110 mile-wide Taiwan Strait. This results from its strong nationalist sentiment that Taiwan must be reunited with the motherland, while also serving as a strong counterpoint to the presence, real or potential, of US forces that might intervene should China attempt to use force or coercion against Taiwan to speed up its return to the mainland. According to China's vision, the return of Taiwan to China is an internal matter and thus it fits into the greater stated doctrine that China will only use its military forces for defensive purposes. Consequently, the steady build-up of naval, air, and missile forces opposite Taiwan is not seen as aggressive or offensive in nature. The US government's position, as noted above, remains for a peaceful resolution of the differences between China and Taiwan. The Taiwan Relations Act continues to allow for the US to provide military equipment and technology to support Taiwan's self-defense. In addition, the US military through various force adjustments and other mechanisms continues its efforts to maintain "the capacity to defend against Beijing's use of force or coercion against Taiwan" (DoD 2009: 41).

The Taiwan Strait is in fact a critical flashpoint in the current global security situation. At present, the PRC seems content to allow the situation with Taiwan to continue *in tenebris*, in a state of uncertainty or ambiguity, especially since the election in 2008 of President Ma Yingjeou, who has offered more conciliatory policies toward the PRC with an easing of tensions. Yet the military build-up continues, and China appears set on increasing its ability either to invade the island or to coerce or intimidate it into bending to Beijing's will. Perhaps nowhere is this

369

threat more apparent than as depicted in the map of China's missile coverage of the Taiwan Strait and Taiwan with both *surface-to-air (SAM)* and short-range ballistic missiles (SRBM) (see Figure 22.5).

According to the DoD 2009 report, China now has more than 1000 SRBM and cruise missiles arrayed opposite Taiwan that could directly attack it and nearby naval forces. While China still possesses only a limited amphibious force with lift capacity likely confined to one infantry division, nonetheless, it is clear that China is working equally hard on its missile and information warfare capacity. This could enable it to deny opposing forces (presumably US) to engage quickly and effectively in the event China does elect to use force or coercion against the island. The map of the outer range of intermediate-range ballistic missiles offers additional evidence of Beijing's growing capacity to extend its offensive power against naval forces at much greater distances from the China mainland.

Various scenarios have been projected for how the PRC might go about attacking Taiwan. China's growing and improving naval, air, ground, amphibious, and missile forces allow considerable flexibility It is also clear, as seen in the accompanying tables (see Tables 22.1, 22.2, and 22.3) that China's ground, air, and naval forces in the Taiwan Strait Theatre are overwhelming in number. Increasingly, as discussed above, the forces are also rapidly modernizing and improving in quality and technical sophistication for modern warfare. One plausible scenario

Figure 22.5
Range of China's SAM and SRBM coverage in the Taiwan Strait and covering Taiwan and adjacent waters beyond. This missile coverage highlights the vulnerability of Taiwan to missile attack from the nearby China mainland.

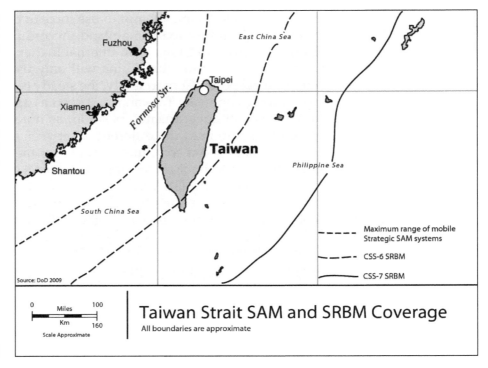

370

Table 22.1: Taiwan Strait military balance, naval forces

Type of ship	China		Taiwan
	Total	East & South Seas Fleet	Total
Destroyers	27	17	4
Frigates	48	39	22
Tank landing ships/amphibious transport dock	27	25	12
Medium landing ships	28	23	4
Diesel attack subs	54	32	4
Nuclear attack subs	6	1	0
Coastal patrol (missile)	70	55	59

Note: The PLA Navy has the largest force of principal combatants, submarines, and amphibious
warfare ships in Asia. After years of neglect, the missile-armed patrol craft is also growing. In the
event of a major conflict, the East and South Seas Fleets would be expected to participate in direct
action against Taiwan. The North Sea Fleet would be responsible primarily for protecting Beijing
and the northern coast, although it could provide mission-critical assets to support the other fleets.
Source: DoD 2009.

Table 22.2: Taiwan Strait military balance, ground forces

	China		Taiwan
	Total	Taiwan Strait	Total
Personnel (active)	1.25 million	440,000	130,000
Group armies	18	8	3
Infantry divisions	19	8	0
Infantry brigades	24	11	8
Mechanized infantry divisions	4	1	0
Mechanized infantry brigades	5	1	3
Armor divisions	9	4	0
Armor brigades	8	3	5
Artillery divisions	2	2	0
Artillery brigades	17	6	5
Airborne divisions	3	3	0
Amphibious divisions	2	2	
Amphibious brigades	3	3	3
Tanks	6700	2800	1100
Artillery pieces	7400	2900	1600

Note: PLA active ground forces are organized into Group Armies. Infantry, armor, and artillery
units are organized into a combination of divisions and brigades deployed throughout the seven
military regions. A significant portion of these assets are deployed in the Taiwan Strait area,
specifically the Nanjing, Guangzhou, and Jinan military regions.
Source: DoD 2009.

Table 22.3: Taiwan Strait military balance, air forces

Aircraft	China		Taiwan
	Total	Taiwan Strait	Total
Fighter	1655	330	390
Bomber/attack	645	160	0
Transport	450	40	40

suggests Beijing would employ stealth and surprise in an attempt to compel a rapid military and diplomatic resolution before any effective foreign power could be brought to bear on the situation. If this did not work, China would likely seek to prevent US involvement or then use its available military assets to bring a rapid end to military engagement. Finally, if it did not succeed in a quick victory, it might pursue a protracted conflict followed by a political settlement. All of these outcomes have risks associated with them, with the possibility of a lengthy conflict being the most potentially damaging to China's global political and diplomatic position in which it would risk a tense and bitter relationship with the US (DoD 2009).

Conclusion: China's military and the future

China, since the reforms of the late 1970s, has undergone a remarkable transformation. Driven largely by unprecedented economic growth, China has managed a far-reaching modernization of its military and strategic missile forces. While Beijing has always asserted that its military will be used only for defensive purposes with a goal of protecting China's security, it is now clear that military modernization enables China to project power beyond its borders and based on new technologies to challenge and deny other powers access to potential battle areas peripheral to China. China is transforming the PLA from a mass "people's army" to a modern well-trained military force that can "fight high intensity conflicts along its periphery against high tech adversaries"—an approach that China refers to as preparing for "local wars under conditions of informationization" (DoD 2009: 1).

Substantial and rapid increases in defense funding have allowed China to purchase advanced foreign weapons while transforming its own forces through improved technology and education, continuing high rates of investment in its economic development as well as in its science and research establishments. This growth has then been transferred into the military, which has modernized its weaponry, technology, and strategic nuclear and missile forces while undergoing major changes in doctrine and organization to allow for combined forces and operations.

This remarkable change in China's economic and military power has far-reaching implications for its neighbors in the western Pacific as well as for the world. The calculus of global power relations is shifting, and this ushers in an era of challenge and change. Dynamic new power shifts can lead to new suspicions and uncertainty, particularly in the case where China does not offer much transparency in allowing others to know the true size of its annual military expenditures. Neighbors such as Russia, India, and Japan as well as smaller Southeast Asian countries

may become increasingly anxious over China's new power and its aggressive search for new sources of energy and mineral resources (Goldstein 2001).

The most likely flashpoint in recent years is Taiwan, and it continues to be a serious and enduring irritant in relations between China and the US. While this issue seems to have quieted since 2008, the Chinese continue to build up threatening military forces and remain strongly and unremittingly committed to restoring Taiwan to Chinese sovereignty. Any assessment of China's growing military capacity as well as its intentions toward Taiwan will raise serious questions as to what this means for US–Chinese relations as well as the future of Taiwan. As China grows stronger, the potential for serious misunderstanding or the use of force is likely to increase, a sobering prospect for all with an interest in maintaining peace and stability in the western Pacific.

References cited

Department of Defense (DoD). 2009. *Military power of the People's Republic of China 2009.* Office of the Secretary of Defense, annual report to Congress. Washington, DC.

Fairbank, J. K. 1992. *China, a new history.* Cambridge, MA: Belknap Press.

Goldstein, A. 2001. "The diplomatic face of China's grand strategy: a rising power's emerging choice." *China Quarterly* 168: 835–64.

Griffith, S. B. 1963. *Sun Tzu, the art of war.* New York, NY: Oxford University Press.

Harding, H. 1993. "The concept of 'Greater China': themes, variations, and reservations." *China Quarterly* 168: 660–85.

Information Office of the State Council of the People's Republic of China. 2009. *China's national defense in 2008.* 20 January. www.china.org.cn/government/whitepaper/node_7060059.htm [accessed 30 April 2010].

Lampton, D. M. 2007. *The three faces of Chinese power: might, money, and minds.* Berkeley, CA: University of California Press.

Pannell, C. W. 2006. "Review, Office of the Secretary of Defense. The military power of the People's Republic of China. 2005. Washington D.C.: annual report to Congress pursuant to the National Defense Authorization Act, fiscal year 2000, 2006." *Eurasian Geography and Economics* 47(4): 499–504.

Samuels, M. 1982. *Contest for the South China Sea.* New York: Methuen.

Sawyer, R. D. (trans.). 1993. *The seven military classics of ancient China.* Boulder, CO: Westview Press.

Scobell, A. & W. Kirby. 2003. *China's use of military force: beyond the Great Wall and Long March.* Cambridge, UK: Cambridge University Press.

Shambaugh, D. (ed.). 2000. *The modern Chinese state.* Cambridge, UK: Cambridge University Press.

——. 2003, *Modernizing China's military: progress, problems, and prospects.* Berkeley, CA: University of California Press.

Strategic Forecasting. 2008. *Taiwan: cruise missiles and warming relations with China.* 29 October.

US Department of State. Bureau of East Asian and Pacific Affairs. 2009. *Profile, People's Republic of China.* January.

Veeck, G., C. W. Pannell, C. J. Smith, & Y. Huang. 2007. *China's geography: globalization and the dynamics of political, economic, and social change.* Boulder, CO: Rowman & Littlefield.

Chapter twenty-three
Ungoverned space and effective sovereignty in the Global War on Terror
Western Pakistan

FRANCIS A. GALGANO

Introduction

> I do not make this decision lightly. I make this decision because I am
> convinced that our security is at stake in Afghanistan and Pakistan. This
> is the epicenter of the violent extremism practiced by *al-Qaeda*.
>
> (President Barack Obama, 1 December 2009, White House 2009)

As the GLOBAL WAR ON TERROR (GWOT) enters its ninth year, the focal point of US military and diplomatic efforts against Islamic terrorism is returning to its starting place in Afghanistan, which was once the cradle of the *Taliban* and former training grounds of *al-Qaeda*. However, of even larger geopolitical importance, the effort is now going to have to potentially incorporate expanded operations in the *Federally Administered Tribal Areas (FATA)* of western Pakistan (DoD 2006; Constable and Witte 2009). In fact, during his speech outlining his Afghan strategy, President Barack Obama indicated clearly that there was a fundamental connection between global terrorism and safe havens that now exist in western Pakistan (White House 2009). President Obama also indicated that securing the FATA is essential to the successful prosecution of the war on Islamic terrorism because these wild tribal lands are now the *center of gravity* for the *Taliban* and *al-Qaeda*—it is believed that it is the sanctuary for Osama bin Laden and second-in-command Ayman al-Zawahiri—and is now the principal training ground for soldiers of the global *jihad* (Bajoria 2007; Constable 2009; Constable and Witte 2009; White House 2009).

> Since 9/11, *al-Qaeda*'s safe-havens [in Afghanistan and Pakistan]
> have been the source of attacks against London and Amman and
> Bali. The people and governments of both Afghanistan and Pakistan
> are endangered. And the stakes are even higher within a nuclear-

armed Pakistan, because we know that *al-Qaeda* and other extremists seek nuclear weapons, and we have every reason to believe that they would use them.

(President Barack Obama, 1 December 2009,
White House 2009)

Pakistan (see Figure 14.1) finds itself straddling the fault line between Islamic terrorism and the rule of global law. From the perspective of the military geographer, the link between the FATA and the war on terror is of fundamental importance because it manifests the salient geographic dynamics that characterize modern conflict and *asymmetrical warfare*. For the US and its allies, engaging the *Taliban* and *al-Qaeda* in the FATA has become *the* conflict in the GWOT because many recent terrorist attacks can be traced directly to this region, and it has become the new base of operations for terrorist organizations and other *violent non-state actors* (Cordesman 2007, 2009; Sappenfield 2008; Siddique 2009). Finally, it is becoming increasingly clear that the fundamentalist movement emanating from this region is having a destabilizing effect on Pakistan, which is a nuclear state (Kyl 2009).

Undoubtedly, the resurgence of the *Taliban* and reconstitution of *al-Qaeda* in the FATA region signals not only a threat to Afghanistan, but to Pakistan as well (Constable 2009). The seminal predicament for the US and its allies is that they must somehow contend with a violent terrorist organization within the sovereign territory of a nominal ally, thus making operations against the *Taliban* and *al-Qaeda* fundamentally problematical. The dilemma is compounded further because until recently, the Pakistani government has been indifferent about pursuing an aggressive policy toward terrorist organizations within the FATA—its sovereign territory—and its intelligence service is directly aiding the *Taliban* (National Security Archive 2007; Sappenfield 2008; Cordesman 2009).

Thus, the role of the FATA in the War on Terror is essential to understanding links between *ungoverned space* and *effective sovereignty*, and the future of regional and global security (Garamone 2004; Jacoby 2004; Tallent 2005; DoD 2006; Galgano 2007). Military geographers can provide an important vantage point from which to examine these issues because matters of governance and effective sovereignty are of paramount importance in this region. Military operations have demonstrated that US, NATO, and Pakistani forces can win virtually any serious open battle with the *Taliban* and *al-Qaeda*; however, events have also demonstrated that tactical victories alone cannot win the war on either side of the Afghan–Pakistan border (Cordesman 2007). It is also becoming increasingly clear, as was the case in Vietnam, that tactical military victories will be largely irrelevant unless the Afghan and Pakistani governments can create competent governance and assert

375 effective sovereignty on both sides of this contested border, but

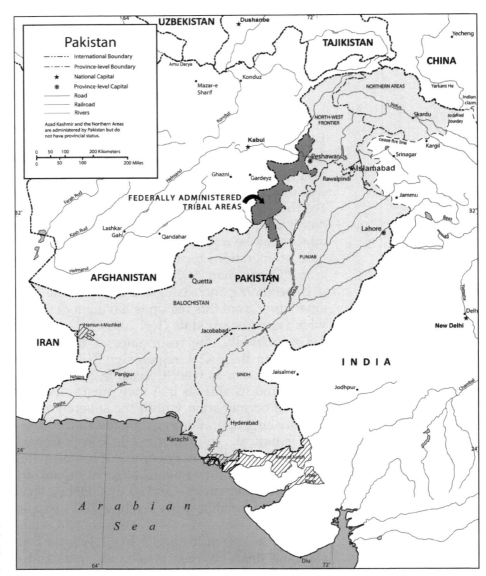

Figure 23.1
Map of the Federally Administered Tribal Lands of Afghanistan.

especially in the FATA (Cordesman 2009). It is clear, however, that the *Taliban* and *al-Qaeda* must be defeated militarily before any diplomatic efforts will succeed (Bajoria 2007; Cordesman 2009).

Ungoverned space and the GWOT in Pakistan

Instability in weakly governed areas of Afghanistan and Pakistan is having a clear and debilitating effect on regional stability and is influencing US strategy to meet threats to its security. Events throughout the world since 9-11 have clearly demonstrated that the new security menace is transnational in nature and characterized by an enemy without territory and borders (Thomas and Casebeer 2005). Furthermore, this transnational security menace has adroitly exploited regions of the world where government control is absent or weak (Tallent 2005). This global dynamic fosters growing threats to regional security including the export and franchising of terrorism, proliferation of weapons of mass destruction, uncontrolled arms and drug trade, and piracy on the seas (Thomas 2006; Galgano 2009).

Ungoverned spaces are areas where government control is largely absent and merit attention because humanitarian disasters and ethnic conflict can affect them severely, or violent non-state actors can exploit them as sanctuaries largely without fear of interference (Galgano 2007). Because Pakistan is a nuclear state, and the *Taliban* is committed to taking it over for its own purposes, the tribal lands of western Pakistan are perhaps the most problematic and dangerous ungoverned areas in the world (Miskel and Norton 1997; Garamone 2004; Jacoby 2004; Tallent, 2005; Galgano 2007; Cordesman 2009).

Apprehension over ungoverned areas has been elevated because of US military operations in Afghanistan and Iraq; transnational extremists such as *al-Qaeda* are increasingly denied their former sanctuaries (Tallent 2005). Consequently, they are now more reliant on leveraging and franchising indigenous and affiliated terrorist groups worldwide, and violent non-state actors such as the *Taliban* and *al-Qaeda* are exploiting places where states are already struggling with control, such as Afghanistan and western Pakistan. Both regions are defined by endemic imbalances in the distribution of wealth, staggering health problems, fragile political systems, regressive social systems, and disenfranchised youth susceptible to the lure of extremism (Garamone 2004; DoD 2005; Constable 2009).

The study of weakly governed areas is of vital important to the GWOT because, despite tactical victories, decapitation of terror networks, and other relatively successful military operations, the West has been slow to attack the conditions that foster terrorism (Abbott 2004; Galgano 2007). Therefore, understanding the dynamics of ungoverned areas is important because the established rules of state sovereignty may no longer apply; this new dynamic has been demonstrated clearly, and most recently, along the Afghan–Pakistani border (Rosenthal 2004; Siddique 2009).

The Federally Administered Tribal Areas

In the context of the GWOT, Pakistan occupies a position of great geostrategic importance, bordered by Iran, Afghanistan, China, India, and the Arabian Sea (see Figure 14.1). Pakistan's essentially ungoverned and remote FATA region (see Figure 23.1) has become the principal training ground for *al-Qaeda* and the base for the *Taliban*'s insurgency against Afghanistan and Pakistan (Cordesman 2009). Furthermore, the

Taliban is making efforts to establish a parallel government in the FATA, and the common border between the two states is now one of the most contentious and dangerous areas in the world (Bajoria 2007; Siddique 2009). The FATA is the epicenter of Islamic extremism in the region and the springboard for exportation of violence on a regional and global scale. In a 2008 report, the UN indicated that more than 80 percent of all suicide bombers in Afghanistan and Pakistan were recruited or trained in the FATA (Cordesman 2007; UN 2007). On a global scale, the train bombings in Madrid (2004) and London (2005), and the Mumbai attacks (2008), were planned, staged, and co-ordinated in the FATA as well (Black 2008).

Pakistan's boundary with Afghanistan is about 2250 kilometers long (see Figures 14.2 and 23.1). Along its northern extent, it runs along the high, rugged, ridges of the Hindu Kush and Pamirs. The modern boundary between the two states was drawn in 1893 by British diplomat Sir Henry Mortimer Durand as a means to divide and weaken the eleven Pashtu tribes that dominate the region, and to turn Afghanistan into a buffer zone between the British and Russian empires (Library of Congress 1994; Bajoria 2007). This boundary, called the *Durand Line*, became the official Afghan–Pakistani border when Pakistan became independent in 1947. Nevertheless, its legitimacy has been disputed by the Pashtu tribes that straddle the border since it effectively divides the ethnic group. Afghanistan, too, has rejected the Durand Line because it feels that it was imposed by Great Britain, thus nullifying its claim to the Pashtu lands in western Pakistan, which they view as a natural extension of their territory (Bajoria 2007). More importantly, Afghans are apprehensive over the Durand Line because its division of the Pashtu tribes has fueled their desire to establish a separate state and it has in effect destabilized the eastern region of the country (Siddique 2009).

The semi-autonomous tribal lands of the FATA (see Figure 23.1) consist of seven so-called agencies: Bajaur, Mohmand, Khyber, Orakzai, Kurram, and North and South Waziristan. The remote, mountainous territory of the FATA runs along the Afghanistan border, and the region is populated by fiercely independent Pashtu tribes. Although the Pashtu tribes elected to join Pakistan rather than India after it gained independence in 1947, Islamabad historically has had negligible control over the region (Bajoria 2007).

Thus, the FATA is a classic ungoverned space. The border is poorly controlled and the *Taliban* routinely makes incursions from Pakistan into Afghanistan. The region is characterized by invasive corruption, poverty, lawlessness, and violence. Even though Pakistan's constitution imparts executive authority over the region to the president, the governor of the North West Frontier Province (see Figure 23.1) controls the FATA by managing bureaus that administer and deliver services such as health care and education in the tribal areas (Library of Congress 1994). However, actual power in the FATA rests with each of their political agents or magistrates, who represent the Pakistani federal government. The magistrates exercise control (such that it is) over the tribes through a set of archaic colonial-era Frontier Crimes Regulations that were established by the British (Bajoria 2007). These colonial-era laws are quite repressive and individual tribesmen in the FATA have limited rights—the laws are typically used by federal authorities as a political weapon, and have long been a source of animosity between Pashtu tribal leaders and Islamabad. Instead of imparting a measure of control, the Frontier Crimes Regulations have established conditions that degrade effective governance within the region and have promoted distrust, resentment, and disorder. Furthermore, government officials have shown little regard for the Pashtu tribes and limited accountability for their actions. This has fostered inherent political instability, pervasive violence, capricious rule of law, and endemic corruption (Kaufmann et al. 2003). Actually, the colonial laws permit federal political agents to impose collective punishment on tribes for crimes committed by an individual, and the magistrates can indiscriminately hand down prison sentences and other legal judgments without due process or right of appeal (Bajoria 2007; Siddique 2009).

The lack of government accountability in the region is exacerbated by pervasive corruption and a near absence of social infrastructure. Nepotism and favoritism are effectively law of the land, and selected tribal leaders known as *maliks* are given economic incentives, doled out by federal magistrates, in exchange for their loyalty. Magistrates collect and distribute tax revenue with little oversight from Islamabad, and tribes suffer from a lack of development and oppressive poverty, which only intensifies conditions that facilitate radical activities in the region (Siddique 2009). For example, development data indicate that only 17 percent of the population is literate, and the distribution of health care is equally dismal. In the FATA, there is only one doctor for every 8000 people as compared with one doctor per 1500 people in the rest of the country (Bajoria 2007).

Erratic application of divisive laws, endemic corruption, and pervasive inequities in infrastructure have enabled the proliferation of extremist Islamic views and the radicalization of many of the region's dis-enfranchised male population. There are only 102 high schools in all of the tribal lands. This vacuum has been filled by more than 300 *madrasas*, or Muslim schools, which are operated by *Wahhabist* clerics, and the number is growing. The alarming proliferation of these religious schools reflects the growing power of Islamic extremism in the tribal lands (Siddique 2009). There is a profusion of extremely poor, disenfran-chised, uneducated young men who are easily radicalized in the *madrasas* and are recruited and exploited by extremist Islamic groups with little trouble. Thus, the region exhibits characteristic indicators of an ungoverned area that is susceptible to polarizing, radical violence that
can be exploited by violent non-state organizations (Bajoria 2007).

Given these conditions, religious extremism and radical, anti-Western violence are significant problems in the FATA and, consequently, the tribal lands have become a melting pot for jihadists from all over the world (Bajoria 2007). In addition to the *Taliban* and *al-Qaeda*, the tribal lands are host to Chechen groups, and organizations such as the *Islamic Movement of Uzbekistan* (National Security Archive 2007). The *Taliban* has exploited the area's pervasive lack of governance and is now attempting to establish a parallel government in the region (Siddique 2009). Since the beginning of the Afghanistan war in 2001, key members of the *Taliban* have advanced into leadership roles, particularly in North and South Waziristan and Bajaur. The emergence of the *Taliban* has disturbed the political balance in the FATA and there have been cases of tribal leaders being executed for challenging the *Taliban*'s growing power or for working too closely with the Pakistani Army (Bajoria 2007).

It is important to note, however, that the *Taliban*'s religious extremism is not a new dynamic in the tribal lands, and, for decades, the Pashtus have practiced various forms of fundamentalism and exhibited highly conservative social values that predate contemporary counterterrorism efforts in the region (Constable 2009). This is compounded by the reality that, for most of the region's Pashtu population, being Pakistani citizens is secondary to their Pashtu identity, and they regard foreigners, including the Pakistani Army, with extreme suspicion (Bajoria 2007). This problem has been exacerbated since the 9/11 terrorist attacks. The region came under US scrutiny after the *Taliban* and *al-Qaeda* took refuge in the FATA. As a result, President Musharraf ordered a series of half-hearted offensives designed to eliminate terrorist organizations in the region, but these efforts largely failed. The failure was because the military actions were, in effect, window dressing, and became increasingly unpopular with the Pakistani Army in which Pashtus are the second largest ethnic group, and because the *Taliban* continues to receive direct support from the Pakistani intelligence agency (National Security Archive 2007).

These circumstances make Pakistan a particularly dubious ally and, thus, the FATA represents a very dangerous area where ungoverned space is being exploited. The problem is further compounded because it is within the sovereign territory of a so-called ally that has thus far lacked the political will to prevent its territory from being used as a springboard for violent attacks by terrorist organizations. Given this reality, the question facing the US, and for that matter the rest of the global community, is what do we do to eliminate, or at least mitigate the danger represented by this region?

Effective sovereignty

Our overarching goal remains the same: to disrupt, dismantle, and defeat *al-Qaeda* in Afghanistan and Pakistan, and to prevent its capacity to threaten America and our allies in the future.

(President Barack Obama, 1 December 2009, White House 2009)

The existence of ungoverned space in Pakistan is now playing a major role in the GWOT as *al-Qaeda* exploits the FATA to prosecute global *jihad* by attacking Western interests and promoting mass murder (Tallent 2005; Constable and Witte 2009; White House 2009). Thus, to respond effectively to the danger posed by a violent non-state actor operating from ungoverned space, a threatened state may be required to challenge the long-established rules of diplomacy and doctrines of international relations (Rosenthal 2004). In other words, does the threat of attacks emanating from ungoverned space in a sovereign state challenge the longstanding notion of sovereignty, and can one state intervene in another's ungoverned space? This paradigm has been termed effective sovereignty doctrine, which contends that, in a situation within which US national security may be threatened by a government's failure to exercise adequate control over an ungoverned area, the US reserves the right to take action deemed necessary to ensure its security (Isacson et al. 2004; Armstrong 2005).

Not all responses to effective sovereignty problems compel military action. In some instances, government leaders and non-governmental organizations have been able to remedy problems through peaceful means using established diplomatic and international protocols. In such cases, well-established doctrine is reasonable as it imparts the normative guidance that is needed (Balch 1910; Rosenthal 2004). However, the actions of *al-Qaeda* and the *Taliban* in the FATA, coupled with the feckless response of the Pakistani government, have clearly demonstrated that longstanding and well-established diplomatic protocols, as well as international doctrines and the principles they engender, must be considered in light of the new global circumstance (Galgano 2007). Specifically, that the serious threat posed by *al-Qaeda*, with the avowed goal of promoting mass murder, must be dealt with using direct military force even if that means military action without the consent of the territorial sovereign (Rosenthal 2004; ASIL 2009). Thus, government leaders may be faced with the very real necessity of having to employ military force to subdue a violent non-state actor operating within an ungoverned area of a sovereign state, perhaps even that of a so-called ally, such as Pakistan (Hoffman 2005; Sullivan 2006).

The FATA has been the training, planning, and staging site for a number of terror attacks (Bajoria 2007; White House 2009). The principal dilemma is that Pakistan has demonstrated little desire to intervene and prevent the lawless use of its territory. More importantly, and of direct bearing on the issue of effective sovereignty, is that the Pakistani government, through its intelligence service (ISI), has directly and materially aided the *Taliban* since 1996. Furthermore, it is believed that key leaders in the ISI and the Pakistani Army are still supporting the *Taliban* and perhaps even *al-Qaeda* with intelligence, weapons, and money even as the Pakistani government alleges to take action to pacify the FATA (National Security Archive 2007; DeYoung and Warrick 2008).

As a result, the US has been forced to employ direct military intervention in the FATA, mostly using aerial drones (ASIL 2009).

Such attacks are the manifestation of direct military action, which the US pursued during the Bush and now Obama administration. The US position is that it has the right to self-defense and use pre-emptive military action when deemed necessary. In fact, the DoD published a classified order in 2004 that gave broad authorization for US military forces to conduct direct operations against *al-Qaeda* and the *Taliban* within the borders of some twenty countries (ASIL 2009). Although the US began promoting its effective-sovereignty doctrine as early as 1995, the 2004 DoD order implies a rather broad interpretation of the right to self-defense (Abbott 2004; Hoffman 2005; Thomas 2006; ASIL 2009). In concert with this new paradigm, the US has conducted more than a dozen "secret" ground operations in Syria, Pakistan, and Somalia since 2004 (Schmitt and Mazzetti 2008); it has carried out an estimated twenty-six missile attacks in Pakistan during 2008 alone (ASIL 2009). One such operation, a heli-borne cross-border attack by a small US force into Syria from Iraq, drew strong protests from Syria in the UN. In addressing the justification for the attack against jihadists operating against US forces from Syrian territory, US officials referred to comments from President Bush's 2008 address to the UN General Assembly:

> To uphold the words of the Charter in the face of this challenge, every nation in this chamber has responsibilities. As sovereign states, we have an obligation to govern responsibly, and solve problems before they spill across borders. We have an obligation to prevent our territory from being used as a sanctuary for terrorism and proliferation and human trafficking and organized crime.
>
> (President George Bush, 23 September 2008,
> White House 2008)

It is clear that the Obama administration will pursue this doctrine in Pakistan as well—it has authorized numerous drone attacks against suspected *Taliban* and *al-Qaeda* targets in Pakistan since January 2009 (ASIL 2009). As indicated in his December 2009 speech, it appears that President Obama will continue to authorize cross-border attacks into the FATA because the Pakistani government has demonstrated that it has little means and even less political will to force a showdown with terrorist organizations operating there. The sobering reality is that Pakistani-led operations in the FATA have become increasingly unpopular and the Pakistani Army is reluctant to pursue these operations to placate the West (Bajoria 2007; Constable 2009).

Although the use of economic and diplomatic protocols have worked to solve effective sovereignty issues in the past—most notably in Latin America—these aspects of diplomacy do not appear to be a viable solution in the FATA (Manwaring 2002; Talbot 2002; Correll 2003;

Isacson et al. 2004; Bajoria 2007). The Pakistani government has endeavored to work out a series of ceasefires, treaties, and aid accords with the *Taliban* since 2004. In every instance, the agreements have fallen apart, or have been simply renounced by *Taliban* leaders once they have used them to provide cover for a new offensive of their own (Bajoria 2007). It is clear that the *Taliban* and *al-Qaeda* intend to use a perversion of Shari'a as a pretext for prosecuting a reign of terror and to justify their goals. They will continue to plan global *jihad*, kill with impunity, and labor to establish a parallel government in the FATA to serve their violent purposes (Sappenfield 2008). Furthermore, the *Taliban* and *al-Qaeda* will not rest until they topple the Pakistani government and turn Pakistan into a fundamentalist state (Cordesman 2009). Experts agree that the area must be pacified by military force *combined* with political agreements to solve the region's complex issues (Bajoria 2007).

Classification of ungoverned space in the FATA

The existence of ungoverned areas is not a new phenomenon and, clearly, their exploitation by transnational actors has a longstanding history as well (Thomas and Casebeer 2005). The compelling problem that we now face is the potential for ungoverned space to be used as a springboard for disruptive or perhaps catastrophic activities by terrorist organizations (Talent 2005). Furthermore, dynamics of the modern world, i.e. telecommunications, the internet, banking and money transfers, and travel, have aided non-state actors and make it much easier for them to exploit remote areas of the world where governance is weak.

A classification system is important and useful because government leaders and military commanders as well as directors of non-governmental organizations and intergovernmental bodies have to contend with ungoverned spaces along a broad spectrum of responses, i.e. humanitarian assistance and nation-building activities to direct military intervention (Correll 2003). Thus, ungoverned areas must be viewed functionally to determine the distinctive relationships between the nature of "ungovernance" and the activities of the violent non-state actor(s). Given this requirement, Galgano (2007) developed a two-tiered classification scheme to organize ungoverned spaces based on their type (i.e. genetically) and function (see Figure 23.2). This classification scheme considers a genetic hierarchy (physical and non-physical) as well as a functional construct based on government and non-state actor interaction within the region.

The FATA has all of the attributes of physical ungoverned space (Galgano 2007): it is a remote, undeveloped territory that is considered a frontier region by the Pakistani government. Even given the FATA's geographic proximity to Islamabad, Pakistani federal authorities have essentially been unable or unwilling to develop infrastructure and exert control over the region. Development indicators suggest that, at every level, the FATA and its population lags well behind the rest of the state

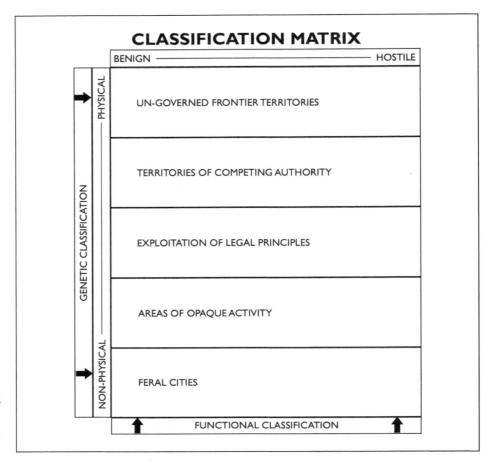

(Library of Congress 1994; Sappenfield 2008). Consequently, the FATA's Pashtu tribes manifest a high level of poverty and can be easily exploited or recruited by organizations such as the *Taliban* and *al-Qaeda* (Tallent 2005). The area has very little infrastructure and is susceptible to devastating humanitarian and natural disasters as well. Furthermore, this type of ungoverned space characteristically extends over the frontier borders of neighboring states—in this case Afghanistan—creating difficult sovereignty issues, thus making unified responses and control more difficult.

Galgano's (2007) functional categories of ungoverned space offer five basic classifications: 1) ungoverned frontier territories; 2) territories of competing authority; 3) exploitation of legal principles; 4) areas of opaque activity; and 5) feral cities. These functional classifications have to be considered given that human processes are typically very complex and, thus, it is difficult to place ungoverned spaces into discrete categories. Indeed, an analysis of the governance dynamics in the FATA indicates that there is a great deal of overlap between the functional classifications. Nonetheless, an assessment of ongoing dynamics within the FATA suggests that it is fundamentally a territory of competing authority, but also manifests conditions indicative of an ungoverned frontier territory and the exploitation of legal principles.

As a physical ungoverned space, the FATA exhibits conditions consistent with an *ungoverned frontier territory*. The region is very rugged, remote, and has little government-sponsored infrastructure such as roads, airfields, water distribution, electrical grids, schools, hospitals, and other features common to modern society (Bajoria 2007). This type of region is ideal for non-state actors seeking concealment or separation from a state's security apparatus. Humanitarian disasters in these regions are particularly problematic because a responding government or non-governmental agency may have to expend enormous effort simply to establish an infrastructure in order to bring relief supplies into the region (Galgano 2007). This was evident during the 2005 earthquake in northern Pakistan, during which the combination of remoteness and lack of infrastructure essentially required all relief supplies to be flown into the area. The lion's share of this mission was accomplished by US Army aviation units (Thompson and Halter 2006). In terms of security operations, the Pashtu lands span the border region between Afghanistan and Pakistan, and there is little control exerted by either sovereign entity. Furthermore, the near lack of basic infrastructure and government presence means that the indigenous population is usually impoverished and day-to-day survival and security is a matter of personal initiative (Galgano 2007).

Principally, the FATA is a territory of competing authority. This type of ungoverned area is typical of a sovereign state's unwillingness to exercise authority over part or whole of a country (Whelan 2005; Galgano 2007). In the case of the FATA, federal authorities use taxation and colonial-era laws to selectively control the region and, consequently, it has become disenfranchised, alienated, and susceptible to exploitation. The Pashtu people identify more closely with their ethnic identity than they do with the Pakistani government; government agents have systematically alienated the population through invasive corruption, erratic and malicious application of antiquated laws, and lack of accountability. Problems in the region were exacerbated following the Russian invasion of Afghanistan when millions of Pashtu refugees moved into the FATA. The crushing poverty and lack of education proved to be fertile ground for the Wahhabi *madrasas* that moved into the area and established a *de facto* education system. Thousands of young men were indoctrinated and radicalized by the imams teaching at these religious schools, and they became willing recruits of the *Taliban*, *al-Qaeda*, and other fanatical organizations (Siddique 2009). These conditions have been exploited further by the *Taliban* as they have moved into the area following Operation Enduring Freedom in 2001. They have in effect begun to establish a parallel government by

385

providing a rudimentary health care system, a security force, and other government-like services—in effect establishing a competing authority in the region (Siddique 2009). The *Taliban* has also instituted a set of their version of Shari'a laws that ban video stores, drinking, co-mingling of men and women in public, and other very strict interpretations of the Koran. Additionally, they have enacted Shari'a laws barring women from shopping, banning widows from seeking government aid, and ending coeducation (Constable 2009; Siddique 2009). Pakistan's government officials have reported that the *Taliban* is looking to expand its authority throughout the Pashtu tribal lands to include the whole of the North West Frontier Province (Siddique 2009).

Finally, adjunct to their establishment of a competing authority in the FATA, the *Taliban* has begun to exploit legal principles. The absence of an effective federal presence in the FATA has offered the *Taliban* the opportunity to manipulate legitimate government processes to serve its own violent ends. Throughout the FATA and now in the North West Frontier Province, members of the *Taliban* are taking over, or are being "elected" to low-level government positions, thus in effect legitimizing their hold over the region. In addition, they are assassinating tribal leaders that challenge its authority, and are replacing them with leaders that are more amenable to *Taliban* control (Siddique 2009).

Thus, the *Taliban* and to some extent *al-Qaeda* are adroitly using the power vacuum in the FATA to establish a "legitimate" parallel government structure. In this lawless area the *Taliban* has been able to assimilate legal norms. They have filled a power vacuum and established themselves within legitimate activities and government positions such as magistrates, police, and the judicial system to provide cover for their operations. Their emplacement of clinics and schools has given them credibility among a population that has been essentially ignored for generations by the Pakistani government (Sappenfield 2008). Given these conditions, it is easy to understand why local tribes now provide security, logistics, and sanctuary for extremist organizations in the FATA. Furthermore, attempts by Western security forces and the Pakistani Army serve only to antagonize further the people of the region because they give the very real appearance that they are trying to dismantle the only benefactors these people have ever had.

Summary and conclusions

The fundamental problem in the Southwest Asian Theater of the GWOT is that the war that actually exists is not the war that the West wants to fight, or is even willing to accept as reality at this juncture. US analyses—along with that of its NATO allies—replicate the same errors that were made in the assessments of the conflict in Iraq (Cordesman 2007). What

we fail to grasp, or are simply unwilling to yet accept, is that the struggle for Afghanistan and the tribal lands of Pakistan is a war of attrition, which the *Taliban* can win by controlling the weakly governed space and the populations that live there. The *Taliban* is seeking to deny the Pakistani government control over this territory and will not rest until control is achieved and they have developed a solid base from which to topple the central government. The war in the FATA is also an ethnic struggle that is inextricably linked to the Pashtu population (Cordesman 2007).

The US, and frankly much of the world, face a clear set of traditional, disruptive, catastrophic, and irregular threats that have and will continue to emanate from ungoverned space in western Pakistan. Traditional challenges include epidemics, natural disasters, and famine, which are usually best handled by non-governmental organizations, although military units have the equipment and training to operate in austere environments and have increasingly been asked to intervene in such cases. This was evident during the 2005 Pakistani earthquakes.

Disruptive and irregular challenges are activities by violent non-state actors that include piracy on the open ocean, narco-trafficking, weapons trade, industrial piracy, or actions such as smuggling and slave trade. In these cases, military units are best used for training indigenous police forces to address the problem from within. However, using US soldiers within another sovereign state in order to prevent these types of activities would be highly problematic and seriously blurs the line between law enforcement and military operations.

Catastrophic challenges are the most likely serious threat to regional and global stability: they include the use of ungoverned space to plan and launch devastating terrorist attacks such as the 9/11 attack in New York City and others in London, Madrid, and Mumbai. The scenario that creates even more anxiety is one in which a weakly governed area is used to develop weapons of mass destruction such as dirty bombs, nuclear, biological, and chemical weapons. This is clearly the concern in Pakistan should the state fall to the *Taliban* along with its armed forces and nuclear arsenal. Catastrophic challenges may entail the presence of terrorist training bases or perhaps even a stockpile of aircraft, ships, or other weapons once belonging to the former state sovereign that may be used as weapons against the US or its overseas interests. In this scenario, direct military intervention appears to be the only option.

The principal challenge to the DoD is that it is normally in the business of reacting to military crises and not traditionally equipped or staffed to plan for and deal with the challenges presented by ungoverned space and the emerging doctrine of effective sovereignty. However, in order to succeed in the GWOT, the US must deal with the roots of terror and not simply rely on spectacular military operations and other high-profile actions. Thus, military and civilian leaders within the DoD and other government agencies must develop plans to contend with ungoverned spaces by understanding their functional classification and by using non-military options where appropriate and, thus, avoid situations becoming crises. Finally, the US simply cannot become directly involved in every potential lawless area on earth.

Therefore, to support long-term US strategy in reducing the threat from ungoverned space the DoD should begin to focus on stability-enhancing strategies that promote civil control over ungoverned areas and assist in the development of more professional security forces within developing or weak states. In that context, the DoD should focus its efforts on developing better trained indigenous military forces, which will, in the long term, be more effective in the GWOT. This doctrine would include: enhanced civil control and defense reform (i.e. the development of appropriately sized, funded, and equipped armed forces with improved transparency and accountability); enhanced military professionalism (i.e. institutionalized training for a disciplined army with a professional ethic and the conduct of legitimate missions while respecting the law and human rights); capacity building that entails appropriately equipped and well-led military forces to effectively reduce ungoverned space; and finally providing humanitarian assistance and inculcating indigenous forces with the tools and mission awareness to do the same (Galgano 2007).

Irrespective of passive and diplomatic means of improving the level of governance, the US and the West must accept that, in the end, they must fight and destroy the *Taliban* and *al-Qaeda*. Because they are violent non-state actors, we have no reasonable expectation that we can rely on formally accepted diplomatic protocols. Furthermore, they have renounced all attempts to negotiate. The plain truth is that we have to subdue the *Taliban* because, in practice, they are inextricably linked to *al-Qaeda*. By allowing the *Taliban* to expand their control in the FATA we will only broaden the opportunities for *al-Qaeda* to exploit this sanctuary, provide them with additional security, and ultimately give them the time and strategic space to fully reconstitute and project their influence and violence around the world.

References cited

Abbott, P. K. 2004. "Terrorist threat in the tri-border area: myth or reality." *Military Review* (September–October): 51–5.

American Society of International Law (ASIL). 2009. "Reported U.S. directive authorizing clandestine attacks on al Qaeda in numerous countries: U.S. strikes in Syria and Pakistan draw protests." *American Journal of International Law* 103(1): 161–3.

Armstrong, N. 2005. "Crying wolf." *International Studies Review* 45(4): 3–14.

Bajoria, J. 2007. "Pakistan's tribal areas." Council on Foreign Relations, 26 October. www.cfr.org/publications/11973/ [accessed 28 October 2009].

Balch, T. W. 1910. "The Arctic and Antarctic regions and law of nations." *American Journal of International Law* 4(2): 265–75.

Black, I. 2008. "Attacks draw worldwide condemnation." *Guardian* (28 November). www.guardian.co.uk/world/2008/nov/28/mumbai-terror-attacks-international-response [accessed 30 April 2010].

Constable, P. 2009. "The Taliban tightens hold in Pakistan's SWAT region." *Washington Post* (5 May). www.washingtonpost.com/wp-dyn/content/article/2009/05/04/AR2008050400189/ [accessed 15 October 2009].

Constable, P. & G. Witte. 2009. "Pakistan wary of Afghan strategy." *Washington Post* (3 December). www.boston.com/news/world/asia/articles/2009/12/03/Pakistan_wary_of_obamas afghan_strategy.htm [accessed 3 December 2009].

Cordesman, A. H. 2007. *Assessing the Afghan–Pakistani conflict.* Washington, DC: Center for Strategic and International Studies. http://csis.org/publication/assessing-afghan-pakistani-conflict [accessed 30 April 2010].

——. 2009. *Winning in Afghanistan: how the U.S. will win or lose the war.* Washington, DC: Center for Strategic and International Studies. http://csis.org/publication/winning-afghanistan-1 [accessed 30 April 2010].

Correll, J. T. 2003. "European Command looks south and east." *Journal of the Air Force Association* 86(12): 26–34.

Department of Defense (DoD). 2005. *The national defense strategy of the United States of America.* Washington, DC: US Government Printing Office.

——. 2006. *The national military strategic plan for the War on Terror.* Chairman of the Joint Chiefs of Staff. Washington, DC: US Government Printing Office, www.defenselink.mil/qdr/docs [accessed 12 October 2009].

DeYoung, K. & J. Warrick. 2008. "Pakistan and U.S. have tacit deal on airstrikes." *Washington Post* A1 (23 September).

Galgano, F. A. 2007. "A geographic analysis of ungoverned spaces." *Pennsylvania Geographer* 44(2): 67–90.

——. 2009. "The borderless dilemma of contemporary maritime piracy: its geography and trends." *Pennsylvania Geographer* 47(1): 3–33.

Garamone, J. 2004. *Defense intell chief outlines world security climate.* Washington, DC: American Forces Information Service, 24 February. www.defenselink.mil [accessed 8 September 2009].

Hoffman, M. H. 2005. "Rescuing the law of war: a way forward in an era of global terrorism." *Parameters* (summer): 18–34.

Isacson, A., J. Olson, & L. Haugaard. 2004. *Blurring the lines, trends in U.S. military programs with Latin America.* Washington, DC: Latin America Working Group Education Fund, Center for International Policy and Washington Office on Latin America.

Jacoby, L. E. 2004. *Current and projected national security threats to the United States.* Statement for the Record, Senate Select Committee on Intelligence. Washington, DC: US Senate, 24 February. www.dia.mil/publicaffairs/Testimonies/statement12.html [accessed 21 August 2009].

Kaufmann, D., A. Kraay, & M. Mastruzzi. 2003. *Governance matters III: governance indicators for 1996–2002.* The World Bank, World Bank Institute, Global Governance Department and Development Research Group.

Kyl, J. 2009. General McChrystal's strategy for victory in Afghanistan. National Ledger (12 October). http://nationalledger.com/artman/publish/article_272628415.shtml [accessed 28 October 2009].

Library of Congress. 1994. *Pakistan.* Library of Congress Country Studies, Washington, DC: US Government Printing Office. http://memory.loc.gov/cgi-bin/query2/r?frd/cstdy:@field(DOCID+pk0038) [accessed 30 April 2010].

Manwaring, M. G. 2002. *Nonstate actors in Columbia: threat and response.* Strategic Studies Institute, US Army War College, Carlisle Barracks, Pennsylvania.

Miskel, J. F. & R. J. Norton. 1997. "Spotting trouble: identifying faltering and failing states." *Naval War College Review* 50(2): 79–91.

National Security Archive. 2007. *Pakistan: the Taliban's godfather?* George Washington University, 14 August, www.gwu.edu/-nsarchiv/NSAEBB/NSAEBB227/index.htm [accessed 28 September 2009].

Rosenthal, J. 2004. "New rules for war?" *Naval War College Review* 58(3/4): 91–101.

Sappenfield, M. 2008. "Foreign jihadists in an ungoverned tribal belt kill leaders, recruit locals." *Christian Science Monitor* (28 February). http://csmonitor.com/2008/0228/p06s02-wosc.htm [accessed 30 April 2010].

Schmitt, E. & M. Mazzetti. 2008. "Secret order lets U.S. raid al-Qaeda in many countries." *New York Times* A1 (10 November).

Siddique, A. 2009. "Worries in Pakistan that Taliban imposing 'parallel' government." Radio Free Europe/Radio Liberty (6 January). http://rferl.org/articleprintview/1367060.html [accessed 30 April 2010].

Sullivan, B. 2006. *Fighting the long war—military strategy for the war on terrorism.* Presentation to the Executive Lecture Forum, Radvanyi Chair in International Security Studies, Mississippi State University, 2 July.

Talbot, I. 2002. "Democracy, terrorism and brinksmanship." *Asian Survey* 43(1): 198–207.

Tallent, H. B. 2005. *Statement to the House International Relations Committee, Subcommittee on International Terrorism and Nonproliferation.* Washington, DC: US House of Representatives, 10 March. wwwa.house.gov/international_relations/109/tal031005.htm [accessed 10 September 2009].

Thomas, T. S. 2006. "Control roaming dogs: governance operations in future conflict." *Military Review* (January–February): 78–85.

Thomas, T. S. & W. D. Casebeer. 2005. *Turbulent arena: global effects and non-state adversaries.* INSS Occasional Paper 58, USAF Institute for National Security Studies, US Air Force Academy, Colorado Springs, Colorado.

Thompson, W. & S. Halter. 2006. "Aviation warfighters excel during disaster assistance operations in Pakistan." *Army Aviation* 55(2): 40–3.

United Nations (UN). 2007. *Suicide attacks in Afghanistan (2001–2007).* New York, NY: United Nations.

Whelan, T. 2005. "Rethinking the future nature of competitions and conflict: Africa's un-governed space: a new threat paradigm." 19 December 2005. www.jhuapl.edu/POW/rethinking/SeminarArchive/121905/121905_WhelanNotes.pdf [accessed 10 June 2009].

White House. 2008. *News release, President Bush addresses United Nations General Assembly.* 23 September. http://georgebush-whitehouse.archives.gov/news/releases/2008/09/20080923-5.html [accessed 18 September 2009].

——. 2009. *Remarks by the President in Address to the Nation on the way forward in Afghanistan and Pakistan.* United States Military Academy, West Point, New York, 1 December. www.whitehouse.gov/the-press-office/remarks-president-address-nation-way-forward-afghanistan-and-pakistan [accessed 30 April 2010].

Contributors

FRANCIS A. GALGANO received a BS from the Virginia Military Institute in 1980. He later earned a master's and doctoral degree from the University of Maryland at College Park in 1989 and 1998 respectively. He retired from the Army as a Lieutenant Colonel after 27 years in 2007—at that time, he was serving on the faculty of the US Military Academy. He is presently the Chair of the Department of Geography and the Environment at Villanova University. Dr Galgano has co-edited two military geography books and has authored a number of publications on various geographical subjects.

EUGENE J. PALKA received a BS from the US Military Academy at West Point in 1978, and subsequently earned a master's degree in geography from Ohio University and a PhD from the University of North Carolina at Chapel Hill. He is a colonel in the US Army and a Professor of Geography. He currently serves as Professor and Head of the Department of Geography and Environmental Engineering at the US Military Academy at West Point. He has previously authored or co-authored numerous books, book chapters, instructor's manuals, and professional articles on various topics in geography.

DOUGLAS E. BATSON is a Political Geography Analyst with the National Geospatial-Intelligence Agency (NGA). Mr Batson holds a Master of Education from Boston University and has earned bachelor's degrees in history and geography from Excelsior College. His interests in human terrain analysis and Turkic toponymy stem from his 23-year career in the US Army Reserve. Email: Douglas.E.Batson@nga.mil.

KENT HUGHES BUTTS is a Professor of Political Military Strategy and the Director of the National Security Issues Group at the Center for Strategic Leadership, US Army War College. A graduate of the US Military Academy, he holds a master's degree in Business Administration from Boston University, an MA and PhD in Geography from the University of Washington, and was a John M. Olin Post-Doctoral Fellow in National Security at the Center for International Affairs,

Harvard University. He formerly held the Army War College George C. Marshall Chair of Military Studies. His primary research focus is the geopolitics of natural resources. Email: Kent.Butts@us.army.mil.

MARK W. CORSON, Department of Geology/Geography, Northwest Missouri State University, Marysville, Missouri. Dr Corson received a BA in Government from the University of San Francisco in 1983 and earned an MA in Geography and a PhD from the University of South Carolina. He is currently an Associate Professor of Geography at Northwest Missouri State University. Dr Corson is an Army Reserve officer with experience in Iraq. Email: mcorson@nwmissouri.edu.

WILLIAM W. DOE III, Warner College of Natural Resources, Colorado State University, Fort Collins, Colorado. Dr Doe is the Associate Dean for Research, an environmental geographer, and former US Army engineer officer with research expertise in military lands management and warfare ecology. He received his BS from the US Military Academy, MSCE from the University of New Hampshire and PhD from Colorado State University. Email: william.doe@colostate.edu.

JOSEPH P. HENDERSON, Department of Geography and Environmental Engineering, United States Military Academy, West Point, New York. Lieutenant Colonel Henderson received a BS in Geography from the US Military Academy in 1987, and later earned his master's (1997) and PhD (2006) from the University of Tennessee. LTC Henderson has research interests in the area of climatology and geomorphology. Email: joseph.henderson@us.army.mil.

JOSEPH P. HUPY, Department of Geography and Anthropology, University of Wisconsin–Eau Claire. Dr Hupy is an Assistant Professor of Geography. He holds a BS degree in Geography with emphasis in GIS and Remote Sensing from Central Michigan University and an MA in Geography from New Mexico State University with a focus on Applied Geomorphology. He completed his PhD at Michigan State University in 2005. His research interests include the impact of warfare on the physical environment. Email: HUPYJP@uwec.edu.

AMY RICHMOND KRAKOWKA, Department of Geography and Environmental Engineering, US Military Academy, West Point, New York. Dr Krakowka is an Assistant Professor of Geography with research interests in resource geography and environmental security. She received a BS in Environmental Studies from the State University of New York College of Environmental Science and Forestry. She received both an MA in Energy and Environmental Analysis and a PhD in Geography from Boston University. Email: amy.krakowka@usma.edu.

SARAH JANE MEHARG, Department of Politics and Economics, Royal Military College of Canada. Dr Sarah Jane Meharg is Adjunct Professor at the Royal Military College of Canada and the Senior Research Associate at the Pearson Peacekeeping Centre in Ottawa, Canada. She is Canada's leading post-conflict reconstruction expert and specializes in the research and implementation of advanced technologies for reconstruction initiatives. Dr Meharg focuses on economic acceleration in regions experiencing economic transitions, including post-conflict and post-disaster environments such as Afghanistan, Haiti, and the Balkans. Email: mehargs@pcpcanada.com.

STEVEN OLUIĆ, Office of the Dean, US Military Academy, West Point, New York. LTC Oluić is an Assistant Dean at West Point and a former Associate Professor in the Department of Geography, US Military Academy. His research interests include Balkan regional geography, radical Islam in Europe, and US Balkan Muslim diaspora communities. LTC Oluić received a BA in Geological Science from Case Western Reserve University, an MS in Environmental Science from the University of Cincinnati, and a PhD in Geography from Kent State University. Email: steven.oluic@us.army.mil.

CLIFTON W. PANNELL, Department of Geography, University of Georgia, Athens, Georgia. Dr Pannell is Professor of Geography and Associate Dean of Arts and Sciences emeritus with research interests in the economic, urban, and political geography of contemporary China. He has served as visiting professor at the US Military Academy, West Point, and the University of Hong Kong. Pannell received the BA and MA degrees in Political Science from the University of North Carolina, Chapel Hill, and University of Virginia respectively. He received the PhD in Geography from the University of Chicago. Email: cpan@uga.edu.

HENDRIK A.P. SMIT, Department of Military Geography, Faculty of Military Science, University of Stellenbosch, South African Military Academy, Saldanha, South Africa. Commander Smit is an Officer in the South African Navy and a lecturer in Military Geography. He is the departmental chair of the Department of Military Geography and has a research interest in historical military geography. He received a BA, BA Hons (*Cum Laude*) and a Master's in Geography and Environmental Studies from the University of Stellenbosch. As a former infantry officer, he saw active service on the northern Namibian border during 1986 and 1987. Email: hennies@ma2.sun.ac.za.

WILEY C. THOMPSON, Department of Geography and Environmental Engineering, US Military Academy, West Point, New York. LTC Thompson is an Assistant Professor of Geography and Deputy Department Chair with research interests in disaster response and civil–military co-ordination. He received a BS in Geography from West Point and earned an MS and PhD in Geography from Oregon State University. Email: wiley-thompson@usma.edu.

Glossary

Aardvark holes: holes made by the burrowing activities of the aardvark, a nocturnal, ant eating animal. Serious injuries can occur when accidentally stepped in by people, horses, or pack animals.

Absolute location: a way of describing the position of an object or place by using a precise co-ordinate system or other means of establishing an exact location.

Aeolian: geomorphic processes associated with wind action.

Agent: A disease-causing organism, including animals and viruses, ranging in size from microscopic one-celled organisms to parasitic worms and insects.

Air bridge: the employment of aviation assets to reconnect isolated communities in conditions where overland transportation systems have been disrupted or are inoperative.

Aircraft carrier: a warship designed for deploying and recovering aircraft, thus acting as a seagoing airbase.

Alluvial basin: usually a river basin made of loose, unconsolidated sediments.

Alluvial soil: fine, unconsolidated, fragmental material laid down by a stream, comprising silt, sand, and gravel.

al-Qaeda: an Islamic terrorist organization founded some time between 1988 and 1990. It operates as a violent non-state actor, and at its core is a fundamentalist Sunni movement calling for global *jihad* and murder of people who adhere to the ideals of Western liberal society. *Al-Qaeda* has attacked civilian and military targets in various countries, the most notable being the September 11 attacks in 2001, in which they murdered more than 3000 people in New York City and Washington, DC.

Ambient air temperature: the temperature in any part of the atmosphere immediately surrounding a specific entity.

Amebic dysentery (amoebiasis): an infection of the intestine caused by an amoeba called *Entamoeba histolytica*, which, among other things, can cause severe diarrhea. Amoebae are parasites that are found in contaminated food or drink. They enter the body through the mouth when the contaminated food or drink is swallowed. The amoebae are then able to move through the digestive system, take up residence in the intestine, and cause an infection.

Amphibious operation: An attack launched from the sea by naval and landing forces embarked in ships, involving a landing on a hostile shore.

Anglo-Boer War: the war in southern Africa between the two Boer republics, the Zuid Afrikaansche Republiek (ZAR) and the Orange Free State (OFS), and Britain. The war started on 9 October 1899 and ended on 31 May 1902.

Anthropogenic: effects, processes, or materials that are derived from human activities, as opposed to those occurring in biophysical environments without human influence.

Anticyclonic: a high-pressure system characterized by descending air and divergent winds.

Antiterrorism operations: defensive measures used to minimize the vulnerability of individuals and property to terrorist attacks.

Archipelago: a chain or cluster of islands that are formed tectonically.

Arctic: the region around the earth's North Pole. The Arctic includes the Arctic Ocean (which overlies the North Pole) and parts of Canada, Greenland (a territory of Denmark), Russia, the US (Alaska), Iceland, Norway, Sweden, and Finland.

Area defense: used to retain terrain and is designed to draw the enemy into a well-developed series of positions to break up enemy forces by concentrated firepower.

Area of Responsibility: a geographic area assigned to a unified combatant command.

Armored fighting vehicle: a light-armored fighting vehicle designed for the transport of infantry. They usually have only a machine gun, although variants carry recoilless rifles, anti-tank guided missiles, light cannon, or mortars.

Arms control operations: support treaties and enforcement agencies. Military forces can assist in locating, seizing, and destroying weapons after hostilities, or escort deliveries of weapons and *matériel* to preclude loss or unauthorized use, inspecting and monitoring production and storage facilities, or training foreign forces to secure weapons and facilities.

Assault: To make a short, violent, well-co-ordinated attack against an objective.

Asymmetrical warfare: a war between belligerents whose relative military power, or whose strategy or tactics, differ significantly. Such warfare often involves strategies and tactics of unconventional warfare, within which the weaker combatants attempt to use strategy to offset deficiencies in quantity or quality. This is in contrast to *symmetric warfare*, where two powers have similar military power and resources, and rely on tactics that are similar overall, differing only in details and execution.

Atabrine: a medicine made of quinacrine hydrochloride, used to treat malaria.

Athlete's foot: a fungal infection of the skin that causes scaling, flaking, and itching of affected areas. It is typically transmitted in moist areas where people walk barefoot, such as showers or bathhouses. Although the condition typically affects the feet, it can spread to other areas of the body, including the groin.

Atoll: an island of coral that encircles a lagoon partially or completely.

Attack: an offensive operation that destroys or defeats enemy forces, seizes and secures terrain, or both.

Attack helicopter: a military helicopter armed for attacking targets on the ground such as enemy infantry, armored vehicles, and structures, using automatic cannon and machine-gun fire, rockets, and precision guided missiles.

B-1: a low-level US attack bomber.

Ba'ath Party: the Arab Socialist Ba'ath Party was founded in Damascus as a secular Arab nationalist movement to unify Arab countries in one state and to combat Western colonial rule that dominated the region. In Arabic, Ba'ath means renaissance. The Ba'ath Party came to power in Syria on 8 March 1963 and has held a monopoly on political power since. Later that same year, the Ba'athists gained control of Iraq and ran the country on two separate occasions, briefly in 1963 and then for a longer period lasting from July 1968 until 2003. After the fall of Saddam Hussein during the course of the 2003 Iraq War, the Coalition Provisional Authority banned the Iraqi Ba'ath Party in May 2003.

Bacillary: is a type of dysentery caused by shigellosis. Bacillary dysentery should not be confused with diarrhea caused by a bacterial infection. One characteristic of bacillary dysentery is blood in stool, which is the result of invasion of the mucosa by the pathogen.

Base Realignment and Closure (BRAC): a series of congressionally mandated consolidations and closures of military installations in the US in the 1990s due to downsizing of the military after the Cold War.

Battalion: a unit of about 500–1500 soldiers, usually consisting of between three and six companies and typically commanded by a lieutenant colonel.

Battlespace: includes the environment, factors, and conditions that must be understood to successfully apply combat power, protect the force, or complete the mission. This includes: enemy and friendly armed forces; infrastructure; weather; terrain; and the electromagnetic spectrum within the operational areas and areas of interest

Biomass fuel: solid, liquid, or gaseous fuel obtained from lifeless or living biological material. It is a renewable energy source based on the carbon cycle, unlike other natural resources such as petroleum, coal, and nuclear fuels. Common biomass fuels are wood, animal waste, and residual agricultural products.

Black powder: term used to describe the primitive form of black gunpowder, which was used until the advent of smokeless gunpowder in the 1870s.

Boer: literally 'farmer,' but used to indicate the inhabitants of the two Boer Republics, the ZAR and OFS, regardless of their profession.

Bomber: an aircraft designed to attack ground targets by dropping bombs.

Bosniaca: all documents in any format written or published about BiH in every territory or in any language regardless of the author's origin.

Bošniak or Bošnjak: term denoting Bosnians who are Muslim and also used to identify Bosnian Muslims living in other regions of the former Yugoslavia. This community looks to Sarajevo as the center of their religion in the region.

Break-bulk: a shipping term for any loose material that must be loaded individually.

Brigade: a tactical formation made up of between two and six battalions. It includes about 5000 soldiers and many heavy weapons such as tanks and artillery.

C-130 Hercules: a medium-size military transport aircraft capable of carrying a 41,790 pound payload.

C-17 Globemaster: a large military transport aircraft capable of carrying a 170,900 pound payload.

C-27J Spartan: a medium-size military transport aircraft capable of carrying a 25,353 pound payload.

Cadastre: normally a parcel-based, up-to-date land information system containing a record of interests in land (e.g. rights, restrictions, and responsibilities). It usually includes a geometric description of land parcels linked to other records describing the nature of the interests, the ownership or control of those interests, and often the value of the parcel and its improvements.

Campaign: a planned series of battles designed to achieve a strategic objective.

Cantonment: the built-up or "garrison" area of a military installation (distinct from the training or testing areas) that includes facilities for military personnel, administration, and tactical vehicle parks, as well as basic infrastructure to support these facilities and military family housing.

Cape Colony: British crown colony to the south and west of the two Boer republics.

Carpet bombing: wide-area bombing strategy developed to saturate as much area of ground as possible with heavy explosives. The term originated in World War II in the heavy-bomber strategic bombing campaigns, but was highly implemented in the Second Indochina War.

Center of gravity: this is defined as the source of power that provides moral or physical strength, freedom of action, or will to act.

Centripetal force: those forces that tend to bind or unite a state. Some examples are a strong leader or shared ideological or religious beliefs.

Četniks: term that was first used to identify "freedom fighters" against Ottoman invaders. It is commonly used to denote the Serbian nationalist and Royalist guerilla forces that fought the Axis in 1941 to 1945. It is typically a term of derision for Serbs during Yugoslavia's fall in the 1990s.

CH-47 Chinook: a heavy-lift military helicopter capable of carrying 33,000 pounds of cargo or thirty-three personnel.

Coastal plain: an area of flat, low-lying land adjacent to a seacoast and separated from the interior by other features

Cold War: term given to the continuing state of political conflict, military tension, and economic competition existing after World War II (1939–45), between the USSR and the US from 1945–91. Even though the two powers' military forces never officially clashed directly, they expressed the conflict through proxy wars, military alliances, a nuclear arms race, espionage, and technological competition.

Collateral damage: unintentional or incidental injury or damage to persons or objects that would not be lawful military targets in the circumstances ruling at the time. Such damage is not unlawful so long as it is not excessive in light of the overall military advantage anticipated from the attack.

Combatant Command: the six regional/geographic areas of the world defined by the US Department of Defense for deployment of operational forces under joint (all military services) command by a senior (four-star) general or admiral. The six Combatant Commands are: the US Northern Command (USNORTHCOM), US Southern Command (USSOUTHCOM), US European Command (USEUCOM), US Africa Command (USAFRICOM), US Central Command (USCENTCOM), and US Pacific Command (USPACOM).

Combatant Commander: military leader of a Unified Combatant Command.

Combined arms teams: tactical units made up of infantry, tanks, and artillery.

Commandant: Boer military rank. A commandant was the leader of a commando, consisting of the armed men of a district or town. It must be remembered that most Boer soldiers were not professional soldiers, but belonged to the citizen force. At this stage of the war, most of the officers were elected by the men serving under them.

Community assistance: a broad range of activities that provide support and maintain a strong connection between the military and civilian communities.

Company: a military unit, typically consisting of 75–200 soldiers. Most companies are formed of three to five platoons, although the exact number may vary by unit type and structure.

Compartmentalization: occurs when terrain features and the structure of the land surface combine to restrict movement of military forces into defined corridors.

Concentration camp: system of confining civilians from the two Boer republics, especially women and children, in camps. This system was aimed at denying Boer soldiers from obtaining food from the women on farms and to weaken the resolve of the Boers to keep on fighting. The fact that more civilians died in these camps than soldiers on the battlefields caused great bitterness towards the British after the war among the defeated Boers.

Conflict transformation: the process of reducing the means and motivations for violent conflict while developing more viable, peaceful alternatives for the competitive pursuit of political and socioeconomic aspirations.

Continental law: law inspired by old Roman law, the primary feature of which was that laws were written into a collection; codified, and not determined, as is English common law, by judges. The 1804 Code Napoleon is a well-known example of civil law.

Continental shelf: is the extended perimeter of each continent and associated coastal plain, and was part of the continent during the glacial periods. It is covered by relatively shallow seas and gulfs during interglacial periods, such as the current epoch.

Continentality: the tendency of land to experience more thermal variation than water, due to the land's lower specific heat capacity. Continental climate also tends to be dryer than oceanic climates as there is less moisture input to the atmosphere from evaporation.

Corps: a large operational formation consisting of several divisions.

Counterinsurgency: military term for the armed conflict against an insurgency by forces aligned with the recognized government of the territory in which the conflict takes place.

Counterterrorism: offensive measures taken to prevent, deter, and respond to terrorism. Military forces usually participate in the full array of counterterrorism actions, including strikes and raids against terrorist organizations and facilities.

Creep: a form of down-slope movement caused by gravity and water.

Cruise missile: a guided missile that carries an explosive payload and uses a propulsion system, usually a jet engine.

Cruiser: provides primary air defense to a fleet and carries an array of missiles.

Cultural property: understood as interchangeable with the term cultural heritage, as defined by the UNESCO Convention Concerning the Protection of the World Cultural and Natural Heritage.

Customary tenure: an informal, agreed to, or established-by-custom relationship of people to land, often allocated without written documents.

D-Day: a generic military term that refers to the date that a military operation is to begin. More familiarly and in the popular media, it also refers to 6 June 1944, which was the invasion of Normandy during World War II.

Defensive operations: not a decisive form of warfare; a commander will resort to a defensive strategy to defeat an enemy attack, buy time, economize forces, or develop conditions favorable for offensive operations.

Deflation: the removal of fine-grained sediments from the ground surface by wind.

Demonstration: an attack or show of force on a front where a decision is not sought. It is made with the aim of deceiving the enemy. It is similar to a feint except that enemy contact is not sought.

Dendritic drainage pattern: the most common form of drainage pattern; it looks like the branching pattern of tree roots. It develops in regions underlain by homogeneous material, i.e. the subsurface geology has a similar resistance to weathering so there is no apparent control over the direction the tributaries take. Tributaries join larger streams at an acute angle.

Dengue fever: an acute febrile disease (meaning fever), found in the tropics, and caused by four closely related virus serotypes. It is also known as breakbone fever. Dengue is transmitted to humans by the *Aedes aegypti* or more rarely the *Aedes albopictus* mosquito, which feed during the day. The disease manifests as a sudden onset of severe headache, muscle and joint pains, fever, and rash.

Department of Defense (DoD): the branch of the federal department charged with co-ordinating and supervising all agencies and functions of the government relating directly to national security.

Desertification: the degradation of land in arid and dry sub-humid areas, resulting primarily from man-made activities and influenced by climatic variations. It is principally caused by overgrazing, overuse of groundwater, and diversion of water from rivers for human consumption and industrial use, all processes fundamentally driven by overpopulation.

Destroyer: a fast and maneuverable warship intended to escort larger vessels and defend them against attackers such as submarines and aircraft.

Disease: the alterations of living cells or tissues in such a way as to jeopardize their survival in their environment.

Distance: in an absolute sense, the linear measurement between places. In a relative sense, it is typically thought of in terms of time.

Division: a large military unit, usually consisting of around 15,000 to 20,000 soldiers.

Dolerite (diabase): a basic igneous rock, usually dark colored and fine or medium textured.

Domestic support operation: use of military units and capabilities to supplement the resources of local governments and organizations.

Donga: a steep-sided gully in southern Africa, produced by soil erosion.

Drift: a shallow part of a river, usually with firm underwater conditions, used as a regular crossing point. Drifts sometimes indicated the only places where a river could be crossed with safety.

Durand Line: refers to the border between Afghanistan and Pakistan. It was established after the November 1893 Durand Line Agreement to serve as the frontier line of the British sphere of influence. It is named after Henry Mortimer Durand, the Foreign Secretary of colonial British India at the time.

Dust storms: large weather hazards that transport massive volumes of dust held in suspension.

Dysentery: a disorder of the digestive system that results in severe diarrhea, with mucus and blood in the feces. If left untreated, dysentery can and usually will be fatal.

Eastern Schism: the separation of medieval Christendom into the Western, Catholic, and Rome-centered, and Eastern, Orthodox and Constantinople-centered, churches. The year 1054 is normally associated with the break; however, the schism was a process that occurred over decades, leading to the estrangement of the Catholic West from the Orthodox East.

Ecocide: refers to any large-scale—usually anthropogenically induced—destruction of the natural environment.

Ecoregion: a geographic region or ecosystem resulting from large-scale predictable patterns of climate, which in turn affect the kinds of soils, vegetation, and other natural environmental characteristics. These regions are defined as various levels within a hierarchical classification system, such as Bailey's ecoregional classification system, which uses Domains, Divisions, and Provinces as the levels of classification.

Effective sovereignty: the ability of a state to provide control over its territory and organizations emanating from its territory.

Emergency Management Cycle: a model that depicts the full cycle of activities from the hazard event through response and mitigation back to an enhanced state of rebuilt structures and systems that are better prepared to resist future events.

Encroachment: term coined by the Department of Defense in the early twentieth-century century to define the impacts of commercial and residential development on adjacent military installations to include safety, noise, light, and broadband interferences that limited military activities inside the fence line. The term was also used to describe the impacts of environmental regulation and protection of natural and cultural resources on military readiness.

Endemic: disease carried by many hosts in a condition of "near equilibrium," without causing rapid and widespread deaths. It does not cause immediate death but gradually weakens the health and wellbeing of the host.

Engle Act of 1958: named after Congressman Clair Engle of California, this act established a key principle that DoD withdrawals of areas in excess of 5,000 acres required an Act of Congress, with the attendant public hearings.

Envelopment: a form of maneuver in which the attacker attempts to avoid direct contact with enemy defenders by seizing objectives in the enemy rear.

Environmental determinism: the view that the physical environment, rather than social conditions, determines culture. Those who hold this view say that humans are strictly defined by stimulus–response (environment–behavior) and cannot deviate.

Environmental matrix: a methodology for studying operating environments that accounts for the sum of all factors which operate at a place, and which can have an effect on the successful execution of any operation.

Environmental security: environmental risk analysis based on multi-faceted linkages between anthropogenic and natural processes that destabilize the environment and contribute to instability or conflict. The fundamental components of environmental security include: 1) environmental processes that undermine governments and promote instability; and 2) environmental processes that trigger civil conflict.

Epidemic: sudden and severe outbreak of a disease.

Erg: a desert landscape formed of a sea of sand.

Ethnic cleansing: the planned and systematic removal of one national or ethnic group from territory coveted by another group. It routinely involves mass expulsion, atrocity, and destruction of the expelled group's symbols—religious structures, monuments, and cultural markings.

Ethnicity: typically defined as a combination of a people's customs, language, and religion, and its racial heritage.

Exclusive economic zone: under the law of the sea it is a zone over which a state has special rights over the exploration and use of marine resources. It stretches from the seaward edge of the state's territorial sea out to 200 nautical miles from its coast. In casual use, the term may include the territorial sea and even the continental shelf beyond the 200 mile limit.

Exploitation: an offensive operation intended to disorganize the enemy in depth, and disintegrate integrity of their dispositions to the extent that they have no alternative but to surrender.

Explosively formed penetrator: a device with a self-forging warhead, or a self-forging fragment, which is a special type of shaped charge designed to penetrate armor.

Federally Administered Tribal Areas: areas bordering Afghanistan comprising a region of some 27,220 km². The area is colloquially referred to as Pakistan's Tribal Belt.

Fighter: a military aircraft designed primarily for attacking other aircraft.

Floodplain: an area beside a river that is flooded when water levels in the river rise because of high rainfall.

Foreign humanitarian assistance: missions usually conducted to relieve the results of natural or man-made disasters.

Foreign internal defense: includes participation by civilian and military agencies of one government to free and protect the society of another government from subversion, lawlessness, and insurgency.

Formal region: a substantial area within which a legitimate generalization of commonality may be made with respect to an attribute.

Forward operating base (FOB): a secured forward position that is used to support tactical operations. A FOB may or may not contain an airfield, hospital, or other facilities. The base may be used for an extended period of time. A FOB also reduces reaction time and increases time on task to forces operating from it.

Frontal attack: engages the defenders along their entire front and seeks to destroy or fix an enemy in place.

Frontal dust storm: a storm generated by frontal activity.

Full-spectrum operations: operations conducted by military forces across all spectrums of conflict (i.e. low-intensity combat to total war) to peacetime operations (e.g. stability and support operations).

Functional region: a spatial system with interdependent components; its defined geographic extent is a function of the dynamics of the system under study.

Genocide: in 1948, the *Convention for the Prevention and Punishment of the Crime of Genocide* defined genocide as any of the following acts committed with intent to destroy, in whole or in part, a national, ethnic, or religious group: 1) killing members of the group; 2) causing serious bodily or mental harm to members of the group; 3) deliberately inflicting on the group conditions of life calculated to bring about its physical destruction in whole or in part; 4) imposing measures intended to prevent births within the group; and 5) forcibly transferring children of the group to another group.

Geographic Information System (GIS): captures, stores, analyzes, manages, and presents data that is linked to location. Technically, a GIS is a system that includes mapping software and its application to remote sensing, land surveying, aerial photography, mathematics, photogrammetry, geography, and tools that can be implemented with GIS software.

Global Positioning System (GPS): a US space-based global navigation satellite system. It provides reliable positioning, navigation, and timing services to worldwide users on a continuous basis in all weather, day and night, anywhere on or near the earth.

Guomindang: Nationalist Chinese Party of Chiang Kai-shek that has ruled Taiwan for most of the last 65 years.

Haboob: a type of intense dust storm commonly observed in the Sahara Desert, as well as across the Arabian Peninsula, throughout Kuwait, and in the most arid regions of Iraq. It is associated with thunderstorms.

Hadj: a religious pilgrimage that is the fifth pillar of Islam, a moral obligation that must be carried out at least once in their lifetime by every able-bodied Muslim who can afford to do so. The *Hadj* is a demonstration of the solidarity of the Muslim people, and their submission to Allah (God).

Hamada: a desert landscape with an entirely rocky and impermeable surface.

Health: a state of complete physical, mental, and social wellbeing (not merely the absence of disease or infirmity).

Host: the organism infected by the disease agent. After being afflicted by an infectious disease, a host (person, animal, bird, or arthropod) supports the disease organism by providing lodgment or subsistence.

Howitzer: a type of artillery piece that is characterized by a relatively short barrel and the use of comparatively small explosive charges to propel projectiles at trajectories with a steep angle of descent.

Hyperthermia: where the core temperature of the human body rises to 39°C (102°F) or above.

Hypothermia: where the core temperature of the human body drops below 35°C (95°F).

Identicide: a strategy of warfare that deliberately targets and destroys cultural elements through a variety of means in order to contribute to eventual acculturation, removal, and/or total destruction of a particular identity group, including its contested signs, symbols, behaviors, values, heritages, places, and performances.

Improvised explosive device: a bomb constructed and deployed in ways other than in conventional military action.

Impuzamugambi: a Hutu militia in Rwanda formed in 1992 and one of the two that perpetrated much of the 1994 genocide. The term means "Those who have the same goal" or "Those who have a single goal" in the Kinyarwanda language.

Indirect fire: method of artillery fire employed with the advent of long-range, cylinder-shaped shells that were propelled by high-explosive propellants. Prior to indirect-fire methods, artillery gunners used open sights on their guns.

Infiltration: a form of tactical-level maneuver during which the attacker uses small units to exploit gaps in the enemy defense to reach and occupy a position of advantage in the enemy rear.

Informal settlements: areas where groups of housing units have been constructed on land that the occupants have no legal claim to, or occupy illegally (also called slums, squatter settlements camps, *favelas*, or shanty towns).

Informationization: the development of advanced information technology as part of modern military equipment and the modern military battlefield.

Interahamwe: the largest and most important of the Hutu militia that participated in the 1994 genocide. It had the backing of the Hutu-led Rwandan government and was believed to have been supplied and trained by the Rwandan Army. The term means "Those who stand/work/fight/attack together."

Intervisibility lines: small, almost imperceptible undulations on the desert floor that can effectively conceal small forces and individual vehicles from being observed by other units at ground level.

Irredentism: the policy of states or political leaders to extend their state's boundaries or cultural influence into neighboring territories inhabited by their co-nationals or ethnic brethren.

Islamic Movement of Uzbekistan: a militant Islamist group formed in 1998 by former Soviet paratrooper Jumna Namangani and the Islamic ideologue Tahir Yuldashev. Its objective is to overthrow the current Uzbek government and create an Islamic state under Shari'a.

Island arc: a type of archipelago formed by plate tectonics as one oceanic tectonic plate subducts under another and produces magma. Island arcs that develop along the edges of a continent (for example large parts of the Andes/Central American/Canadian mountain chain); may be known as a volcanic arc.

Joint Army Navy Intelligence Series (Janis): A series of jointly produced intelligence reports assembled by the US Army and Navy during World War II.

Joint commands: unified military commands made up of two or more services.

Jungle rot: a lesion occurring in cutaneous leishmaniasis caused by a variety of micro-organisms, including mycobacteria. Ulcers occur on exposed parts of the body, primarily on the lower. These lesions may frequently develop on pre-existing abrasions or sores, sometimes beginning from a mere scratch.

Key terrain: any locality or area, the seizure or retention of which affords a marked advantage to either combatant.

Krajina: regions of Croatia and western Bosnia inhabited by Serbs since the fourteenth century. They correspond to the Habsburg Empire's military districts where Serbs and other Christians fleeing Ottoman oppression settled, serving as frontier guards against the Ottomans in return for freedom of religion and significant autonomy.

Kunai grass: a dense, tall grass found throughout tropical regions of the Pacific.

Land administration: formal systems necessary to register land and property, and hence to provide secure ownership and interests in land, investments, and other private and public rights in real estate.

Land tenure: the relationship, whether legal or customary, among people with respect to land. Land tenure is an institution, i.e. rules invented by societies to regulate behavior and determine who can use what resources for how long, and under what conditions.

Landlocked state: a state that is surrounded by land without a coastline or port, which typically disadvantages the state in terms of trade, economic development, and interaction in a globalizing world.

Laterization: older term used to describe irreversible hardening of soils, often in tropical climates, into a brick-like consistency.

Law of the Sea Treaty: the United Nations Convention on the Law of the Sea—or UNCLOS—is also called the Law of the Sea Treaty. It is the international agreement that resulted from the third United Nations Conference on the Law of the Sea, which took place from 1973 through 1982. UNCLOS defines the rights and responsibilities of nations in their use of the world's oceans, establishing guidelines for businesses, the environment, and the management of marine natural resources.

Lifelines: systems or networks that provide for the circulation of people, goods, services, and information upon which health, safety, comfort, and economic activity depend.

Line of contact: a general trace delineating the location where two opposing forces are engaged.

Line of operation: a line that connects a military force from its base to its objective. A line of operation can be a terrain feature, such as a river or terrain corridor, or a cultural feature, such as a road or canal.

Liquefaction: transformation of a granular material from a solid state into a liquefied state as a consequence of increased pore-water pressure.

Lomonosov Ridge: an unusual underwater ridge of continental crust in the Arctic Ocean, which spans 1800 km from the New Siberian Islands over the central part of the ocean to Ellesmere Island of the Canadian Arctic islands. The width of the Lomonosov Ridge varies from 60 to 200 km, and it rises 3300 to 3700 m above the seabed. The minimum depth of the ocean above the ridge is 954 m. The Russians claim that the underwater Lomonosov Ridge and Mendeleev Ridge are extensions of the Eurasian continent.

Macrogeography: large-scale analysis of military problems and environments, usually at the strategic and operational level of war.

Madrasa: this term is derived from Arabic and refers to any type of school. However, since 9-11, usage has referred to extremist Sunni religious schools that have radicalized young men throughout the Middle East and Southwest Asia. Students in the *madrasa* are called *talibs*, and such men became the *Taliban* in Afghanistan in the mid-1990s.

Mainland beaches: a beach formed directly along the seaward edge of a landmass—the beach is not backed by a bay or lagoon.

Malaria: a vector-borne infectious disease caused by protozoan parasites. It is widespread in tropical and subtropical regions, including parts of the Americas, Asia, and Africa. The disease is caused by protozoan parasites of the genus *Plasmodium*. Five species of the plasmodium parasite can infect humans; the most serious forms of the disease are caused by *Plasmodium falciparum*. Malaria caused by *Plasmodium vivax*, *Plasmodium ovale* and *Plasmodium malariae* causes milder disease in humans that is not generally fatal. A fifth species, *Plasmodium knowlesi*, causes malaria in macaques but can also infect humans. Usually, people get malaria by being bitten by an infective female *Anopheles* mosquito. The parasites multiply within red blood cells, causing anemia (light-headedness, shortness of breath, tachycardia, etc.), as well as other general symptoms such as fever, chills, nausea, flu-like illness, and, in severe cases, coma and death.

Malik: an Arabic word meaning king. The term *malik* is used in Afghanistan and the tribal areas of Pakistan, especially among the Pashtu, for a tribal leader or a chieftain. *Maliks* serve as *de facto* arbiters in local conflicts, interlocutors in state policy-making, tax collectors, heads of villages, and town councils.

Malnutrition: food intake insufficient in quantity or deficient in quality to sustain life at optimal conditions of health. Malnutrition results from deficiencies in protein, vitamins, or minerals within a person's diet. Caloric intake may be adequate, but the lack of a well-balanced nutritional diet has a negative impact on the body's ability to function.

Malthusian: a concept named after Thomas Robert Malthus (1766–1834), a British scholar, influential in political economy and demography. The term is linked to the theory that societal improvements result in population growth that, he states, sooner or later are checked by famine, disease, and widespread mortality.

Meander: a twist or loop in the stream channel pattern of a river.

Medical geography: subfield of geography that uses the concepts and techniques of the discipline to investigate health-related topics. It explains the distribution of health and disease, and identifies efficient ways to intervene and distribute trained personnel and technology to provide effective health care.

Meeting engagement: occurs when an attacking force in motion engages an enemy at an unexpected time and place.

Microgeography: small-scale geographic study of terrain features.

Microterrain: small irregularities in terrain that can be used by soldiers or military units for a distinct advantage. These are typically small undulations in the terrain, drainage ditches, or other such features of small relief.

Military installation: a federal land area managed by the Department of Defense for the purpose of conducting military training and testing activities in support of the national defense mission. A typical military installation includes the cantonment area (barracks, motor pools, administrative areas, housing areas, etc.) and a range area for live-fire, maneuver, and other military-specific activities.

Military lands: federal lands controlled by the four Armed Services (Army, Air Force, Navy, and Marine Corps) in the fifty states and territories. These lands consist of both deeded ownership from the federal government and lands that are "withdrawn" by congressional approval from the overall federal land inventory. These lands typically reside within the boundaries of a military installation.

Military Lands Act of 1986: Public Law 99-606, authorizing DoD several large land withdrawals in the west, but limiting these withdrawals to fifteen years and requiring the preparation of extensive Environmental Impact Statements (EIS).

Military operating environments: a portion of the earth's surface within which a military operation occurs. The environment size and scale is a function of the operation and level of war, and is influenced by the totality of the physical and human landscape.

Military Operations Other Than War: includes the use of military capabilities across a range of operations that fall short of outright war. Military operations other than war focus on deterring war, resolving conflict, promoting peace, and supporting civil authorities in response to domestic crises.

Millet: an Ottoman term for non-Muslim religious communities in Ottoman-conquered territories. The *millets* were led by the community's religious leader and possessed a great deal of power, setting their own laws and collecting and distributing their own taxes—however, this should not be confused with having any equality with their Ottoman overlords.

Mobile defense: focused on destroying attacking forces by permitting the enemy to advance into a position that exposes him to counter-attack.

Mortar: a cheap, simple indirect-fire weapon, usually carried by infantry troops. Mortars fire explosive shells at very high arcs, but over relatively short ranges.

Movement to contact: designed to develop the situation and establish or regain contact.

Mujahedeen: foreign Islamic fighters that supported the beleaguered Muslim forces in Bosnia, 1991 to 1995. These Islamic fighters also brought their radical Islamic ideologies and goals of establishing an Islamist base in Europe. Several of the 9/11 hijackers served in Bosnia during the war.

Natal: British crown colony to the south and east of the two Boer republics.

Nation: a group of people sharing common cultural characteristics such as ethnicity, history, language, or religion that binds them closely together. In most cases a common homeland or territory is associated with the nation.

National Command Authority: in the US, this is the legal war-making authority consisting of the President and Secretary of Defense.

Nationalism: the political mobilization of a nation to pursue a national goal; this may be territory, human rights, or political power.

Nation-building: the process of constructing or structuring a national identity using the power of the state. This process aims at the unification of the people or peoples within the state so that it remains politically stable and viable in the long run. Nation-building can involve the use of propaganda or major infrastructure development to foster social harmony and economic growth.

Nation state: a political territorial unit in which the nation and state are congruent; the territorial state matches the area settled by a national group. Slovenia is a good example.

Noncombatant evacuation operations: used to relocate threatened civilian noncombatants from locations in a foreign state to secure areas. Typically, these operations involve citizens whose lives are in danger either from the threat of hostilities or a natural disaster.

Northern Cape: semi-arid region of the Cape Colony situated in the interior of southern Africa.

Northwest Passage: a sea route through the Arctic Ocean, along the northern coast of North America via waterways amidst the Canadian Arctic Archipelago.

Offensive Operations: the decisive form of war, designed to destroy or defeat an enemy, secure important terrain or resources, or expel enemy forces from a region.

Operation Enduring Freedom (OEF): official name used by the US government for its war in Afghanistan and Iraq, together with three smaller military actions, under the umbrella of its Global War on Terror (GWOT).

Operational art: the process by which commanders effectively use resources to achieve strategic objectives.

Operations: any form of military endeavor with an objective start and finish time.

Operations in support of diplomatic efforts: used to establish peace and order before, during, and after conflicts and may incorporate preventive diplomacy, peacemaking, and peace-building.

Orange Free State (OFS): one of the two Boer republics involved in the Anglo-Boer War against Britain. During the war the OFS was led by President M. T. Steyn.

Oxisol: tropical soil, often reddish in color. These soils are considered among the oldest of the soil orders, containing high amounts of secondary oxide clays.

409 **Pandemic**: a global spread of a disease.

Peace enforcement operations: enacted to apply or threaten military force to compel compliance with resolutions or sanctions designed to maintain or restore peace. Peace enforcement operations normally do not require the consent of all parties.

Peace operations: encompass peacekeeping operations and peace enforcement operations conducted to support diplomatic efforts to establish and maintain peace.

Peacekeeping operations: undertaken with the consent of all major parties to a dispute. They are used to aid the implementation of ceasefire agreements, or to support diplomatic efforts.

Penetration: an attack designed to rupture enemy defenses on a very narrow front to dislocate the defensive system.

Permafrost: soil at or below the freezing point of water (0°C or 32°F) for two or more years. Most permafrost is located in high latitudes (i.e. land in close proximity to the North and South Poles), but alpine permafrost may exist at high altitudes in much lower latitudes.

Peshmerga: the term used by Kurds to refer to armed Kurdish fighters. Literally meaning "those who face death," the *Peshmerga* forces of Kurdistan have been in existence since the advent of the Kurdish independence movement in the early 1920s.

Physiography: the subfield of geography that studies physical patterns and processes of the earth—the forms, patterns, and structure of the natural landscape.

Platoon: a small tactical formation made up of several squads.

Polar projection: a very useful map projection in which all distances measured from the center of the map along any longitudinal line are accurate. Many maps of the North and South Poles are made from polar projections.

Pom-poms: converted 37 mm caliber machine guns, firing 1-pound, percussion-fused shells.

Primate city: the leading city in its country or region, disproportionately larger than any others in the urban hierarchy.

Pursuit: a type of offensive operation designed to trap an enemy attempting to escape.

Quinine: a natural white crystalline alkaloid that has fever-reducing, antimalarial, painkilling, and anti-inflammatory properties. Originally discovered by the Indians in Peru, the bark of the cinchona tree was first brought to Europe by the Jesuits. Quinine was the first effective treatment for malaria caused by *Plasmodium falciparum*, appearing in therapeutics in the seventeenth century. It remained the antimalarial drug of choice until the 1940s, when other drugs replaced it.

Raid: an operation, usually small in scale, involving a swift penetration of hostile territory to secure information, confuse the enemy, or to destroy installations. It ends with the planned withdrawal of the raiding force.

Rapprochement: in international relations this term connotes the re-establishment, or desire thereof, of cordial relations between countries.

Rayah: an Ottoman Turkish term to denote the non-Muslim taxpaying communities in the Ottoman Empire. Literally means "flock" or even "cattle."

Reg: a gravel desert surface.

Regiment: similar to a brigade. A tactical formation made up of between two and six battalions, and includes about 5000 soldiers and many heavy weapons such as tanks and artillery.

Region: an area on earth's surface delineated by specific criteria.

Relative location: provides the military geographer with the position of a place or phenomenon relative to the location of other places or phenomena.

Relief operations: used to support the efforts of state, local, and host nation authorities after a disaster. These operations focus on recovery of critical infrastructure and on the wellbeing of supported populations.

Reservoir: refers to a large number and concentration of hosts in a population, from which a disease may expand or diffuse. The infectious agent normally lives and multiplies within the reservoir. Thus, a reservoir may serve as a continuing source of possible infection for humans.

Retrograde operations: employed to move units away from the enemy to gain time, preserve forces, or preclude combat under unfavorable circumstances.

Revolution in Military Affairs (RMA): Chinese viewpoint on the far-reaching changes in military technology, forces, and doctrine brought about by the remarkable advances in science and technology that have been applied to all facets of military affairs.

RH-53: a specialized version of the Sikorsky CH-53 Sea Stallion helicopter.

Rift Valley fever: caused by a virus spread by the bite of infected mosquitoes, and can cause several different syndromes. Usually sufferers have either no symptoms or only a mild illness, with fever, headache, myalgia, and liver abnormalities. In a small percentage of cases (@ 2 percent) the illness can progress to hemorrhagic fever syndrome or meningoencephalitis (inflammation of the brain). Patients who become ill usually experience fever, generalized weakness, back pain, dizziness, and weight loss at the onset of the illness. Typically, patients recover within 2–7 days after onset.

Ringworm: a fungal infection of the skin in humans and domestic animals. Those that cause parasitic infection feed on keratin, the material found in the outer layer of skin, hair, and nails. These fungi thrive best on skin that is warm and moist. It is associated with severe itching, which can lead to infection once the area is scratched.

Riverine operations: operations conducted by forces organized to cope with and exploit the unique characteristics of a riverine area and inland waterways.

Rogue wave: relatively large and spontaneous surface waves that are a threat even to the largest ships. They are more precisely defined as waves whose height is more than twice the significant wave height (SWH), which is itself defined as the mean of the largest third of waves in a wave record. Rogue waves seem to occur in deep water or where a number of physical factors such as strong winds and fast currents converge. This may have a focusing effect, which can cause a number of waves to join together.

Roll-on/roll-off: also called ro-ro ships, these vessels are designed to carry wheeled cargo such as automobiles, trucks, semi-trailer trucks, trailers, or railroad cars that are driven on and off the ship on their own wheels.

Roma: Europe's largest and poorest minority community. Also called gypsies or Romani, the Roma is an ethnic group tracing its origins to medieval India that has been historically discriminated against. The greatest concentrations of Roma are in Central and Southeastern Europe.

Rome plow: heavy, often armored, tractor equipped with a specially designed blade for bulldozing down trees. These specialized tractors were heavily utilized in the Vietnam War for land-clearing operations.

RPG: a rocket-propelled grenade designed by the Soviet Union. The weapon includes a hollow launcher tube, which is reloaded after firing with a large conical hollow-charge grenade. The grenade is propelled by a small rocket and is capable of destroying most armored vehicles except for modern tanks.

Rural–urban divide: concept that highlights the cultural, economic and social differences, most often perceived, between the cosmopolitan urbanites and allegedly backwards rural populations.

Rwandan Patriotic Front (RPF): formed in 1987 by the Tutsi refugee diaspora in Uganda, this political and paramilitary organization operated against the Hutu-led government in Rwanda and eventually invaded and stopped the genocide in 1994.

Saltation: a specific type of particle transport by fluids such as wind or water. It occurs when loose material is removed from a bed and carried by the wind, before being transported back to the surface. Examples include pebble transport by rivers, sand drift over desert surfaces, soil blowing over fields, or even snow drifting over smooth surfaces.

Scale: representation of a real-world phenomenon at a certain level of generalization.

Scrub typhus: a form of typhus caused by *Orientia tsutsugamushi*. Although it is similar in presentation to other forms of typhus, it is caused by an agent in a different genus, and is frequently classified separately from the other typhi. Symptoms include fever, headache, muscle pain, cough, and gastrointestinal symptoms. More virulent strains of *O. tsutsugamushi* can cause hemorrhaging and intravascular coagulation.

SCUD: a series of tactical ballistic missiles developed by the Soviet Union during the Cold War and exported widely to other countries. SCUDs are generally inaccurate and have different models with ranges between 180 and 500 km.

Second Island Chain: extension of China's maritime reach far beyond the traditional First Island Chain that included the East and South China Seas and Taiwan into the western Pacific Ocean as far as Guam and western New Guinea. This is part of the current doctrine of China's maritime defensive perimeter.

Security assistance: refers to a cluster of programs that support national objectives by providing equipment, military training, and other defense-related services to foreign nations.

Selva: dense tropical forest, often associated with broadleaf canopy forests of equatorial regions.

Shamal: a northwesterly wind blowing over Iraq and the Persian Gulf region, often strong during the day, but decreasing at night. This weather effect occurs anywhere from one to several times a year, mostly in summer but sometimes in winter. The resulting wind typically creates large sandstorms that impact Iraq, although most sand is picked up from Jordan and Syria. This type of dust event is caused by frontal activity.

Shanghai Communiqué (Joint Communiqué on the Establishment of Diplomatic Relations): the enabling treaty that established diplomatic relations between the US and China signed by President Jimmy Carter in 1979.

Shi'a: the second largest denomination of Islam, after Sunni Islam. The followers of Shi'a Islam are called Shi'as or Shi'ites. Shia Muslims believe that Ali Muhammad's cousin and son-in-law was the first of the Imams and was the rightful successor to Muhammad and thus reject the legitimacy of the first three Rashidun caliphs.

Show of force operations: used to bolster and reassure allies, deter potential aggressors, and gain or increase influence.

Siege: the action of an armed force that surrounds a fortified place and isolates it while continuing to attack with the intention of conquering by attrition or assault. Sieges occur when a city or area cannot be easily taken, and refuses to surrender.

Site: the characteristics of the local setting or internal aspects of a place. In the military geographic context, it may include such attributes as relief, climate, vegetation, soil composition, mobility potential, street patterns, and the availability of water.

413 **Situation**: the external locational attributes of a place.

Soilscape: term used to describe the soils aspect of a geographic landscape.

Spoils of war: any profits extracted as the result of winning a war or other military activity.

Squad: the smallest tactical unit, consisting of eight to ten soldiers.

Stability and support operations: military operations other than direct warfare designed to promote stability and permit local authorities to establish a secure environment.

Stability operations: an overarching term encompassing various military missions, tasks, and activities conducted outside the US in co-ordination with other instruments of national power to maintain or re-establish a safe and secure environment, and provide essential government services, emergency infrastructure reconstruction, and humanitarian relief.

Stateless nation: a political term used to imply that a group, usually a minority ethnic group, is a nation, and is entitled to its own state, specifically a nation state for that nation.

Strategic geometry: the critical arrangement of key terrain, strategic objectives, and movement corridors on the military landscape.

Strategy: defined as the art and science of developing and using political and military force as needed during peace and war to achieve national objectives.

Subduction: the process of one lithospheric plate descending beneath another.

Subduction zone: a long, narrow belt in which subduction takes place.

Submarine: a ship that can operate independently underwater, as distinct from a submersible that has only limited underwater capability.

Subsidence: a downward shift of the earth's surface with respect to sea level.

Subsistence farming: self-sufficient farming in which farmers grow only enough food to feed their family. The typical subsistence farm has a range of crops and animals needed by the family to eat during the year.

Sunni: the largest denomination of Islam.

Sunni Triangle: a densely populated region of Iraq to the northwest of Baghdad that is inhabited mostly by Sunni Muslim Arabs. The roughly triangular area's corners are usually said to lie near Baqubah (on the east side of the triangle), Baghdad (on the south side), Ramadi (on the west side), and Tikrit (on the north side). Each side is approximately 125 miles long. The area also contains the cities of Samarra and Fallujah. The area was a center of strong support for former Iraqi president Saddam Hussein's government; starting in the 1970s many government workers, politicians, and military leaders came from the area.

Support operations: the use of military units to assist civil authorities as they prepare for, or respond to, crises and to relieve suffering.

Support to civil law enforcement: activities related to counterterrorism, counter-drug operations, civil disturbances, and general support to civil law enforcement organizations. Military support involves providing resources, training, or augmentation within the bounds of the law.

Support to counter-drug operations: the use of military forces to interdict drug shipments along national borders and a form of domestic support operations.

Support to insurgencies: the NCA may employ forces to support insurgencies that oppose regimes that threaten national interests or regional stability. These are operations normally given to Special Forces (i.e. Green Berets, Navy Seals, etc.).

Surface-to-air missile (SAM): short-range anti-aircraft missiles.

Suspension: the process by which fine-grained sediments are held aloft over great distances by wind.

Systematic geography: a specific aspect of the physical or human landscape, rather than a defined space.

Tactics: defined as the employment of units in combat.

Taiwan Relations Act: US law that followed the Shanghai Communiqué and established informal relations with Taiwan. It also allowed the US to sell military equipment to Taiwan for defensive military purposes.

Taliban: a radical Sunni Islamist movement that governed Afghanistan from 1996 until late 2001, when it was removed from power by US forces during Operation Enduring Freedom. It has since regrouped in the tribal areas of western Pakistan and revived as a strong insurgency movement governing at the local level and fighting a guerrilla war against the governments of Afghanistan, Pakistan, and the NATO-led International Security Assistance Force.

Tank: a tracked, armored fighting vehicle designed for front-line combat that combines offensive and defensive capabilities.

Task force: a combined arms force, usually about the size of a battalion.

Technical vehicles: a term used to describe civilian mini-pickup trucks armed with machine guns and grenade launchers. The term stems from the Somali crisis of 1992–3, during which warlords armed common civilian vehicles in this fashion.

Terrain analysis: the collection, analysis and evaluation, and interpretation of geographic information on the natural and man-made features of the terrain, combined with other relevant factors, to predict the effect of the terrain on military operations.

Territorial sea: a belt of coastal waters extending, at most, twelve nautical miles from the baseline (usually the mean low-water mark) of a coastal state.

Thermoregulatory processes: those processes that enable the body to maintain a stable core temperature, regardless of the temperature of the air surrounding the body.

Tidal range: the vertical distance between the high-tide line and low-tide line. Tidal range is significant, especially given the slope of a beach—the flatter the beach slope, the greater the area exposed at low tide, which is an important consideration during amphibious landings.

Traverse: a legal term for travel or passing across, over, or through.

Trellis drainage pattern: a drainage pattern that looks similar to a common garden trellis. Trellis drainage develops in folded topography like that found in the Appalachian Mountains of North America. Short tributary streams enter the main channel at obtuse angles as they run down sides of parallel ridges called anticlines. Tributaries join the main stream at nearly right angles.

Trench: a ditch dug by soldiers to provide shelter against enemy fire.

Tsunami: a long-period ocean wave usually caused by sea-floor movements during an earthquake, submarine volcanic eruption, or submarine landslide. The word is Japanese for "harbor wave."

Tundra: a biome where the tree growth is hindered by low temperatures and short growing seasons. There are three types of tundra: Arctic tundra, alpine tundra, and Antarctic tundra. In tundra, the vegetation is composed of dwarf shrubs, sedges and grasses, mosses, and lichens.

Turab: the name given to an intense wind and dust storm from the south (in the Middle East), as opposed to the shamal, which originates from the north and northwest.

Turning movement: a variation of the envelopment in which the attacking force passes around the enemy's principal defensive positions to secure objectives deep in his rear to force the enemy to abandon his position or divert major forces to meet the threat.

Undernutrition: lack of calories or the quantity of food intake. Like malnutrition, undernutrition renders a person more susceptible to other maladies, and thus lowers the state of health.

Unexploded ordnance (UXO): explosive weapons that did not explode when they were employed and still pose a risk of detonation, potentially many decades after they were used or discarded.

Ungoverned space: an area that is outside of the effective control of a sovereign government and thus can be affected by severe humanitarian disasters, or exploited by violent non-state actors such as terrorist groups, narco-traffickers, and crime syndicates.

Unified combatant commands: a joint military command composed of forces from two or more services and assigned a geographic or functional mission.

Unified Modeling Language (UML): a standard notation for the modeling of real-world objects as a first step in developing an object-oriented design methodology.

Unmanned aerial vehicles: aircraft flown remotely by a pilot on the ground (it is not an autonomous aircraft) and can serve in a reconnaissance role and fire missiles.

Ustaše or Ustashe: Croatian fascists that participated in the perpetration of the Nazi Holocaust. The Ustaše-led Independent State of Croatia, 1941–5, was an ally of Germany and responsible for the extermination of between 300,000 and 700,000 Serbs, Roma, and Jews.

Usufruct: a legal term for the right to use and enjoy the profits and advantages of something belonging to another as long as the property is not damaged or altered in any way.

Vector: a carrier of a disease that is capable of transferring the latter between hosts. The agent often goes through life cycle changes in form within the vector. The habitat of the vector may determine the location of the disease. Biological vectors (such as insects or rodents) are alive and provide the habitat within which an agent can develop or multiply prior to becoming infective. By comparison, non-biological or mechanical vectors such as water, soil, food, or fecal matter are not essential for the agent's life cycle but may serve as a vehicle for transmitting the infectious agent.

Veld(t): open or uncultivated grassland in southern Africa.

Violent non-state actors: refers to an organization that uses illegal violence (i.e. not *officially* sanctioned by a state or inter-governmental body such as the UN) to achieve its goals. This is problematic because traditional forms of diplomacy are often ineffective with non-state actors because normal state structures do not exist. Examples are: warlords, insurgents, terrorists, militias, pirates, and criminal organizations like the Mafia or Yakuza.

Wadi: an ephemeral streambed in a desert environment. A wadi is typically steep-walled with a flat sandy bottom.

Wahhabism: a sect attributed to Muhammad ibn Abd-al-Wahhab, an eighteenth-century scholar from modern Saudi Arabia. Wahhabists are dedicated to a strict and radical interpretation of the Koran.

Westphalian system: the concept of nation state sovereignty based on two principles: territoriality and the exclusion of external actors from domestic authority structures.

Williwaws: sudden blasts of wind descending from a mountainous coast to the sea. The word is of unknown origin, but was earliest used by British seamen in the nineteenth century. The williwaw results from the descent of cold, dense air from the snow and ice fields of coastal mountains in high latitudes, accelerated by the force of gravity. Thus the williwaw is considered a type of katabatic wind.

Withdrawal: a planned operation in which a force in contact disengages from an enemy force.

World Climatic Region (WCR): a classification of land areas on a global scale that equates to the Domain classification level (four classes) of Bailey's ecoregional classification system, and which is used to compare military installations in the US as analogs to deployment areas worldwide.

Zuid-Afrikaansche Republiek (ZAR): one of the two Boer republics involved in the Anglo-Boer War against Britain. During the war the ZAR was led by President Paul Kruger.

Index

University Readers™

Reading Materials Evolved.

Introducing the

SOCIAL ISSUES COLLECTION

A Routledge/University Readers Custom Library for Teaching

Customizing course material for innovative and excellent teaching in sociology has never been easier or more effective!

Choose from a collection of more than 300 readings from Routledge, Taylor & Francis, and other publishers to make a custom anthology that suits the needs of your social problems/ social inequality, and social issues courses.

All readings have been aptly chosen by academic editors and our authors and organized by topic and author.

Online tool makes it easy for busy instructors:

1. *Simply select your favorite Routledge and Taylor & Francis readings, and add any other required course material, including your own.*

2. *Choose the order of the readings, pick a binding, and customize a cover.*

3. *One click will post your materials for students to buy. They can purchase print or digital packs, and we ship direct to their door within two weeks of ordering!*

More information at www.socialissuescollection.com

Contact information: Call your Routledge sales rep, or
Becky Smith at University Readers, 800-200-3908 ext. 18, bsmith@universityreaders.com
Steve Rutter at Routledge, 207-434-2102, Steve.Rutter@taylorandfrancis.com.